CANADIAN M̶ PEOPLES:
REPRESENTIN̶G̶ R̶E̶L̶I̶G̶I̶O̶N̶ A̶T̶ H̶O̶M̶E̶ A̶N̶D̶ ABROAD

Christian missions and missionaries have had a distinctive role in Canada's cultural history. With *Canadian Missionaries, Indigenous Peoples*, Alvyn Austin and Jamie S. Scott have brought together new and established Canadian scholars to examine the encounters between Christian (Roman Catholic and Protestant) missionaries and the indigenous peoples with whom they worked in nineteenth- and twentieth-century domestic and overseas missions.

This tightly integrated collection is divided into three sections. The first contains essays on missionaries and converts in Western Canada and in the Arctic. The essays in the second section investigate various facets of the Canadian missionary presence and its legacy in east Asia, India, and Africa. The third section examines the motives and methods of missionaries as important contributors to Canadian museum holdings of artifacts from Huronia, Kahnawake, and Alaska, as well as China and the South Pacific.

Broadly adopting a postcolonial perspective, *Canadian Missionaries, Indigenous Peoples* contributes greatly to the understanding of missionaries not only as purveyors of Western religious values, but also as vehicles for cultural exchange between Native and non-Native Canadians, as well as between Canadians and the indigenous peoples of other countries.

ALVYN AUSTIN is an adjunct professor in the Department of History at the University of Toronto and the Department of History at Brock University.

JAMIE S. SCOTT is an associate professor in the Religious Studies Program at York University.

Canadian Missionaries, Indigenous Peoples

Representing Religion at Home and Abroad

*Edited by Alvyn Austin
and Jamie S. Scott*

UNIVERSITY OF TORONTO PRESS
Toronto Buffalo London

© University of Toronto Press 2005
Toronto Buffalo London
Printed in Canada

ISBN 0-8020-3951-0 (cloth)
ISBN 0-8020-3784-4 (paper)

Printed on acid-free paper

Library and Archives Canada Cataloguing in Publication

Canadian missionaries, indigenous peoples : representing religion at home and
abroad / edited by Alvyn Austin and Jamie S. Scott.

Includes bibliographical references and index.

ISBN 0-8020-3951-0 (bound)   ISBN 0-8020-3784-4 (pbk.)

1. Missions, Canadian – History.   2. Missionaries – Canada – History.
I. Austin, Alvyn   II. Scott, Jamie S.

BV2121.C3C365 2005   266'.00971   C2004-906134-8

University of Toronto Press acknowledges the financial assistance to its
publishing program of the Canada Council for the Arts and the
Ontario Arts Council.

This book has been published with the help of a grant from the Canadian
Federation for the Humanities and Social Sciences, through the Aid to
Scholarly Publications Programme, using funds provided by the
Social Sciences and Humanities Research Council of Canada.

University of Toronto Press acknowledges the financial support for its
publishing activities of the Government of Canada through the
Book Publishing Industry Development Program (BPIDP).

University of Toronto Press acknowledges the financial support for this book
from: Currents in World Christianity, University of Cambridge, funded by
the Pew Charitable Trusts of Philadelphia; York University; and the (late)
University of Toronto–York University Joint Centre for Asia Pacific Studies.

Contents

Acknowledgments

We, the editors and authors, would like to thank above all the Currents in World Christianity (CWC) project, which brought us all together. CWC was based at the Centre for Advanced Religious and Theological Studies, University of Cambridge, under the direction of Brian Stanley, and funded by The Pew Charitable Trusts of Philadelphia. This book is a result of their vision. The opinions expressed in this volume are those of the authors and do not necessarily represent the views of The Pew Charitable Trusts.

Currents in World Christianity was the successor to the North Atlantic Missiology Project, which created an international community of mission scholars. CWC became the most intensive and extensive modern scholarly assessment of the history and impact of British- and North American–sponsored Christian missions between 1740 and 1968. It focused, in its own words, 'on the complex inter-relationship between the mission theology, theory and policy,' giving 'full weight to both the social, economic and political contexts within which mission theory was forged, and to the deeply held theological convictions which motivated the movement.' The CWC conferences in England, Scotland, the United States, and South Africa may prove to be as pivotal in (re)writing the history of missions as the great missionary conferences of a century ago were in shaping the modern missions enterprise.

The editors wish to thank Brian Stanley, whose grace and scholarship brought together this vast circle of scholars and friends.

CWC selected York University as its Canadian node, under Jamie S. Scott and Alvyn Austin. This allowed us to present four full-day seminars under the broad title 'Missions and Empires' in 1999–2001. At

York University, the planning committee included Peter M. Mitchell, Margo S. Gewurtz, and William Westfall. We would particularly like to thank Shirley Lee and Bernie Frolic of the (late) Joint Centre for Asia Pacific Studies, who took care of a multitude of arrangements.

With deepest gratitude, we would like to acknowledge the archives of the United Church of Canada, the Presbyterian Church in Canada, the Anglican Church, and the Quebec-based Society of Jesus (Jesuits). These are, quite simply, among the great repositories of Canadian history. Yet they have faced difficulties with budget cuts and space restrictions. We would like to put in a word on their behalf. Eleven of the twelve papers in this volume rely on research done in the United Church and Anglican (General Synod) Archives in Toronto, and in the regional archives in Nova Scotia and British Columbia. We have been privileged to live in their precincts, among friends, the best archivists in Canada.

We would also like to thank the Royal Ontario Museum, the Redpath Museum at McGill University, and the Maritime Museum of the Atlantic.

Looking back at Canadian historiography over the last few decades, it is astounding how the United Church Archives in particular has shaped our view of Canada's past. Since the 1960s, when social history was just beginning, they have provided documents and images pertaining to political movements, temperance, architecture, education, the university question, and the settlement of the West. Those haunting images of immigrants and urban poor – the 'men in sheepskin coats' – came from the UCA, as did the documentation for first-wave feminism. With this book, we reveal the equally haunting images of Canada's encounter with the international world, the missionary movement.

CANADIAN MISSIONARIES, INDIGENOUS PEOPLES

Introduction

ALVYN AUSTIN AND JAMIE S. SCOTT

In 1969, John King Fairbank, the distinguished Harvard sinologist, in his presidential address to the American Historical Association, called the missionary 'the invisible man of American history,' standing at the sidelines, the messenger, the bridge between East and West. Yet, he continued, the missionary movement was the most important intercultural experiment in history. No apologist for Christian missions, Fairbank saw their significance in cultural and political history. Historians took up Fairbank's 'assignment for the '70s' (as his address was titled), with a different, secular agenda, and gradually, one by one, the mission archives have been opened and the rich historical documentation they contain has been decoded.[1]

In Canada, John Webster Grant, the eminent church historian, wrote his path-breaking 1984 study of the four centuries of home missions to the Natives, *Moon of Wintertime: Missionaries and the Indians of Canada in Encounter since 1534*. In it, he astutely noted that today, unlike a century ago, it is no longer the Natives, but rather the missionary who needs to be explained.[2]

This volume, *Canadian Missionaries, Indigenous Peoples*, takes Grant's observation to the next stage, to reintroduce the converts back into the dialogue so they can help explain not only themselves but the missionary, the missionized and the missionizers. It takes a multifaceted approach to what has become a highly political topic, the nature and role of Christian missionaries who were appointed by various Protestant and Roman Catholic churches to work in Canada or in foreign fields. It examines their impact from a variety of perspectives, including gender, cross-cultural exchange, ethnography, museum collections, and biographical discourse. The twelve authors represent a wide range of disciplines, including Canadian Native and social history; the history of China, Japan and Oceania; international relations; religious studies; anthropology; art history; feminism; and post-colonial and cultural studies. In seeking to inform the reader about the complexity and multivalent nature of the missionary experience, this volume, we hope, makes an important statement concerning a topic that has been much discussed but often misunderstood.

As a colony in the French and British empires, Canada had a unique history both as a missions-receiving and missions-sending nation, in two languages, cultures, and religions: English Protestants and French-Canadian and English Roman Catholics. The Canadian contribution to the world missionary enterprise, like its contribution to the First World War, was 'more than its bit.' It has been said that in proportion to their size and resources, the churches of Canada sponsored more missionaries at home and abroad than any other nation in Christendom.[3] Consequently, missions have had a larger impact on Canadian identity than they did in, say, the United States.

Within the methodological context of a conversation between more traditional mission studies and contemporary scholarship in post-colonial and cultural studies, each author focuses on one aspect of missions, a snapshot or a case study that illustrates the complex encounter between missionaries and converts. The chapters range widely in time and space, from the Red River (Winnipeg) in 1820 to the Second World War in China and Japan more than a century later. Some give voice and agency to the converts; others try to decode the contradictory, ambiguous, and shifting role of Canadian missions at home and around the world.

From the 1880s, in the absence of formal diplomatic relations, the missionary movement was Canada's foreign policy. It was also the way that many Canadians, French and English, learned about the larger world. Who can estimate the impact of a returned missionary from the South Seas or inland China, wearing native dress and displaying his collection of little 'idols,' speaking to a rural congregation in Nova Scotia or Saskatchewan? The movement ended – or seemed to end – in 1949, when the Communists founded the People's Republic of China and expelled all the foreign missionaries. Among the supposed 'lessons to be learned from China,' a topic that preoccupied mission studies through the Cold War, was that the missions movement had been a tragic mistake: it was cultural imperialism. This was what Jesse Arnup, the secretary of the Board of Overseas Missions of the United

Church, declared when the last missionary left China and the United Church closed the books.

By 1969, twenty years later, when Dr Fairbank made his famous remark, missionaries were indeed invisible; they had disappeared from the radar of popular culture or academic history. Worse, they had become a historical embarrassment.

Initially, during the 1970s and 1980s, when 'mission studies' was first becoming a field of academic endeavour, scholars all over the world approached the multinational, multilingual, multicultural missionary movement from all directions at once. Area specialists concentrated on foreign missions, the influence of 'us' over 'there.' Native historians untangled the relationship between missions, government, and the Native peoples. Another fruitful study was the mission bureaucracy at home, the vast fund-raising and recruiting societies, such as the Student Volunteer Movement (SVM) and the Women's Missionary Societies (WMS).

Since the majority of missionaries were women, either married or single, 'Women's Work for Women' attracted the attention of feminist scholars, who analysed the exporting of the domestic two-spheres ideology. R. Pierce Beaver, an American church historian, in his pioneering study, *All Loves Excelling* (1968, revised 1980), claimed extravagantly that the WMS societies were 'the first feminist movement in North America and stimulated the rise of various other streams in the nineteenth-century struggle for women's rights and freedom.'[4]

Considering their history, the archival resources for Canadian missions are vast. The earliest Protestant mission propaganda consisted of letters published in British magazines, such as the Church Missionary Society *Intelligencer*. These adventure stories of the 'missionary heroes of the cross' are revisited by several authors in this book. They formed a distinct genre of Sunday school literature, a pious version of the *Boy's Own Annual*. The epitome was Hiram A. Cody's biography of Bishop Bompas, *An Apostle of the North, Memoirs of the Right Reverend William Carpenter Bompas* (1908), which is a Robinson Crusoe story set in the icy Arctic wastes.

The most important synthesis in the new missions history was John Webster Grant's *Moon of Wintertime*, which introduced the idea of the 'encounter' between the dominant culture and the Native populations. Grant was the professor of Church History at Emmanuel College, the United Church seminary, and he brought a critical assessment from within the institution, quite different from the hagiography of the earlier generation. In fact, he concluded, Christianity may belong to the Indian past. 'The bonds attaching Indians to the churches are fragile, and perhaps in some cases irretrievably broken.'[5] That was before the sad revelations about the residential schools and the lawsuits brought by thousands of former students charging physical and sexual abuse and cultural genocide. These lawsuits have threatened to bankrupt the Anglican Church as well as Roman Catholic orders, such as the Oblates.

Grant's colleagues – John Moir at Knox College and C.T. McIntire of the Centre for Religious Studies – edited a volume in 1988 entitled *Canadian Protestant and Catholic Missions, 1820s–1960s*, which summed up the approaches and themes at the time. The primary paradigm was missions as a manifestation of Canadian nationalism. Most chapters focused on the home front, on mission theory and urban missions to identifiable ethnic groups: Protestant missions to French Canadians and Jews, and English Catholic missions to Irish and Ukrainian Catholics. Two chapters examined overseas missions in India and Trinidad; none looked at Canadian Natives.[6]

Meanwhile, independently, other scholars were approaching Canadian missions from the perspective of Chinese history. The pivotal event was the creation of the 'Canadian Missionaries in East Asia Project' at York University in the late 1970s, by Peter M. Mitchell, the son and grandson of China missionaries, and Margo S. Gewurtz, who has a chapter in this book. They compiled oral histories and organized the first scholarly conferences on Canadian foreign missions. Several authors in this book have been associated with this project over the years. It was an international effort, with strong relations with Institutes of Canadian Studies in China. Soon, the United Church and Anglican Archives were inundated with scholars from China, Taiwan, Korea, all seeking to recover their own historical documents which had been destroyed by the wars of the twentieth century.

The first – but unpublished – study to come out of the East Asia Project was John W. Foster's doctoral dissertation, 'The Imperialism of Righteousness: Canadian Protestant Missions and the Chinese Revolution, 1925–1928' (1977), which, as its title implies, was a Marxist interpretation of cultural and religious imperialism, the dominant paradigm in Chinese studies in the 1970s.[7] Alvyn Austin's *Saving China: Canadian Missionaries in the Middle Kingdom, 1888–1959* (1986) presented a more sympathetic interpretation and a broader perspective of Protestant and Catholic missions. But, as Austin stated, this was a history of Canadians, rather than a history of Christianity in China. A.

Hamish Ion wrote a trilogy on Canadian and British missions in the Japanese Empire, which included Japan, Taiwan, Korea, Manchuria, Occupied China, and Hong Kong, from the 1870s to the end of the Second World War. Meanwhile, personal accounts were published regularly, as the older generation of pre-war missionaries were writing their memoirs, as well as scholarly biographies of Bishop William Charles White, James Endicott, and Robert McClure, who were all 'legends' of China missions.[8]

China was always the most significant foreign field, but throughout the 1980s, important studies opened worlds of missions. Ruth Compton Brouwer wrote on Presbyterian women in India. Her *New Women for God: Canadian Presbyterian Women and India Missions, 1876–1914* examined the history of the India mission from a feminist perspective.[9] Rosemary Gagan examined Methodist women in the Canadian West, West China, and Japan in her monograph *A Sensitive Intelligence: Canadian Methodist Women Missionaries in Canada and the Orient, 1881–1925*. Gagan concluded that the 'most accomplished recruits, socially and intellectually, were sent to the politically visible stations of the Orient where they flourished as professional altruists,' while 'the least qualified women ... were consigned to work among Canada's indigenous peoples and immigrants.'[10]

In the 1990s, missions history came into contact with new ideas from the social sciences, such as historical anthropology, discourse analysis, post-colonial literature, and gender and cultural studies. These spoke of complex encounters – J.W. Grant's word again – between two cultures, the colonizers and the colonized, the missionaries and the missionized. This was a two-way street, a dialogue that, as Susan Neylan notes in chapter 4, was 'not necessarily a mutually beneficial conversation between Native and missionary, but it was a dialogic encounter nonetheless.' Reconstructing this conversation – perhaps with a 'hermeneutic of suspicion' – has produced a more nuanced, more ambiguous history of missions than either the missionary hero stories or the dialectic Marxist could imagine.

The pioneers of this new school of mission history were John and Jean Comaroff, who examined the London Missionary Society's (LMS) operations in Southern Africa. With a cast of characters that included the local tribes, the British administration and military, British and Boer settlers, and LMS missionaries, the Comaroffs carefully unwound the delicate interlacings of missionary intentions and, as far as they may be discerned, the motives of the missionized Tswana. 'The long conversation ... proceeded on two levels from the very beginning. Most overt was the tangible attempt to convert the Africans, to overwhelm them with arguments of images and messages, thereby to establish the truth of Christianity. Only partially distinguished from this in the evangelical enterprise was the effort to reform the indigenous world: to inculcate in it the hegemonic signs and practices – the spatial, linguistic, ritual, and political forms – of European culture.'[11]

Our vision as editors and authors is shown in the tripartite structure of this book: Part I on home missions to Native Canadians; Part II, on foreign missions to the heathen overseas; and Part III, a trip to the museum to look at the souvenirs – the 'curios' – the missionaries brought home to explain the Other to Canadian church people.

Part I: The Home Fields begins with two ideas, two seemingly benign tropes that have been part of Christianity since 'Adam delved and Eve span' – cultivation and motherhood – and examines what happens when these seeds were planted by the missionaries as state policy.

Jamie S. Scott starts off with the trope of 'cultivation,' which runs through Christian scriptures from the Garden of Eden, when Yaweh commanded Adam that he must cultivate the soil from which he had been taken. The metaphors grow: planting, reaping, sowing; harvesting souls; scattering the good seed on stony ground; even the term 'mission field' itself. These metaphors of 'the Bible and the plough' assumed a particular resonance in evangelical Christian mission thought and practice at the height of nineteenth-century British colonial and imperial expansion, at once expressing and embodying church–state relations from the metropolitan centre to the far-flung outposts in the Canadian Arctic.

'The discursive logic of the figure of cultivation leads down a violent path,' Scott notes, as transforming nomadic Native peoples into settled, middle-class Canadian citizens became a missionary goal, blurring the boundaries between sociopolitical and theological agendas. The end result was the residential school – based on the reform school model used for recalcitrant youth at home – where each inmate was forced to cultivate the soil from which he had been taken, in a little plot demarcated by a wicker fence.

Myra Rutherdale examines the equally potent metaphor of motherhood among Anglican women missionaries in British Columbia and the Northwest Territories. Looking at the public reports and private let-

ters of 130 women, some English, some Canadian, who served between the 1860s and the 1950s, Rutherdale analyses the self-representations, perceptions, and discursive strategies the women used to write mission and to create their self-identity as mothers. The discursive logic of motherhood also led down a violent path, when these unmarried women became 'mothers' by adopting 'motherless mites' in the residential schools and hospitals. By reshaping Native childhood and family life in the mould of Christian marriage, these women became moral guardians of their charges, going so far as to condone interracial marriage as a way of resolving 'the Indian problem.' By constructing their identity in gender terms, Rutherdale concludes, they also constructed their own racial identity as 'white mothers' – a telling phrase – in the anything-but-family-like residential schools and hospitals.

One underlying theme in both chapters is the tension between the mission bureaucracy (and behind that, the government) in the metropole – whether London or Toronto – and their agents in the fields. These themes – race, gender, and bureaucracy – are picked up by the next two chapters, which introduce two of the most unusual missionaries in nineteenth-century British Columbia, and in the process, recover two lost voices which will surely delight twenty-first-century readers.

Gail Edwards's chapter focuses on the Rev. William Henry Pierce, one of the colourful characters of the BC coast. He was of mixed race, the son of a Scottish Hudson's Bay Company employee and a Tsimshian mother, who became a candidate for the Methodist ministry. As both a Native convert and a Methodist missionary, Pierce was an exemplar of the missionary enterprise as well as a signifier of the triumph of the missionary project of civilizing and converting. Yet, despite (because of?) his marriage to a white missionary, he was never accepted by the other white missionaries, who designated him as a 'Native minister' exclusively to Native communities. Pierce came into confrontation with the missions bureaucracy when F.C. Stephenson and his wife, Annie, the founders of the Young People's Forward Movement for Missions, encouraged him to write his autobiography. Pierce laboured at it for years, but Stephenson lost interest when he discovered it was not the heroic Methodist story with which he wanted to thrill the people at home. To put it bluntly, Pierce was not white enough to pass for a 'real' missionary.

Susan Neylan examines the life of Alexander Wellington Clah, a full-blood Coast Tsimshian, who happened to be W.H. Pierce's uncle. Also a candidate for the Methodist ministry, he provides an Aboriginal perspective on the missionizing process. He accepted the new sources of spiritual power, material wealth, and modes of authority offered by Christianity, while retaining a Tsimshian belief in dreams and portents, the raising of the dead, and visions of the afterlife. Clah's self-proclaimed mission was to walk from one settlement to the next, driven not by wages or fame, but by faith. 'I Believe what God will Said in my heart to teach the poor people. alrounds sometimes I walk 200 miles. Some 300. some 400 miles.' Clah wrote a daily journal from the 1850s to 1909, and as this example shows, his distinctive syntax presents a beguiling counterpoint to missionary narratives. Although literate converts like Clah were privy to the same metaphors, literary devices, and common texts characteristic of the Euro-Canadian discourse on mission work, Neylan shows how he manipulated, rejected, or challenged those conversations, particularly when asserting land rights of his people. 'Did you ever see a Christian take land from another Christian, and sell it, not letting him know anything about it?' he said to the Indian agent.

Part II: Over the Seas and Far Away picks up the themes articulated

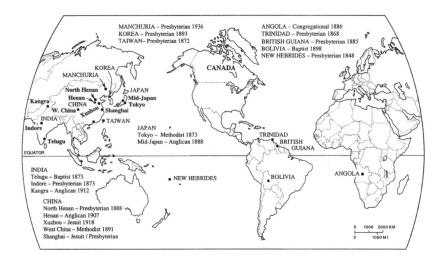

for home missions and transplants them in the foreign missions, under quite different circumstances. Within this broad context, two chapters focus on China missions, while the other two broaden the perspective to the international world between the wars.

Before we discuss these chapters, a brief history of Canadian missions overseas is necessary. The first Canadian Protestant foreign missionaries were sent in 1844 from Nova Scotia, which was still a tiny colony that had barely achieved responsible government. The Secessionist Presbyterians sent the Rev. John Geddie and his wife Charlotte to the Scottish mission in the New Hebrides (now Vanuatu) in the South Pacific. This small but neglected effort is described in two chapters in Part III, by Barbara Lawson and Arthur Smith. That same year, the Nova Scotia Baptists sent Richard Burpee and his wife to join their American colleagues in Burma, which grew into the Canadian Baptist mission in India. By the 1870s, Ontario Presbyterians had established missions in Taiwan, then a part of the Chinese Empire, and in India, while the Anglicans had started work in Mid-Japan.

Since Canadian Protestants were relative latecomers to foreign missions, they had to accept out-of-the-way places (like Trinidad) or get shoehorned into existing fields where British or American societies were already working (such as West China in Sichuan [formerly spelled Szechwan] province). By 1920, the five mainline denominations claimed responsibility for 40 million 'heathens' around the world and sponsored 400 missionaries in China, 200 in India, and 150 in the Japanese Empire.[12] In addition, several hundred Canadians worked in multinational, interdenominational 'faith missions' such as the China Inland Mission and the Sudan Interior Mission. The Methodists alone raised $1.3 million for missions, of which $300,000 went to West China to support 194 missionaries, in what was reputedly the largest mission in the world, with its showplace West China Union University.[13]

The Methodist church, consolidated as a national body in Toronto, concentrated on two large professional missions in Japan and West China. The Presbyterians, more diverse in church organization, had a string of missions from Trinidad and British Guiana (now Guyana) to India, Korea, China, and Taiwan. The Anglican Church established daughter dioceses in Henan (formerly spelled Honan), China; Kangara, India; and Mid-Japan. The Baptists had India and Bolivia, while the Congregationalists, the smallest of the national denominations, had a mission in Angola.

Alvyn Austin looks at the career of a very proper missionary, the Rev. Edward Wilson Wallace, who – 'as much as any one man,' according to Jesse Arnup – made Christian education in China 'respectable.' The son of the professor of New Testament at Victoria College, Wallace was sent by the Methodist church in 1906 to found a daughter of the University of Toronto, West China Union University. On his arrival, he was assigned a larger task, creating an entire school system from kindergarten to university for three provinces of West China. Austin considers the models of education that Scott and Rutherdale discuss for the home missions. But Wallace's purpose was different: he hoped to create English-speaking elite citizens of the New China. To this end he constructed a system of private religious schools, parallel to but not recognized by the Chinese state system.

Margo S. Gewurtz's chapter provides the feminist counterpoint to Wallace's male school system. She takes us to the Presbyterian mission in North Henan to meet the first convert, an opium addict and *yamen* runner (magistrate's enforcer) who was known to generations of Canadians as Old Blind Chou (pronounced 'Old Blind Joe'). The official histories describe his conversion when the missionary doctor performed a cataract operation in public view. When the bandages were removed, Chou reportedly shouted, 'Once I was blind, now I can see.' Missionary accounts edit this event: one leaves out his opium addiction, another elevates his occupation to 'police constable.' Yet each makes the missionary – not the convert, who has much more to lose – the hero on his *agon*, his spiritual quest. With a hermeneutic of suspicion used in feminist biblical scholarship, Gewurtz reconstructs the conversion of Chou and places him in his own family context. In the telling and retelling of the missionary narratives, key actors are written out: not only Chou's wife and mother, but the missionary women themselves, who were instrumental in converting the family.

Ruth Compton Brouwer takes us into the international missions bureaucracy in the interwar years, examining the careers of three professional women: Dr Belle Choné Oliver of India, Dr Florence Jessie Murray of Korea, and Margaret Wrong of Africa. After the horrors of the First World War and the violence of nationalism in the fields, foreign missions were reinventing themselves: *Re-Thinking Missions* was the title of a famous report in 1932. One outcome of these diverse new ambitions was that some Western professional women became colleagues of their male counterparts and mentors and colleagues of modernizing, non-Western men. Brouwer's argument is aptly summed up by the title of her recent monograph, *Modern Women Modernizing Men: The Changing Missions of Three Professional Women in Asia and Africa, 1902–1969* (2003).

Oliver, Murray, and Wrong were participants in a multifaceted process of modernizing missions so as to make them responsive to the 'demands of the hour.' Moving beyond 'women's work for women' in mission work did not automatically mean moving beyond older styles of missionary evangelism. Nonetheless, the gender shift was part of a larger pattern that ultimately had that effect. 'Were my subjects unwitting participants in a process of secularizing missions?' Brouwer asks provocatively.

A. Hamish Ion takes an equally international perspective of the interwar years by examining Canadian Protestant missions in various parts of the expanding Japanese Empire. From the Sino-Japanese War in 1895, when Japan seized its first colony, Taiwan, the Japanese Empire came to include Sakhalin, the Liaotung Peninsula, Korea, the mandated Pacific Islands, and Manchuria (renamed Manchukuo), as well as much of north and coastal China. Canadian missions were located in every area except the islands, and the experience of each mission was different, depending on its identification with Japanese *tennō*-centred ('Emperor worship') nationalism. In Japan itself, Canadian missionaries – as British subjects – aligned themselves with their Japanese Christian friends, who wanted to be patriotic citizens. In Taiwan, the redoubtable George Leslie Mackay welcomed the Japanese occupation in 1895 because it got rid of the corrupt Qing government. Twenty-five years on, Canadian missionaries were key leaders of the anti-Japanese nationalist movement in Korea. In the colonies, the class-consciousness of their underclass and indigenous converts reinforced the missionaries' opposition to the Japanese colonial authorities.

Part III: Bringing It All Back Home returns to Canada to look at the souvenirs the missionaries brought to 'represent' their encounter with the Other. Missionary ethnography, or the analysis of collections made by missionary amateur anthropologists, is a relatively new and exciting field. However, as the controversial experience of the Royal Ontario Museum's *Into the Heart of Africa* exhibit (1989–90) indicated, it, too, is a highly charged political issue.

France Lord takes this book in a completely different direction with her examination of the missionary collections of the Jesuits of Quebec from the 1840s to the 1950s. The history of French-Canadian Roman Catholic missions followed a different trajectory from those of Canadian Protestants, which is, unfortunately, beyond the scope of this book. Briefly, as the French orders were brought into Quebec by Bishop Bourget in the 1840s, such as the restored Jesuits and Oblates, French Canadians increasingly took over home missions to the Canadian Natives.

The first Québécois missionaries entered foreign missions as individual members of French orders ('immergées dans les entreprises étrangères,' according to Cardinal Bégin). Two Sisters of Providence went to Chile in 1853, followed by Jesuits to Zambezi in 1883, Holy Cross Fathers to the Holy Land, and White Fathers to Africa. Important foundations were established before 1920, such as the Soeurs Missionnaires de l'Immaculée-Conception and the Missions Étrangères de Québec.

The main impetus for Quebec foreign missions came after the First World War, when Pope Benedict XV internationalized the predominantly French missions of the church. French-Canadian foreign missions grew rapidly, sending out at least one hundred new missionaries a year, until by 1950 they outnumbered Canadian Protestants: 2000 missionaries in forty countries, with twenty Canadian bishops or vicars apostolic. Their numbers continued to expand through the 1960s, the years of the Quiet Revolution in Quebec, until they peaked at 5256 in 1971 in one hundred countries, of whom over 2000 were in Africa.

The missionary collections of the French-Canadian Jesuits encapsulate this history, from an unexpected angle. When the restored Jesuits were invited back to Quebec in 1843, they were granted their old fields in Huronia, Ontario, and Kahnawake (formerly spelled Caughnawaga), near Montreal. The fathers did not make an ethnographic collection of Indian artifacts as such, but they did assiduously collect documents and relics that pertained to predecessors in New France. By preserving these documents, such as the *Jesuit Relations*, which had been suppressed for a century, they had a profound impact on the writing of Canadian history, which persists today in such hero stories as the film *Black Robe*. In 1903, the French-Canadian Jesuits were granted their first foreign mission, to Alaska, and in 1918 the diocese of Xuzhou, China.

Previous chapters discuss the tension between the metropole and the field, but the demands of the Procureur des missions, the chief financial officer in Quebec City, were extreme by any standard. The Procureur would send shopping lists to China for specific items to stock the Jesuits' private museum, the Musée d'art chinois, and the 'curio shop' attached to it. These orders included such things as a peasant's outfit, 600 fans, back scratchers, and cigarette holders, all of which were to be sold at a profit. The objects gained a different meaning in each locale where they were displayed: in the museum, the Collège de Sainte-Marie, the curio shop, or the *expositions missionnaires*, the multimedia spectacles that attracted hundreds of thousands of people.

Barbara Lawson and Arthur Smith have written complementary chapters on two missionary collectors in the New Hebrides, Canada's first foreign mission. Lawson considers the collection of the Rev. Hugh Robertson: 125 artifacts 'sparsely documented and idiosyncratically gathered' that he donated to the Redpath Museum, the natural history museum attached to McGill University. She examines the collection not only for what it contains, but for what it does not contain. Robertson collected ethnically 'pure' objects that reflected the rapidly dying native culture. Thus, his collection does not contain many 'hybrid' objects that showed the intrusion of British trade goods. Critical consideration reveals intercultural processes and subtleties that are lost when one merely looks to these objects for tangible evidence of an unnegotiated cultural past. In other words, missionary collections were the product of a transaction between missionary and natives, part of the international money economy whereby old objects were replaced by modern consumer goods.

Arthur Smith takes us to the islands of Iririki and Aneityum, where the Rev. Joseph Annand worked for forty years. Smith picks up the theme of cultivation and gardens discussed by Scott in chapter 1, describing how Annand tried to replicate a miniature Kew Gardens in the South Pacific to teach the indigenous people about agriculture. The Annand collection, which ended up in the Royal Ontario Museum, was more eclectic than Robertson's, and included ferns and butterflies, adzes, a walking stick, a mouth organ, and 'pudding bowls,' but few 'fetishes' or weapons. Smith does for the benign idea of 'curios' what Scott does for metaphors of cultivation and Rutherdale does for motherhood; curios were not value-neutral, sentimental souvenirs, but were graphic, almost toxic 'representations' of 'heathen customs.'

Linfu Dong concludes this book with a chapter on the Rev. James Mellon Menzies, who became one of the foremost scholars of ancient China and a founder of scientific archaeology in China. Menzies had a unique career. After graduating in Civil Engineering, he went on to study for the ministry at Knox College. Sent to the Presbyterian mission in North Henan in 1910, he was stationed at Zhangde (formerly spelled Changte, now called Anyang), where he made a discovery that would change his life. He identified the so-called 'Waste of Yin,' which had been the site of the ancient Shang dynasty (also called Yin, 1200–1045 BCE), the first historical dynasty. The fields were littered with tiny white fragments, which turned out to be 'oracle bones,' ancient bones and tortoise shells that had been incised with the earliest form of Chinese writing. For fifteen years, Menzies was the self-appointed custodian of the Waste of Yin, encouraging the peasants not to dig for 'treasure' until it could be scientifically excavated by the Academia Sinic starting in 1928. Anyang is considered one of the most important archaeological sites in the world.

While working as an evangelist during the day, Menzies devoted his free time to archaeology. There are some 150,000 oracle bones or fragments in existence, and Menzies assembled a personal collection of 50,000, by far the largest collection in the world. In order to decipher the oracle bone script, he had to immerse himself in Chinese scholarship to study the changes in Chinese calligraphy over time. One ideograph in particular absorbed Menzies' scholarship, the name of the supreme deity of the Shang people, *Shangdi*, which is usually translated as 'Lord on High.' (*Shangdi* is used by Protestants to translate Jehovah God Almighty.) For Menzies, archaeology was not an end in itself, but rather a way of extending the scope of Christian missions and establishing Christianity within Chinese culture.

'I have directed my life,' Menzies wrote to Sidney Smith, president of the University of Toronto, 'endeavouring to convince the peasants, students and scholars of North China that there is no contradiction involved in being a true Chinese, proud of his cultural tradition, a true scientist searching for truth wherever it may be found and a true Christian living a Christian life in his own Chinese society. This was but the expression of the three great passions of my life, my Sinophilia, my scientific bent, and my missionary purpose.'

The same may be said – in different times and places – of other people in this book.

NOTES

1 John King Fairbank, 'Assignment for the '70s,' *American Historical Review* 74.3 (December 1969): 861–79.

2 John Webster Grant, *Moon of Wintertime: Missionaries and the Indians of Canada in Encounter since 1534* (Toronto: University of Toronto Press, 1984).

3 Alvyn J. Austin, *Saving China: Canadian Missionaries in the Middle Kingdom, 1888–1959* (Toronto: University of Toronto Press, 1986), 85.

4 R. Pierce Beaver, *All Loves Excelling: American Protestant Women in World Missions* (Grand Rapids: Eerdmans, 1968), revised as *American Protestant Women in World Mission: History of the First Feminist Movement in North America* (Grand Rapids: Eerdmans, 1980).

5 Grant, *Moon of Wintertime*, 266.

6 J.S. Moir and C.T. McIntire, eds, *Canadian Protestant and Catholic Missions, 1820s to 1960s: Historical Essays in Honour of John Webster Grant* (New York: P. Lang, 1988).

7 John W. Foster, 'The Imperialism of Righteousness: Canadian Protestant Missions and the Chinese Revolution, 1925–1928' (PhD dissertation, York University, 1977).

8 Lewis C. Walmsley, *Bishop in Honan: Mission and Museum in the Life of William C. White* (Toronto: University of Toronto Press, 1974); Stephen Endicott, *James G. Endicott: Rebel Out of China* (Toronto: University of Toronto Press, 1980); Munroe Scott, *McClure: The China Years* (Markham, ON: Penguin, 1979). See also Linfu Dong, *Cross Culture and Faith: The Life and Work of James Mellon Menzies* (Toronto: University of Toronto Press, 2005).

9 Ruth Compton Brouwer, *New Women for God: Canadian Presbyterian Women and India Missions, 1876–1914* (Toronto: University of Toronto Press, 1990).

10 Rosemary Gagan, *A Sensitive Intelligence: Canadian Methodist Women Missionaries in Canada and the Orient, 1881–1925* (Montreal/Kingston: McGill-Queen's University Press, 1992).

11 Jean and John Comaroff, *Of Revelation and Revolution: Christianity, Colonial-*

ism, and Consciousness in South Africa, vol. 2: *The Dialectics of Modernity on a South African Frontier* (Chicago: University of Chicago Press, 1997), 311.

12 Compiled from H.C. Priest, *Canada's Share in World Tasks* (Toronto: Canadian Council of Missionary Education Movement, 1920), and other sources.

13 Foster, *Imperialism of Righteousness*, 555.

PART I

The Home Fields

Chapter 1

Cultivating Christians in Colonial Canadian Missions

JAMIE S. SCOTT

Introduction

In a seminal statement of the policy which dominated the nineteenth-century evangelizing of the Christian Missionary Society (CMS), Henry Venn, the society's chief secretary in its formative years, 1841–72, couches his celebrated 'three-self' principles in these terms:

> If the elementary principles of self-support and self-government and self-extension be thus sown with the seed of the Gospel, we may hope to see the healthy growth and expansion of the Native Church, when the Spirit is poured down from on high, as the flowers of the fertile field multiply under the showers and warmth of summer.[1]

One historian of missions, David Bosch, associates Venn's policy with the development of the notion of mission as 'inculturation.'[2] Late nineteenth-century issues of the CMS's principal organ, the *Intelligencer*, reverberate with this policy of inculturation. In one lead article, for example, George Ensor draws upon this discourse to associate 'Missions and Civilization.' Invoking the conceits of both Enlightenment progress and Christian eschatology, Ensor argues 'that the connection of Christianity and Civilization is not accidental but essential, not external but vital; for the soil in which alone the plant of a permanent and progressive Civilization will root is that of the moral being, and it is the function of Christianity alone to prepare and subdue that soil into readiness for its implantation.'[3]

As Bosch has pointed out, by the end of the nineteenth century the evangelical missionary movement was divided between those who argued 'that evangelism preceded civilization' and those who argued 'for introducing civilization as a precondition for evangelism.'[4] In either case, though, the discourse of 'cultivation' lubricates the slippage between the salvific and the civilizing agendas of Christian colonialism. This chapter explores this discourse at work and at play in Canada's domestic mission fields.[5] It focuses upon three texts: John West's *The Substance of a Journal During a Residence at the Red River Colony, British North America, in the Years 1820–1823* (1824), William Carpenter Bompas's *Diocese of the Mackenzie River* (1888), and Nicholas Flood Davin's *Report on Industrial Schools for Indians and Half-Breeds* (1879). West's *Journal* plants the seeds for a century of evangelical efforts to civilize the Native peoples of British North America, while Bompas's *Diocese* and Davin's *Report*, virtually two generations later, reflect the discursive interplay that developed between the institutional policies of church and state for cultivating Native peoples in the ways of the new Dominion of Canada. The chapter closes with some remarks on the ambiguous outcomes this doubled civilizing agenda occasioned in relations between Native and non-Native cultures, focusing on the mixed messages at once embodied and expressed in the institution that came to be known as the residential school system.

Cultivating Christians in the 'Wide Waste Howling Wilderness'

Posted in 1820 to the Red River settlement – later Winnipeg, in the province of Manitoba – the Rev. John West became the first CMS missionary to British North America. Methodist and Moravian missionaries had operated in Upper and Lower Canada in the late eighteenth and early nineteenth centuries, after the Thirteen Colonies' War of Independence, and continued to do so, along with other denominations, throughout the nineteenth century. The English-based, evangelical Anglican CMS took the lead in establishing mission stations in the prairie, Arctic, and northwest regions of British North America.[6] Appointed by the Hudson's Bay Company (HBC) as chaplain to the settlers and traders of the Red River colony, West also showed much enthusiasm for converting Native peoples. Published in 1824 after his return to England, West's *Journal* gives a first-hand account of the efforts of early nineteenth-century 'British Christians' to export 'the advantages of civilized and social life, with the blessings of Christianity.' It states that West's evangelical mission is to attempt 'to seek the instruction, and endeavour to meliorate the condition of the native Indians' – goals wholly articulated in the language of cultivation.[7]

Literally and figuratively, West couches his mission in the language of landscape and cultivation. He is fully aware of the profound attachment of the Native peoples to their physical environment. When, for example, West suggests to a Native chief that he 'remove his tribe to a distance from their native soil,' the chief rebuffs the missionary: '"We were born," said he, "on this ground, our fathers lie buried in it, shall we say to the bones of our fathers, arise, and come with us into a foreign land?"' But reading the landscape in and through a totally different cultural vocabulary, West sees only 'wilderness.' Thus named as 'uncultivated' in non-Native terms, the landscape becomes 'uncultured' in spiritual and ethical terms – a 'heathen and moral desert.' In a completion of the rhetorical circle, West looks forward to the day when 'this wide waste howling wilderness [will] blossom as a rose, and the desert become as a fruitful field!' He likens 'the seed of instruction that is now sown' to 'the sure word of Prophecy,' which lies 'buried, waiting for the early and the latter rain.' And his confidence in the future success of his mission seems boundless: 'Christianity shall burst upon the gloomy scene of heathenism, and dispel every cloud of ignorance and superstition, *till the very ends of the earth* shall see the salvation of the Lord [emphasis in the original].' West's determination to lead Native peoples 'to the culture of the field as a means of subsistence' and the evangelical warrant for the Christian transformation of 'this wild waste of heathenism' develop a kind of dialectical isomorphism.[8] To cultivate the heath is to convert the heathen, and vice versa.

The discursive logic of the figure of cultivation leads down a violent path, however, and tellingly, the *Journal* reports Native compliance with this violence. West describes a conversation with a converted chief. Presumably representing his people in the traditional way of such things, it is the chief who first speaks the violence that must be done upon his own people for their own good. He admits of 'a great many willows to cut down, and roots to remove ... before the path [of Christianity] will be clear to walk in.' Written as direct, not reported speech, the words of the chief place civilizing Christian missionaries, rude Natives in need of civilizing, and sympathetic readers of the *Journal* on the same ideological page. West then continues the chief's line of thought, picking up on the figure of land-clearing: 'The axe, however, is laid to the root of the tree, in the establishment of schools, as a means of instruction and of diffusing Christian knowledge in this wilderness.'

Of course, it is a very tough love indeed that understands education in terms of the axe at the root, but the non-Native narrative has already co-opted the Native chief himself as thinking along these lines. In practical terms, West's 'instruction' entails establishing 'the principle, that the North-American Indian of these regions would part with his children, to be educated in the white man's knowledge.'[9] Having co-opted the chief's voice, the civilizing missionary thus seems to enjoy Native support for seizing Native infants, before traditional ways have corrupted their souls, to rear them in non-Native ways, isolated from the temptations of Native life.

Drawing extensively upon the discourse of cultivation, two further passages articulate this pedagogy in some detail. In the first passage, West describes how fellow settlers have warned him of the difficulty of teaching Native people 'Christianity or the first rudiments of settled and civilized life.' The agricultural figure persists:

> I determined not to be intimidated, not to 'confer with flesh and blood,' but to put my hand immediately to the plough, in the attempt to break in upon this heathen wilderness. If little hope could be cherished of the adult Indian in his wandering and unsettled habits of life, it appeared to me, that *wide and most extensive field*, presented itself for cultivation in the instruction of the native children. [emphasis in the original][10]

Refusing the warnings of actual 'flesh-and-blood' farmers, the missionary becomes the cultivator of civilized ways among the Natives, whose own social and cultural traditions constitute a 'heathen wilderness' – a 'wide and most extensive field' awaiting the civilizing violence of Christian education. At the same time, though, civilizing the Natives means putting an end to their 'wandering and unsettled habits of life,' in other words, making real 'flesh-and-blood' farmers of them. Once again, the discourse of cultivation lubricates the slippage between the literal and the figurative, blurring the boundaries between the salvific and the sociocultural aspects of the Christian civilizing agenda.

Having articulated the strategic goals of this Christian civilizing agenda, West spells out the tactics in the second passage. At the 'Church Mission School,' writes West,

> the Indian children ... have already made most encouraging progress in reading, and a few of them in writing. In forming this establishment for their religious education, it is of the greatest importance that they should

be gradually inured to the cultivation of the soil, and instructed in the knowledge of agriculture. For this purpose I have allotted a small piece of ground for each child, and divided the different compartments with a wicker frame. We often dig and hoe with our little charges in the sweat of our brow as an example and encouragement for them to labour; and promising them the produce of their own industry, we find that they take great delight in their gardens. Necessity may compel the adult Indian to take up the spade and submit to manual labour, but a child brought up in the love of cultivating a garden will be naturally led to the culture of the field as a means of subsistence: and educated in the principles of Christianity, he will become stationary to partake of the advantages and privileges of civilization.[11]

Here, West returns the agricultural figure full circle to the literal business of teaching Native children gardening as a prelude to making them 'flesh-and-blood' farmers. Notice, too, that not only are Native children taught to cultivate the ground, but this ground is divided into 'different compartments with a wicker frame.' Native education is thus infused with the Protestant ethic of personal responsibility and the capitalist spirit of individual ownership.[12] Elsewhere West talks of 'agriculture' as 'an important branch in the system of instruction,' and of the delight Native boys take 'in hoeing and planting their separate gardens.' His *Journal* closes in appropriate agricultural terms: 'Not my will, however, but His be done, who alone can direct and control all Missions successfully, to the fulfillment of His prophetic word,' he writes, 'when "The wilderness shall be become a fruitful field"; and "the desert shall rejoice and blossom as the rose."'[13]

From the Red River Settlement to the Residential School

John West returned to England in 1823, and did not set foot in British North America again. Published just over fifty years later, however, Bompas's *Diocese of the Mackenzie River* reveals the extent to which the agricultural coupling of material and spiritual responsibilities had come to dominate the Anglican missionary agenda at the institutional level in the Dominion of Canada, newly confederated in 1867. Bompas left England in 1865 to serve the CMS for forty years in Canada, becoming the first Bishop of Athabasca in 1874, of Mackenzie River in 1884, and of Selkirk in 1891. The long career of this 'Apostle of the North' epitomizes CMS activity in the Pacific Northwest and the

Muscular Christianity in its Anglican form: Bishop William Carpenter Bompas, the 'Apostle of the North,' helping to work a raft in his Diocese of the Macken-zie. From a painting by John P. Campbell.

Canadian Arctic, and his *Diocese* was intended to raise funds from a wider audience for maintaining and expanding CMS influence in those regions.[14] Bompas thus locates missionary activity among the various Native peoples of his ecclesiastical domain within their geographical, botanical, zoological, climatic, economic, sociological, and political contexts. At the same time, though not purely an account of missionary activity in the Mackenzie River, the *Diocese* nonetheless revolves around such evangelical concerns.

In a telling passage, Bompas cites the journal of Alexander Mackenzie, the young, late eighteenth-century explorer for whom the diocese and the great northern river running through it are named. In 1801 Mackenzie published his *Voyages from Montreal on the River St. Lawrence, through the Continent of North America, to the Frozen and Pacific Oceans; in the Years, 1789 and 1793.* Mackenzie prefaces the *Voyages* with a brief history of the Canadian fur trade, in which he attributes the 'failure' of seventeenth-century Récollet and Jesuit missions among the Native peoples of colonial New France 'to a want of due consideration in the mode employed by the missionaries to propagate the religion of which they were the zealous ministers.' The Roman Catholic missionaries adapted themselves to the Native way of life, he argues, and thereby 'acquired their contempt rather than their veneration.'[15] Mackenzie goes on to offer his own suggestions for successful missionizing:

If they had been as well acquainted with human nature, as they were with the articles of faith, they would have known, that the uncultivated mind of an Indian must be disposed by much preparatory method and instruction to receive the revealed truths of Christianity, to act under its sanctions, and be impelled to good by the hope of its reward, or turned from evil by the fear of its punishments.[16]

Like West's *Journal*, Bompas's *Diocese* draws here upon the discourse of cultivation to contrast the strengths of European civilization, founded upon 'the revealed truths of Christianity,' with the shortcomings of Native traditions – 'the uncultivated mind of an Indian.' Again echoing West, Bompas adopts the words of Mackenzie's *Voyages* to slip easily from the theological benefits of Christian civilization – 'impelled to good by the hope of its reward, or turned from evil by the fear of its punishments' – to the socioeconomic benefits of farming:

They [the French Roman Catholic missionaries] should have began [*sic*] their work by teaching some of those useful arts which are the inlets of knowledge, and lead the mind by degrees to objects of higher compensation. Agriculture so formed to fix and combine society, and so preparatory to objects of superior consideration, should have been the first thing introduced among a savage people: it attaches the wandering tribe to that spot where it adds so much to their comforts; while it gives them a sense of property, and of lasting possession, instead of the uncertain hopes of the chase, and the fugitive produce of uncultivated woods.[17]

As their own documents reveal, Mackenzie's judgment upon Roman Catholic missionaries in New France is somewhat misplaced; as for Mackenzie, so for the French Jesuits, civilizing and settling Native peoples are inseparable tasks.[18] But more to the point, like West, with his small garden allotments 'for each child,' divided one from another into 'different compartments with a wicker frame,' Mackenzie espouses a typically individualist Protestant emphasis on personal property and possession – a way of thinking likely foreign to the more communitarian sensibility cultivated by the Roman Catholic missionaries in the reductions of seventeenth-century New France.

As for West, so for Mackenzie's ventriloquizing Bompas, 'agriculture' must replace the 'uncultivated woods' if 'a savage people' are to be transformed into civilized Christians. But in some ways, Bompas seems to push this discursive association between the theological and the socioeconomic further than West. In the *Diocese*, the discourse of cultivation seems almost to displace the realities of physical geography. Though Bompas is well aware of the difficulties of farming in the north, for example, he ignores differences in climate and terrain, and recommends modelling evangelistic policy in the Canadian subarctic on that in Manitoba. There, writes Bompas, 'the missionary success realised appears greatly owing to the efforts made to encourage the Indians to settle and farm, at the same time that they have been indoctrinated with the truths of the Gospel.' Like Mackenzie and West, Bompas laments that 'it is foreign to the Indian nature to remain long in one place,' noting that although 'vegetable crops might be grown in the southern part of the [Mackenzie River] diocese, the Indians have not yet found patience and perseverance enough to continue to cultivate these.'[19] In other words, the temporary failure of non-Native agriculture in the Canadian subarctic has little to do with the unsuitability of climate and terrain, and everything to do with the immaturity of Native culture – the inability of Native people to apply themselves 'yet' to European modes of cultivation.

The word 'yet' is important here, for it expresses the hope – even expectation – attendant upon a Christian eschatology cast in terms of nineteenth-century notions of moral and spiritual development. One day, so Bompas seems to be saying, the Native people of the Diocese of the Mackenzie River will attain moral and spiritual maturity, and their disciplined application to farming and the resulting fruitfulness of their fields will testify to these developments. On that day, church and state will recognize Native Canadians as equal to non-Native Canadians because on that day Native Canadians will be recognizable as civilized Christians. Drawing once again upon the figure of cultivation, an undated clipping from the Anglican periodical *Canadian Churchman* puts it this way: 'There is a certain dignity about the Indian that marks him off from the negro, who in adaptability his superior, is his inferior in those qualities, which, when cultivated and developed place him on a level of acknowledged equality with civilized peoples.'[20] Indeed, the inseparable synchronicity between settlement and farming on the one hand, and 'the truths of the Gospel' on the other, rooted as they are in the discourse of cultivation, prompts Bompas to prophesy that '[f]or resources to be consumed in the country, agricultural produce will probably in the end prove the most reliable, notwithstanding the severe climate.'[21]

For Bompas, settlement, with its attendant emphasis on property and possession, is the bridge that links the socioeconomics of colonial civilization with the Christian ideology of moral cultivation. In so writing, Bompas is expressing the view that colonization, civilization, and cultivation go hand in hand at both the ideational and the material levels. In the words of Comaroff and Comaroff, 'sedentary agriculture, it was believed, was both a cause and an effect of civility and advancement, the fountainhead of productive society and moral community.' Following a pattern repeated around the empire, this view saturates late nineteenth-century writings about the mission fields. Settled in one place and firmly anchored there out of economic self-interest, the nomadic Native Canadian is saved from the temptations besetting vagrant criminal classes – classes 'of shifting populations: of shifty, shiftless people wandering about sans property, propriety, or a proper place in the body politic.'[22]

Further, West's understanding of education as the key to the cultivation of Christian civilization among Native peoples comes to dominate CMS policy in Canada. Like West, Bompas laments the lack of any 'educational system' in his diocese, and like West, he links farming, schooling, and the saving of souls in a common discursive economy.[23] In a chapter entitled 'Church of England Missions,' Bompas writes:

> And yet education is here the main hope of Missionary success, for the minds of the natives need to be trained and enlarged by education to appreciate better the spiritual truths of the Gospel.
>
> In connexion with the diocesan school it appears very desirable to set on foot an industrial farm for the purposes of encouraging the Indians to agricultural pursuits by setting an example of it, and training some of the youths to this work. It seems very desirable in such a wild Indian country as this, Christianity should not be presented to the natives in separation from some of the blessings it usually brings in its train, in regard to a more civilised and comfortable and less precarious earthly existence.[24]

Understanding the processes of civilization in and through the language of cultivation thus permits Bompas to represent schooling in agriculture as essential not only to the salvation of young souls, but also to the conversion of Native 'earthly existence' into something 'comfortable and less precarious.' Transforming nomadic Native peoples into settled middle-class Canadian citizens becomes a missionary goal, further blurring the boundaries between sociopolitical and theological agendas. In Mariana Valverde's words, 'the perfect sociology, perfectly applied, will realize the Kingdom of God on Earth.'[25]

Also couched in figures of cultivation, Canadian federal programs for the assimilation of Native peoples into non-Native ways of life meet this missiological agenda halfway. Davin's *Report* epitomizes this discursive two-way street. Davin served in various capacities in Conservative governments under Prime Minister John A. Macdonald, one of the architects of Confederation. His *Report* worked as a blueprint for formal cooperation between the churches and the federal government in the establishment and maintenance of a nationwide system of educational institutions for Native children. Described by John Milloy as 'a manifesto for residential education' and 'the "official" justification for the concerted attack by church and state upon Aboriginal culture,' the *Report* originated in Davin's investigations into policies for the education of Native Americans in the United States.[26] Davin had met Carl Schurz, the American Secretary of the Interior, and E.A. Hayt, Commissioner of Indian Affairs, who recommended industrial schools for Native Canadians. Davin speaks approvingly of American institutions where, 'in addition to an English education, the boys are instructed in cattle-raising and agriculture; the girls in sewing, bread-making, and other employments suitable for a farmer's wife,' though 'in the case of the boys, agriculture is principally aimed at, cattle-raising requiring but few hands.'[27] The *Report* tells of Cherokee Indian leaders who agree with American officials: ostensibly Christianized in mission schools by the 1860s, and known as 'the most civilized tribe in America,' the Cherokees seemed living proof of how an aggressive educational policy might speed up the process of assimilating Native peoples into non-Native society.[28]

A staunch British imperialist, Davin recommends that the Canadian federal government take advantage of the start already made on civilizing Native children in schools run by missionaries, for 'the Indians have their own ideas of right and wrong, of "good Indians" and "bad Indians," and to disturb this faith, without supplying a better, would be a curious process to enlist the sanction of civilized races whose whole civilization, like all the civilizations with which we are acquainted, is based on religion.'[29] At the same time, Davin is unwilling to waste public monies; these institutions must become 'self-supporting in a few years.' Their best chance for such self-sufficiency lies in the quality of the soil available to them for cultivation. At the Anglican school near Prince Albert, Saskatchewan, 'the land is wonderfully fertile'; Methodist Old Bow Fort, Alberta, possesses 'a vast tract of the finest grazing soil in the world'; and 'the land is excellent' at Presbyterian Riding Mountain, Manitoba. But of the Roman Catholic school at Qu'Appelle, Saskatchewan, Davin writes: 'The soil, it is true, is generally poor, but where the river narrows it leaves a good deal of fair land.' In a sort of metaphorical slippage, theological denominationalism comes to permeate the very soil, it seems, as Davin presumably writes with an eye to the Protestant temperament of his political masters.[30]

In succeeding paragraphs, Davin continues to interlace the logics of these socioeconomic, political, and theological agendas. The success of the proposed industrial residential schools, he argues, will depend on the government's ability to attract not only the teacher with 'force of character' and 'a knowledge of farming,' but above all, the teacher with 'not only the energy but the patience of an enthusiast.' Here, the term 'enthusiast' – meaning, literally, 'filled with the spirit of God' – will have been widely understood to indicate evangelical missionary.[31] And in a final gesture, Davin brings this discursive logic full circle by suggesting that public costs might be further reduced if such teachers are offered 'a percentage on the reduction in the cost of management.'[32] In the last analysis, as Sarah Carter so succinctly puts it, 'missionaries came to be increasingly relied upon as agents of assimilation, particularly because they financed themselves.'[33]

Less and less confident after Confederation about the ability of day schools in Native communities to implement the Christian civilizing agenda, the main Christian denominations – whether based in England, France, Scotland, Quebec, or Ontario – all entered into agreements with the Canadian government's Department of Indian Affairs to develop Davin's system of industrial and residential schools.[34] By 1931, there were 44 Roman Catholic, 21 Anglican, 13 United Church, and 2 Presbyterian schools dotting the Canadian landscape, mostly in the prairies and British Columbia.[35] In most cases, church and state cooperated to locate these schools without regard for the ability of Native families to visit their children or of the children to spend holidays with their families – an institutionalized expression of West's 'principle, that the North-American Indian ... would part with his children, to be educated in the white man's knowledge.' As the Annual Report of the Department of Indian Affairs put it in 1889, 'the boarding school disassociates the Indian child from the deleterious home influences to which he would otherwise be subjected' and 'reclaims him from the uncivilized state in which he has been brought up.'[36]

Federal and ecclesiastical officials received a good deal of public support for this policy, too, particularly in the influential press. Popular magazines trumpeted the wisdom of bringing to bear the combined authority of church and state on the chronically troubled issue of relations between Canada's Native and non-Native communities. In 1891, for example, an article by 'Iota' on 'The Government and Indian Education' in *The Week* argued that reserve day schools were not enough to solve 'the Indian problem,' while 'the boarding industrial school' had 'overruling advantages':

> In the first place the children are always present; they get their lessons every day, not once or twice a month; they are taught to love cleanliness and punctuality, things impossible in their own homes. They have a constant example of the unremitting work with which the white man purchases his. They are given sound constitutions by good food and sufficient clothing, bathing and ventilation. They are given a good practical knowledge of that great civilizer the English tongue, and with this and the bringing together of various tribes in one school, the old tribal enmities are broken up and the child that came into the school a filthy, ignorant

little Cree or Ojibway or Sioux, thinking his language, his village, his tribe, the perfection of all creation, is sent out an English-speaking Canadian. Besides this he has the benefit of the example of good living set before him by Christian men and women and his mind is still further braced by the hand training which he receives.

Above all, Iota concludes, 'the combination of Government and Missionary Society seems to work well, and the pupils turned out feel the white man has done what is fair by him, and that he henceforth must earn his own living.'[37]

In reality, however, daily life in the residential schools was scarcely 'fair.' Essentially, Davin's program drew upon the same English common law doctrine of *parens patriae* (parent of the country) invoked in Great Britain and the United States to justify the public institutions built to house, hide, and tame the increasingly large numbers of destitute children cast up in the wake of late eighteenth- and nineteenth-century urbanization and industrialization.[38] If the state deemed natural parents incapable of providing the essential elements of an appropriate physically and morally healthy upbringing, so the *parens patriae* argument went, then the state must assume these responsibilities. Reciprocal benefits flowed from such an arrangement: state intervention served the best interests of disadvantaged children, who were fed, clothed, and prepared for constructive roles in civilized society, as well as the best interests of civilized society, which might reasonably expect to profit economically and spiritually from the rehabilitation of a generation of youngsters otherwise condemned to wasted lives of petty crime and chronic incarceration. As Juanita de Barros has noted, the founders of these reformatories 'aimed to remove young offenders from "contaminating" contact with adult criminals, to save them from joining the "criminal classes," and to inculcate industriousness.'[39] In the last analysis, however, the emphasis fell on industriousness. The result: the cities of Great Britain and the United States spawned a rash of 'factory-like institutions' where, in the words of E. Brian Titley, 'neglected or delinquent children were trained by brutal regimen for the menial roles they were destined to play in the system of production.'[40]

At once penitential and penitentiary in ethos, the civilizing program of Davin's residential schools was modelled on these industrial reformatories. In Anne McGillivray's summary words, 'the perishing child and the dangerous child were to be reformed by corporal punishment, regimentation and surveillance, isolation from kin and culture, cultural devaluation, religious indoctrination, education tailored to social status and child labour.'[41] In the residential schools, evangelical educators cultivated the values 'vital for effective functioning in the capitalist economy ... in a relentless program of behaviour modification which involved the ringing of bells to indicate time periods and the liberal infliction of corporal punishment.' The missionaries imposed 'a military form of discipline,' cut the hair of Native children, and dressed them in non-Native styles of clothing to create 'the illusion that cultural transformation had taken place.' The children were also forced to abandon 'the use of Indian languages in favour of English.'[42]

Significantly, such efforts to cultivate non-Native habits of mind were coupled with 'practical instruction in trades and agriculture for the boys and in domestic skills for the girls.' Before long, this part of the curriculum 'took precedence over the academic program ... in accordance with the economic role envisaged for the Indians by both church and state.'[43] Missionaries and government officials alike 'absorbed the axiom that agriculture made men peaceful, law-abiding, and amenable to education – at once civil and servile.'[44] Partly to equip the boys for their return to the reserve, partly to help the schools become self-supporting, 'training in agriculture and/or gardening was even more important than trades instruction and was almost universally provided.'[45] But in both cases, the unquestioned ideological association of cultivation with civilization – an association at work, as we have seen, on both sides of an educational agenda initially conceived in terms of 'the bible and the plough' – blinded both church and state to the fact that this training was of little use on many reserves and of little effect on school budgets.[46]

Conclusion

A trope of cultivation runs through Christian scriptures, from Yahweh's post-Edenic injunction to Adam 'to cultivate the soil from which he had been taken' (Genesis 3:23) to Jesus' parable of the sower (Mark 4:1–20). From the earliest expressions of ecclesiastical hope, this trope furnished a discursive ethos within which Christian theologians articulated the growth of the church. The Gospel of John records the missionary dictate of Jesus himself in just such terms: 'My father is honoured in this, that you produce much fruit; then you will be my disciples' (John 15:8). Among the church fathers, Tertullian writes famously of the blood of the martyrs as the seed of the church, while

Augustine reiterates the apostle Paul's confidence that barbarian nations will accept the gospel and join the church 'as she bears fruit and grows throughout the world.'[47]

As we have seen, this trope assumes a particular resonance in evangelical Christian mission thought and practice at the height of nineteenth-century British colonial and imperial expansion, at once expressing and embodying church–state relations from the metropolitan centre to the far-flung outposts of the CMS in the Canadian northwest and subarctic. As Nicholas Thomas has noted, 'the distinctiveness of evangelical colonialism arises not from the terms or metaphors of its propaganda, if these are taken in isolation, but from narratives in which these tropes have specific meanings, and from practices which were inflected, if not wholly shaped, by the terms of missionary rhetoric.'[48]

Permeating Venn's policy statements about 'the elementary principles of self-support and self-government and self-extension' being 'sown with the seed of the Gospel,' as well as West's *Journal*, Bompas's *Diocese*, and Davin's *Report*, the discourse of 'cultivation' at once describes and determines the character of a particular congress of narratives shaping 'meanings' and 'practices' in nineteenth- and early twentieth-century Canada.

Cultural historian Raymond Williams provides some insight into the way in which this discursive interplay between the evangelical and imperial projects likely owes something to the common roots of such notions as culture, colony, and cultivation in the Latin word *colere*. He points out that *colere* carries a range of interrelated meanings: first, 'to inhabit,' from which, by way of the Latin cognate *colonus*, we derive the English 'colony'; second, 'to cultivate,' from which, by way of the Latin cognate *cultura*, we derive the English 'culture,' first in the sense of 'tending, nurturing, husbanding,' and eventually in the anthropologist's sense of all that a society cultivates as essential to civilization; and third, 'to honour and worship,' from which, by way of the Latin *cultus*, we derive the English 'cult.'[49]

In a related vein, Frieda Knobloch stresses that the word 'agriculture' has a specific history, too. Originating in 1603, about the same time as the verb 'colonize,' Knobloch writes, 'agriculture ... is not a generic designator for how any society produces food or even how Europeans produced food a century or two before that.' As such, she continues, 'Euro-Americans have tended not to see indigenous food production [like wild-rice gathering] as agriculture at all, indicating the cultural specificity of this word.' Furthermore, the two words, colo-

nization and agriculture, 'work together: colonization is about enforc-
ing landownership through a new, agricultural occupation of lands
once used differently,' which 'brings about the 'improvement' of land
newly under cultivation – it brings culture to wilderness.'[50] These discursive associations, at once literal and metaphorical, combine and
recombine with the force of an apparently irresistible logic, a logic
which in turn circles around to justify the self-imposed civilizing mandate of church and state alike to bring 'culture to wilderness.'

Correctly, I think, Carter concludes that 'the ultimate goal [of Canadian federal policy] was to bring about the cultural transformation of
the Indian to eventually achieve their total assimilation into white
society.' 'The three basic means to this end,' Carter continues, 'were
missionaries, schools, and agriculture.'[51] As we have seen, however, it
is the discourse of cultivation that blurs, blends, and binds the distinct
mandates among these constituencies into a common cause. Still, it
would be misleading to suggest that church and state were always
and everywhere successful in their shared policy of cultural assimilation, sustained though it was over many decades across the geographically diverse regions of the developing nation of Canada. In this
respect, Stephan Collini has reminded us of 'the complexity of culture.' There is no question but that we need to be aware of unequal
distributions of power and influence of one kind or another in relations between European colonial and imperial officers and their cultural others, Collini argues, but we also need to keep in mind the
dangers of slipping into too easy an opposition between marginalized Native peoples and their silencing oppressors, between a dominant centre and an alienated periphery. Just as 'the centre' is not
monolithic in its intentions, so too, different marginal groups 'in a culture are never self-contained or purely oppositional, but share concepts and values and engage in constant commerce, often intelligible
and profitable commerce, with their cultural neighbours, including
the most powerful ones.'[52] In other words, the complex entanglements
of historical process produce inevitably ambiguous results, even
under the most apparently one-sided conditions of cultural encounter, conflict, and occasional accommodation.

Bearing this caveat in mind, I would like to close by invoking a
couple of vignettes that taken together exemplify the ambiguous legacy of the CMS agenda for cultivating Canada's Native peoples in the
ways of non-Native Christian civilization. The first vignette opens in
1892, when the CMS missionary, the Rev. Thomas Jabez Marsh,

arrived from Toronto to join Bompas in the Diocese of the Mackenzie River. The following year, Bompas sent Marsh to establish a small Anglican mission in the Northwest Territories on the south shore of the Great Slave Lake, close to today's town of Hay River, 1130 km north of Edmonton and 494 km south of Yellowknife. Within a decade, St Peter's mission at Hay River included a mission house, a church (St Peter's), a small hospital, and a boarding school for forty students from the surrounding Chipewyan, Slave, Dogrib, Yel-lowknife, Beaver, Mountain Indian, and Tukudh communities.[53] In 1907, a keen and energetic thirty-two-year-old missionary, the Rev. Alfred James Vale, took over from Marsh. Vale was appointed missionary in charge and principal of the school. He served in these capacities from 1907 to 1927. From 1894, when it opened with five students, until 1937, when it burned down, the Hay River residential school exemplified the nationwide system of residential institutions; it included a large three-storey main building, warehouses, cottages, barns, boatyards, and several acres of vegetables and field crops.[54]

In the second vignette, twenty-five years after Vale's retirement, as church and state began to regroup after the traumas of the Second World War, St Peter's mission survived only as a delapidated church, a warehouse, and a cemetery. Writing in the October 1950 issue of the Anglican periodical *The Arctic News*, the Rev. Donald B. Marsh (no relation to Thomas Jabez Marsh), Bishop of the Arctic, recalled the Hay River residential school 'of Northern fame.' All that 'remains of that great school is a pit and a few piles of scrap wood,' he laments; it has been replaced by 'a $250,000 four-roomed government day school' in the modern, mainly non-Native settlement of Hay River, across the river, built, ironically enough, on Vale Island, named for the former long-time missionary principal of Hay River residential school. 'Some of our Hay River people we have lost,' continues Marsh, and 'there has been no one to marry the young couples save a Roman Catholic priest.' 'The Anglicans and many others are asking for "a minister,"' notes Marsh. 'We who have had such a glorious heritage at Hay River,' he encourages, 'should surely respond to this challenging call. The little historic church, the mission house and the work are all there, but – WHO WILL GO?'[55] Three years later, the call unheeded, Marsh's tone turns nostalgic, even resigned, as he hearkens back in romanticizing, bucolic terms to the former glory of 'the great white painted school' which served as 'the main educational centre for the Mackenzie River Indians; filled with children from Alberta and even from the far

Cultivating Christianity in Canada's Far North: Rev. Alfred James Vale (centre) and Native boys at the Hay River residential school ploughing with sled-dogs because there were no larger beasts, circa 1915. (Note the boys are wearing military-style uniforms.) Vale's photograph albums contain many images of farming, gardens, and prize potatoes.

reaches of the Arctic coast' and 'surrounded with green fields in which were grazing cattle and roaming horses.'[56]

Finally, however, in 1956, Vale himself, long since retired to Vancouver, was invited back to spend a month at St Peter's mission and to serve as chaplain to Marsh at the dedication of a new church. Following 'The Bishop's Letter,' the October 1956 issue of *The Arctic News* contained a short interest piece from Marsh titled 'A Veteran Returns.' The article describes Vale's visit to Hay River, where he 'was missionary and teacher ... for some twenty years.' 'To the Eskimos and Indians,' writes Marsh, 'he was father, counsellor and friend' – the man of God who 'loved them and won them to Christ.' But the most vivid image in the piece contrasts the planting and harvesting of potatoes then and now. Now, in the early 1950s, Marsh contrasts the dog ploughs of 1908, when Vale was residential school principal, with 'the roaring purr of a diesel ... tractor.' 'Civilization moved North!' exclaims Marsh proudly.[57]

But in the contrast of dog sled with diesel engine lies another story. Early in his tenure as principal of Hay River residential school, Vale himself had proudly written that his 'boys, with the exception of three days ploughing did all the work in raising one Thousand bushels (1000) of Potatoes, also cared for a garden which yielded 200 cabbages, 15 bu of Turnips, 5 bu of Beets 3 bu of carrots and 2 bu of Parsnips and also some flowers.'[58] Now, the stirrings of Venn's moral and spiritual self-sufficiency, which their boyhood labours were supposedly designed to arouse in the pupils of Hay River residential school, have yielded to virtually indentured dependency upon the impersonal ministrations of a centralized government bureaucracy. 'The potato field,' writes Marsh, 'was being prepared for the Indians by a representative of the Indian Department,' while 'not far away was the great house excavated by that same tractor and filled with potatoes that the Indians had been paid to gather the year before.'[59]

Meantime, though, according to Marsh, Vale remained 'proud of the little patches around the houses where the Indians had made their own gardens' – evidence that 'they learned the need for cultivation' – and the civilizing influence of Hay River residential school 'has spread to Aklavik, Tuktoyaktuk, Coppermine, Cambridge Bay, Fort McPherson, Fort Simpson, Fort Smith, Fort Resolution, Yellowknife and Fort Wrigley through its pupils who now live and work in these settlements and who are highly respected members of their communities.' Indeed, Marsh quotes a riverboat purser who would take freight on trust only from Native shippers who 'went to Hay River School,' a trapper who singles out a Native man on the riverbank as 'superior to all the rest ... because he went to Hay River School.' A 'dogteam driver,' Joe, confessed that when first he was sent as a youngster to the residential school, he was 'very homesick,' but that Vale would explain how God disapproved of misdeeds, so that 'now whenever I want to do something wrong I can feel his hand on my shoulder and hear him say, "Don't do anything you would be ashamed to do before God,"' and that helps me not to do bad things.' Most pleasing, from Marsh's episcopal perspective, memories of Hay River residential school 'still linger in the minds of pupils such as the Rev. James Edward Sittichinli, Indian deacon, and his wife Julia; the Rev. Thomas Umaok, Eskimo deacon, and his wife Susie on the Arctic coast; James and Sarah Simon of Fort McPherson, as well as catechists, interpreters and other native workers in the North.'[60]

As these vignettes illustrate, the policy of cultivating Christians in colonial Canada ultimately produced oddly mixed results. On the one hand, as McGillivray has noted, government efforts to transform nomadic Natives into settled citizens 'was geared to peasant farming in a machine age.' On the prairies, for example, non-Native farmers 'bought and shared the new gigantic steam engines for the agricultural conquest of the plains,' while '[Native] reserve farmers worked with horse and hand tools.' What is more, Native farmers were unable to raise money to purchase expensive modern machinery, because treaties with Ottawa forbade them from taking out mortgages on reserve lands.[61] The Comaroffs have noted analogous contradictions in the evangelical civilizing program in Africa, where an early nineteenth-century romanticized ideal envisioning free yeoman farmers, domestic housewives, and the nuclear family farm paradoxically 'presupposed the social order of industrial capitalism, itself centred on the urban middle-class household.' The result: by the close of the nineteenth century, in Canada, southern Africa, and elsewhere throughout the imperium, Native males were often reduced to manual labour and their wives to domestic service, or the family were left trying to eke out a livelihood subsistence-farming on the uneconomic fringes of an increasingly mechanized, centralized, and commercialized colonial agronomy.[62] On the other hand, missionary religious indoctrination, as epitomized in the residential school curriculum and its effects on such Native Canadians as Marsh's dog-team driver, Joe, and the various Native Canadian ministers and converts Marsh lists, succeeded in cultivating the seeds of Christian spirituality in fertile Native souls, only to abandon young enthusiasms to the stresses of economic dependency and ecclesiastical anachronism, as the fate of Hay River's St Peter's Anglican mission illustrates. As a symbolic reminder of these mixed messages, the Manitoba Museum of Man and Nature in Winnipeg still holds Donald B. Marsh's collection of approximately 500 Native artifacts, where, presumably, they await either restoration or repatriation.

NOTES

I wish to thank the Social Science and Humanities Research Council of Canada for funding this research.

1 Henry Venn, 'The Organization of Native Churches,' in Max Warren, ed., *To Apply the Gospel: Selections from the Writings of Henry Venn* (Grand Rapids, MI: Eerdmans, 1971), 71.

2 David Bosch, *Transforming Mission: Paradigm Shifts in Theology of Mission* (Maryknoll, NY: Orbis Books, 1991), 450.

3 George Ensor, 'Missions and Civilization,' *Church Missionary Society Intelligencer* (August 1891): 553, 564.

4 Bosch, *Transforming Mission*, 297.

5 John L. Comaroff and Jean Comaroff, *Of Revelation and Revolution: Christianity, Colonialism, and Consciousness in South Africa*, vol. 2: *The Dialectics of Modernity on a South African Frontier* (Chicago: University of Chicago Press, 1997), details the pervasive presence of this discourse of cultivation in the writings of the nonconformist London Missionary Society among the Tswana of southern Africa. In some ways, this paper reiterates in the Canadian context the work of the Comaroffs in colonial Africa.

6 For a contemporary outline of CMS activities in Canada, see Eugene Stock, *One Hundred Years, Being the Short History of the Church Missionary Society* (London: Church Missionary Society, 1898), 87, 103–4, 116, 165, 171. For a more recent and expansive history, see T.C.B. Boon, *The Anglican Church from the Bay to the Rockies: A History of the Ecclesiastical Province of Rupert's Land and Its Dioceses from 1820 to 1950* (Toronto: Ryerson Press, 1962). For a historical overview of Christian missions to the Native peoples of Canada, see John Webster Grant, *Moon of Wintertime: Missionaries and the Indians of Canada in Encounter since 1534* (Toronto: University of Toronto Press, 1984).

7 John West, *The Substance of a Journal During a Residence at the Red River Colony, British North America, in the Years 1820–1823* (1824; reprinted Vancouver: Alcuin Society, 1967), v, vi, 3, 109, 2, 43, 29.

8 Ibid., 155.

9 Ibid., 95, 14–15.

10 Ibid., 13–14.

11 Ibid., 150–1.

12 Comaroff and Comaroff, *Dialectics of Modernity*, 133, describe the southern African mission garden, 'itself a master symbol of civilization and British-ness,' which at first stands 'between the Christians and hunger, perhaps even starvation,' but which 'was also an exemplary appropriation of space ... an icon of colonial evangelism at large.'

13 West, *Journal*, 91, 209.

14 The sobriquet 'Apostle of the North' repeats the title of Hiram A. Cody's biography of Bompas, *An Apostle of the North, Memoirs of the Right Reverend William Carpenter Bompas, with an Introduction by the Most Reverend S.P. Matheson* (London: Seeley, 1908).

15 William Carpenter Bompas, *Diocese of the Mackenzie River* (London: Society for Promoting Christian Knowledge, 1888), 34; citing Alexander Macken-zie's *Voyages from Montreal on the River St. Lawrence, through the Continent of North America, to the Frozen and Pacific Oceans; in the Years, 1789 and 1793; with a Preliminary Account of the Rise, Progress, and Present State of the Fur Trade of that Country* (1801; edited by W. Kaye Lamb, Cambridge: Cam-bridge University Press, 1970), 67.

16 Bompas, *Diocese*, 36; citing Mackenzie, *Voyages*, 67.

17 Bompas, *Diocese*, 35; citing Mackenzie, *Voyages*, 67.

18 Cornelius J. Jaenen, for example, quotes Récollet Father Hennepin: 'But chiefly it should be endeavour'd to fix the Barbarians to a certain dwelling Place, and introduce our Customs and Laws amongst them, further'd by the assistance of zealous People in Europe, Colleges might be founded to breed up young Savages in the Christian Faith, which might in turn con-tribute very much to the Conversion of their Countrymen.' Quoted in 'Edu-cation for Francization: The Case of New France in the Seventeenth Century,' in Jean Barman, Yvonne Hébert, and Don McCaskill, eds, *Indian Education in Canada*, vol. 1: *The Legacy* (Vancouver: University of British Columbia Press, 1986), 45–63, 47; citing L. Hennepin, *A New Discovery of a Vast Country in America* (London, 1698), 2.

19 Bompas, *Diocese*, 34, 40, 41.

20 Quoted in James R. Miller, *Shingwauk's Vision: A History of Native Residential Schools* (Toronto: University of Toronto Press, 1996), 187.

21 Bompas, *Diocese*, 100.

22 Comaroff and Comaroff, *Dialectics of Modernity*, 123.

23 Bompas, *Diocese*, 33.

24 Ibid., 34.

25 Mariana Valverde, *The Age of Light, Soap, and Water: Moral Reform in English Canada, 1885–1925* (Toronto: McClelland & Stewart, 1991), 107.
26 John S. Milloy, *A National Crime: The Canadian Government and the Residential School System, 1879–1986* (Winnipeg: University of Manitoba Press, 1999), xiv.
27 Nicholas Flood Davin, *Report on Industrial Schools for Indians and Half-Breeds* (Ottawa: n.p., 1879), 2.
28 William G. McLoughlin, *The Cherokees and Christianity, 1794–1870: Essays on Acculturation and Cultural Persistence* (Athens, GA, and London: University of Georgia Press, 1995), 3.
29 Davin, *Report*, 14. On Davin's life and opinions, see C.B. Koester, *Mr. Davin, MP* (Saskatoon: Western Producer Prairie Books, 1980).
30 Davin, *Report*, 3, 13–16.
31 Ibid., 15. As the mythological and literary resonances in his narrative poem *Eos, A Prairie Dream; and Other Poems* (Ottawa: Citizen Printing & Publishing Co., 1884) make clear, Davin was a scholar of classical Greek and Latin. He would have been aware of the evangelical implications of the term 'enthusiast.'
32 Davin, *Report*, 3, 13–16.
33 Sarah Carter, *Lost Harvests: Prairie Indian Reserve Farmers and Government Policy* (Montreal/Kingston: McGill-Queen's University Press, 1990), 23.
34 For critical histories of this system, see especially Miller, *Shingwauk's Vision*, and Milloy, *A National Crime*. For an account of parallel practices in the United States, see R. Douglas Hurt, *Indian Agriculture in America: Prehistory to the Present* (Lawrence: University Press of Kansas, 1987). Though he has very little to say specifically about church-run schools, Anthony F.C. Wallace, *Jefferson and the Indians: The Tragic Fate of the First Americans* (Cambridge: Belknap Press of Harvard University Press, 1995), 336, argues that federal educational policy for Native Americans produced ambiguous results. On the one hand, prolonged exposure to non-Native culture inevitably made those Native Americans who returned to their reservations 'agents of cultural change'; on the other hand, however, the failure of non-Native authorities to make 'allowances for tribal distinctions' in the schools probably ended up helping to create a Native sense of cultural solidarity.
35 For statistics on the dispersal of residential schools and attendance by province, see Anne McGillivray, 'Therapies of Freedom: The Colonization of Aboriginal Childhood,' in Anne McGillivray, ed., *Governing Childhood* (Aldershot: Dartmouth, 1997), 154–5.
36 Quoted in J.R. Miller, *Skyscrapers Hide the Heavens: A History of Indian–White Relations in Canada* (Toronto: University of Toronto Press, 1989), 196.

37 'Iota,' 'The Government and Indian Education,' *The Week* 8.24 (15 May 1891): 378, 379.
38 For the role of *parens patriae* in the development of the reform school movement in Europe and North America, see Steven Schlossman, 'Delinquent Children: The Juvenile Reform School,' in Norval Morris and David J. Rothman, eds, *The Oxford History of the Prison: The Practice of Punishment in Western Society* (New York: Oxford University Press, 1995), 363–89. For the transformations in the legal and political status of Native children in Canada, see McGillivray, 'Therapies of Freedom,' 135–99.
39 Juanita de Barros, 'Metropolitan Policies and Colonial Practices at the Boys' Reformatory in British Guiana,' *Journal of Imperial and Commonwealth History* 30.2 (May 2002): 1.
40 E. Brian Titley, 'Indian Industrial Schools in Western Canada,' in Nancy M. Sheehan, J. Donald Wilson, and David C. Jones, eds, *Schools in the West: Essays in Canadian Educational History* (Calgary: Detselig Enterprises, 1986), 133.
41 McGillivray, 'Therapies of Freedom,' 151.
42 Titley, 'Indian Industrial Schools,' 141.
43 Ibid., 143.
44 Comaroff and Comaroff, *Dialectics of Modernity*, 123–4.
45 Titley, 'Indian Industrial Schools,' 143.
46 See J.R. Miller, 'The Policy of the Bible and the Plough,' in Miller, *Skyscrapers Hide the Heavens*, 189–207.
47 Maurice F. Wiles and Mark Santer, *Documents in Early Christian Thought* (Cambridge: Cambridge University Press, 1975), 259.
48 Thomas, *Colonialism's Culture*, 8, 135. In its analysis of the trope of cultivation in Canadian missionary discourse, this chapter owes much to Thomas's approach to colonial and post-colonial cultural history.
49 See Raymond Williams, *Keywords: A Vocabulary of Culture and Society* (New York: Oxford University Press, 1976), 76. Comaroff and Comaroff, *Dialectics of Modernity*, 123, 443 n.15, draw attention to Williams's work, suggesting that 'historical connections among the concepts of culture, cultivation, civilization, and evolution' also carry implicitly colonial and racist assumptions.
50 Frieda Knobloch, *The Culture of Wilderness* (Chapel Hill: University of North Carolina Press, 1996), 4, 5. In these respects, Knobloch's work has significant implications not only for the role of missionaries in promoting non-Native forms of food production, but more widely, for present-day ecological theologies and their various efforts to reclaim the traditional wisdom of Native modes of food production for a less invasive, less predatory

approach to farming, forestry, and fishing. Knobloch notes, too, the especially devastating effects of non-Native agricultural theory and practice
upon the North American landscape and its Native inhabitants, particularly 'the breaking plow' and absolute notions about 'good' and 'bad'
plants – 'weeds and not-weeds' – which have 'nothing to do with the individual identities of the plants involved' or their 'noncommercial value'
(117). More to the point, she stresses that the socially and culturally disruptive consequences of an agriculture 'which underscored again and again
the emphasis on "efficiency," commercial value, and greatness of scale – as
well as the accompanying marginalization of noncommercial forms of
agriculture and the arrangement of women, Native Americans, and farm
laborers in their respective places in an elaborate social hierarchy represent
choices made by the powerful and bargains made by the less powerful'
(74).

51 Carter, *Lost Harvests*, 23.
52 Stephan Collini, 'Grievance Studies: How Not to Do Cultural Criticism,' in
    English Pasts: Essays in History and Culture (Oxford: Oxford University
    Press, 1999), 252–68, esp. 263–4.
53 For Marsh's years at Hay River, see the 'Introduction and Biographical
    Sketch' to Janet Pennington, 'Marsh, Reverend Thomas Jabez: An Inven-
    tory,' NWT Archives, Culture and Heritage, Department of Education,
    Culture and Employment, Government of the Northwest Territories, Yel-
    lowknife, Northwest Territories (June 1993), http://pwnhc.learnnet.nt.ca/
    research/findingaids/N–1988–039.pdf. Accessed 24 October 2003.
54 Vale's photograph albums in the Anglican Church General Synod Archives
    are a visual source for his agricultural efforts, including fields of potatoes
    and cabbages, and small individual garden plots.
55 *Arctic News* (October 1950), 4; emphasis in the original.
56 *Arctic News* (October 1953), 10.
57 *Arctic News* (October 1956), 4, 3.
58 Quoted in Miller, *Shingwauk's Vision*, 258–9.
59 *Arctic News* (October 1956), 3.
60 Ibid., 3–5.
61 McGillivray, 'Therapies of Freedom,' 142. For a thorough analysis of the
    effects of the policies of the Canadian federal government on Native farm-
    ers on the prairies, see Carter, *Lost Harvests*.
62 Comaroff and Comaroff, *Dialectics of Modernity*, 136.

Chapter 2

Mothers of the Empire: Maternal Metaphors in the Northern Canadian Mission Field

MYRA RUTHERDALE

Introduction

Identity and self-identity have increasingly become a focus for historical and sociological discussion. How do people see themselves, and are their identities fluid or contingent upon time and place? When I started to read the primary sources on the lives of 130 or so Anglican women who worked in Aboriginal communities in northern British Columbia, the Yukon, and the Northwest Territories in the late nineteenth and early twentieth centuries, I wondered how women missionaries wrote about and saw themselves. How did they and the mission agencies reflect upon their mission work? Through an analysis of the self-representations, perceptions, and discursive strategies women used to write mission, it became evident that one of the most pervasive identities used to describe and justify their work was maternity. Maternal metaphors were frequent in diaries, letters, and articles produced in the northern mission fields.

The women in this study were part of a mission frontier in northern Canada. They were all Anglican. Many were teachers or nurses hired by the Anglican Church to help convert Aboriginal peoples to Christianity; others were missionary wives who accompanied their husbands to mission stations across the north. A little less than half of the women came from England with the Church Missionary Society (CMS), and the rest were mostly Canadian, and hired by the Missionary Society for the Church of England in Canada (MSCC).

The image of missionary women as 'mothers' was constantly remarked upon. They were described as mothers of the church, mothers of children in residential schools, and mothers of junior clergy. The idea that missionary wives could be 'mothers' to the church or to those who attended the church was remarkably consistent. Parent societies and male missionaries reinforced the maternal metaphor. When the Rev. William Collison was preparing to marry Marion Goodwin in England before they left for his first mission in the diocese of Caledonia in northern British Columbia, the CMS committee approved her because she would be a 'true mother to the infant church at Metlakatla.'[1] At the death of Mrs Ridley, Bishop William Ridley of the Diocese of Caledonia claimed the Tsimshian felt 'orphaned.'[2] When Stella Du Vernet, wife of the second Bishop of Caledonia, died in 1929 she was described as a 'real mother to the clergy, and indeed to the hundreds of young men who were trying to establish themselves in this new land.'[3]

Historians and mission scholars have long recognized the existence of the discourse of maternity in the mission fields of East Asia, India, and Africa. Jane Hunter, who writes on missionary women in China, describes the exportation of American domesticity and suggests that 'the interaction between "the home and the world" [is] a fertile ground for both further empirical and theoretical inquiry.'[4] Margaret Jolly considers the connection between motherhood and empire in an intriguing case study of two colonizing women in the South Pacific, and argues that gender had a major influence in colonial encounters. White women related differently to Aboriginal women than did their male colleagues. Women could relate to each other because of their common experiences as women. The rules of engagement in colonial settings encouraged detachment rather than intimacy between races, yet the 'mother–daughter' relationship introduced a parallel norm and at the same time allowed for some detachment:

> The symbolic constitution of the relationship between colonizing women and colonized women in the familial mode as that between mother and daughter was a poignant but strategic expression of the tension between superordination and identification, between detachment and agonized intimacy, between other and self.[5]

Implicit in the construction of the image of motherhood was the understanding that women were guardians of morality. In her study of matrons and rescue workers in the American west, Peggy Pascoe identifies certain patterns in what she calls a search for women's 'moral authority': 'its origins in a "women's culture" rooted most firmly among white middle-class women, its use of the female values of that culture to strengthen the social authority of women, and its assumption that those values applied (or should apply) to women of ethnic minority groups as well as to white women.'[6]

Of course, motherhood rhetoric was also employed in noncolonial settings. As historian Anna Davin has shown, the links between empire, motherhood, and race were constantly reinforced in early twentieth-century England.[7] Barbara Caine's history of Victorian feminism argues that this maternal ideology was both binding and liberating for women: 'feminists found in early Victorian domestic ideology not only a set of ideas which they had to combat, but also one which helped them to negotiate with liberalism and with the gendered nature of the public sphere.'[8] Caine links evangelical religion with an extended idea of domesticity, which ultimately provided some women with a wider sphere: 'From a statement of the limitations women face and of their necessary domestic confinement, it thus moves to the demand that women carry first into their homes and then into the wider society something of the religious zeal and fervour which other missionaries were taking to the heathen in the foreign lands.'[9]

A maternal identity was especially strategic in northern Canada. Ironically it allowed women more freedom to practise their ministry than they would have had in either southern Canadian dioceses or in England. Like Pascoe's rescue-home matrons, women missionaries saw themselves as the purveyors of a Christian womanhood which, once introduced, would appeal to all. Women missionaries developed 'mother–daughter' relations with young Aboriginal women in mission houses, hospitals, and schools, and they attempted to mother Aboriginal children, yet there is no evidence that they felt sisterly solidarity with Aboriginal women their own age.

Mothers of the Empire and 'Their' Children

Kathleen Martin went into the field conscious that she would be on her own, the only Anglican missionary in Fort Selkirk, Yukon. In 1916 she was encouraged by a minister in Vancouver to contact Bishop Isaac O. Stringer, bishop of the diocese of the Yukon, about working in the north. A trained teacher, Martin claimed to feel 'drawn to the work amongst the Indians.' She had no mission training, but had taught Sunday school in Vancouver for a number of years. When Bishop Stringer responded to her inquiry he confessed he was short-staffed because of the First World War and in need of a man for the Carcross school: 'The Rev. W.T. Townsend who now teaches the school has volunteered as Chaplain for the front, and his name has gone in with my approval. I had thought of having a man, but it is possible that a lady teacher might do.'[10] As it turned out, Martin was needed instead at Fort Selkirk, where there was an Aboriginal catechist, Jonathon Wood, but no other missionary nearby. Bishop Stringer described Fort Selkirk, north of Whitehorse, as a 'rather lonely place,' but assured Martin that there were two white women, probably traders' wives, in the village. Except for occasional trips to the 'outside,' Martin stayed in the Fort Selkirk area until the early 1950s, almost forty years.

Martin delighted in mothering the children in the village. At one poignant moment when she felt discouraged about the impact of her work, Martin claimed to be cheered by a visit from Peter McGinty, chief of the Selkirk band who wanted to know how long Martin would be staying there. He wanted her to continue her work, as did others in the village. 'I really did intend going out in the summer to stay,' reported Martin to Bishop Stringer, 'but the Indians won't even consider it. I scold them, order them around, spank their youngsters, and do all sorts of queer and unheard of things, but still they seem to want me to stay.'[11]

And, when she was on furlough in Vancouver in 1928, she wrote to the bishop to tell him that she was anxious to return: 'I miss the children very much, no one seems to need a "white mother" here.'[12] This was a critical moment in her self-identification. Martin obviously revelled in her status as a mother to Aboriginal children, and identified herself as a 'white mother.' The maternal identity was important to her self-perception. And so too was her identity as a white woman. She, however, did not see any contradiction in the fact that the children she mothered were not biologically her own. In fact, at least in the context of her mission work, she quite clearly defined the norm for motherhood as unmarried white women.

Like Martin, Selina Bompas cared for several Aboriginal children at various mission homes throughout the Yukon and identified herself as 'Mama Bompas.'[13] She grew attached to the children, especially the babies. Her first was an infant named Jennie. While nursing the baby in the fall of 1876, Bompas disclosed her emotional need: 'The dear babe is still very delicate and has needed constant watching and care ever since she came to me a year ago. Still, she has been a great blessing and comfort to me, and I know not what I should have done on some

Selina Charlotte Bompas, with one of the many children who passed through her hands and who gave her purpose and the reconstituted identity as 'Mama Bompas.'

of these long dreary nights without her little hand patting my face, and her bright little face cheering many an anxious hour.'[14] When Jennie died in 1877, Bompas remarked that she had 'from the first viewed the Indian children as my especial charge.'[15]

Bompas was always pleased to have new children in her home, but sometimes they prompted bittersweet longings for former charges, who had returned to their parents or had died: 'It was very merciful of God to let me have charge of another little Indian child [named Mary],' she wrote. 'It was very painful at first, as she is just the age of my little Lucy the year we went to Fort Norman, and one seemed living over the past again, and at times almost forgot the interval of deep sorrow.'[16] Mary reminded Bompas of Lucy's 'quaint Indian ways,' suggesting the tendency to construct racial identity. Yet she herself undoubtedly gained a sense of accomplishment and self-identity through her motherhood role. In 1900 Bishop and Selina Bompas moved to Cariboo Crossing in the southern Yukon, where he planned to open two new missions. When they decided not to take any more children into their home Selina confessed great sadness, stating that she had grown so fond of caring for children that she 'had lost an object in life.'[17]

Florence Hirst claimed similar feelings while nursing Inuit children in the Pangnirtung mission hospital on Baffin Island in the winter of 1936. She described how she felt about a tiny infant girl in her charge. The little baby, Betty, was portrayed as the 'darlingist little thing I ever saw.' She said that she was never happier and described her routine: 'I feed her – bath her dress her – scold her and love her – She is the sweetest softest most cuddlesome little thing. A real Eskimo – covered with blue spots and brown skin. I think she smiled at me yesterday.'[18] Hirst felt entirely fulfilled in her work with Betty. In contrast to her interactions with other patients, she was able to cuddle and love Betty, even if that meant occasional scolding.

Hirst's elation was consistent as three days later, she related: 'I don't think I was ever so happy in my life before as I am with the sole care of this little motherless mite, Oh she is a pet. Fat and sleepy, and soft and cuddlesome! I just love her with all my being.'[19] Betty improved steadily during her three-month stay at the hospital. Hirst lamented the day when she would have to return Betty to her father, but sadly the infant died unexpectedly. Hirst wrote in her diary: 'She passed away in her sleep ... with a faint smile on her face, and her little hand up above her head, just as Prue left her. It must have been her heart, which is not unlikely when one realizes just what background she had.'[20]

At the time of Betty's death Hirst was devastated. She felt a certain emptiness. She missed bathing and feeding her and wrote that she felt 'completely lost' without the child to pamper. Her identity, in part, was shaped by her self-perception as a 'mother.' Hirst's description also epitomizes Christian grandiloquence. It seems to assume the Inuit might not care for a motherless infant and suggests once again that racial barriers were constructed to suit circumstances since, presumably, the community and extended family had nurtured the child. Nevertheless, Prudence Hockin, a nurse at the Pangnirtung hospital, and Hirst both achieved a sense of purpose through mothering 'motherless mites.' When Hockin's charge Rhoda left the hospital Hirst claimed that 'It well nigh broke our hearts, for we felt that we were more to the child than her own mother – we had cared for her since she was 7 weeks old, and she was now one year.'[21]

Reconstituting Family Life

Like mission homes and hospitals, northern schools also provided a setting for women missionaries to construct themselves as mothers. Schools varied depending on both the location and population. Lessons took place in either mission homes, separate buildings designated as Indian Day Schools, or in residential schools. In general, the missionaries tried to establish an educational setting at each station. The earliest schools seemed concerned with projecting a positive, though culturally specific, image of family life. The image of a happy family was important. In discussing life at the residential school in Hay River, Northwest Territories, for example, the Rev. Thomas Marsh described Miss Orr, the teacher, as a perfect mother who busied herself 'mothering the little children in every way, seeing that they are kept clean and their clothes mended, that the sick are brought to Mrs. Marsh or me, as the case may be and seeing to all the other cares that a family of twenty-two or twenty-three children must bring.'[22]

A short time later, a travel writer, Agnes Deans Cameron, arrived for a brief stay at Hay River before returning home to relate her 'adventures' in the Canadian north. In *The New North: An Account of a Woman's 1908 Journey through Canada to the Arctic*, she wrote that Hay River was the 'most attractive' mission in the north. She felt the Anglican school was full 'of earnest and sweet-hearted women bringing mother-love to the waifs of the wilderness, letting their light shine where few there are to see it.'[23]

One of the primary aims of the mission schools was to teach children about Christianity as early as possible. A clear articulation of this goal was missionary William Hogan's colourful prescription for creating Christians in the Queen Charlotte Islands: 'I believe the great secret of success, in all missions is in getting hold of the young of both sexes & training them from six years old till fifteen & implanting the bible teaching doctrinarily deep in their hearts.'[24] Several missionary women from England attempted this at Metlakatla, British Columbia. In 1898, for example, Mildmay-trained missionary Alice Tyte wrote to the secretary of the CMS apologizing for not having time to write earlier, and describing her work: 'I know that you will understand that with a family of twenty five one has a heartful, headful and handful, with very little leisure time to sit quietly and write even to our dear ones and the many loving and sympathetic friends in the homeland.'[25] The image of family life was important for Tyte's self-perception as a mother figure.

Of course, the descriptions of children taken from their real mothers and sent to residential schools challenge the image of missionaries as mothers. What is painfully obvious is that missionaries involved in Aboriginal education believed that what they were doing was justified. Otherwise they could not have stayed in mission work. Two striking accounts written twenty years apart suggest the torment of the children as they became accustomed to their new environments. Their resistance and painful struggle are obvious. Writing for a juvenile audience in 1908, Selina Bompas described a typical first-year experience, and how difficult the first year of school was for the 'Indian child.' According to Bompas boys and girls were equally resentful of being forced indoors. Boys however were eager to go off on the hunt with their male kin and could hardly contain themselves if they caught sight of men readying to leave the village: 'He will start to run after the hunter, and if caught and sent back to school, he will cry and yell until the whole camp is roused, and tearful sympathizing mothers rush in to know who is dealing this harshly with their darling.'[26] Girls too felt trapped in classroom settings: 'The girls are equally resentful of restraint, and look upon a closed door or window as their natural enemy.'[27] In Bompas's view the children resented the constraints of school because of where and how they were 'born and bred.' She concluded her comments with a story about a girl named Frisky who escaped through her bedroom window and ran away because she felt like picking berries.

In 1928 Ethel Catt wrote of escorting three children from Herschel Island in the High Arctic to attend the school at Hay River. Catt shepherded them and other children from surrounding mission stations, from Fort Chipewyan down to Hay River. She began with three siblings, George, John, and Mary, who ranged in age from five to nine years old. None could speak English and all were frightened. Before they left, John ran away and had to be dragged back to the mission. George sat on the bottom of the gangplank and refused to go on to the boat, and had to be carried on. Once aboard he promptly locked himself in the washroom. Finally, as Catt was putting them to bed aboard the ship they began to cry. As Catt wrote: 'I tried talking, singing, coaxing, but nothing would do & of course they did not know a word I said.' They made it to Hay River, and some time later Catt concluded that though these three 'creatures' resisted being 'harnessed,' they had 'fallen into school ways beautifully and will make fine men and women.'[28]

Scenes like this were repeated time and time again across the north as children were taken to residential schools. In 1928 Miss Ridgeway at Carcross school in the Yukon described the difficulty of the situation. In her report to the Woman's Auxiliary she complained that she was overwhelmed with work: 'I have 36 children to teach – from those who do not know one word of English and scream at the oppressiveness of a roof over their heads for the first time to seniors in Grade Six.'[29]

Residential schools left Aboriginal children 'betwixt and between' two cultures and unable to cope adequately in either white or Aboriginal worlds.[30] Students experienced traumatic disruption in their childhood and adolescent development. Worse, the teachers deliberately tried to alienate them from their own languages and cultural practices. Yet despite the obvious discordance between children's real needs and the residential school environment, missionary women and men persisted in the belief that they were improving Aboriginal children, and that such schooling would produce, as Catt put it, 'fine men and women.'

Missionaries in northern villages were instructed by their bishops to be on the lookout for children to attend schools, but if parents refused to send their children there was very little that could be done. Many Aboriginal people did resist. When students returned home for the summer they often spoke of their terrible experiences and parents

Metaphors of motherhood in Canada's High Artic: Bessie Quirt and Inuvialuit girls at Shingle Point school, Northwest Territories. Scenes like this were repeated throughout Canada's home missions.

sometimes refused to let them return in the fall. Missionaries denied the rumours and defended the schools. At any rate, in the scramble to 'civilize and Christianize' Aboriginal children these emotions were covered up. Rather than allowing Aboriginal mothers to raise the children, 'mothers of the Empire' became surrogates in residential schools run by the Anglican Church from Hay River on Great Slave Lake to the Chooutla School at Carcross.

The metaphor of maternity persisted well into the 1930s. Toronto-born deaconess Mabel Jones declared her pride when eight children were confirmed at the Shingle Point school: 'This beautifully solemn Service always stirs one to the depths, but perhaps this Service had special meaning for us in that those who were confirmed, with one exception, were our boys and girls whom we had the privilege and responsibility of mothering for several years at school. We felt something of the awe mixed with joy of real parents when their children stand forth and publicly make Christ their choice.'[31]

Mothering 'motherless mites' became for many women a way to justify their work in the north. Convinced that their benevolence was necessary, they secured their positions by reformulating themselves as mothers. While it is tempting to be critical, one must also recognize that the women's responses to the children appeared to be based on close, intimate bonds.

Mothers of the Empire Remake Marriage and Motherhood

One recurring theme in mission literature focused on how Aboriginal children were raised. In order to identify themselves as superior mothers, British and Canadian missionaries sometimes devalued Aboriginal women's maternal skills. Their most common complaint was that Aboriginal mothers were weak disciplinarians. Typical was an article entitled 'Indian Girls and Women,' in the *North British Columbia News* in 1912. Aboriginal women were lax with their children, the author claimed: 'Unselfish she slaves for her husband and her children, without thinking of herself at all. Not that she attempts to train the children in ways of obedience, for the child pleases itself entirely, its will is never crossed. The children please themselves whether they attend school or no the parent never compels.'[32] Similarly, Sarah Stringer, who began her work in the north in 1896, said in an address to the women of Winnipeg's Canadian Club in 1931 that Inuit parents 'never punish a child; when they ask them to do something they do not persist in having them do it; the parents ask them why no, but they do not insist.'[33] Parents, but most usually mothers, were thought to be weak and passive with their children.

By contrast, in the mission schools the children were subjected to a life of discipline and strict regimentation. The curriculum for girls stressed household management and childrearing: preparation for marriage and a life of household labour was the objective. A matron of the Ridley House for 'white and half-breed' children at Metlakatla claimed: 'The girls do cooking, sewing dressmaking, laundry and household work. The boys take their share of the housework, clean the boots and knives, saw and chop the wood, and in the spring and summer do some gardening.'[34] Although both girls and boys were taught how to speak, read, and write English, the emphasis for girls was on household management.[35] In the same letter in which the Rev. William Hogan insisted that Bible knowledge be implanted 'doctrinarily deep in the hearts' of Aboriginal children, he also emphasized the value of teaching girls domestic duties: 'This is followed out here most admirably under Miss Dickinson who is so thorough going and energetic. Her life and self sacrifice cannot but tell upon the lives of those Indian girls from the various tribes along the coast: she trains them so that they may be able to take care of their own houses in days to come & prepares them in all household duties.'[36]

Some seven years later, in 1905, the Rev. J.H. Keen noted that this rigid routine continued to be followed by the students at the Indian girls' school at Metlakatla. The girls usually entered at the age of ten, and it was hoped they would stay until they reached sixteen or seventeen. Their daily routines at the home were very clock-oriented. 'It is now 4:30 p.m. and they have work to do before tea,' Keen stated. 'A large basket full of stockings is brought in and distributed and these the girls proceed to mend. At other times of the day we might have seen them washing their clothes, or scrubbing the floors, or cooking or learning dress-making.'[37] Keen believed the girls would 'become true Christians' and, equally important, good housewives under the guidance of the women teachers. According to Margaret West, the pupils began their day at 6 a.m. and then met in a large playroom 'for united prayers and praise to God, who has, for the time being, permitted us to be one family and we often pray that the lessons we learn together at these morning meetings may sink deeply into our hearts and bring forth fruit into our lives.'[38] West wanted the school to function like a family home. She believed herself to be the mother of a unified family. Clearly, institutional life did not at all correspond to family life, but the family ideal remained a constant ideological gloss and moral model.

Marriage preparations for Aboriginal girls had a certain irony. Here young girls were being prepared for marriage by women missionaries, many of whom were unmarried themselves and who may have been attracted to the mission field because it appeared to offer freedom from prescribed roles in their own societies. Missionaries wanted Aboriginal girls to marry, and apparently they had some influence. Florence Eden-shaw, a Haida woman from Masset on the Queen Charlotte Islands, remembered play-acting weddings with her playmates:

> Once Phoebee, Emma [Matthews], Douglas and I decided to play wed-ding in the woods. 'You want to marry Douglas?' 'No.' They ask another one. 'No.' They were all shy. 'Who's going to marry Douglas?' No one said anything. 'Florence you marry him.' 'OK.' We got somebody's veil to take to the woods. Phoebe and Emma put flowers at the front of the veil. They worked at it for quite a while and then they put flowers on their hats that they made out of skunk cabbage leaves, and they made bouquets. All the bridesmaids followed me down to the village. I don't remember if we pretended to have a feast or not. I must have been ten or eleven.[39]

'Pretending to have a wedding' was no doubt a common game for North American children in the first decade of the twentieth century, but, as Margaret Blackman has observed, it is significant that Eden-shaw and her friends were not pretending to be at a potlatch, nor were they mimicking the traditional winter dance. They were acting out a Christian ceremony, complete with veils and corsage, modeled wholly on the expectations of missionaries.

Missionaries were pleased when Aboriginal women, especially those under their care, chose to participate in a Christian wedding cer-emony. In the 1970s, Angela Sidney, a Tagish-Tlingit elder, remem-bered a conversation with Mrs Watson, an Anglican missionary who taught at the school in Carcross, that took place in 1916:

> 'I understand that you are married.'
> I said 'Yes.'
> 'Did he give you a ring?'
> 'Yes, he gave me one – his own ring – one time when we went to cache.'
> 'Are you married in church?'

I said, 'NO.'

'Well, you know what?' she said. 'You're not supposed to be like that. You've got to get married in church!'

Well, I told her I didn't mind, but my husband wouldn't want it – not to get married in church.

Mrs Watson waited for George Sidney to come home from work that evening:

'I understand you're married,' she told George.

'Yes, Angela Johns.'

'Well, you know you've got to get married.'

'We are already married, Indian way. Its just as good, isn't it?'

'That's not good enough,' she told him. 'You've got to marry her white man way. I raised that kid!' she told him.

The belief that there was an 'Indian way' and a 'white man way' was based on the fact that most Aboriginals did not feel it necessary to have church-sanctioned marriages. The 'white man way' meant that a religious ceremony would take place. In this case, not only did Mrs Watson convince George that a Christian ceremony was necessary, but, as Angela recalled, she also bought her a cream-coloured linen suit, white shoes, a hat, and a string of pearls: 'she told me everything I should wear.' Watson had her way and the Sidney's were married – twice. Angela Sidney's story of how Watson insisted upon a Christian marriage, supplied the clothing, and then on the day of the wedding acted as a parent by giving away the bride, is illustrative of how intensely involved missionary women could become in Aboriginal women's lives. Yet, Angela Sidney did not recall the story with bitterness: in fact, at the beginning of the conversation she said 'Oh, she was so kind, she loved me up and everything.'[40] Both Florence Edenshaw and Angela Sidney give testimony to the persistence of the missionary's desire to ensure that the young girls they came into contact with would become married. And marriage was not enough: their relationships had to be sanctified by Christian marital ceremonies.

Missionaries encouraged Aboriginal girls to marry because they hoped that once family life was established Aboriginal people would end their seasonal migrations and settle permanently in villages. When an Aboriginal girl married, a feeling of accomplishment and satisfaction was expressed. Elizabeth Wilgress sent a photograph to *The New Era* in 1908 with a description of a young girl named May Kai who married at Hay River: 'We are very glad to see her married though she is only sixteen. Her husband is the son of the headman of the village.'[41] Similarly, Sarah LeRoy at Hay River wrote to the *Letter Leaflet* that she was pleased when one of her former students married: 'You will be interested to hear that Laura is married. You know she left the school last July. She wrote me a letter saying she was busy in her new home. We are always glad to hear of the girls being married, as they are open to many temptations in their free life.'[42] This was a typical response. It was generally agreed that Aboriginal girls educated by the Anglicans would make good wives, but if they remained single, the girls would face evil temptations. Their 'morality' was guarded by their 'surrogate mothers.' Yet, some like Kathleen Martin realized the options for Aboriginal women were limited. She confessed to Bishop Stringer that it was 'a pity to have the girls marry so young and yet it is the only way for them if they remain in camp.'[43] Her implication was that if the girls remained single and stayed at Selkirk they might become pregnant.

Concern about chastity and the 'many temptations' of young Aboriginal women stemmed in part from the arrival of white settlers. White men working in construction camps in northern British Columbia or mining for gold in the Yukon caused missionaries great fear and anxiety. They represented a threat to the aim of Christian missions and were therefore carefully scrutinized and regularly criticized. Settlers, too, represented the evils of white society and a disruption of the harmony missionaries were trying to achieve. If white miners would not attend church, or show any outward signs of living Christian lives, how could missionaries be critical of Aboriginal peoples? How could they claim they represented a world where everyone was civilized and Christian when these miners openly defied them? As whites began to come to the north in larger numbers, especially after the turn of the twentieth century, this problem became exacerbated.

In the May 1895 edition of the *Canadian Church Magazine and Mission News* Selina Bompas expressed her grave concern about the impact of gold miners in Forty Mile Creek, the winter headquarters for many newly arrived white men. Bompas expressed her fear that miners would have a bad influence on Aboriginal women. While she conceded that some miners were respectable, others of a 'very different type' caused her anxiety:

> And thus our Indians, being brought into contact with the white man, fall in only too easily with his taste for luxury, love of gambling, coarse, vile language, and for the miserable and ruthless degradation of women. Our

American citizen would scorn to marry an Indian; indeed, by an iniquitous law of his country, he is forbidden to do so. But the higher law of God he can set aside and ignore. The sweet, oval face and laughing eyes of our Indian girl pleases him; he knows that she can be made as deft with her hands, as tidy and orderly, as skillful with her needle as any white woman. She is sadly, deplorably vain, poor child, and a gay shawl or two, a pair of gold earrings, will sorely tempt her, as the bag of flour has tempted her father to wink at the transaction.[44]

Bompas saw herself as a moral guardian over unsuspecting Aboriginal women, fearing the 'inclinations' of white men. Her statement showed her contempt for white men who ignored Christianity, and also positioned her as the protector over the morality and sexuality of Aboriginal women.

Veteran missionary Bishop William Ridley was equally worried about gold-seekers and Aboriginal peoples near Atlin, British Columbia: 'These children of the forest grow into fine types of humanity until Americanized by contact with lustful whites who disgrace their nominal Christianity and degrade the Barbarians.'[45] Likewise, Elizabeth Soal at Hazelton, in north central British Columbia, wrote to the *North British Columbia News* in 1916 when this town was home to about 200 white newcomers: 'One very sad feature of the work here, is the very adverse influence of so many of the white men in their neglect of the Sabbath and holy things. As a result the attendance of the Indians at divine service has been reduced very considerably, but we still have great hopes for the future, for by the Grace of God we are doing our best to teach the children the way of truth and thus we sow in hope and trust in Him for the increase.'[46] Kathleen Martin expressed similar anxieties. In Selkirk she was known, she asserted, to 'have it out' with white men who ignored the Sabbath.[47]

Despite the fear of white men's moral danger, there seems to have been very little resistance to interracial marriage. This lack of concern reaffirms the missionaries' aspiration to see Aboriginal women married. They frequently commented on mixed-race marriages in non-judgmental terms. Selina Bompas was very pleased to announce the marriage of Julia Sims, who had been adopted as a young girl by the Rev. Sims and raised for a short period by her. According to Bompas, Julia had been 'uncivilized' and 'hopelessly bad and possessed of every evil propensity.' 'But,' Bompas insisted, 'God's grace prevailed at last, and man's extremity is God's opportunity. Julia is now the wife of a white man, Mr. Horsefall, a very pleasing and respectable man. They were married about eighteen months ago by Bishop Reeve, have one little daughter, and appear to be contented and happy as possible, and Mr. Horsefall said to me when calling on us at Moseyed a few weeks ago since, "a man could not have a better wife."'[48]

The same enthusiasm was demonstrated by Kathleen Martin when in 1921 her Aboriginal maid, Alice, married a white man. Bishop and Mrs Stringer were in the village for a short pastoral visit, so the Bishop performed the marriage ceremony himself: 'My Indian maid Alice, was married on Tuesday evening to one of the white men here and they went off in a launch on Wednesday for a honey-moon trip up the McMillan River.'[49]

Aboriginal women's marriages to white men went unopposed, in part at least, because it was hoped they would contribute to Euro-Canadian assimilation. Lay worker C.F. Johnson, the supervisor of the Dawson Hostel for Half-Breed Children, reported on a marriage between a hostel resident and a white trading post manager: 'We have just had word of the marriage of one of our girls to the manager of a small trading post in the far north. She was a very capable young woman and will make a real home for the man she married. Her last six months at St. Paul's Hostel were spent in the kitchen where she received a training which will now be of inestimable value.' Johnson speculated that with many more White men coming 'into the country,' there would be more intermarriage: 'The process of assimilation is going on around us, slowly but surely, so that in the course of time there will be no native problem.'[50] Whether or not assimilation was a shared goal among missionaries, it was quite obvious that missionary women in particular felt responsible for the moral development or sexual control of Aboriginal girls. This was reflected in their desire to see them married in Christian ceremonies and settled.

Training Aboriginal girls as domestic servants was considered an acceptable alternative to sending them back to their families. Mary Mellish, a teacher in Moosehide, reported to *The New Era* in 1905 that she had a six-year-old girl living with her whom she was training: 'she is not at all pretty but is smart, and in time will make a good servant; there is such an improvement in her already.'[51] In the same year it was reported in the *Letter Leaflet* that three young women from the Chooutla school at Carcross were employed as domestic servants in Whitehorse. One worked for Sarah Stringer.[52] In 1923 the same paper mentioned Gladys Roberts, who was graduating from Carcross school:

Our other graduate is Gladys Roberts, who has been in school for the last twelve years and has done very well in her class room work. She has been trained for domestic service, and will we hope, have a good influence wherever she goes. She is returning to Moosehide, near Dawson, to her parents, but hopes, after spending a short time at home, to take a place of service in Dawson, and earn her own living.[53]

Other young women returned to their villages and worked as aides in the smaller schools. In a report from Rampart House and Old Crow, the Rev. McCullum mentioned that he was being assisted in the school work by Magi Daniel and Eunuch Ben, 'two graduates of the Carcross Residential School.'[54]

Missionaries did not offer a variety of options for young women's independence, and that was certainly never their stated objective. Like the matrons in Pascoe's study, their goal was to introduce Christian womanhood and to protect and nurture the morality of Aboriginal women on an increasingly changing frontier. At the same time that they tried to create their own identities as mothers and moral guardians, women missionaries also attempted to reinforce a domestic, familial ideal and identity for the young women they contacted. Marriage, motherhood, or domestic service were all seen as positive choices for Aboriginal women.

Conclusion

Motherhood became a part of missionary women's identity, and to a significant degree it justified their work. Being a 'mother' to 'motherless mites' and young Aboriginal women gave them a feeling of superiority. The maternal image lent a sense of status and freedom and created boundaries of maternal authority that gave women missionaries a feeling of self-worth and responsibility. Ironically, this identity could imply extended roles for women because it represented a position of both authority and protection. The discourse of motherhood points out many of the ironies inherent in northern missions. Motherhood became a dominant discourse used in a context that had been constructed as masculine. Furthermore, although the rhetoric of motherhood implied limited roles, instead it provided women with opportunities to expand their experiences in the multifaceted work at and beyond the mission stations. The motherhood image was most strategic and ironic for those women who were not mothers themselves:

women who had turned to mission work as an alternative to traditional roles. These women transcended gendered expectations but
relied on traditional rhetoric to construct their identities.

Reading through their diaries and letters reminds us how missionary women positioned themselves as mothers and what the tragic
implications of those identities were. They employed the metaphors of
motherhood and family to organize a sustained structural intrusion
into the lives of northern Aboriginal peoples. The identity allowed
missionary women to give shape to their lives, to construct a persona
that they thought justified their work. Tragically, in constructing their
identity as 'mothers' – a seemingly benign image – they also became
aware – sometimes for the first time – that they were 'white.'

NOTES

1 William Henry Collison, *In the Wake of the War Canoe* (1915, reprinted and
edited by Charles Lillard, Victoria, BC: Sono Nis Press, 1981), 18.
2 'Diocese of Caledonia,' *The New Era* (April 1904), 123.
3 'Death of Mrs. Du Vernet,' *North British Columbia News* (January 1929), 916.
4 Jane Hunter, 'The Home and the World: The Missionary Message of U.S.
Domesticity,' in Leslie Flemming, ed., *Women's Work for Women: Missionaries
and Social Change in Asia* (Boulder: Westview Press, 1989), 159. The most
complete analysis of the shifting roles of American missionary wives and
single women is Dana Lee Robert, *American Women in Mission: A Social History of Their Thought and Practice* (Macon, GA: Mercer University Press,
1996).
5 Margaret Jolly, 'Colonizing Women: The Maternal Body and Empire,' in
Sneja Gunew and Anna Yeatman, eds, *Feminism and the Politics of Difference*
(Boulder, CO: Westview Press, 1993), 104.
6 Peggy Pascoe, *Relations of Rescue: The Search for Female Moral Authority in
the American West, 1874–1939* (New York: Oxford University Press, 1990),
209.
7 Anna Davin, 'Imperialism and Motherhood,' *History Workshop Journal* 5
(Spring 1978): 10–12.
8 Barbara Caine, *Victorian Feminists* (New York: Oxford University Press,
1992), 43.
9 Ibid., 44.
10 Anglican Church of Canada, General Synod Archives, Toronto (GSA),
Stringer Papers, Series 1 1-A-5, 'Stringer Martin/Cowaret Correspondence,'

letter from Martin to Stringer, 9 February 1916; letter from Stringer to Martin, 15 March 1916.

11 Ibid., letter from Martin to Stringer, 6 August 1923.

12 Ibid., letter from Martin to Stringer, 15 October 1928.

13 'Letter from Mrs. Bompas – (Continued),' *Letter Leaflet* (December 1893), 59.

14 Ibid., 69.

15 Charlotte Selina Bompas, *A Heroine of the North: Memoirs of Charlotte Selina Bompas (1830–1917), Wife of the First Bishop of Selkirk (Yukon), with Extracts from her Journal and Letters,* compiled by S.A. Archer (London: Society for Promoting Christian Knowledge, 1929), 76.

16 Ibid., 136.

17 Ibid., 165.

18 GSA, Diocese of the Arctic Collection, M71–4, box 12, 'St. Luke's Mission, Pangnirtung, Florence Hirst Journals,' 20 February 1936.

19 Ibid., 23 February 1936.

20 Ibid., 21 April 1936.

21 Ibid., 10 January 1938.

22 'Life at Hay River Mission,' *The New Era* (August 1907), 274.

23 Agnes Deans Cameron, *The New North: An Account of a Woman's 1908 Journey through Canada to the Arctic* (New York: Appleton, 1910), revised and edited by David R. Richardson (Saskatoon: Western Producer Prairie Books, 1986), 131.

24 CMS Papers, Correspondence outgoing, Reel A 123, Letter from Hogan to parent committee, July 1893. Microfilm copy in National Archives of Canada.

25 Ibid., Reel A 125, Letter from Tyte to parent committee, 1 March 1898. Mildmay was the Anglican Deaconess house in London, England, where women trained for parish and mission work. There was a similar house in Toronto.

26 Selina Bompas, 'The Carcross School Children,' *The New Era* (July 1908), 256.

27 Ibid.

28 'Mackenzie River,' *The Living Message* (12 May 1928), 149.

29 'Yukon,' *The Living Message* (February 1928), 41.

30 See Ken Coates, 'Betwixt and Between: The Anglican Church and the Children of Carcross (Chooutla) Residential School, 1910–1955,' *BC Studies* 64 (1984–5): 27–47; Celia Haig-Brown, *Resistance and Renewal: Surviving the Indian Residential School* (Vancouver: Tillacum, 1988).

31 'The Arctic: Bishop Fleming Visits Anglican Eskimo Children at Shingle Point,' *The Living Message* (October 1934), 312.

32 'Indian Girls and Women,' *North British Columbia News* (October 1912), 38–9.
33 GSA, Stringer Papers, Series 2 2–B, 'Sarah Ann Stringer Talks, Addresses,' Address to Winnipeg's Canadian Club Women, November 1931.
34 'Caledonia,' *Letter Leaflet* (January 1906), 71.
35 For an illuminating treatment of the education of Aboriginal girls in an all-girls, mixed-race school in Yale, British Columbia, see Jean Barman, 'Separate and Unequal: Indian and White Girls at All Hallows School, 1884–1920,' in Veronica Strong-Boag and Anita Clair Fellman, eds, *Rethinking Canada: The Promise of Women's History* (Toronto: Copp Clark Pitman, 1986), 215–24.
36 CMS Papers, Correspondence outgoing, Reel A 123, letter from Hogan to parent committee, July 1893.
37 J.H. Keen, 'Children At Metlakatla,' *The New Era* (June 1905), 218.
38 Ibid.
39 Margaret Blackman, *During My Time: Florence Edenshaw Davidson, A Haida Woman* (Seattle: University of Washington Press, 1982), 88.
40 Julie Cruikshank, *Life Lived Like a Story: Life Stories of Three Yukon Elders* (Vancouver: UBC Press, 1990), 113–14.
41 'Hay River – Needs and Anxieties,' *The New Era* (April 1908), 141–2.
42 'Mackenzie River,' *Letter Leaflet* (June 1917), 244–5.
43 GSA, Stringer Papers, Series 1 1–A-5, 'Stringer Martin / Cowaret Correspondence,' letter from Martin to Stringer, 10 January 1924.
44 *Canadian Church Magazine and Mission News* (May 1895), 104.
45 'Miners and Indians,' *Canadian Church Magazine and Mission News* (December 1900), 267.
46 'Hazelton,' *North British Columbia News* (July 1916), 27.
47 GSA, Stringer Papers, Series 1 1–A-5, 'Stringer Martin /Cowaret Correspondence,' letter from Martin to Stringer, 26 January 1918.
48 'Letter from Mrs. Bompas – July 1900,' *Letter Leaflet* (January 1901), 74.
49 'St. Andrew's Selkirk,' *Northern Lights* (1921), 4.
50 'Dawson, St. Paul's Hostel,' *Northern Lights* (May 1929), 11–12.
51 'Selkirk,' *The New Era* (October 1905), 377.
52 'Selkirk,' *Letter Leaflet* (April 1905), 155.
53 *Letter Leaflet* (April 1923), 129.
54 'Rampart House and Old Crow,' *Northern Lights* (1927), 4.

Chapter 3

'The Picturesqueness of His Accent and Speech': Methodist Missionary Narratives and William Henry Pierce's Autobiography

GAIL EDWARDS

In *From Potlatch to Pulpit*, the autobiography of William Henry Pierce, an Aboriginal convert and a Methodist missionary, the editor included the following ambiguous tribute:

> To the present writer, who has known a good deal of him and his work over long years, William Henry Pierce is an outstanding figure among a noble band of heroic missionaries. Brave men who, on our own shores, laboured under conditions already difficult for us to visualize, who travelled great distances by canoe or mountain trail; who suffered privation, exposure and danger, for no earthly reward, but solely to bear the glad news of the gospel to their fellow man, when that fellow man was scarcely other than a savage ... His career is surely unique. When one recalls his birth, his bringing up in a heathen village with the most pagan influences about him, separated from his father, and his mother dead. Confronted almost daily with the most savage and cruel scenes – what a marvel that he became what he did become![1]

Why did the writer consider Pierce both an exemplar of the missionary enterprise and a signifier of the triumph of the missionary project of civilizing and converting? The late nineteenth-, early twentieth-century Methodist Church of Canada constructed missionary heroes – male and female – in its magazines, pamphlets, and biographies. By emphasizing the missionary as a romanticized figure of bravery and duty, the Methodists sought to create and sustain interest in the missionary enterprise in British Columbia among a metropolitan readership. At the same time, these missionary narratives constructed the 'Aboriginal Other,' who could be civilized, converted, and made literate only through the unremitting toil and personal intervention of the

Rev. William Henry Pierce, with his wife Margaret Hargrave Pierce, and their son. Pierce, the son of a Hudson's Bay trader and a Tsimshian woman, became a 'picturesque' Methodist missionary along the British Columbia coast in the early 1900s.

binary opposite, the missionary hero. Thus, the complexities and tensions in the autobiographical narrative of William Henry Pierce, who was at one and the same time Methodist missionary hero and Aboriginal Other, raise important questions about the role that literacy and the discursive norms of Methodist print culture played in the construction of missionary biographies, and in the multiple and conflicting identities of Aboriginal Methodist converts.

In order to disseminate information about missions, and to sustain interest in support for mission work, the Missionary Society of the Methodist Church of Canada embarked on an ambitious program of publications. A steady stream of annual reports, pamphlets, magazines, teaching aids, Sunday school literature, biographies, and autobiographies describing work in particular mission fields flowed from the Methodist missionary presses. The publications were designed to capture the interest and imagination of the reader through letters from missionaries describing the challenges and triumphs of their work; narratives of successful revivals, deathbed conversions, and the awful fate of the unconverted; news from the sponsoring society; and appeals for funds and material goods.[2]

From the outset, Methodist missions in British Columbia were heavily reliant on funding from groups and individuals far removed from the mission fields. The first Wesleyan Methodist missionaries had been sent to British Columbia from Ontario, arriving on the west coast in January 1859, with partial funding from the English Wesleyan Methodist Missionary Society. However, the primary support for British Columbia missions came from the Missionary Society of the Canadian Methodist Church, centred in Toronto, and from funds raised by individual congregations in Ontario. Individual missionaries were also responsible for raising funds locally, and were required by the Doctrines and Discipline of the Methodist Church to report on the financial position and spiritual development of their missions. The steady flow of letters and reports that were sent from the British Columbia Conference, and from individual missionaries, to the central headquarters in Toronto, frequently reiterated the need for additional funds for mission projects. The letters also reminded the Society of the self-sacrifice and hard work of the missionaries in the field, who were labouring in locations and among peoples far removed geographically and spiritually from the more genteel surroundings of central Canada, while simultaneously reinforcing their connection with and continuance of the norms of Methodist worship and discipline 'at home.'[3]

In the face of competing missionary claims for funding from more exotic locations like China and Japan, the missionaries in British Columbia sought to present their work as a heroic struggle for the souls of the unconverted, and situated themselves as agents directly guided by divine will, while at the same time triumphantly announcing their successes to stimulate donations and demonstrate their own ability to effect conversions. In order to dramatize the struggle, Aboriginal peoples were presented as uniformly barbaric and heathen savages living in the sin and degradation common to all who had not yet converted, but with the potential for conversion and salvation available to all who repented of their sins. Within these narratives, despair and hopefulness were held in tension. If whole communities were converted and civilized, then the missionary's work was, in effect, completed and his position made redundant. On the other hand, readers would be discouraged from donating if the situation in a particular missionary station were utterly hopeless and no progress towards the conversion of the community could be expected or was realized.

The missionary emerges in these letters and reports as a conduit for the salvation of the unconverted, as a teacher, guide, and moral arbiter. The missionary's identity as a hero was constructed through a series of dualities and oppositions between the self and Other, as Myra Rutherdale clearly articulates in the previous chapter of this book.[4] The missionary's own position as civilized, educated, literate, and European was contrasted with the uncivilized, uneducated, and illiterate Aboriginal Other, in an appeal to the commonsense racism of colonial discourse.[5] The Aboriginal convert was reconstructed through a similar series of binary oppositions. The unconverted lived in a state of disorder. Illiteracy, personal uncleanness, uncontrolled sexuality, intoxication, communal habitation, and an economy based on migratory patterns of hunting and gathering were all symbols of the savage.[6] As the missionary brought order and godliness, the converted subject would be inculcated into literacy, cleanliness, chastity, temperance, nuclear family housing, and nonmigratory agricultural subsistence.[7]

The Methodist missionaries, who were required by the doctrine and discipline of the Methodist Church to abstain from snuff, tobacco, and alcohol, and to be free of personal debt, were particularly incensed by what they believed to be Aboriginal intemperance and profligacy. They viewed the rituals of the potlatch as the flagrant violation of the sanctity of personal property and the accumulation of capital, and worked vigorously with federal government Indian agents to enforce the 1884 ban on the potlatch.[8] Aboriginal converts were required to renounce their former tribal practices, and were watched carefully for evidence of backsliding. Attending a potlatch, singing traditional songs, or calling on a medicine man to cure a sick family member were all signs that the Aboriginal convert's commitment to Methodist Christianity was wavering. The missionary narratives frequently describe the struggles of individual missionaries against recurrences of Aboriginal practices in convert communities, describing the missionary's opposition to traditional practices and beliefs in the language of battle.

Methodist missionaries were charged with preaching God's word and teaching all non-Christians of the errors and sinfulness of their ways as a means of stirring them to repentance, leading them to conversion. However, the Methodist belief in the power of direct experience with the word of God as a means of effecting conversion was challenged when the missionaries interacted with the Aboriginal peoples of British Columbia, who had rich oral literatures, but no written languages, and no fixed culture of the printed word. The Methodist practice of itinerancy, in which missionaries moved to new postings every two or three years, meant that the missionary who sought to preach the gospel to Aboriginal peoples was faced with a series of pressing decisions about language and literacy. By the time a missionary had acquired even a small measure of fluency in the indigenous language of the nation in which his mission was located, he could find himself moved to a new station, among a different nation who spoke a different, completely unrelated language. Not surprisingly, while some Methodist missionaries engaged in translation work and taught converts to read in their indigenous languages, the majority of missionaries taught English to the Aboriginal communities they sought to evangelize as the best means by which Christian teaching could be inculcated.[9] For Methodists, learning English and interacting with print culture were valuable skills that would hasten the process of inculturation of Aboriginal people into Christian and civilized norms of behaviour.[10] The ownership of a Bible, the ability of a convert to memorize and recite biblical verses and sing hymns from memory, whether in their own language or in English, were all signs of successful evangelism.[11] The disciplinary act of Bible reading, however, was the primary signifier of the efficacy of conversion, and a commitment to Protestant norms of worship. The ability to read Scripture was a signifier of conformity to new Eurocentric and Methodist norms of behaviour and marked Aboriginal converts as civilized and Christianized. Conversely, failure of converts to learn to read was noted with disfavour in missionary reports, even by missionaries whose own English was perhaps somewhat less than entirely grammatically correct.[12]

In the process of their education in Methodist norms of behaviour, Aboriginal converts also replicated the particular cadences of Methodism. Methodist missionary discourse was explicitly shaped by the language of John Wesley's sermons, diaries, and hymns, which all ordained Methodist ministers read as part of their education. Methodist missionaries were encouraged to model their missionary practices (and expectations of mission) directly on Wesley's descriptions of his own work. The fervent revivalist nature of Methodism in British Columbia, seen as rather old-fashioned by central Canada, was particularly noticeable in Aboriginal missions. Converts were encouraged to preserve earlier Methodist traditions like the class meeting, camp meetings, and love feasts.[13] Aboriginal conversion narratives, as reported by the missionaries, were distinctively Wesleyan. The converts described their former state of sinfulness, the joy of their conversion, and the blessings that had been bestowed upon them since their conversion. These narratives were at one and the same time formulaic and individual – variations on a familiar theme. The predictable patterns of deathbed speeches, exhortations by the converted to unbelieving friends and family members, and pleas to renounce tribal customs structured the narratives of lived Aboriginal experience within missionary expectations of the transformation wrought by conversion.[14] Just as the physical body of the convert would be disciplined to new norms of cleanliness and order, so too the speech of the convert would be disciplined to new ways of describing and interpreting the self and experience.

The autobiography of William Henry Pierce exemplifies the tensions embodied in the Aboriginal convert, who was required to learn new discourses and new forms of the presentation of the self. Pierce was born in 1856, in Fort Rupert in northern coastal British Columbia. In the complex world of post-contact Tsimshian culture, Pierce was careful to note his family connections to new sources of power. His Scottish father was an employee of the Hudson's Bay Company. Through his mother's family, his adopted uncle was Arthur Wellington Clah, who was the first language teacher and interpreter for the Anglican missionary William Duncan.[15] After his mother died, Pierce was taken by his grandfather to live with his maternal family at Fort Simpson (later

Port Simpson). There he received brief initial schooling in English from the famous Anglican missionary William Duncan. He later became a cabin boy on the Hudson's Bay Company's steamer *Otter*, and was given further instruction in English by the captain.[16]

During a visit to Victoria as a young man, Pierce was converted during a Methodist revival meeting. In Pierce's words, 'One night I attended the service and listened to the words of Rev. Thomas Crosby, and that night I gave my heart to God. I felt that a great weight had been lifted off my shoulders. I went back to the meetings and the more I saw of them [i.e., the Methodists] the more I liked them.'[17] He began his career in evangelism the very night of his conversion, when he left the meeting to exhort a friend to kneel and pray with him.[18] The Methodists in Victoria provided further opportunities for his education, and eventually hired Pierce to act as an interpreter at Port Simpson. Pierce's work as a lay evangelist and interpreter led to his assignment to various Aboriginal communities as a preacher and teacher. The Methodist missionary periodical the *Missionary Outlook* began to report on Pierce's work and, on occasion, to print his letters, 'as evidence that God is sending forth some "living epistles" among the dark tribes on the coast.'[19]

In 1883, the minutes of the Port Simpson District Ministerial Session and Annual District Meeting noted that the Methodist ministers of the district agreed to receive Pierce on trial as a candidate for ministry, noting that he 'has labored among the Indians as an Evangelist for the past seven years and has been an instrument of much good to his fellow men, and has had considerable education, and is in every way fitted as a Candidate for the ministry ... And whereas Bro. Pierce is not able to attend this District meeting on account of the steamer not calling at his Mission as expected, he be recommended to be received by the Conference on trial as a Candidate for the ministry for the Indian work of British Columbia.'[20]

The resolution noted Pierce's 'considerable education.' While few of the Methodist missionaries in British Columbia had a university education, candidates for the ministry were expected to have sufficient formal education to complete the course of reading that constituted their education for ministry.[21] Pierce was proud of the level of education that he had achieved. In one of his earliest published letters, he said 'I feel a thirst for knowledge,' although he was also careful to attribute success in his learning to God, continuing, 'I pray to God that He will teach me by His grace to know more of His will.'[22] Throughout his letters, he framed his thirst for knowledge within the higher priority that he placed on his mission work: 'I would like to be a man of high education. But saving souls is better.'[23] At the same time, in his letters and autobiography, he carefully described his various opportunities for study, and expressed gratitude to his teachers, who had provided him with the means for self-advancement.[24]

However, his educational attainment was called into question in the 1884 minutes of the Port Simpson annual district meeting, which noted that Pierce was 'not sufficiently educated to take the regular course of study.' These deficiencies were determined not to be a barrier to his candidacy only because he was 'intended for the native work entirely.' Despite the concern, a committee was formed to examine him, and Pierce 'passed a fairly creditable examination in his first year's course considering the great disadvantages he has labored under in acquiring an English education.'[25] Subsequent minutes again drew attention to his educational deficiencies and special status as an Aboriginal candidate for ministry who would serve exclusively as a missionary to Aboriginal communities, while simultaneously praising his efficiency, usefulness, enthusiasm, and knowledge of the Doctrines and Discipline of the Methodist Church.[26] In his autobiography, Pierce stated only that he had been part of the first ordination class of the British Columbia conference, and made no mention of his special status, or the apparent challenges that he faced in passing the ordination examinations.[27]

Pierce's missionary career after his ordination was spent in various coastal Aboriginal communities. His autobiography describes his successes at inculcating Christianity and civilization among the Heiltsuk peoples of Bella Bella, the Nuxalk peoples of Bella Coola, and the Gitxsan peoples of Kispiox on the Upper Skeena River. In the pattern familiar from the missionary narratives, Pierce noted with pride that when the Heiltsuk chiefs decided to allow their people to become Christian, the consequent physical and social transformation of the village was immediate and dramatic:

Each family selected a lot on which to build his Christian house and instead of wearing blankets as their only article of clothing, the men desired to buy suits of clothes and boots. The women bought shawls and some material to make dresses for themselves and the children. Week by week the change became more apparent and in a short time the village became transformed.[28]

At Bella Coola, Pierce participated with approval in an Aboriginal convert's personal transformation. The convert and his family renounced their tribal customs by burning their 'heathen treasures,' that is, their ceremonial dance regalia.[29] Unlike some of his white missionary peers, Pierce understood that the destruction of the regalia not only was a personal rupture with the past, but also dislocated the family within Nuxalk society. As he stated in his autobiography, the convert's bonfire was 'a great sacrifice ... [that] meant that the traditions of his family would be wiped out.'[30]

This doubling of sensitivity to, and simultaneous rejection of, Aboriginal traditions permeated the second half of the autobiography, in which the editor gathered together a collection of Pierce's notes on the beliefs and practices of the northern coastal First Nations in a section titled 'Conditions, Habits and Customs Before Christianity Was Introduced.' Christianity marked a temporal disruption, in which the past of 'superstition or old Heathen beliefs' was transformed into the modern and rational present. Pierce was ambiguous about his own subject position as an Aboriginal convert. His early life with his Tsimshian grandparents marked him as Aboriginal, and in his autobiography he described his work as a translator for the missionaries at Port Simpson and Laxgalts'ap, which depended on his fluency in Tsimshian and Nisga'a. However, his narratives of his own missionary work are silent on his position as an Aboriginal convert preaching to Aboriginal communities, and indeed, it is not clear from his autobiography whether he himself had to employ translators to communicate with the Heiltsuk and Nuxalk peoples.[31]

Pierce was an ambivalent missionary hero who both confirmed and contradicted the established pattern of missionary narratives. Pierce and his fellow missionaries wrote of their work for immediate publication in the denominational missionary magazines the *Missionary Outlook* and the *Missionary Bulletin*. The magazines were distributed to an interested metropolitan readership, who were encouraged to take a personal interest in the work of missionaries in the field, extending to the practice of a church group 'adopting' a missionary.[32] Accounts of missionary triumphs and challenges were also widely disseminated through the Missionary Society's pamphlets and teaching aids.

In 1910 Pierce started to write an autobiographical sketch, at the request of the Missionary Society in Toronto, which made no further use of it.[33] Subsequent extended correspondence between Pierce and his wife and Frederick Clarke Stephenson and his wife Annie Stephenson, of the Methodist Young People's Forward Movement for Missions, reveals Pierce's repeated attempts to expand and revise the manuscript, and his increasing frustration as publication was promised and then repeatedly delayed.[34]

The correspondence also indicates the extent to which the manuscript was a collaboration between Pierce and his wife, Margaret Hargrave Pierce, a former missionary school teacher whom Pierce had married in 1890. In 1919, the Pierces sent a letter to the Stephensons stating that progress on the manuscript was slow. While they had written chapters on 'Indian life before the whites or missionaries came,' they had not yet begun to write the chapters on mission work (what they called the 'Mission Work and Spiritual part') and had 'come to the conclusion that we must move a little quicker.'[35] Subsequently, they sent the completed chapters to the Stephensons in Toronto, although Margaret noted that it had taken 'a long, long time to finish the little that we have done, but we are really trying now to hustle more.' Delays had been caused by Pierce's busy schedule, and she noted that she was planning to 'do some of it even if Mr. P. is not always here.' The Stephensons had arranged for manuscript to be typed, and the Pierces noted that they were hoping to keep the typist very busy.[36]

The next round of correspondence between the Pierces and Annie Stephenson six years later, in 1925, indicated that they were at work again on the manuscript, and had completed further sections, which Mrs Stephenson had returned with a transcribed typewritten copy.[37] A year later, Mrs Stephenson wrote to Margaret that she had received suggestions about the best arrangement of the manuscript, but was very busy with preparations for the first General Council of the new United Church of Canada.[38] Late that same year, Pierce himself wrote to Mrs Stephenson, noting that he had received many requests for the book, and hoping that it would be made 'as attractive as possible.'[39]

By 1928 the letters from the Pierces had changed – the former chattily informal tone of friendship had shifted to something more terse and businesslike: 'The enclosed I received today and thought I would pass it on to you to read. That is only one of many inquiries re the book. I should like to hear from you what is your idea on the matter and what is your intention? How long do you think it will be before you have the opportunity of getting it done. Kindly let me hear from you.'[40] The letter remained unanswered until May 1933, when Annie Stephenson wrote to the Pierces: 'Were you ever thoroughly ashamed of yourselves? If you were you know what I feel like now.'[41] She blamed the inability of the Missionary Society to publish the manuscript on the lack of funds for publishing, and the limited sale of missionary literature during a time of financial hardship.

Stephenson's acknowledgment of the failure of the Society to publish Pierce's autobiography, after her five years of silence on the subject, and twenty-three years after he started writing the sketch, was spurred by the news that the Methodist minister and publisher J.P. Hicks had arranged for publication of the manuscript by a local Vancouver printer, as a tribute to the elderly Pierce, who had retired in 1932. In 1929, the archivist of the British Columbia Conference, John C. Goodfellow, had contacted Pierce after meeting him during the Conference to ask about his knowledge of traditional Aboriginal beliefs regarding astronomical events.[42] Two years later, Goodfellow wrote to Pierce inquiring about the progress towards publication of his autobiography, and invited him to address the Conference Historical Committee at their meeting in Victoria, on 'some phase of the work covered by your book.'[43] Evidently, the interest in the manuscript among members of the British Columbia Conference was sufficient to prompt Hicks, the editor of the *Western Recorder* periodical, to move to find a publisher, and the autobiography finally saw print in 1933.

In his autobiography, Pierce spoke of his close association with the other Methodist missionaries in northern British Columbia, whom he clearly regarded as his missionary peers. In return, their narratives of their own work only briefly mention Pierce as 'our native brother,' who took charge of a mission until a white missionary could be sent.[44] The failure of the Missionary Society to publish Pierce's autobiography, despite repeated promises that the work would see print, highlights the ambiguity of his status as missionary hero and Aboriginal Other, in comparison with the earlier lionization in print of Thomas Crosby, the (white) Methodist exemplar of missionary-as-hero on the north Pacific coast.

The marriage between the half-Tsimshian Pierce and the Englishwoman Margaret Hargrave was highly unusual in late nineteenth-century British Columbia, and seems to have been met with silent disapprobation by Alexander Sutherland, the formidable head of the Missionary Society in Toronto. Unlike the marriages of other missionaries in the field, the Pierce-Hargrave marriage was not reported in the *Missionary Outlook*, and for a period of approximately five years after the marriage, no letter from Pierce was published.[45] Sutherland made no mention of Pierce in his reports on his official visits to British

Columbia, and made somewhat disparaging remarks about Mrs Pierce in his private correspondence. In Sutherland's view, Pierce was indelibly marked as both ordained missionary and Aboriginal Other. In a letter to Edith Griffin, a schoolteacher who had volunteered to teach at Kispiox, he stated:

> My own private opinion is that a man should be sent to teach the school at Kishpiax. A lady could not make her home in an Indian house. The missionary in charge is a mixed blood but educated in English schools, and speaking English readily. His wife is a White woman but I have heard that the state of her health is such that she can give but little attention to household matters.[46]

Correspondence between Sutherland and various missionary officials indicated that the Society found it impossible to place a teacher at Kispiox because Pierce was at one and the same time a brother missionary and an Aboriginal man, and therefore not to be trusted to behave decently when living in close proximity to a white woman.[47]

Pierce's dual identity was raised again in 1909. The Gitxsan peoples of the Upper Skeena were seriously concerned about the incursion of surveyors and workers who were preparing to lay the tracks for the Grand Trunk Pacific Railway. The preparations for the construction of the railway and increasing European settlement in the Upper Skeena focused the attention of the Gitxsan peoples on their ongoing struggle with the government to recognize their rights to land claims in the area, and they began to agitate vocally for the settlement of their claims. In response, the European settlers in the area became alarmed, and mobilized the support of the Indian agent for the region, who interpreted the concerns of the Gitxsan peoples as evidence of a potential Aboriginal insurrection. Correspondence between George Raley, missionary at Kitimat, and the Superintendent of Missions Alexander Sutherland in Toronto made it clear that for Sutherland and Raley, Pierce's primary identity was Aboriginal Other, whose loyalty to the government had been disputed by the Indian Commissioner. Raley stated that although 'his testimony was favorable to Mr. Pierce,' he had serious concerns. 'I do not doubt Mr. Pierce's loyalty to the Government or the church, but his judgment is that of an Indian rather than a White man and may be faulty at times.'[48] The following spring, over the protests of the Kispiox Aboriginal converts, Pierce was reassigned to a new post, Port Essington, at the mouth of the Skeena River, safely away from any land claims controversy, where he and Mrs Pierce were to remain until his retirement in 1932.[49]

By the time of his death in 1948, Pierce was widely recognized as a pioneer missionary in British Columbia. At the same time, the praise never failed to remind the reader of Pierce's doubled identity, describing him as 'the Indian missionary orator,'[50] the 'Indian Half-Breed [who] was [the] spear-thrust of coast missions,'[51] and a 'colorful British Columbia-born cleric of Indian descent.'[52] The editor of *From Potlatch to Pulpit*, J.P. Hicks, wrote encouragingly to Pierce about his work, while privately writing, 'Perhaps we expect too much of him. He may not have the business mind, and outlook, that WE have,'[53] 'WE' being Hicks's white clergy peers, Pierce being Aboriginal and therefore unable to understand business. Despite a lifetime of work in the cause of promoting Christianity and Euro-Canadian cultural norms, Pierce had never ceased to be reminded that his mission was as 'an Aboriginal Indian, with attractive abilities and passionate ministerial devotion, [who worked] among his people in the North.'[54]

In his final tribute to Pierce, Hicks's ambiguous and slightly patronizing editorial note in *From Potlatch to Pulpit* articulated the power and limitation of the print culture of missionary narratives, while simultaneously constructing and deconstructing Pierce as a Methodist missionary hero, who embodied both the missionary's transformative faith and the Aboriginal Other's need for transformation:

> Only the merest glimpse has been here given of the more recent years of Mr. Pierce's ministry – which he did not record in his manuscript – though it may not be necessary to write more. Only those who have met him, heard him give addresses, or in conversation relate his experiences and his views on life – Christian life, his own field of labour, public life, and the Church's responsibility, can really form any idea of the picturesqueness of his accent and speech – and of his approach to any subject; his shrewd observation; his unconscious, but compelling humour; or the intensity of his Christian devotion. His original, quaint illustrations are captivating, though impossible of realistic reproduction.[55]

NOTES

1 William Henry Pierce, *From Potlatch to Pulpit: Being the Autobiography of the Rev. William Henry Pierce, Aboriginal Missionary to the Indian Tribes of the*

Northwest Coast of British Columbia, edited by Rev. J.P. Hicks (Vancouver: The Vancouver Bindery, 1933), 103–4.

2 For an overall examination of the role of missionary biographies see Terrence L. Craig, 'The Missionary Lives: A Study in Canadian Missionary Biography and Autobiography,' *Studies in Christian Missions*, vol. 19 (Leiden: Brill, 1997).

3 The most authoritative history of Canadian Methodist missions is Neil Semple, *The Lord's Dominion: The History of Canadian Methodism* (Montreal/Kingston: McGill-Queen's University Press, 1996), chapters 11 for Home Missions and 12 for Foreign.

4 See also Myra Rutherdale's article, 'Revisiting Colonization through Gender: Anglican Missionary Women in the Pacific Northwest and the Arctic, 1860–1945,' *BC Studies* 104 (Winter 1994): 3–23, and her monograph, *Women and the White Man's God: Gender and Race in the Canadian Mission Field* (Vancouver: University of British Columbia Press, 2002). For a broader discussion of dualism in colonial discourse, see Abdul R. JanMohamed, 'The Economy of Manichean Allegory: The Function of Racial Difference in Colonialist Literature,' *Critical Inquiry* 12 (1985): 59–87; Homi K. Bhabha, 'The Other Question: Stereotype, Discrimination and the Discourse of Colonialism,' in *The Location of Culture* (London and New York: Routledge, 1994).

5 Jacques Derrida argues that the writing of one culture about another always involves a violence 'of difference, of classification, and of the system of appellations.' *Of Grammatology*, trans. Gayatri Chakravorty Spivak (Baltimore: Johns Hopkins University Press, 1976), 107. Ann Laura Stoler, 'Cultivating Bourgeois Bodies and Racial Selves,' in *Race and the Education of Desire: Foucault's History of Sexuality and the Colonial Order of Things* (Durham, NC: Duke University Press, 1995), draws attention to the contingency by which racial identities are constructed in colonial discourse.

6 The Methodist missionary discourse made it clear that the binary distinctions were predicated on the fundamental difference between 'heathen' and Christian. See for example, *Missionary Outlook* 9 (1889): 89: 'The things we abhor in their lives and customs are not distinctly Indian. They are the inevitable accompaniments of heathenism, and only serve as evidence that Indians were such. Filth, noise, want of principle, lack of intellect, greediness, inordinate desire for revenge, will always exist where paganism does, and while it does. It is part of it.'

7 Single-family housing was a particular preoccupation among missionaries. The need to encourage settled residences and agricultural pursuits among Aboriginal converts is a persistent theme in Canadian missionary narratives, and is a central goal of Canadian Aboriginal educational

policies into the twentieth century, as Jamie S. Scott's chapter in this book indicates.

8 See Douglas Cole and Ira Chaikin, *An Iron Hand upon the People: The Law against the Potlatch on the Northwest Coast* (Vancouver and Toronto: Douglas & McIntyre; Seattle: University of Washington Press, 1990).

9 A notable exception to this policy was Thomas Crosby, who made an explicit decision to learn to preach in the indigenous language of the people whom he evangelized, stating that 'In all my work since then I have experienced that in no way can one properly preach the truth to a people except in their own language.' See *Among the An-ko-me-nums: Or Flathead Tribes of Indians of the Pacific Coast* (Toronto: William Briggs, 1907), 56.

10 See, for example, Charles Reddick, missionary at Kitimat, to the Rev. Alexander Sutherland, 30 December 1907: 'One very encouraging thing is that many of even the middle aged men are ambitious to become like the white men. Some want to learn to read and write. I am going to start a night school, and hope to help them some. Not many men here, but what have some fund of English, and many have a larger vocabulary than they like to own. I hope to do something in the way of getting them to use English, by the night school. It seems to me the wisest course to discourage their use of their own language all I can, and to encourage English all I can. Consequently, while I am trying to learn the language, yet I do not plan to use it more than really necessary.' United Church Archives (UCA), Methodist Church of Canada, Missionary Society, Alexander Sutherland Papers [cited as Sutherland Papers], box 6, file 98, 'Correspondence re Kitimat Mission 1905–1908.' Sutherland was Secretary of the Missionary Society from 1878 until it was reorganized in 1906. He remained Foreign Secretary until his death in 1910.

11 See, for example, Thomas Crosby's report on mission work at Port Simpson, *Fifty-Seventh Annual Report of the Missionary Society of the Methodist Church of Canada* (Toronto: Methodist Mission Rooms, 1881), xiii: 'We have had as many as sixty and eighty old people meet after the Sabbath morning service to commit to memory the text in their Aboriginal tongue ... At the same hour there is a large gathering of young or middle-aged people with their Bibles in the Church, memorizing the [Biblical] text both in English and Tsimpshean.'

12 See, for example, George Read, lay missionary at Hartley Bay, BC, to Alexander Sutherland, 3 February 1906, in Sutherland Papers, 6/107, 'Correspondence re China Hat, 1906–1910': 'The sixteen souls above mentioned when pleaded with and asked to get right with God came boldly to the front and kneeling down cried with tears to Our Heavenly Father that He for Jesus sake would be merciful unto them and just like Him Glory be

to His ever Adorable Name, forgave them freely ... They attend regular [sic] the means of Grace and are always ready to give their testimony and declare what the Lord has done for their souls ... Some of them I am sorry to say cannot read their Bibles properly neither do they understand the English Language.'

13 See, for example, *Missionary Outlook* 3 (1883): 49: 'Our Brethren on the Pacific Coast preach an old-fashioned gospel, and are blessed with an old-fashioned revival.'

14 For deathbed speeches, see Thomas Crosby, *Up and Down the North Pacific Coast by Canoe and Mission Ship* (Toronto: Missionary Society of the Methodist Church, 1914), 188–90.

15 For A.W. Clah, see the next chapter in this book, by Susan Neylan, 'Eating the Angels' Food'; and also R.M. Galois, 'Colonial Encounters: The Worlds of Arthur Wellington Clah, 1855–1881,' *BC Studies* 115–16 (Autumn/Winter 1997–8): 105–47; and Peggy Brock, 'Building Bridges: Politics and Religion in a First Nations Community,' *Canadian Historical Review* 81, no. 1 (2000): 67–96.

16 Pierce, *From Potlatch to Pulpit*, 11–13.

17 Ibid., 13.

18 The friend, George Edgar, in turn laboured for many years as a lay evangelist and teacher, before being ordained in 1900 for 'Aboriginal Work.'

19 *Missionary Outlook* 1 (1881): 71. The earliest printed letter that mentions Pierce's work is Alfred E. Green, Nass River, dated 21 September 1877, and printed in *Wesleyan Missionary Notices*, 3d ser., no. 16 (Feb. 1878): 271, describing a stop at the 'middle village' during a missionary journey up the Nass: 'It was the first time that that place had been visited by any of your Missionaries, but William Henry, one of Mr. Crosby's young men, had been there two or three weeks teaching school.' Thomas Crosby, in a letter from Fort Simpson, of the same date, 21 September 1877, and printed in the same issue of *Wesleyan Missionary Notices*, in discussing the work on the Nass, stated: 'We have also to keep Wm. Henry Pearce [sic] up there as Interpreter and Assistant-teacher to Bro. Green, and we are told that no means can be had to help to keep him. Three white men who have seen his work for the four months he has been up there, have volunteered to support him for three months, and then we shall hope and trust for the future.'

Brief mentions of Pierce appeared in the *Missionary Outlook* 1 (1881): 24: 'It is really a blessed thing to see how attentively they listen, both old and young, to the word of life, and how lustily they sing the hymns taught them by Wm. H. at the day school. Wm. H. has done good work in the short time he has been here [at Bella Bella].' *Missionary Outlook* 1 (1881): 59: 'Our little Church at Port Essington has been in use some time, but more work has to be done on it when the lumber is well seasoned. I have sent Wm. H. Pierce, who did such good work at Bella Bella before Mr. Tate's appointment, to take charge there.' *Missionary Outlook* 4 (1884): 15: 'Weekeeno is a hard place, but the softening influence of the gospel is equal to the hardest. Bro. Pierce is doing faithful work there, both among whites and Indians.' *Missionary Outlook* 5 (1885): 47: 'Word from Bro. Pierce at Bella-Coola is very good; the Lord is with that brother in very deed.' It is apparent from these brief descriptions of Pierce's stationing and work that he was being used to fill positions that could not sustain a white-ordained missionary or when no other missionary was available.

20 *Minutes of the Port Simpson Ministerial Session and Annual District Meeting*, 1883, Port Simpson District, Toronto Conference, Methodist Church of Canada, in United Church of Canada, BC Conference Archives [UCA (BC)].

21 For a detailed exploration of the educational patterns of Methodist missionaries in British Columbia, see my 'Creating Textual Communities: Anglican and Methodist Missionaries and Print Culture in Nineteenth-Century British Columbia' (PhD diss., University of British Columbia, 2001), chapter 2, 'Education for Ministry and the Print Culture of Anglican and Methodist Missionaries.' Between 1859 and 1900, a total of 133 probationers and ministers were stationed on the various circuits in British Columbia. Their level of educational attainment and progress towards ordination followed traditional Methodist patterns. Of the 133, 60 (45 per cent) had not attended college, or had no record of higher education; 32 (24 per cent) had attended college for at least one year, but had not received a degree; 34 (25 per cent) held one or more earned degrees; 6 (5 per cent) had honorary degrees only; and one held a licentiate in theology.

22 *Missionary Outlook* 1 (1881): 71.

23 Ibid., 174.

24 See, for example, the letter from Pierce printed in *Missionary Outlook* 3 (1883): 191: 'I am thankful to say our brother Mr. Jennings, is trying to improve me in my studies.'

25 *Minutes of the Port Simpson Ministerial Session and Annual District Meeting*, 1884, Port Simpson District, Toronto Conference, UCA(BC).

26 *Minutes of the Port Simpson Ministerial Session and Annual District Meeting*, 1886 and 1887, Port Simpson District, Toronto Conference, which included the resolution heartily recommending him to be ordained and admitted into full connection with the Methodist Church.

27 Pierce, *From Potlatch to Pulpit*, 61.

28 Ibid., 42.

29 Ibid., 45.

30 Pierce's approval of the destruction of dance regalia is echoed in his
    letter to Sutherland, dated 14 February 1908, in Sutherland Papers 5/103,
    'British Columbia Indian Missions: Correspondence re Kishpiox, Upper
    Skeena, 1906–1910,' in which he describes the conversion of a chief at
    Kispiox.

31 Crosby, *Up and Down the North Pacific Coast*, 187, stated 'it was found very
    difficult to keep a regular Missionary [i.e., a white missionary] at Bella
    Bella,' and that 'the Bella Bellas never heard their Missionary preach in
    their own language.'

32 This practice of 'adopting' a missionary by branches of the Epworth
    League, the young adult study and mission group in the Methodist Church,
    was heavily promoted, in particular, by the *Missionary Bulletin*.

33 Pierce, *From Potlatch to Pulpit*, 86.

34 The correspondence regarding the publication of the autobiography can be
    found in 'Printing and Publishing, Correspondence re W.H. Pierce and
    autobiography, 1919–1936,' UCA, Methodist Church of Canada, Young
    People's Forward Movement for Missions, Frederick Clarke Stephenson
    Papers, box 11, file 13 [cited as Stephenson Papers]; and W.H. Pierce vertical
    file, UCA(BC). Evidently, the possibility of publication had been discussed
    for some time prior to the first letter in the file, from M.H. and W.H. Pierce
    to the Rev. F.C. and Annie Stephenson, dated 18 March 1919, which begins:
    'We have not forgotten you, even if we have never written you a personal
    letter for some time past. For quiet a while now it has been our intention to
    write you regarding the book which we hope to finish and publish some
    day.'

35 M.H. and W.H. Pierce to F.C. and Mrs Stephenson, 18 March 1919.

36 Letter from M.H. Pierce to Mrs Stephenson, 14 June 1919, in ibid. J.P. Hicks,
    the editor of *From Potlatch to Pulpit* explained the disjunction in the text
    between the first, autobiographical section, and the second section, which
    focuses on Aboriginal systems of belief and practices, by noting that the
    autobiographical portion ended with the year 1910, and the remainder of
    the manuscript was 'devoted to Indian legends, traditions and customs of
    the pre-white man period – a wealth of information which the future, per-
    haps even more than the present, will value.'
      Judging by the outline of the work, included in a letter from W.H. Pierce
    to Mrs Stephenson, 28 January 1925, in Stephenson Papers, the manuscript
    had attained the form by 1925 that was published in 1933 – a first section

based on the 1910 autobiographical sketch, supplemented by the material in the second section, which the Pierces described in their letter of 19 March 1919, as 'everything we could think of relating to the Indian life before the whites or missionaries came; many legends and traditions exceedingly interesting which have never been known or published by any one – also the history of the different villages along the Skeena right up to Port Simpson.' In this letter the Pierces also stated, 'After this is quite finished, then we begin on the Mission Work and the Spiritual part. This will cover from the time Mr. Duncan arrived, to the present time.' It seems clear that this final section was never written.

As the manuscript of *From Potlatch to Pulpit* does not seem to have survived, it is impossible to determine the extent of the collaboration between Pierce and Margaret in the creation of the book, although external evidence is provided by the dramatic shift in literary style in Pierce's published letters from the early, pre-Margaret period, to the letters written after their marriage. Pre-Margaret, Pierce's preferred style of communication was an exuberant mix of Methodist rhetorical tropes (such as 'a warm heart,' 'seasons of refreshing'), paraphrased quotations from Scripture and popular Methodist hymns, and echoes of Wesley, undoubtedly transmitted in the sermons preached by the white Methodist missionaries. Pierce's sophistication with syntax and grammar varied within a letter, depending on whether he was quoting / paraphrasing another source, or articulating his own wishes: 'God bless you and your family – this is my daily pray. I thank God for answering our pray for the missionary to be send here. I know it is through your helping me since I started to pointing people to the Lamb of God, that I enjoy this blessed religion in my own heart every day, and I wish to thank you for all your great kindness to me.'

Once his published letters resume, subsequent to his marriage to Margaret, the grammar and syntax become much more regular. This may reflect Pierce's growing ease with English – or the hidden editorial hand of Margaret.

37 W.H. Pierce to Mrs Stephenson, 28 January and 23 March 1925, and Mrs Stephenson to Mrs Pierce, 23 April 1925, in Stephenson Papers.

38 Mrs Stephenson to Mrs Pierce, 20 March 1925, in ibid.

39 W.H. Pierce to Mrs Stephenson, 28 October 1926, in ibid. While the majority of the correspondence regarding the book was written by Margaret and signed by Pierce, this letter was clearly in Pierce's own handwriting. Judging by the two very different manuscript hands that appear in the letters, Margaret usually acted as Pierce's amanuensis, as well as engaging in correspondence under her own signature.

40 W.H. Pierce to Mrs Stephenson, 30 July 1928, in ibid. This letter bears a manuscript note, 'Answ. ADS May 12/33.'
41 Mrs Stephenson to W.H. and M.H. Pierce, 12 May 1933, in ibid.
42 John C. Goodfellow, Princeton BC, to W.H. Pierce, 13 June 1929, in W.H. Pierce vertical file, UCA(BC).
43 Goodfellow to Pierce, 6 April 1931. Pierce's talks at the British Columbia Conference became a regular event. William Lashley Hall editorialized in his partial transcript of the diary of pioneer missionary Ebenezer Robson: 'A new name is added to the list, a native son, Indian of mixed blood, Brother Pierce, as he will be generally called, who will continue for half a century as an active missionary among his own people. From time to time Conferences and other gatherings will be enlivened and enlightened with his racy Indian humour, if not always edified; whose guileless naivete, on occasion, will come near shocking more sophisticated ears.' See 'An Old Timer's Diary,' chapter 4 (1883–4), 321, in Ebenezer Robson vertical file, file 1/3, part IV, UCA(BC). See also 'Report of the British Columbia Annual Conference, 1933,' *New Outlook* 9, no. 24 (14 June 1933): 460, in which Pierce's speech was described as 'something of an annual institution in the Conference.'
44 Crosby, *Up and Down the Pacific Coast*, 186. This pattern seems to have been reinforced by the Aboriginal communities, who frequently indicated their preference for white ordained missionaries, despite the language barriers, rather than Aboriginal lay missionaries, fluent in the indigenous language of the community. This preference may have been a reflection of the Aboriginal communities' active strategizing to familiarize themselves with European modes of power. See Brett Christophers, *Positioning the Missionary: John Booth Good and the Confluence of Cultures in Nineteenth-Century British Columbia* (Vancouver: UBC Press, 1998).
45 It is also perhaps surprising to note that although letters from missionary wives featured prominently in the *Missionary Outlook*, no letters from Margaret were ever published, especially given her later voluminous correspondence regarding the autobiography. On similar issues of apparent gender bias in missionary reports, see the chapters by Margo Gewurtz and Barbara Lawson in this book.
46 Sutherland to Miss Edith Giffin, 14 May 1909, 'British Columbia Indian Missions: Correspondence re Kishpiox, Upper Skeena, 1906–1910,' Sutherland Papers, 5/103.
47 See the letter from T. Ferrier to Sutherland, 28 April 1909, in ibid.
48 George Raley to Sutherland, 19 October 1909, in ibid.
49 See also Gail Edwards, '"A Great Unrest Permeates the Indians Here": The

Gitx̲san of the Upper Skeena and "Land Matters," 1906–1910,' unpublished paper presented at the BC Studies Conference, Vancouver, May 2003.

50 'Meeting of the British Columbia Conference,' *New Outlook* 3, no. 25, and whole number 27 (27 June 1927): 18. See also 'Re-establishment of Marine Service on Pacific West Coast,' *New Outlook*, n.s. 9, no. 13 (old series 104, no. 20) (29 March 1933): 276: 'Brother Pierce was a fine raconteur and an orator of the Indian style.'

51 *Daily Colonist* (14 January 1934), 22. Pierce referred to his doubled identity in a speech to the British Columbia Annual Conference in 1933, *New Outlook* 9, no. 24 (13 June 1933): 460: 'Mr. Pierce humorously alluded to his ancestry in stating that while racial mixtures were sometimes said to bring out the bad of both races, in his case the process had been reversed. He had inherited the best elements of the Scotch from his father and the best traditions and qualities of the Aboriginal peoples from his Indian mother.'

52 'W.H. Pierce, First Indian Cleric, Dies,' *Vancouver Sun* (15 April 1948), 11.

53 J.P. Hicks to John Goodfellow, 31 October 1932, in W.H. Pierce vertical file, UCA(BC).

54 'We Heartily Greet Them,' *Western Methodist Recorder* 23, no. 12 (June 1924): 9.

55 Pierce, *From Potlatch to Pulpit*, 97.

Chapter 4

'Eating the Angels' Food': Arthur Wellington Clah – An Aboriginal Perspective on Being Christian, 1857–1909

SUSAN NEYLAN

I wish to tell you that more of the heathen are converted to God, and many more are preparing to renounce heathenism, when the white missionary comes up. The foundation of darkness has been shaking [*sic*] up by God's mighty power ... Our people are busy every day like bees in gathering lots of good Indian food for the winter, also they are eating the angels' food, even the Word of Life.[1]

A Coast Tsimshian man who was having an ample helping of this angel's food was Arthur Wellington Clah. Like William Henry Pierce (Clah's nephew who is the subject of Gail Edwards's chapter 3) or Edward Sexsmith, the Native missionary who described the mission work at Kispiox in 1888 in the above quotation, or, indeed, dozens of other Aboriginal missionaries, catechists, and evangelists throughout northern British Columbia, Clah represents an important aspect of mission history. His perspective on the process of missionization helps to reveal what the transition to Christianity may have meant both ideologically and practically to those at the centre of it.

Among the Tsimshianic-speaking First Nations of northern British Columbia (Tsimshian, Nisga'a, and Gitxsan) the arrival of Protestant missionaries in the mid- and late nineteenth century exposed them to a new source of spiritual power, material wealth, and modes of authority. Aboriginal men and women took an active role in missions as founders, church leaders, preachers, and committed Christians. They participated in the production as well as the consumption of Christianity and what it meant to be Christian. Yet, they never entirely controlled the process of missionization or fully steered the course of mission life. Not necessarily a mutually beneficial conversation between Native and missionary, it was a dialogic encounter nonetheless.

Arthur Wellington Clah, a Tsimshian Christian and Methodist evangelist (and William Henry Pierce's uncle), walked thousands of miles throughout British Columbia spreading the gospel. He kept a diary from 1857 to his death in 1909, and developed a syncretic Christian identity that was evangelical yet also indigenous in nature.

Some Aboriginal converts, like the extraordinary Arthur Wellington Clah, expressed their personal experiences in textual records. These perspectives are diverse examples of how missions were (re)presented and (re)written. Ultimately these multifaceted texts enrich our knowledge of the historical changes taking place during early missionization and what role within those changes Aboriginal evangelists envisioned for themselves. Literate converts, like Clah, were privy to the same metaphors, literary devices, and common texts characteristic of the Euro-Canadian discourse on mission work. Yet, Native writers manipulated, rejected, or challenged those conversations on missions. Aboriginal writings also illustrate simultaneously genuine evangelicalism and an indigenized Christianity. In this paper, I offer some brief illustrations from Clah's journals and his other writings of how he framed his own Christian identity and concerns, particularly when it came to the Canadian appropriation of Tsimshian land.

Arthur Wellington Clah, Tsimshian Christian and evangelist, figures prominently in my research into Native roles in mission work in nineteenth-century northern British Columbia (along the north coast, and the Skeena and Nass river watersheds), because of the rich documentary record on him, including his own voluminous autobiographical accounts.[2] Clah (the anglicized version of his hereditary name ⱡa'ax), traced his family from the Gidestsu nation of Klemtu (China Hat) and inherited the Killerwhale or Blackfish (Gispwudwada) clan and name T'amks (Tdahmuks or Tamks, which was also the name of his house) from his maternal uncle.[3] Clah was a fur trader, leader, and preacher of apparent influence in the Fort Simpson/Lax Kw'alaams area throughout the latter half of the nineteenth century.[4] Clah frequently appeared in the missionary literature, but his association with Euro-Canadians had actually begun earlier through his employment with the Hudson's Bay Company (HBC).

Clah kept a journal, first as a means to learn English, but then to record his life.[5] His journals span nearly fifty years, beginning in the mid-1850s and with regular daily entries almost unbroken from 1861 to 1909.[6] Employed by the HBC, Clah worked as a translator and trader before being hired by the first official missionary to the region, the Rev. William Duncan, who arrived in 1857. Clah was credited with teaching Duncan Sm'algyax (Coast Tsimshian language), and with saving his life during a confrontation with another Tsimshian chief who opposed the missionary's work.[7]

Although an early convert of Duncan's and presumably an adherent to a brand of evangelical Anglicanism, Clah chose to remain in the Fort Simpson area when Duncan moved to Metlakatla, the famous industrial mission and centrepiece of the Anglican Church for a few decades (1862–87).[8] Indeed, by the 1870s, Clah had drifted towards Methodism. He was baptized and became a member of the Methodist Church at Fort Simpson (renamed Port Simpson in 1880), and was associated with the Rev. Thomas Crosby for many years. But in truth, Clah really never adhered to any one denomination of Protestantism. By the 1890s, he even participated in Salvation Army services.

Most of Clah's own evangelism and missionary work was done voluntarily. Despite associations with some of the best-known Euro-Canadian missionaries in the province, his journals are a testimony of his own brand of evangelical faith. This is most explicit in matters where Clah disagrees with Euro-Canadian missionaries over who could teach and interpret Christianity, but also in the unique representations of faith, reflective of Tsimshian life and viewpoints. Christianity was presented as more than merely a belief system; it was offered by Euro-Canadian missionaries as a component for a new society modelled upon Western notions of what constituted 'civilization.' However, this did not mean that converts necessarily accepted the deal as prepackaged. Clah's journal entries also provide good examples of how Christianity became indigenized at the local level – that is, refashioned to mesh with and complement Tsimshian beliefs, interpreted through pre-existing practices – or generally, how the new religion was understood through the filter of Native spiritual systems.

There is no denying the fact that missions to First Nations in British Columbia were part of the process of colonization, and by pointing to the voices of Native Christians, I do not suggest all had equal expression of or access to power. But to view Christianity and Aboriginal religions as opposites is not always productive. While there were many points of difference, at its core, Tsimshian spirituality shared a surprising number of elements with nineteenth-century evangelical Christianity. For example, both were experiential religions, ones that placed individuals in direct contact with nonhuman powers. Both valued transformative religious experiences and marked these spiritual transformations by bestowing new names in special ceremonies (e.g., *yaakw*, or the feast potlatch context for Tsimshian peoples, and baptismal rites for Christian culture).

Syncreticism – combining beliefs or practices of diverse religious forms – came as no surprise. Let me offer a subtle reference to this from

Clah's journals. In 1893, in the middle of a discussion of how the Native expectations for the Wesleyan Methodist Church were not being fulfilled, Clah wrote that one could see Heaven either after death or while asleep.[9] This simple explanation succinctly encapsulated two belief systems held simultaneously and without apparent contradiction within a single individual. Clah described the concept of the Christian afterlife, and also alluded to the Tsimshianic importance allotted to dreams, both as predictions of what might come and literally as conduits to other realms. In this instance, the newer Christianity and the older Tsimshian religious beliefs were complementary rather than oppositional.

In the mission literature, catechisms or baptismal examinations were designed to prompt confessional responses and denunciation, especially of non-Christian practices.[10] This confessional or denunciatory model was embraced by Native converts in their own written works as a way of expressing their depth of faith. For Clah, that measure was found in his constant search for Jesus, paralleled by his own evangelist travels in search of enlightenment. While there was no apparent tradition of public confession among pre-Christian Tsimshian,[11] it was very common to recount and even recreate transformative experiences, such as reenactments of contacts with nonhuman powers. In a letter published in the *Missionary Notices of the Wesleyan Methodist Church* in April 1875, Clah wrote of seeing tracks in the snow and literally tracking Jesus.[12] An encounter with a physical presence of Jesus is reminiscent of 'traditional' Tsimshian narratives of encounters with nonhumans or wonders, during solitary vision quests.

Scholars have examined the relationship between public confession and religious enthusiasm in the larger mission context but may have underemphasized a similar association in written discourses at the individual level. Letters, journal entries, sermons, and religious confessions together 'define the unique identity and culture position of the Christianized Native.'[13] Collectively these may be deemed Christian autoethnographies, after Mary Louise Pratt's concept of those textual strategies in which 'the colonized subjects undertake to represent themselves in ways that engage with the colonizer's own terms. If ethnographic texts are a means by which Europeans represent to themselves their (usually subjugated) others, autoethnographic texts are those the Others construct in response to or in dialogue with those metropolitan representations.'[14]

David Murray in his book *Forked Tongues*, analysed the rhetorical expression of confessional modes of writing as they appeared in Native autobiographies, and connected this kind of expression to the much broader context of imbalanced power relationships endemic to colonial missionization of First Nations.[15] In reading Native-produced texts, Murray claims we gain insight into the complex relation between self-expression in Native autobiographies, freedom, and power.

Confession is an expression of social power relations, according to Michel Foucault, and 'a ritual of discourse in which the speaking subject is also the subject of the statement; it is also a ritual that unfolds within a power relationship, for one does not confess without the presence (or virtual presence) of a partner who is not simply the interlocutor but the authority who requires the confession.'[16] In Roman Catholicism, private confession to a priest is an important dogma, but in Protestant Christianity, confession is a significant recognition of both the private, personal self (privately praying before God), and the public, social self (publicly proclaiming one's Christianity). Even the power of the minister or preacher conformed to his or her ability to remain a supplicant before self, congregation, and God.

In a way, Clah's journal itself was a confessional history.[17] Especially later in life, Clah increasingly defined his purpose behind his daily entries in terms of the recording of history, but a history that was one of moral and spiritual 'evolution' for his people. Each new booklet was inscribed with a brief description of Clah's sense of a history of profound change on the north coast.[18] For his journals from the late 1890s and early 1900s he even included rather lengthy headers for each separate page, with similar confessional gloss:

Clquah.Collams. [Lax Kw'alaams (Port Simpson)] B.C. Jan 1 1894 writen by Arthur Wellington Clah. this Book keeping write how the great Kings work for all nation all of the world for our good or evel ways. Is the great north History about old and New people that we all built Happy for our lord Jesus Christ make us free. But Jesus make up liberty from temptation. this writen for New people to know about old and new Christian inside the man. Same men make two Road inside. Some one Road inside that Reach to Heaven when he die one heart. Two hearted man reach no heaven. this Book written to know Both.[19]

There is no doubt that Clah gained power and authority because of his access to Christianity and his personal relationships with spiritually powerful individuals (missionaries). His own rise to prominence in a 'traditional' sense in the late 1860s – assuming the headship of his lineage as a house chief, holding a potlatch (*yaakw*), and assuming a hereditary name-title, his success at trade – paralleled his rise as a Christian.[20] He not so much demanded his right to interpret religion, as he believed he had the right to do so as an expression of his faith. Part of what it meant to be a Christian was the ability to interpret Christianity. As Peggy Brock in her examination of Clah's Christian nature deftly phrased it, 'Christianity was not experienced as an alien ideology, but as a new Tsimshian form of knowledge. Although its source was from outside Tsimshian society, as were many forms of knowledge, Christianity was expressed in Tsimshian ways.'[21]

How did missionaries who were both Aboriginal and Christian, like Clah, view themselves and their work? As I have noted in my previous study of him, first and foremost, Clah preached out of a sense of personal conviction as a Christian. Clah clearly writes of his evangelistic work in terms of a far-ranging and lifelong pursuit, driven not by wages or fame, but by faith. He wrote that he took his 'wages from god.'[22]

> When I felt stronger in Spirit of God I start walk ... I keep the Holy Bible with me to tell the people about Jesus Christ the lord. Because Jesus Said ... go ye therefore and teach all nations. So I Believe what God will Said in my heart to teach the poor people. alrounds sometimes I walk 200 miles. Some 300. some 400 miles. 8 hundred miles round trips from Cassier. Sometimes go ways up north an alaska u.s.a. telling the friends about our saviour Jesus. But sometimes I came back 3 months. Some came back 4 months. when I came home.[23]

These claims of travelling and evangelizing many miles were no exaggeration. Geographer R.M. Galois has graphed Clah's annual rounds (trading, engaging in wage-labour, hunting, fishing, prospecting, and visiting friends and family) in 1864 and 1873 based on Clah's journal entries. Clah was thirty-three years old in 1864, and according to Galois's calculations, he travelled 6000 kilometres that year. A decade later, at forty-two years of age, his annual rounds totalled approximately 3200 kilometres.[24] Galois located exclusive 'preaching' trips made by Clah during the winter months, which was the 'traditional' religious season in Tsimshian culture.

However, in my reading of these same journal entries I would add that evangelism, bible reading, and holding Sunday services were also facets of Clah's daily life, and occurred regardless of his location or activity; nothing was as consistent or more habitual than these expressions of his Christianity, except perhaps his dedication to making entries in the journals themselves. This point is significant because it shows one of the mechanisms by which Christian knowledge was being spread outside of official mission contexts. Nor were Clah's evangelistic efforts unusual. There were many kinds of church groups (e.g., Epworth Leagues, Band of Christian Workers, or the Church Army) that allowed Aboriginal individuals to go preaching for weeks on end, sometimes without any supervision by church officials. In nineteenth-century British Columbia, there were also indigenous forms of spiritual expression, such as prophet movements, that incorporated, even appropriated, Christian practices and disseminated them outside the formal structures of missionization.[25]

The language Clah used in his journals referenced this mobile aspect of the Tsimshian lifestyle. He frequently wrote about prospecting trips, accompanied, of course, by preaching along the way. He used prospecting terminology when he described inter- or intradenominational rivalry. For example, when recording the conflict between William Duncan and Anglican Church officials – a conflict that placed the Tsimshian at the very centre and was one of the factors behind the 1887 establishment of New Metlakatla in Alaska – Clah wrote that Anglican Bishop William Ridley was 'trying Jump William Duncan's claim. he wished put Duncan out.'[26] He also applied the prospecting metaphor to Aboriginal land claims. In the 1880s, when reserves were being allotted in the north, without any formal treaties or practical consultation with First Nations, Clah commented the 'whit[e] people trying Jump our land to Claim ... [it]. whit[e] people first known Judgment to what Judgment is. I know little myself. If I Jump any friends land to claimed our God punish me Bad at last day.'[27] In effect, Clah presumed a Christian moral code applied and that ultimately God would pass judgment on those who appropriated Native lands.

Tsimshian Christians willingly believed in a Christianity that served their lives and societies in ways unforeseen by mission authorities. One vignette from Clah's journal demonstrates this conviction, and illustrates how, again, converts did not passively receive Christian teachings from non-Natives. In 1880 Clah recorded the reaction of the local missionary at an Anglican mission (Kingaleg) on the Nass River, when Clah's supposedly deceased nephew was brought back to life with a dream from heaven. Clah had excitedly gathered people together to pray, sing, and worship because of this direct intervention of God into their lives. Although the whole event was Christian in motivation and form, the Anglican lay missionary Henry Schutt denounced the event. In a direct challenge to the missionary's authority, Clah validated his nephew's experience by citing biblical precedence and reaffirming his own personal conviction that the Christian god and saviour Christ were active in his own life:

> Calling me in his house. he asking me why I call the people with me. so I say yes. he says what you said to them. so I tell him about what I told the friends about F.S. [Fort Simpson] an metleketlah they want. try make one heart. an about mans dream. Cshutt [Schutt] laughing to me. nobody see the Heaven. an nobody see god. same he told me about moses. that If anybody who dreamed god or Christ stoned or killed dead. so I told him. Mr. Cshutt I think you mistake. I have seen all the dreams on Holy Book. Jacob had a good Dream. John had a good Dream. Joseph good Dream. Cshutt says not now. God sent words long time ago. not now. so I speak to him. you not Believed who make you live now. I Believe myself the great god His with me now. He gave me live. an Spak [speech] and my eyes an mine fut [foot] to walk now. not [long] ago and not yesterday. [but] to night. I Believe His with me Jesus always come see the mens heart. Cshutt says goodnight.[28]

Schutt explained that to distort biblical narratives was dangerous, and that those in the bible who dreamed of God or Christ were, in fact, killed. However, Clah was not misled because he knew the biblical texts too well. He directly refuted Schutt's arguments by citing several examples where that was not the case. Seemingly undermining his own missionary agenda, Schutt insisted that God no longer directly intervened in the lives of humans.[29] The threat of circumventing the 'official' mission representatives as the source of Christian knowledge in this way was an assault on the power of the missionary. Even in this Christian form, the prophet (or in this case, a potential prophet) threatened church hegemony. Clah probably did not see it this way. Most likely, he would have simply explained that he was being a good Christian.

This is not an isolated incident. Clah frequently clashed over the issue of who had the authority to interpret Christianity and certainly was not as deferential towards missionaries as they expected.[30] Indeed, brazen in many of his dealings with non-Natives, this may reflect

Clah's own boisterous personality as well as his Christian nature. In the early 1870s, when William Duncan, the missionary at Metlakatla heard that Clah was preaching Sunday services on his own and holding study sessions, he became quite concerned:

> to day preaching walkd round the places to teaching what Gods words on the bible also News Come up yesterday [from Metlakatla] to Say [William] Duncan laugh at me Because I Teach the people in truth. I making to understan how to Prayer and to Thank God for god looking upon us He gaves us all We want. Some News Said to me If I got licence alright I can preach the people Now I think his little mistake God gave the Licence in our hearts he gaves us One Soul in our hearts to Teach us to love Him an to know him with all our hearts and Keep his commandments Jesus Teach us how to Prayer and how to thank God. He teach us everything.[31]

Clah's comments illustrate both a kind of Native initiative and evangelical understanding of Christianity, but also the typical reaction such perceptions provoked in non-Native missionaries. When challenged by Duncan's opinion that formal training and official sanction were necessary before Clah would be 'licensed' to preach to his fellow Tsimshian, Clah replied that his licence had been granted directly by God. For him there was no need for a church-sanctioned licence to preach; he did not need to be told by any church official how he was supposed to deal with this faith or how to express it.

Clah's right to preach, his right to express his own interpretation of what it meant to be Christian, did not go uncontested. Just as Duncan was perturbed by Clah's unsupervised activities, the Rev. Thomas Crosby's own evangelical Methodism had its limits when it came to Clah's insistence that he, too, should be allowed to preach in the church:

> I went in mission house ... Mr. crosby told me why I not prayer. [pray?] I Never See you Prayer in meeting [either in prayer meeting or praying in meeting]. why whats [what's] the matter. so I told him his wife stand Behine [behind] him. see laughing at me. Because her man Charge to me why not Pray so I told him well. If you wanted me I preach in the Church and you listen to me not only the prayer. I preach very much. he Says Very good. but you not Preach Very longer. so I thinks his [he is] fraiden [afraid or frightened] to me. Because he not I preach longer.[32]

Clah's evangelizing did not necessarily follow the same direction

espoused by the mission or the church; after all he was not in the pay
or under the direct supervision of the church throughout most of his
career as a missionary. But Clah saw his efforts as directly related to the
mission, because he, like others, regarded Christianity as a type of
moral force with the power to equip First Nations with the tools they
needed to survive the tremendous change assaulting their cultures.
Moreover, with Anglicans, Methodists, Salvation Army, and in neighbouring Gitxsan territory, Catholics, Tsimshian could select the best
available choice to suit their needs and agendas.

In 1874, Clah wrote in his journal of the confusion and questions
some Tsimshian had over which denomination and preachers provided the most truthful form of Christianity. Clah responded by insist-
ing that they had the right to select for themselves who taught them
Christianity. His reasoning suggests a very evangelical understanding
of Christianity, and that perhaps a missionary as a 'go-between'
between converts and God was entirely unnecessary:

> Those people wants me to know I If had News to them they expect good
> Minster every days to preach and to teach them right some they Says tom-
> linson [i.e., Anglican missionary, Robert Tomlinson] his [he is] come an
> [and] teach in they wants to know who is the right preacher to telling
> them in Gods words. they Said We Believe God Father If anybody teach
> us right now I get up and tell them I Say all my friends. I have no News to
> telling yous don t to [sic] not troubling ourselfs to what your like to do
> yous not slave Now one thing I have Said to yours Prayer to God love
> him then He will give good minster in here and yous feel happy teach all
> your childrens right way don t teach them Bad one thing I have to telling
> yous friends God Sent Need all round yous and tsimshens now what way
> we go friends. God Father Sent words upon us to stop everything wrong
> Make Him angry stealing liars murder. Jealous fighting Quarling. but god
> Sent words to know Him and to Save Him and to Believe his Son Jesus
> Christ who die for us now Before I left them. they Says wanted me tomor-
> row to teach them right.[33]

Clah's insistence that Native people did not have to be slaves to missionary ideals, that 'god Sent words to know Him,' illustrates his belief
in the centrality of scripture for Native Protestants. Indeed the Bible
was at the core of Protestantism – the word of God, the foundation of
the religion, and the undisputed authority to which Christians turned
to for guidance. Clah was well aware that Christianity was not the

'universal religion' some claimed it to be. Many Tsimshian beliefs still fit into his spiritual map of a world existing alongside Christianity. Clah believed that Christianity was not exclusively a 'white religion' and he frequently found himself evangelizing non-Natives and championing the validity of the Bible.[34] He was quick to point out the inherent incongruity of conversion to Christianity as the true route to equal status for Aboriginal peoples in Euro-Canadian society, especially when it came to Native land.

Without treaties and only minimal consultation with First Nations, reserves were laid out in Tsimshian territory beginning in 1881, when Peter O'Reilly's Indian Reserve Commission visited the north coast at a time when few Tsimshian were even at home.[35] The land issue was a threat with obvious spiritual implications because of the direct involvement of churches on the side of indigenous claims against the government and because of the role Christians played in organizing and voicing Native concerns.

By the end of the 1880s, the Canadian and British Columbia governments accused missionaries of 'stirring up trouble.'[36] Native evangelists, however, needed little prompting. Using Christian organizations, they were in a unique position to disseminate information, coordinate reaction, and voice displeasure about Native land claims. When Victoria newspapers reported on the 1875 government inquiry into the Native Land Question and how it was presented and then summarily ignored by the provincial government, Natives in the city quickly relayed the information from one Native group to another 'with a rapidity that outstrips the mail.'[37] Native Christians learned about Indian policy and governmental intentions from their missionaries, and thus, many were 'able to keep abreast of all the subtle variations in provincial policy.'[38]

Clearly, some Native evangelists facilitated the spread and discussion of land issues directly through their mission work. For example, in his journal entry for 26 December 1889, Clah mentions including lessons on land rights and Canadian law in his sermon. Later, he describes the actions in the following year taken by the village council to remove the missionary who had attempted to enforce the government's position on land rights and local autonomy.[39] Other Native class leaders, church elders, interpreters, and evangelists were, likewise, in a position to act as advocates on Native causes.

Time and time again, the Tsimshian demanded freedom from the confines of Indian agents and the Indian Act, and eloquently defended their position on rights to their own territories.[40] For example, in 1883 Clah reasoned with the Indian agent that Tsimshian lands were protected under God's law (see Appendix). After carefully eliciting an admission from the government representative that Canadian society was governed according to Christian principles and laws, he argued: 'Did you ever see a Christian take land from another Christian, and sell it, not letting him know anything about it?'[41]

In an 1888 sworn affidavit, Clah lamented the loss of his father's lands along the Nass River, where Clah and his family had briefly relocated (1878–81). His land, suggestively renamed 'Canaan,' had been included in a Nisga'a (Kincolith) reserve.[42] Clah complained to the Superintendent General of Indian Affairs, 'I read the Bible and God not approve of Ahab taking land from Naboth. So I don't think that God is pleased with the way the government has taken our land.'[43] Clah's biblical analogy was very apt; in essence, Clah appealed to a Christian moral code for land issues. Just as Naboth had refused to part with his land (what he also termed his father's inheritance) despite the demands from a king, Clah warned that similar behaviour by the Canadian government might likewise result in divine punishment.[44]

For Tsimshianic peoples on the north Pacific coast themselves, the divide between Christian and non-Christian was far less significant than the importance of presenting a unified case for self-determination and autonomy in their own territories. In 1887, Clah attended a meeting in which a group of Nisga'a chiefs discussed strategies to use in their land struggles with the provincial government.[45] Clah recounted the challenges they faced in deciding to either reconcile competing Coast Tsimshian and Nisga'a claims to areas of the Nass River so that they might stand united against the provincial government, or to independently pursue their interests as villages and tribes. One chief addressed the meeting, and while the content of his speech was not noted by Clah, the method by which he chose to validate his opinion offers a powerful image. As the chief spoke, he held a Bible in his left hand, and an eagle feather, a Native symbol of peace, in his right hand. He told the chiefs and elders in attendance that one was not stronger than the other.[46] This image summarizes the predicament confronting Tsimshianic peoples in the late nineteenth-century. At a time when confrontations over cultural practices and land issues saw only dichotomies, they were both Christian and Native. Christian identities were not subordinate or superior to Native ones, but they had become an important part of who Tsimshianic peoples had become after a few decades of missionization. Yet, colonial authorities advocating the appropriation of Native land did not recognize this when it served them better to distance the Aboriginal 'Other' from themselves. Native Christians saw this injustice all too well.

Clah actively reflected upon what it meant to be both a Tsimshian and a Christian in nearly fifty years of daily chronicles. For most of life, his contributions to the dissemination of evangelical Christianity was done on a voluntary basis. His journals were a private record, allowing him the ability to reflect upon Christianization from within. Yet, being an Aboriginal evangelist, it also placed him in a position that enabled him to critique the process. He remained in between 'traditional' and colonial societies, yet part of them both.

> Promise to have Council this evening about Victoria government and canadian government about our land. methodist mission Society promising to help the indian Christianity they give the land in the hand of lawyer. I had told the head Chiefs in Victoria that we waiten them promis. If we lost our land. also we lost our Christian.[47]

As Arthur Wellington Clah expresses his frustration over the Native lands issue, broken promises, and the role played by the Methodists against the government on the Tsimshian's behalf, he also summarizes an important point. In embracing Christianity, Aboriginal people did not entirely forsake connections to their heritage, land, or indigenous cultural expressions. As historian Robert Hefner notes, the crucial aspect of religious conversion 'is not a deeply systematic reorganization of personal meanings but an adjustment in self-identification through the at least nominal acceptance of religious actions or beliefs deemed more fitting, useful or true.'[48] This self-identification is a shifting one, and not the sole reference point for an individual. Religious encounters between Natives and missionaries were dialogic meetings in which both parties changed through the process of translating and communicating their opinions and positions. Yet, while Christianity was not directly imposed upon First Nations, it is important to acknowledge that the relationship was never equal in power, and Christian identities were not always easy ones to define or maintain. Clah's journals offer us a rare glimpse at how one man reflected on his identity as a Tsimshian and as a Christian.

APPENDIX

'A meeting of the Port Simpson People, held December 8th, 1883'[49]

Arthur Wellington (Clah): I want to know if you wish me to ask a question[?]

Mr McKay: Yes any question you like.

Arthur: I have been acquainted with you before this at the Hudson Bay Company. I am well assured that you are a true christian, so now I ask what is your office, a justice of the peace, a magistrate, or an Indian agent?

Mr McKay: I am an Indian agent to attend to anything you wish to ask of the government, and I am also a magistrate.

Arthur: Who are you to help the most, the white people or the Indians?

Mr McKay: If the Indians carry the case to the court of any one else, I will help the Indians if to my court I will do the best I can for both parties.

Arthur: Have you power?

Mr McKay: I can get power. All law abiding people in uniform I call will help me. You do not wish me to bring power from below. There are enough law abiding people here.

Arthur: Who has sent you out here, the Queen, the government or the Victoria government?

Mr McKay: I am sent by the government of Canada, not that of Victoria.

Arthur: I want to know the names of the governors.

Mr McKay: The British Empire has a great number of people. The sun never sets on it, for it is all the world and all this is under the Queen. It is divided into Dominions, Provinces, Colonies, etc. Canada extends from the sea on the one side to the sea on the other. The Governor General of Canada tends to the natives not the Victoria government.

Arthur: Are they all christians?

Mr McKay: Well they ought to be. They are not all but they should be. The Queen, the Governor General & the governors are all christians.

Arthur: Whose law is it that you have brought here: is it God's law or the Queen's?

Mr McKay: The Queen's law is under God's law, and is based on it. The English nation is a christian nation and base their laws on the Bible.

Arthur: We hear you say they are not all christians.

Mr McKay: There are some not christians yet, as it is here. It is a large country, and all are not christians though they ought to be.

Arthur: God has directed you here among your christian brothers. I will tell you what Dr Powell and judge O'Reilly did to us here.

Mr McKay: I will take down everything you say.

Arthur: Did you ever see a christian take land from another christian and sell it, not letting him know anything about it. We have heard that the Queen, that all the people in the west and in the interior across the Rocky Mountains are her children. She calls them such. Is that the way a mother treats her children, takes away their land and not tell them about it? For the Queen we have heard has taken it from us, Skeena, Nass, and all around, and sold it without our knowledge. We call ourselves christians and so have tried to wait patiently. We saw the Whites come here and survey our land, and we have said nothing about it. Only a few years ago we heard that N. and S. America were fighting because they were selling their own brothers as slaves. What is the cause of the war between them; they just fought like dogs. It is God that caused it because they were selling their brothers. Then the Queen sent out two gunboats because she did not like this war. She tried to stop it twas [sic] as it was not right to take and sell their brothers. So I think the war was stopped by the queen. Then she sent out word to all nations that the Indians were free. Mr Duncan brought the news in 1857. We are all free, we are at liberty. I have read in God's book the Bible how the poor are not despised in God's sight. Yet, however great a man may be he is nothing in God's sight if he is not a christian. But the poor if they are christians, have mercies shown them Or can do nothing against the truth, but for the truth.

NOTES

1 E. Sexsmith, Kishpiax [Kispiox], Skeena River, BC, letter dated 22 August 1888, *Missionary Outlook* 8, no. 12 (December 1888): 191.

2 See my *'The Heavens Are Changing': Nineteenth-Century Protestant Missions and Tsimshian Christianity* (Montreal/Kingston: McGill-Queen's University Press, 2003). In particular, sections of this paper draw from chapter 6, 'The Self-Reflections of Arthur Wellington Clah,' 161–74.

3 Wellington Clah (Tamks), 'How Tamks Saved Duncan,' recorded by William Beynon, 1950, in George F. MacDonald and John J. Cove, eds, *Tsimshian Narratives* 2: *Trade and Warfare, Collected by Marius Barbeau and William Beynon*, Mercury series no. 3 (Ottawa: National Museums of Canada, 1987), 210–11; and Arthur Wellington Clah, 'Reminiscences of Arthur Wellington Clah of the Tsimpshean Indian Nation including tribal legends of the time before the Flood, and the coming of the white men, and other Indian lore, etc.,' typescript (hereafter Clah, 'Reminiscences'), Arthur Wellington Clah's Journals (hereafter AWCJ), National Archives of Canada (NAC) MG 40 F11 #A-1709.

4 Gidestsu was a Southern Tsimshian group; however, Clah considered himself a member of the Gispaxlo'ots Nation (Coast Tsimshian) because of connections through his adopted father's lineage. Clah, 'Reminiscences,' 1.
  However, other scholars have classified him otherwise. For example, E.
  Palmer Patterson wrote 'He was a chief of the Gitando tribe of the Coast
  Tsimshian.' 'Neshaki: Kinfolk and Trade,' *Culture* 10, no. 2 (1990): 20.
5 AWCJ, NAC MG 40 F11 #A-1706–1714.
6 Clah's journals begin in the mid-1850s, but entries are sporadic. Despite his
  attempts, Clah's Euro-Canadian education was limited and his use of written English very poor. His grammar is awkward, his capitalization and
  punctuation erratic, and his spelling of words unique. But as language is
  central to understanding the Tsimshian discourse on missions and Christianity, it is important to reproduce Native texts as closely to the originals as
  possible. Therefore, quotations from Clah's journals have been left in their
  original forms, and I apologize for any words I may have unintentionally
  misinterpreted.
7 Much was made of the conflict between Tsimshian chief Ligeex (Legaic)
  and Duncan in the missionary propaganda, where it was described in
  terms of the archetypal 'showdown' between missionary and the shaman.
8 In 1887 over 700 Tsimshian departed for Alaska and established New
  Metlakatla, leaving the old mission site with a hundred or so inhabitants.
  Both Metlakatla communities exist today.
9 'If anyone Breaking our Gods law. or Commandment who man or woman
  Promising to be Gods people Because we keep Promise in church or in
  meeting to See the place of above when we sleep or die.' AWCJ, Monday 18
  September 1893, NAC MG 40 F11 #A-1706.
10 T.O. Beidelman, *Colonial Evangelism: A Socio-Historical Study of an East-
   African Mission at the Grassroots* (Bloomington: Indiana University Press,
   1982), 104–5. Of course, when Native Christians addressed non-Natives, did
   they have any other choice than to frame their transformation as a denunciation of their past lives if they wanted to be considered 'true' Christians?
11 As Margaret Seguin Anderson and Tammy Anderson Blumhagen have
   noted in 'Memories and Moments: Conversations and Recollections,' *BC
   Studies* 104 (Winter 1994): 99, 'neither the "confessional" nor "expose"
   genres are indigenous to Tsimshian *public* discourse (though they are
   probably as widely practiced *privately* among the Tsimshian as anywhere
   else).'
12 Clah, speech recorded in Thomas Crosby, 'Letter dated Fort Simpson, B.C.,
   Jan. 20 1875,' *Missionary Notices of the Wesleyan Methodist Church of Canada*,
   3d. series, no. 2 (April 1875): 38. It is possible that this quotation is by

another man called Clah – Philip McKay Clah – but in spirit, it is certainly in keeping with either man's beliefs.

13 Hilary E. Wyss, *Writing Indians: Literacy, Christianity, and Native Community in Early America* (Amherst: University of Massachusetts Press, 2000), 4.

14 Mary Louise Pratt, *Imperial Eyes: Travel Writing and Transculturation* (New York and London: Routledge, 1992), 7. Hilary Wyss alerted me to this discussion of ethnographic and autoethnographic expressions.

15 David Murray, *Forked Tongues: Speech, Writing, and Representation in Native American Texts* (London: Pinter Publishers, 1991), 48–53; and Neylan, 'The Heavens Are Changing,' 163.

16 Michel Foucault, *History of Sexuality: An Introduction*, vol. 1 (1978), translated by Robert Hurly (New York: Vintage Books, 1990), 61.

17 Neylan, 'The Heavens Are Changing,' 163–4.

18 Clah's awareness and sense of his people's place in an unfolding history extended beyond the north coast area. For example, Clah suggested in one journal entry that God had punished the United States and caused the Civil War because Americans had enslaved Africans, which like the plight of the Tsimshian, resulted in the loss of lands. Attempting to compare the contemporary appropriation of First Nations' land to the plight of black Americans, Clah implied that Africans owned the land in the Americas before they were enslaved. Despite this erroneous assumption, it demonstrates the degree to which Clah's perspective on things was far from 'local.' AWCJ, Saturday 8 December 1883, NAC MG 40 F11 #A-1713.

19 AWCJ, 1 January–3 October 1894, NAC MG 40 F11 #A-1706.

20 For detailed insights into Clah the 'entrepreneur,' see Brian C. Hosmer, *American Indians in the Marketplace: Persistence and Innovation among the Menominees and Metlakatlans, 1870–1920* (Lawrence: University Press of Kansas, 1999), 149, 161.

21 Peggy Brock, 'Building Bridges: Politics and Religion in a First Nations Community,' *Canadian Historical Review* 81, no. 1 (March 2000): 90.

22 AWCJ, Wednesday 4 January 1893, NAC MG 40 F11 #A-1706.

23 Ibid.

24 R.M. Galois, 'Colonial Encounters: The Worlds of Arthur Wellington Clah, 1855–1881,' *BC Studies* 115–16 (Autumn/Winter 1997–8): 129–33 (especially figures 2 and 3).

25 One of the best known during or just before Clah's lifetime was the Wet'suwet'en prophet(s) Bini, who carried a visionary message blending Aboriginal and Christian practices among First Nations throughout the north, including the Tsimshian.

26 AWCJ, Friday 24 October 1884, NAC MG 40 F11 #A-1713.

27 AWCJ, Monday 14 May 1888, NAC MG 40 F11 #A-1714.

28 AWCJ, Saturday 24 January 1880, NAC MG 40 F11 #A-1712.

29 The argument whether 'apostolic gifts' or 'fruits of the Spirit' were with-drawn after apostolic times or remain applicable today is one that goes back to the beginning of Christianity. During and since the Reformation, many Protestants have tried to recreate apostolic Christianity by restoring the 'primitive church' as it existed in the early Christian period. For them, God (and Satan) continue to intervene in human lives through miracles, divine healing, emotional outbursts, shaking and shouting, dreams and visions, exorcism, speaking in tongues, and being 'slain in the Spirit.' Twentieth-century Pentecostals have built a whole theology called 'Resto-rationism,' based on the belief that these 'apostolic gifts' will be restored in the Last Days as a witness to biblical prophecy (this is known as 'the Latter Rain' or the 'Evening Light'). Thus, Henry Schutt took a traditionalist posi-tion that miracles and dreams did not happen in the present time. I kindly acknowledge Alvyn Austin for drawing my attention to this theological debate and to its implications for my interpretation of Schutt's response to Clah.

30 The following two examples also appear in Neylan, 'The Heavens Are Chang-ing,' 162, 171.

31 AWCJ, Sunday 18 January 1874, NAC MG 40 F11 #A-1711.

32 AWCJ, Saturday 17 February 1883, NAC MG 40 F11 #A-1713.

33 AWCJ, 15 February 1874, NAC MG 40 F11 #A-1711.

34 One of my favourite examples is Clah's championing the validity of the Bible to non-Natives he meets along the way during his many travels: 'Mr. McCaullech [a Scots prospector] telling me about people in Europe. some people not Believe Jesus Christ our saviour. some not Believe who our lord God is. not Believed the Holy Bible Himself not Believe the Bible. when McCullech [sic] telling me everything makes me so fraiden [afraid]. Because God knows me an him Speaking against Him. Say Very near half the people in this world not Believe the Bible. no hell and no God. no Jesus. some he Said nobody Know it. so I tell him about the Bible of great god. Say all noncens [nonsense]. I ask him If he Believe Jonah trewt [sic?] our Big Sea and wales [whale] Swallowed him. McCaullech Says I dont Believed wale never Swallowed. Backed wales [whale's] mouth too Small. not Swallowed man. the [that] night I prayer [pray] to my Lord Jesus Christ.' AWCJ, Satur-day 30 May 1883, NAC MG 40 F11 #A-1713.

35 While the initial reserve allotments in 1881 produced immediate and nega-tive response from the Tsimshian, O'Reilly also visited the north coast in 1882, 1888, 1889, 1891, 1893, and 1896 to revise or reassess the reserve sys-

tem. For a discussion of O'Reilly's work, see Kenneth Brealey, 'Travels from Point Ellice: Peter O'Reilly and the Indian Reserve System in British Columbia,' *BC Studies* 115–16 (Autumn/Winter 1997–8): 181–236.

36 Methodist missionaries Reverends A.E. Green and Thomas Crosby were formally banned from attending Reserve Commission meetings in 1888. See the excellent discussion of this and other issues related to Tsimshian land matters in Thomas Bolt, *Thomas Crosby and the Tsimshian: Small Shoes for Feet Too Large* (Vancouver: UBC Press, 1992), 72–94.

37 Sproat to Laird, 30 September 1876, NAC, Department of Indian Affairs, RG 10, vol. 3637, file 7131; cited in Robin Fisher, *Contact and Conflict: Indian-European Relations in British Columbia, 1774–1890* (Vancouver: University of British Columbia Press, 1977), 188.

38 Ibid.

39 AWCJ, 26 December 1889, and 5 February 1890, NAC MG 40 F11 #A-1706.

40 For a general overview of Native land claims in British Columbia, see Paul Tennant, *Aboriginal Peoples and Politics: The Indian Land Question in British Columbia, 1849–1989* (Vancouver: UBC Press, 1990).

41 'Testimony of Arthur Wellington Clah,' Report of Meeting of Port Simpson Indians with Indian Agent, J.W. MacKay, 8 December 1883, NAC RG 10, #C-10105, vol. 3818, file 57837, p. 2. See my Appendix for Clah's testimony in its entirety.

42 As R.M. Galois explains in 'Colonial Encounters,' 142: 'In April 1878, after attempts to settle at Laghco and Aiyansh proved to be unsatisfactory, he built a house on his "father's land" at Laxk'a'ata, near the mouth of the Nass. Here he symbolically re-named Canaan, Clah established, in microcosm, a Native Christian community ... The land however was claimed by the Nisga'a inhabitants of Kincolith, the nearby Anglican mission village. Thanks to the intervention of their missionary, and the ignorance of the Indian Reserve Comissioner, Laxk'a'ata was allotted to the Kincolith Band as a reserve.'

43 Arthur Wellington Clah, 'Affidavit of A.W. Clah (An Indian),' in *Letter from Methodist Missionary Society to the Superintendent General of Indian Affairs regarding the British Columbia Troubles* (Toronto: n.p., 1889), 43.

44 Clah referenced the story of Ahab and Naboth from 1 Kings 21:1–16. Ahab the king of Samaria demanded Naboth's vineyard, who would part with it for neither money nor another plot of land. Ahab and his wife Jezebel plotted against Naboth, had him stoned to death under false accusation of blasphemy, and took his vineyard. However, God (speaking through the prophet Elijah), brought disaster on Ahab's house as punishment for the crime.

45 AWCJ, Saturday 23 April 1887, NAC MG 40 F11 #A-1714.
46 Clah wrote in the margins of his journal that he personally regarded the Bible as the stronger of the two. Ibid.
47 AWCJ, Tuesday 2 June 1891, NAC MG 40 F11 #A-1713.
48 Robert Hefner, 'World Building and the Rationality of Conversion,' in Robert W. Hefner, ed., *Conversion to Christianity: Historical and Anthropological Perspectives on a Great Transformation* (Berkeley: University of California Press, 1993), 7.
49 NAC RG 10, #C-10105, vol. 3605, file 2806, 1–3.

PART II

Over the Seas and Far Away

Chapter 5

Wallace of West China: Edward Wilson Wallace and the Canadian Educational Systems of China, 1906–1927

ALVYN AUSTIN

The Rev. Edward Wilson Wallace was – 'as much as any one man,' according to Jesse Arnup, secretary of the United Church Board of Overseas Missions – responsible for making Christian education in China 'intellectually respectable.' In 1906, Wallace was sent to Sichuan province (formerly spelled Szechwan) in West China to found an overseas daughter of the University of Toronto, West China Union University (WCUU). Once he got there, he was assigned a larger task, creating a 'feeder' board of education for all mission schools in three provinces of western China, from kindergarten to middle school. His twenty-year career in China coincided with the life span of the West China Christian Educational Union (WCCEU): it was founded as he was sailing up the Yangtze in 1906; he became its first full-time secretary in 1913; and it dissolved in 1927, when civil war forced the evacuation of all missionaries. Dr Wallace, as he now was, a widower with a teen-aged son, retired from China.

'The religious interpretation of life provided the foundation of his educational work,' continued Jesse Arnup. 'In his view education was an organ of religion.'[1] But what made the educational systems Wallace created 'Canadian,' and how were they related to the mission school system in Canada described by Jamie S. Scott and Myra Rutherdale in their chapters in this book? Wallace helped create two separate and distinct educational systems, one for the Chinese, and the 'Canadian School in West China,' an expatriate boarding school for the missionaries' own children. The latter followed the Ontario curriculum exactly, mailing the Grade 13 exams to Toronto to be marked. Under the guidance of Lewis Walmsley, later chair of East Asiatic Studies at the University of Toronto, the school taught Latin – out there, a few days'

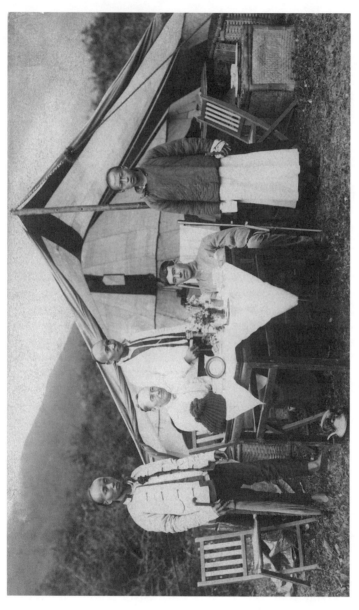

Rev. Edward Wilson Wallace (seated left) and Mrs Davidson in front of his tent in the mountains near Dajianlu (formerly spelled Tachienlu), on the border of Tibet, during his first summer in China in 1907. Wallace of West China helped establish a Canadian system of mission schools in Sichuan province.

march from Tibet – and performed Gilbert and Sullivan pantomimes. 'Adjustable desks and adjustable seats, brought from Canada, gave the children a most comfortable position and a modern appearance to the schoolroom ... Beds and bedding for the boarding-pupils rooms, cutlery, china and glass for the dining-room, and all kitchen furnishings were also brought from Canada.'[2]

On the other side, the Chinese side, Wallace was not building a state educational system, but a union of private religious schools, 'a complete and properly coordinated system of Christian education, parallel to the system of the Chinese government, but with such deviations from it as from time to time seem necessary.'[3] He took two Canadian models with him to China, and created variants on both. Egerton Ryerson's Ontario school system, based on the Irish common school model, was centralized, uniform, and graded. Although on the surface it was a 'secular' system, its underlying ideology, Ryerson stressed, was 'common Christianity,' a broad evangelical Protestant consensus shorn of denominational 'peculiarities.' In reality, Ryerson's system was secular only at the primary and secondary level, while higher education was dominated by church colleges at Queen's and the University of Toronto.

The other model was the industrial school, which had been adapted to the church-run residential schools for Native peoples in Canada. Wallace experimented with a small boarding school, but the industrial school model was not applicable in China for one simple reason: industrial schools were imposed on isolated Canadian Natives to train them to be domestic servants and agricultural labourers. The missionaries had enormous power and prestige, sponsored at the highest level by the Canadian state to solve 'the Native problem.' By contrast, mission schools overseas were meant to educate the new elite, the Christian, English-speaking leaders of the coming church. They would be the preachers, evangelists, biblewomen, nurses, doctors, dentists, YMCA and YWCA workers, the various employees of a multifaceted mission, a 'full-orbed Christianity.'[4]

The West China Field

As latecomers to missions, the Canadian Methodists concentrated on two fields not yet occupied, Japan and West China. Every year from 1906 to 1926 parties of young Canadian missionaries, twenty or thirty at a time, would sail up the Yangtze gorges, 1500 miles inland to Sichuan. In 1905, the West China mission had 30 missionaries (ten couples, eight single women, two men, and several dozen children); by 1920, it had grown to 200 personnel, the majority with university or college education. It had 6000 students in its schools, twice the constituency of the church. They hoped someday to have 200,000 students, one out of every ten children in the province 'securing an education under Christian auspices.'[5]

Of all the parties, none was so remarkable as the first, the '1906 gang,' which included James S. Woodsworth's sister Harriet, Charlie Jolliffe, H.D. Robertson, and Rupert Carscallen (later president of West China Union University and, after his retirement, principal of the Ontario Ladies' College).[6] The natural leader was E.W. Wallace, a tall, thin, bespectacled gentleman, who stands out in photographs from the time. He was twenty-six, the eldest son of Francis Huston Wallace, a noted 'higher critic' and professor of New Testament at Victoria College. His mother was Joy Wilson, the daughter of Bishop Edward Wilson of the Methodist Episcopal church in New Jersey. Born in 1880 at his grandparents' home, Edward Wilson was raised in Cobourg, Ontario, where Victoria College was then located. When Victoria relocated to Toronto and federated with the University of Toronto in 1890, the family moved to 95 Bedford Road in the Annex. E.W. attended Huron Street Public School and Harbord Collegiate, where he won a graduation scholarship to the University of Toronto.[7] He entered Victoria College, but had to take a year off because of illness, and did not obtain his BA until 1904, and BD in 1906.

Like his contemporary, James Mellon Menzies, the subject of Linfu Dong's chapter, Wallace came to public missions through student organizations, the YMCA and the Student Volunteer Movement (SVM). He attended the SVM Convention in Toronto in 1902, one of the great flags-and-bunting occasions,[8] and signed the pledge: 'I will God willing volunteer as a foreign missionary.' He founded the Victoria Student Band, which toured the churches, and in 1903, at the age of twenty-three, he wrote *The Heart of Sz-Chuan*, the first study book published by the Young People's Forward Movement for Missions. In this work, he showed signs of things to come, evincing a certain abstract sympathy for Chinese nationalism. The Chinese, he wrote, 'had good reason to fear and hate the foreigner. Without being asked, without being desired, Western nations have entered China and forced her to open her door to the commerce and religion of other lands.'[9]

Sichuan was 'one of the uttermost parts of the earth,'[10] and the journey took six months from Toronto. By the time Wallace arrived in February 1907, the West China mission had passed its experimental stage. It had four stations – its headquarters in Chengdu, the provincial capital, and stations in Jiading (formerly spelled Kiating, opened 1895), Rongxian (Yuinhsien or Junghsien, 1905), and Renshou (Jenshow, 1905). By 1913, with the acquisition of the London Missionary Society (LMS) mission in Chongqing (Chungking), it had a full complement of ten stations, each with resident evangelistic, medical, and educational work, and a myriad of outstations organized into rural itinerations.

Educational work was still a sideline of evangelism. All the male educational missionaries had to be ordained: in fact, the first non-ordained educationalist, Charles Batdorf, an American teacher at the government middle school, was not hired until 1910. Medical work was secularized from evangelism much earlier. The first medical missionaries had degrees in theology and medicine, but the first non-ordained doctor went out in 1899. Women's work, of course, did not demand ordination.

By 1905 the failing Qing dynasty abolished the old Confucian educational system. With no government schools, there was a 'mass movement to Christianity.' Two hundred young men rushed into the Chengdu school, 'willing to accept any accommodation, eager to study anything' – as long as they could learn English. Schools of every kind, for every age group, sprang up, sponsored by government, gentry, or clan associations. John Livingstone Stewart reported: 'There were Junior Primary, Senior Primary, and Middle Schools for each section of the city. Schools for almost all the prefectures of the province, model schools at each gate, normal schools, kindergartens, colleges, agricultural, medical, law, industrial, military, mechanical and other schools.'[11] Then just as quickly, the government announced it would recognize only government schools, and the students deserted. Six months later when the government schools collapsed, they came back. Though the mass movement may have been ephemeral, it gave the West China mission a vision that would last two generations.

The first step was the formation of the West China Christian Educational Union in October 1906. 'Believing that education in the highest sense cannot exist apart from Christianity,' states the preamble, the union brought together eight mission societies in the provinces of Sichuan, Guizhou, and Yunnan. In addition to the Canadian Methodists, the dominant group, there were the English Quakers, the Church Missionary Society, the LMS, and the China Inland Mission (which included Canadians), and two American denominations, Northern

Baptists and Methodist Episcopals. They agreed on 'the unification and centralization' of education and 'the organization of a Union Christian University.' 'Recognizing the marked advance in the educational aims and methods of the Chinese Government,' the Union recommended 'conformity of the Christian missionary education to the Chinese official scheme ... as is compatible with our Christian ideals.'[12]

The WCCEU issued a standardized, if sketchy, curriculum for junior primary (five years, age 7–12), senior primary (four years, 12–16), and secondary schools (five years, 16–21). In junior primary, students took Chinese classics (eight hours), Chinese grammar and history, arithmetic (six hours), geography, and natural science, with only two hours devoted to religious study. By Grade 5 the students were expected to have memorized the Beatitudes, the Ten Commandments, and a sampling of common Christian texts. The emphasis given to Chinese classics might suggest the schools were not meant to 'denationalize' the Chinese. But these texts were taught not as a way of life, but as a 'subject' according to the rules of higher criticism. 'We urge the study of the Chinese Classics throughout our Educational Course, taught from the modern point of view and with as much foreign co-operation as possible.'[13]

In 1906, when the WCCEU issued its curriculum, no mission school was anywhere near its standards. The Chengdu school was thirteen years old, founded by the patriarch Virgil Hart, who believed that education was 'a very essential part of the propaganda.' He hired three non-Christian scholars on condition that each brought twenty students. In the mornings the boys – and two girls – would memorize the Classic of Filial Piety, and in the afternoons the missionary would try to inculcate 'the fundamental truths of Christianity' and some geography.[14] This remained the model for day schools, and each school had its network of country schools, in varying states of decrepitude, often started by groups of Christians.

Dr Hart also founded an orphanage and boarding school. The Jenny Ford orphanage started when someone found a baby girl lying in the ditch, brought her home, and named her Annie Ford. Once word got out, women would bring babies and try to sell them to the missionaries; occasionally, in these 'adoptions' money and 'presents' would change hands. As for the schooling, Sara Brackbill hoped to 'take advantage of the wonderful memories of these people, and store their minds with eternal truths that shall serve them in times of trouble and temptation.'[15] Several male missionaries also 'adopted' older boys, like Wallace's 'boy' Georgie Bond, sponsored by the mission writer George

J. Bond. 'We trust that this is the nucleus of our coming university,' enthused George Hartwell when the first school opened in 1893.[16]

Wallace the Schoolmaster

The mass movement was at its crest when Wallace arrived. He passed his first term in China (1906–11) out of the limelight, two years at language study in Chengdu and two years at Rongxian. The forced inactivity of language study precipitated a spiritual crisis. Since his only contact with Chinese was his servants – and he went through three houseboys in three weeks – his first impressions were filtered through the eyes of others. Coming 'face to face with an intelligent non-Christian people,' he was forced to 'let go as non-essential ... many ideas and beliefs and practices that have grown up about Christianity in Europe and America. For our message is not "my belief about Christ" but "Christ," not "my limited understanding of God" but "God revealed in Christ."'[17]

The more he learned of the Chinese church, though, he absorbed the missionaries' distrust of the mass movement. 'It would sicken you,' he wrote, 'to see how the Church is used by vile men, so that ... respectable people won't darken its doors.'[18] To his father, the theologian, he described agonized theological debates with Confucian scholars. He disagreed with 'the poor ignorant heathen method ... Surely a system that has produced such a settled people, with a by-no-means low standard of morality ... must be God's way of preparing for Jesus Christ.'[19] He came to a simple, pragmatic compromise. He would make a deliberate effort to 'orientalize' himself, to enter 'into the daily life of the people – not,' he emphasized, like the China Inland Mission, 'by eating their food, wearing their clothes, or living in their houses, but by being interested in what interests them, and showing the common manhood underneath the diverse extremes.'[20]

In September 1908 the council assigned Wallace to Rongxian, a county town of 30,000 people, 160 kilometres south of Chengdu in one of the richest rice-growing areas in China. Rongxian had been opened in 1905 by the eccentric Dr William E. Smith and his wife. Wallace moved the twenty-three boys out of the 'filthy cramped quarters' to a newly constructed building in the mission compound, next to Mrs Smith's girls' school.[21] This allowed him to take in boarders, four 'adopted' boys and the gatekeeper's son. Within six months he had five country schools with 230 students, all more or less following the

WCCEU curriculum. He was brimming with new ideas: 'order, discipline and obedience ... I don't want a lot of little canting prigs but a bunch of healthy manly Christian boys.' When the boys went wild because foreigners had a reputation of a 'loving heart and therefore we will allow them to do whatever they please – a most perilous doctrine in a school' – he turned to discipline, guiltily, for he was not a violent man. 'I administered the bamboo to four delinquents yesterday,' he reported to T.E.E. Shore, the FMB secretary. 'They can't quite understand how I can punish them without first working myself up into a rage, or how I can treat them five minutes after as though nothing has happened. Impartial, impersonal justice is rather a new idea.'[22]

Using the same rationale as missions in northern Canada, Wallace convinced himself of the value of boarding schools. He could supervise the students by precept and example rather than by lectures and memorization. The boarding schools would train 'a thoroughly suitable native ministry ... who from their first education have been under Christian influence,' and Christian teachers, 'not only for our schools, but to man the Chinese schools.'[23] Unlike government schools, which provided free tuition and board, mission boarders paid fees, which helped subsidize the cost. Moreover, those who could not pay and were supported by missionaries had to sign a pledge to work for the mission after graduation.

Before long Wallace was conducting inspections of the dormitory, 'peeping under the beds and looking in the corners for dirt.'[24] He introduced physical training, precision drill, and Indian clubs, and provided military-style white uniforms with peaked caps. His greatest triumph was a field day of government and private schools in the city, when he toured 1500 people, including some Chinese dignitaries, through his house, to the strains of a victrola. 'Our school is in a peculiar position,' he told his family:

> It is not a poor school exactly, though we have plenty of poor children, nor is it a rich man's school, though we have a few boys from comfortable homes. Nor again is it a church school for the great majority of the boys come from outside the church ... Of course I want it to get most of the children of the Christians in the city ... After that I prefer the boys from middle-class and rich homes, as a rule, for they are more likely to go on and take a full course, while the poor boys may only come for a year, do very well and give great promise, and suddenly they disappear.[25]

Except for Mr Gung, whose 'main qualification is that he is a Christian,'[26] Wallace's Chinese teachers were a mixed bag of non-Christians, poor scholars 'of no standing either socially or, too often, morally in the community.'[27] Yet, he wrote admiringly, 'there are no men anywhere doing more noble, if unpretentious, work than these same country Chinese school masters, who with no training themselves in foreign subjects, and underpaid and often over-criticized, are laying the foundations for the new China.'[28] But by spring Wallace was ready to fire them all. The teachers decided to celebrate Confucius's birthday, according to the government decree, despite his strict instructions. When he found out and reprimanded them, they lost face and warned the boys 'to beware of the Church, that England first sent a few missionaries to India and so acquired that influence which resulted finally in the conquest of India. Nice isn't it?' Not nice, but true. Other missionaries did fire teachers for 'disrespect for Christianity.' The Rev. George Sparling, vice-president of WCUU, felt that 'unless the teachers show, at least some respect for our teaching, it will be useless to persuade the scholars of the truth of our message.'[29]

'Hammering away alone,' Wallace missed the real action of mission education, which was happening in Chengdu. The West China Christian Educational Union was registering schools and curricula. The Women's Missionary Society (WMS), expanding faster than the General Board, was opening schools for girls and women of all ages. Most were junior primary taught by male Chinese teachers, poorer than the boys' schools, but by 1910 the WMS had a high school and women's embroidery classes. Working at several levels at once – primary, middle, and college – West China Union University opened in 1910 in a one-storey lath-and-plaster building with upturned Chinese gables.

Wallace did not attend a WCCEU meeting until 1909, at which he was elected chair and part-time secretary. His first assignment was to draw up regulations for the conduct of examinations. The questions would be mailed on special paper to each school in sealed envelopes, and the answers, identified by number, would be returned to Wallace in envelopes which showed 'the name of the Candidate, School, Grade of School, Subject, Year, Date, and Place, and shall have a place for grading.'[30] Ironically, within walking distance of WCUU, the old Confucian examination halls, tens of thousands of small huts where the scholars used to sit for the state exams, were being demolished.

In 1910 Wallace was assigned to Chongqing, the commercial hub of

Sichuan, to open a union middle school. He supervised the construction of a two-storey foreign-style boarding school for forty boys, with airy classrooms and a teacher's study-bedroom. He also started a five-week course for teachers, the first normal school in Sichuan. But the West China mission generously granted furloughs after five years, and Wallace left Sichuan in April 1911. He returned to Canada via the Holy Land, where he met his father, and joined the rest of the family in Germany. Francis Huston had been a delegate to the World Missionary Conference in Edinburgh in 1910, which marked the high tide of ecumenical cooperation, and he introduced his son to prominent educators in Germany, France, and Britain. This furlough proved pivotal in Wallace's life, for he took graduate training at the New York Teachers' College, the birthplace of progressive education, under the famous professors John Dewey and Paul Monroe. The following summer, he made a working tour of schools in Britain. On a personal level, he met and married Rose Cullen of Baltimore, a teacher in a Protestant school in Paris. He wrote sweet love letters and said, 'my heart had many rooms, in each of which one friend was welcome, but none could enter any but his own.' He invited Rose to 'enter my soul ... and dwell in all the rooms.'[31]

Wallace the Ideal Teacher

All through Wallace's furlough, the news from Sichuan was 'disquieting.' While he was touring Europe, a local riot had mushroomed into the Chinese revolution, which overthrew the Qing dynasty and established the Republic of China in October 1911. The situation was so serious that the entire West China mission was forced to evacuate 1500 miles to the coastal cities, the third time in its history.

In early 1913, after a two-year leave, Edward and Rose sailed for China accompanied by Dr Monroe, his mentor at Columbia Teachers' College, who was going to inspect Christian educational institutions in China, Japan, and the Philippines. When they arrived in Shanghai, the China Continuation Committee was holding a special conference on education. As one of the few with practical experience in the hinterland, Wallace was seconded to write 'the findings ... a crystallization of crystallizations.'[32]

A 'thorough convert' to New Education, Wallace wrote optimistically in an article called 'The Ideal Teacher' (1913), an inspirational piece of Dewey-ite faith in the future. 'The primary aim of education being the formation of character, it follows that the first requirement in the ideal teacher is character.' The first requirement is 'a contagious Christian character ... crystal clear sincerity ... [and] a magic attraction' he called 'winsomeness.' The second requisite was 'a contagious love of knowledge.' He should not teach ancient history, but 'the men and the problems of this third year of the Republic of China. The principles of democracy; the differences between the parties; the financial and industrial needs of the country; railways and city parks, crops and standards of living; – these are some of the things that will have a large place in his interests.'[33]

By the time the Wallaces reached Chengdu in June 1913, the revolution was 'as dead as a doornail.'[34] Sun Yat-sen had come and gone, and Yuan Shikai now called himself emperor. As the Republic of China fell apart, Sichuan was divided by nine contending warlords. Wallace's second term was filled with 'storm and stress': between 1911 and 1937 Sichuan suffered 400 civil wars, large and small. Against this background the WCCEU had to negotiate, not a stable society and not anarchy either, but an emerging police state that depended on shifting, personal relations with the authorities. The university 'Senate is a very youthful body,' wrote Wallace, an oldster of thirty-three. 'So we shall have to feel our way.'[35] As for the provincial educational authorities, they 'completely ignored' the Christian schools. 'There is little active opposition, and as little recognition.' When the government announced it would recognize 'institutions under "foreign control" that were doing effective work,' Wallace admitted that 'recognition will involve a certain amount of investigation of our work (should we fear that?), and perhaps some general oversight.'[36] By the 1920s government registration became the dominant issue of Christian education. (Compare the Chinese situation with that in Japan in Hamish Ion's chapter 8.)

Wallace was secretary of the Educational Union and professor of education at WCUU, so his work was divided 'partly for the primary and secondary schools, and partly for the university, thus providing a link between the two departments, and helping to prevent the fatal gap that sometimes exists between school and college systems at home.'[37] Living in a compound near the university, Wallace started an ungraded model school, 'my little Dewey school.' Here the teachers could learn pedagogical skills not on 'the "theoretical student" in our system, but the actual boys and girls in the very real society of China today, and endeavour to make our system fit their varying needs rather than to try to force them all into our mould.'[38] The WCCEU expanded to rapidly fill the vacuum, from 42 schools with 1000 students in 1907, to 270 schools and almost 10,000 students in 1916. These numbers represented less than half the mission schools in Sichuan, Yunnan, and Guizhou.

Wallace was not entirely successful in converting even the liberal missionaries to New Education. Even within the West China mission, 20 per cent of the schools (27 out of 127) were 'unregistered, and usually ungraded.'[39] The CMS, the Quakers, and the Americans were active, but the China Inland Mission (CIM) refused to register. 'The CIM has never been "hot-hearted" over education,' Wallace wrote. 'It has rather distrusted it as a work of the devil, and hence to be used most sparingly and in homeopathic doses.'[40] Nevertheless, the CIM did operate 100 schools in West China, most copied from the 'ragged schools' of east end London. Among liberal missions, Wallace became a prominent spokesman, introducing Chinese into leadership roles within the educational structure.

Looking back on his first term as a bachelor, Wallace remembered an infectious college humour, a 'natural boyish religion'[41] of men 'working together at a common task with others in the spirit of Christian brotherhood.'[42] Now, to his disappointment, his work became increasingly bureaucratic. He travelled constantly, inspecting schools in three provinces and attending conferences downriver. Betweentimes, he was secretary, registrar, treasurer, and chief examiner for the WCCEU, mailing out hundreds of exams in the spring and marking them in the summer. As corresponding editor of the *Educational Review of China* and the *International Review of Missions*, he disseminated his ideas throughout China and beyond. As early as 1918 Wallace was approached by the China Christian Educational Association, an ineffectual organization in Shanghai, to become its secretary. He was proud of being 'Wallace of West China,' he confided to his father. 'That is some educational system. It is a man's work to help it along ... For some time I rather felt that perhaps my work here would be done by 1920! ... But there is so much to do, so little done, that I see a lifetime of service ahead of me.'[43]

Our West China Mission (1920) summarized four 'hindrances' to mission education: incompetent teachers, insufficient supervision, lack of continuity, both of missionaries and students, and inadequate plant. Well-to-do students could afford to pay fees, but the Christians, who were mostly among the rural poor, felt the mission had an obligation to educate their children, whether they could pay or not. Subsidies were a drain on mission finances, and a loan would foster 'a spirit of dependence, of a desire to get much and give little in return, and loads a boy with debt – a big handicap at the beginning of life.'[44] The solution was a 'self-help scheme ... by which these boys might be able to pay their own way.' At Renshou the mission bought a five-acre 'farm,' and every day at four o'clock the boys would march through town with their hoes and shovels to work their allotments. The first year's profit, growing vegetables and cotton, netted 18,000 cash ($5 gold). Another station specialized in 'foreign vegetables for sale (we have nothing native on the place except fig trees).'[45]

The girls' schools were of a whole other order. If boys' education was built from the university down, the girls' was from the orphanages up. The WMS schools, from primary to middle school, usually had a boarding school and orphanage: in Chengdu, for example, the flagship of the WMS had fifty boarders and 'fifteen day pupils from the Orphanage ... The pupils all learn to cook, and sew, and keep their homes neat and clean.' Although they followed the WCCEU curriculum, academic learning was not the goal, rather 'that faith in God and loving service for others are of more value than knowledge gained from books.'[46] This rationale – that good works are better than scholarship – permeated women's work. Since they did not attract the children of rich families, the WMS turned their schools into houses of industry. In Mrs Quentin's kindergarten, a model Montessori class, the children were taught 'handwork of all kinds, including paper-cutting, folding, weaving, sewing, [and] moulding,' along with 'easy Chinese characters' and drawing with crayons. Mrs Burwell stressed that 'white work requires white hands,' as she taught crocheting and embroidery. Clean hands inspired 'cleaner clothes, and so meant better health generally.'[47]

In 1919, WCUU was rocked by the nationwide May Fourth movement. The students organized a public meeting and demanded to carry the 'university flag, (with our name on it)' in the parade. The Chinese faculty, who supported the students, voted to 'trust our men with the flag,' and on the morning of the rally, Wallace reluctantly gave it to them, along with a sermon on their duty 'as individuals ... as patriots, as students of the only university in West China and hence natural leaders, and as Christians.' When the Chinese vice-president harangued the students, warning of 'the danger of misusing the reputation of the institution,' they refused to accept the flag and kicked the foreigners out of the meeting.[48] A week later, asking rhetorically 'when will China be able to get her house in order?' Wallace wrote of the life-and-death struggle between modern ideas and 'the dead weight of the customs of centuries galvanized into activity by the cursed spirit of the times, "made in Japan."' In the end, he was reduced to quoting Kipling:

> Right is right since God is God,
> And right the day must win;
> To doubt would be disloyalty,
> To falter would be sin.[49]

Wallace the Educational Bureaucrat

During his second furlough of 1920–1, E.W. Wallace finished his MA at Columbia Teachers' College and was granted an honourary DD by Victoria College, an unexpected honour. He returned to China in the fall of 1921 alone, since Rose suffered from bronchial problems and stayed home with five-year-old Edward, known as Ebbie, until the following May. As Wallace sailed on the *Empress of Asia* from Vancouver, it carried 'an overpowering list of high class attractions.' John D. Rockefeller and his entourage, including Wallace's mentor, Paul Monroe of Columbia, were going to attend the opening ceremonies of Peking Union Medical College, the most modern medical complex in China, which had been funded by $5 million from the Rockefeller Foundation. Wallace himself was a member of the Burton Commission, under Ernest D. Burton of the University of Chicago, which had the ambitious agenda of creating a national system of Christian education.[50] As the only educational missionary on board, Wallace was constantly in demand. He helped organize a roster of speakers, including Dr Monroe on 'national education' and YMCA secretary T.Z. Koo on 'What the Chinese student is thinking.'[51]

During the fall of 1921 Wallace travelled extensively with the Burton Commission through north and central China, visiting 400 or 500 schools and speaking to thousands of educators. When Burton fell sick, Wallace was elected chairman pro tem, and was thus largely responsible for the final report on primary and secondary education, which was presented to the great Shanghai Missionary Conference in May 1922. 'What should be the place of Christian education in China?' Wallace asked the learned assembly. At first, education had helped dispel prejudice and open the way for the gospel. Later it built the church, providing education that was 'thoroughly Christian in spirit and method' for children and adults. Now, as the percentage of Christian students was declining, a larger purpose had evolved, 'of permeating the life of Chinese society with Christian ideals, even though individuals are not led to allying themselves with the Christian community.' In a breathtaking leap of faith, Wallace proclaimed the coming kingdom, 'making China a nation Christian in principle and practice, and of elevating her national life in all possible ways.'[52]

In another leap he dealt with the conundrum of church and state: 'Is there a permanent place in China for Christian schools, or are we to expect the gradual absorption of our schools into the government system?' he asked rhetorically. 'Is there in the educational system of any country a place for private schools, including those that are founded and conducted by religious bodies?' In 'an unequivocal, Yes,' the commission answered that education in China had always been private, and when 'the educational needs are far beyond the ability of the Government ... the widest range of private educational experimentation' was needed. Mission schools must be 'thoroughly good schools,' he wrote,

> patriotic and national in atmosphere and influence, avoiding all exotic and foreign characteristics, promptly and fully meeting all government requirements, and co-operating with government education in all practicable ways, and at the same time furnishing a healthy variant from the uniform standard, and producing for the changing life of China a Christian group, forward-looking and thoughtful, disciplined and self-controlled. In building up in China Christian education of this type we may be assured that we are building for a long future.[53]

Here was Wallace's vision for his third and last term in China: his little Dewey school magnified to a national scale.

The pressure for Wallace to stay in Shanghai came from the China Christian Educational Association and the home board. As Jesse Arnup put it, 'educational missions throughout China were awake to their opportunity and obligation. Casting about for a leader they came to Szechwan where this great experiment was being worked out.'[54] Wallace's personal satori came during a concert of the *Leonora Overture*, and he answered 'Ready,' on condition he be allowed one year in Chengdu to wrap up his work with the WCCEU. With Rose and Ebbie now with him, Wallace found it as hard to leave Sichuan 'as it was to leave Canada at first ... Szechwan has grown into the very texture of my life ... Now, people in other parts of China hear about our work, and when I meet them they sometimes say "Oh, you are Wallace of West China."'[55]

In May 1923 the Wallaces returned to Shanghai, where Wallace was promptly elected president of the Canadian Association of China. The senior Canadian in Shanghai was Dr Donald MacGillivray, one of the founders of the Presbyterian mission in North Henan (see Margo Gewurtz's chapter 6), who was head of the Christian Literature Society, purveyor of histories, apologetics, novels, and such magazines as the *Christian Farmer*. Like Timothy Richard, his predecessor, MacGillivray had a reputation for being a 'crypto-Buddhist' because he embraced Chinese philosophical syncretism. Thus, two Canadians, too progressive for their own missions, were in change of Christian education for all China.

Shanghai in the 1920s, a colonial enclave behind 'barb wire and sandbags,' was no place to cooperate with the Chinese government. 'Unconsciously,' Wallace wrote, one acquired 'a bureaucratic viewpoint after some months in Shanghai, which is in some ways the worst place in China for centralizing Christian efforts.' His letters and journals sound the same, a round of 'tiffin committees' and musical concerts, interspersed with trips into the interior.[56]

At the same time, Shanghai offered ringside seats for the awakening dragon, as the student movement, which Wallace had helped create, spiralled out of control. The missionary conference of 1922 sparked the opposite, the creation of a Student Anti-Christian Movement, which grew more revolutionary each year. Wallace himself was reading 'radical books,'[57] trying to understand the students even though he felt the nationalist, anti-imperialist, anti-Christian movement was a communist plot, 'allied we have good reason to believe with the bolshevist movement here ... We may have our backs against the wall before the summer, to protect our schools.'[58] More than once he was called upon to explain to Chinese and foreigners alike the other side, 'the side of the Municipal Council and the average Britisher in Shanghai. I told them that I by no means agreed with that side, but that in all fairness they should understand it, and I put it as fairly as I could.' Meanwhile he continued to chase the chimera of government recognition, 'making representations to the various authorities and attempting to win "clarifications" of the regulations.'[59]

Rose died of pneumonia in November 1924, a few days after their twelfth anniversary, and Wallace and eight-year-old Ebbie moved in with a succession of missionary couples.

On 30 May 1925 British police fired on a workers' strike in Shanghai, killing nine people, which sparked riots throughout China. Wallace refused to comment until the 'facts' were clear, for 'there seems to be a most lamentable disregard of the facts.'[60] 'It is a most difficult situation, when the keenest Christian men are, inevitably, leaders in the national movement, which, for the time, is decidedly "anti-foreign." Foreigners demand that Chinese Christians, or at least the Chinese church, should "keep out of politics," just as in other times they criticize the same men because they do not work to set China's house in order.'[61] By 1927, the escalating civil war between the Guomindang (formerly spelled Kuomintang or Nationalist) armies and the northern warlords (known in Chinese history as the Northern Expedition) forced the evacuation of all missionaries – almost 9000 throughout China – from the inland provinces. Though Britain's threat of war was 'questionable,' Wallace noted that most of his Chinese colleagues and members of the National Christian Council (NCC) were 'convinced nationalists, though not members of "the party," and they are bothered when we missionaries find it difficult to express our sympathy because of our "reservations" in the matter of the excesses of the left wing. We have not yet found a complete common understanding.'[62]

There was much discussion in those dark days of the cleavage between 'the Chengdu mind' and 'the Shanghai mind.' Although the West China mission was in no immediate danger, the entire staff of over 200 missionaries and children were evacuated downriver at great expense, except for five Canadians, known as 'the Chengdu Five,' who refused to leave, even when a telegram came: 'Whatinhellisdelaying-youfivemen?' The men in Chengdu refused to push big issues like extraterritoriality and government registration, or discuss bolshevik infiltration of the revolution, preferring to trust the good will of the Chinese authorities.[63]

Despite his best intentions, Wallace typified the Shanghai mind. Throughout the 1920s he had tried to promote Chinese Christian leaders by encouraging the China Christian Education Association to employ Chinese principals and university presidents. Many times he was the only foreigner in a meeting of Chinese educators. Now, with the clock ticking, he tried feverishly to devolve the CCEA to his colleague, the co-general secretary Sanford Chen, and to Earl Willmott, a left-wing refugee from Sichuan who was willing to work under the Chinese.

Wallace and son Ebbie left Shanghai in April 1927, his work in China finished. He did return to China once more, for a few weeks in May 1928, travelling via the Jerusalem Missionary Conference. 'In place of the rather tense and heated atmosphere of 1926,' he wrote his father, 'there was a sense of security and quiet that was almost startling ... The meetings were largely prepared for and conducted by the Chinese ... I was delighted at the grasp of the problem of Christian education and their evident determination to hold fast to its Christian character.' The day he formally handed the China Christian Educational Association to Sanford Chen happened to be the day the hated sign was removed from the public parks: 'No dogs or Chinamen allowed.' So, Wallace noted, 'one of the sorest spots in international relations here is removed.'[64]

Conclusion

In 1930, Wallace, aged fifty, accepted the position as Chancellor of Victoria College, where he remained until his death. 'As head of the church's greatest college,' stated his obituary, he was known for his 'trained mind and fine character.' In particular, 'he defended stoutly the freedom of his associates to think and speak for themselves on the issues of the day.' He supported the Student Christian Movement when it espoused pacifism and left-wing politics, and in 1938, when two professors were accused of being communists, he said, 'I haven't heard anything about Communism here. I'm sure I would have learned about it if the charges were true.'[65]

We get an oblique, unflattering glimpse of this older Chancellor Wallace from the letters of Northrop Frye, the eminent literary critic who was then an assistant professor at Victoria College. (In passing, it is remarkable how many 'mish kids' from West China and Japan appear in these letters; this is confirmed by the student biographies in the Vic yearbooks in the 1930s.) Frye found Wallace cold and distant, and nick-named him 'The Chank.' Wallace 'winced' when someone told thim that the girls in the Margaret Addison residence were hanging 'out on the streets at night. Why, there are so many men around, and sometimes one of them might speak to the girls.' Frye concluded, 'The Chancellor lacks the gift of torrential sympathy, I sometimes feel.'[66]

In September 1939, tragically the very day Canada entered the Second World War, Wallace gave the valedictory address to a conference entitled 'The North American Indian Today,' which shows the overlapping and contradictory themes of the chapters of this book on Home

Missions and those on Foreign Missions. The conference was organized by his brother, Paul A.W. Wallace, who grew up in his shadow.
Eleven years younger (born 1891), Paul was head of the English
department at Lebanon Valley College in Pennsylvania, a 'kind, cheerful, scholarly gentleman.' He became an expert on the history of the
Iroquois and Six Nations Confederacy, and a prominent spokesman for
the Native point of view in North America. The summation of his life's
work was an extraordinary book entitled *The White Roots of Peace*
(1946), which the historian Donald Smith described as a 'wise and
beautiful' book that speaks in the cadences of holy scripture. Writing at
the end of the Second World War, he presented 'the United Nations of
the Iroquois, the famous Indian confederacy that was a model for, and
an incentive to, the transformation of the thirteen colonies into the
United States of America.'[67]

The conference, held at the University of Toronto, brought together
seventy Canadian and American government officials, missionaries,
and academics. This was 'the first conference ever held to discuss
Indian welfare and the first Canadian scholarly conference to invite
Indian delegates.' Its purpose was 'to reveal the actual conditions
today of the white man's Indian wards, and in a scientific, objective
and sympathetic spirit, plan with them for their future.'[68]

Ever the clergyman, Edward Wilson Wallace stated that 'Christian
motives' would resolve the problem of social and racial relations. The
missionary and the scientist must work together, one 'to study and
describe the present situation' scientifically, and the other to dream of
'something better for the Indian than is now.' Whites and Indians must
work together too, for 'the time must come, and soon,' when the Indians will take the lead. 'I know whereof I speak,' he said in conclusion.
'I passed through, in the Christian movement in China of the last quar-
ter of a century, the successive stages of missionary domination, the
first training of Chinese leadership, the hesitations and fears when the
Chinese began to demand effective control of their own church and
schools, and the coming of the happy situation when Chinese leadership became a reality and we who were missionaries were proud to follow their lead as colleagues, no longer as masters.'[69]

Then the most extraordinary thing happened. The Indian delegates
walked out. While the conference was passing resolutions concerning
'the psychological, social, and economic maladjustments of the Indian
populations of the United States and Canada,' the Indians met sepa-
rately to pass their own resolutions. While appreciative, 'they did not

need government officials, missionaries, white sympathizers, or Grey Owls to speak for them.' Now we talk, you listen, they said.[70] To E.W. it must have seemed like 1919 all over again, when the Chinese students refused to carry the school flag.

Though his life abounded in ironies, Edward Wilson Wallace was not an ironic man. Rather – like the mission movement in general – his career was an example of the law of unintended consequences. The mission schools, in China as in Canada, were agents of cultural imperialism, which established white, Western, educated, and male as the norm, and denigrated 'the other,' the dark, shifty, shiftless, uneducated Natives. Wallace's lack of interest in women's education was consistent throughout his career. And yet, by the 1920s the mission schools had trained the next generation of revolutionaries who overthrew missionary imperialism. Nothing shows this irony more graphically than the two occasions when Wallace's audience walked out, leaving the white men talking to themselves and passing unwanted resolutions. Post-colonialists would call this the revolt of the subalterns.

Edward Wilson Wallace died on 20 June 1941, full of honours; with him ended an era. Frederick Clarke Stephenson, friend and colleague for forty years, founder of the Young People's Forward Movement for Missions, died three months later. Edward Junior died in 1944, shot down over Malta during a bombing mission.

NOTES

1 Rev. Jesse H. Arnup, obituary in Edward Wilson Wallace (EWW) biography file, in United Church Archives (UCA), Toronto. The most complete source is the EWW Papers in UCA, cited by box and file, as well as relevant West China mission correspondence and published material concerning the West China Education Union.

2 *Our West China Mission: Being a Somewhat Extensive Summary by the Missionaries on the Field of the Work during the First Twenty-five Years of the Canadian Methodist Mission in the Province of Szechwan, Western China* (Toronto: Methodist Missionary Society, 1920), in Lela A. Ker, 'Departmental Surveys: The Canadian School,' 371–7, quote at 373. For a history of the Canadian School, see Brockman Brace, ed., *Canadian School in West China* (Toronto: Canadian School Alumni Association, 1974).

3 *Our West China Mission*, 36.

4 Michael Gauvreau and Nancy Christie, *A Full-Orbed Christianity: The Protes-*

tant Churches and Social Welfare in Canada, 1900–1940 (Kingston/Montreal: McGill-Queen's University Press, 1996).

5 Ibid., 358. The standard history of Canadian missions to China is Alvyn J. Austin, *Saving China: Canadian Missionaries in the Middle Kingdom 1888–1959* (Toronto: University of Toronto Press, 1986).

6 C.J.P. Jolliffe and his brother Richard Orlando founded a missionary dynasty that eventually numbered fifty members in China. H.D. Robertson joined the Chinese Labour Corps in France during the First World War, and was translator for the Canadian delegation at the founding of the United Nations. He retired in 1946.

7 *The Harbordite* (6 June 1981), 11.

8 Austin, *Saving China*, 96–7.

9 E.W. Wallace, *The Heart of Sz-Chuan* (Toronto: Young People's Forward Movement for Missions, 1903), 76.

10 Arnup, quoted in Austin, *Saving China*, 53.

11 J.L. Stewart, 'Educational Work,' annual report for 1907, in UCA, Methodist Church of Canada, Foreign Mission Board (FMB), West China Mission correspondence, box 18/file 178. (Cited as WCM correspondence.)

12 West China Christian Educational Union (WCCEU) *Annual Report*, 15–19 October 1906. The WCCEU reports are in WCM correspondence, box 18.

13 WCCEU *Annual Report*, 1908, 'Proceedings of the Acting Board of Education, Committee on Primary and Secondary Education,' 13.

14 *Our West China Mission*, 315.

15 WCCEU *Annual Report*, 1913, 36.

16 George Hartwell, annual report for 1893–4, 11, in WCM correspondence, 8/61.

17 EWW, Tachienlu (now Dajianlu, near Tibet), to mother, 11 August 1907, in EWW Papers, 2/16A.

18 EWW to father, Francis Huston Wallace, 31 August 1907, in EWW Papers, Papers, 2/16A.

19 EWW to father, 5 January 1908, in EWW Papers, 2/17.

20 EWW to family, 23 November 1908, in EWW Papers, 2/20.

21 EWW to family, 14 September 1908, in EWW Papers, 2/19.

22 EWW to T.E.E. Shore, FMB secretary, 31 May 1909, in WCM correspondence, 18/179.

23 Ibid.

24 EWW to family, 5 October 1908, in EWW Papers, 2/20.

25 EWW to family, 8 September 1909, in EWW Papers, 3/22.

26 EWW to Shore, 31 May 1909, in WCM correspondence, 18/179.

27 EWW to family, 2 November 1908, in EWW Papers, 2/20.

28 EWW to family, 6 June 1909, in EWW Papers, 3/21.

29 G.S. Sparling to Shore, 12 July 1911, in WCM correspondence, 18/178.

30 WCCEU *Annual Report*, Committee on Primary and Secondary Education, October 1908, 3–5.

31 EWW to Rose Cullen, 17 May 1912, EWW Papers, 3/26.

32 EWW to family, 18 March 1913, EWW Papers, 3/26.

33 WCCEU *Annual Report*, 1913, 43–7.

34 EWW to family, 21 September 1913, in EWW Papers, 3/28.

35 EWW to family, 27 June 1913, EWW Papers, 3/27.

36 WCCEU *Annual Report*, 1917, 16.

37 WCCEU *Annual Report*, 23–8 October 1913, 5.

38 EWW to family, 5 December 1915, in EWW Papers, 3/34.

39 *Our West China Mission*, 37–8. The registered schools included 72 boys' schools (64 lower primary, 12 higher primary, 2 union middle), and 22 schools for girls (16 lower, 5 higher, and one middle school).

40 EWW to Rose Wallace, 24 February 1917, EWW Papers, 4/37.

41 EWW to family, 19 February 1911, in EWW Papers, 3/24.

42 EWW to father, 20 February 1919, in EWW Papers, 4/41.

43 EWW to father, 15 September 1918, in EWW Papers, 4/40.

44 *Our West China Mission*, 323–4, chapters by J.L. Stewart, 'Departmental Surveys: Education,' 305–58, and C.R. Carscallen, 'West China Union University,' 358–70.

45 Ibid., 335.

46 Ibid., Miss C.E. Brooks, 'Station Surveys: Women's Work,' 246–64, quote at 248.

47 Ibid., 332, 336.

48 EWW to father, 25 May 1919, in EWW Papers, 4/41.

49 EWW to father, 1 June 1919, in ibid., 4/41.

50 A university administrator, Burton was a lifelong missions advocate who 'brought to his task a mind of unusual clarity and discriminating judgment, together with a remarkable ability for sympathetic understanding of individuals.' EWW, 'The China Educational Commission, An address delivered at the National Christian Conference, May 9, 1922,' in EWW Papers, 5/48.

51 EWW, 'China Educational Commission 1921,' personal journal, 28 August 1921, 2, in EWW Papers, 4/46.

52 EWW, 'China Educational Commission,' address at National Christian Conference. See also China Educational Commission, *Christian Education in China: A Study Made by an Educational Commission Representing the Mission*

Boards and Societies Conducting Work in China (New York: Foreign Missions Conference, 1922).

53 EWW, address to NCC.

54 Arnup, obituary in EWW biography file, UCA.

55 EWW to father, 8 April 1923, in EWW Papers, 5/51.

56 EWW to father, 6 December 1925, in EWW Papers, 5/51. For tiffin committees, see 7 January 1925, in ibid., 5/59.

57 EWW to father, 1 January 1923, in EWW Papers, 5/59.

58 EWW to father, 7 January 1925, in EWW Papers, 5/59.

59 EWW to father, 20 August 1925, in EWW Papers, 5/59.

60 Ibid.

61 EWW to father, 10 October 1925, in EWW Papers, 5/59.

62 EWW to father, 15 February 1927, in EWW Papers, 6/67.

63 Austin, *Saving China*, 208. The most comprehensive examination of the relation of the various Canadian missions to Chinese nationalism is John W. Foster, 'The Imperialism of Righteousness: Canadian Protestant Missions and the Chinese Revolution, 1925–1928' (PhD diss., York University, 1977), which also has excellent biographical entries for individual missionaries.

64 EWW to father, 7 June 1928, in EWW Papers, 6/71.

65 Arnup, obituary, in EWW biographical file, UCA.

66 Northrop Frye, *The Correspondence of Northrop Frye and Helen Kemp, 1932–1939*, edited by Robert D. Denham, 2 vols. (Toronto: University of Toronto Press, 1996), 860, 856.

67 Donald Smith, 'Paul Wallace and The White Roots of Peace,' Introduction to Paul Wallace's republished *The White Roots of Peace* (originally published 1946; fourth publication, Ohsweken: Iroqrafts, 1998), 17, 32, 34.

68 Donald Smith, 'Now We Talk – You Listen,' *Rotunda* (Fall 1990), 48–52.

69 C.T. Loram and T.F. McIlwraith, eds, *The North Amerian Indian Today: University of Toronto–Yale University Seminar Conference, Toronto, September 4–16, 1939* (Toronto: University of Toronto Press, 1943), 339–44.

70 Smith, 'Now We Talk – You Listen.'

Chapter 6

'Their Names May Not Shine':
Narrating Chinese Christian Converts

MARGO S. GEWURTZ

Introduction

One of the most difficult yet important issues emerging from the study of the impact of the Western missionary movement on China is to understand how the Christian church was built, and by whom. The version of Foreign Mission Board publications and missionary literature gives the simplistic answer: the missionaries. But this claim obscures the reality of a Sino-Western partnership in the creation of a Chinese church, and hides the identity of those Chinese who responded to the message of the missionaries and built the church within their home communities, often against great opposition. The objective of my research is to reveal the Chinese side of this partnership. Specifically, it is about some of the men and women who were the converts in the mission field established in North Henan (formerly spelled Honan) by the Presbyterian (later United) Church of Canada after the first group of missionaries and their wives was sent to China in 1888.

In its sixty-year history, the mission reported some 6000 converts on its rolls. Of these, I have amassed information in a database on some 1500 named individuals. With the data I have on many of the peasant men, women, and children who comprised the bulk of church membership, I have been able to reconstruct glimpses of church membership, village by village, over a span of decades. My methodology enables me to place Christianity in its Chinese setting, and thereby ascertain how it took root in these rural communities, and why churches developed in some villages but not in others that may have been close by.

Because of the paucity of documentation, it has been almost impossible to collect materials pertaining to anything of the cognitive or faith aspects. It is important to ask what the converts actually believed and what ideas drew them to this new foreign sect in the face of often fierce local opposition, even ostracism.[1] Despite the lack of definitive answers, I have had some success in showing that the early converts could in part be characterized by their marginal status, a marginality not defined by economic status but by an inability to conform to the norms of Confucian patriarchal society, whether through opium addiction, failure to have a son, sectarian and hence suspect heterodox religion, or gender inequality.[2]

Nonetheless, there is little in the way of direct testimony or documentation. What is available are numerous missionary accounts of the converts – the 'Miracle Lives,' to cite the title of one such account. But how can these be used and what sort of accounts are they? To answer that, I have employed traditional tools of critical historical method as well as borrowing from narratology and discourse analysis. Such an approach asks us to confront the ability of modern secular intellectual discourse to comprehend the religious commitments of an earlier age.

This paper is divided into two parts. In the first, I employ a variety of heuristic analyses to the narratives of the life and conversion of the first convert, Chou Lao Chung, or 'Old Blind Chou,' his honorific and more usual title. These will explore both the historicity and fictionality of these accounts. Above all, however, I will attempt to penetrate the meaning that Christianity had for this important figure, the Abraham of the new church. But what of Sarah, for the first female convert was Chou's wife? Here we encounter the difficulty that for the female converts no extended narratives exist of the sort routinely found for the males. Hence, the second part of the paper deals with this absence, and applies to it a 'hermeneutics of suspicion' derived from feminist biblical criticism.

The First Convert: 'Old Blind Chou'

I begin with my own narrative; that is, with what I have reliably pieced together from a variety of sources concerning the life of the very first convert, Chou Chung-ch'ing (pinyin Zhou Zhongqing [?]), known by the honorific Old Chou, or better in Chinese Lao Chou.[3] Old Chou was born in 1836 in a village about three Chinese miles from the town of Xun, the county or *xian* capital. Hence, the county town is known as Xun Xian (formerly spelled Hsün Hsien). He was a *yamen* runner, spe-

Lao Chou, Old Blind Chou, the first convert in North Henan (seated right), with his wife, two sons, a daughter-in-law, and a grandson, circa early 1900s. Chou, an opium addict and *yamen* runner, was cured by the missionary doctor and reportedly said, 'Once I was blind, but now I see.'

cifically a policeman, someone hired by the county magistrate to serve summonses, catch robbers and thieves, and perform such other policing functions as required by the magistrate's office, or *yamen*. Such persons were feared and hated by the local populace as they were almost always seeking bribes or extortion to supplement their very meagre income. Policemen occupied the most inferior position of all the runners, and were looked down upon by the intelligentsia and the common people.[4]

When he was in his late forties, Chou's sight began to fail, and by the time he met the Canadian missionaries at the annual Great Fair held in Xun Xian in 1889, he had been blind for six years. Chou was also an opium smoker, having been addicted for some twenty-five years. There is likely a connection between his low status and occupation and his addiction. Opium smoking was a great scourge in North China at the time, and many early converts were addicts. But it was to seek a cure for blindness that brought Old Chou to the missionaries. He met the evangelist with the eponymous name of Jonathan Goforth, who was accompanied by Dr William McClure. Unfortunately for Chou, the missionaries were about to leave, and although Dr McClure said he could cure him, he would need to supervise him afterwards for about ten days.

He promised they would return the following year, but in 1890 it was actually Dr James Frazer Smith who returned and performed North Henan's first cataract operation, enabling Chou to regain his sight. Chou and his son Chou Te-wen (pinyin Zhou Dewen [?]), also an opium addict, both began studying the gospel, and by 1891 asked to be admitted to the church, but the baptism was delayed for one year until both were cured of their addiction. On Sunday 26 June 1892 father and son were baptized and became the first converts. Mrs Chou and her daughter-in-law became the first female converts when they were baptized in 1894.[5] Chou's younger brother and many others in their village also converted. Both Old Chou and his wife served as paid evangelists in the new church. Old Chou died at age 78 (1914) and his wife at age 74.

To be blind and then to see: what better story and metaphor could there be? While all the convert narratives necessarily retell this core story, not all give it the same prominence. And what of the opium addiction or the corrupt *yamen* official lifestyle? Some stories omit opium altogether, and we shall see the curious transformation of *yamen* runner into scholar in at least one account. Narratology distinguishes between the chronological story that is told, or the 'totality of the narrated events,' and the way the story is told, or narrative discourse.[6] It asks us to look at what elements are stressed, and what are the 'gaps, absences, and silences which constitute the traces of the metaphysical assumptions of ... textual systems.'[7] I intend here to analyse the story of the 'life' of the convert, or more accurately the circumstances of conversion, and the narrative discourse of three major accounts of Chou's life: Jonathan and Rosalind Goforth's *Miracle Lives of China*, published in the United States in 1931; the Rev. Murdoch Mackenzie's *Twenty-Five Years in Honan*, published in Toronto as an anniversary book in 1913; and Dr James Frazer Smith's 1937 memoir, *Life's Waking Part*. I have found earlier variant accounts from the 1890s in letters by Mackenzie and Smith and the Rev. Donald MacGillivray.

All three narratives are traditional 'I' narratives in which the focalizer, the one who speaks the narrative, claims first-hand experience, but only Goforths' and Smith's are monologic, defined as a discourse mode wherein the voices of all the characters are subordinated to the authoritative voice and controlling purpose of the author.[8] Even the Goforths' narrative is monologic, despite their extensive use of dialogues as a stylistic element, so that their work reads like a series of mini-plays. But what is seen in these dialogues is that the focalization always derives from an external focalizer, one outside the narrative of the text. The Goforths are omniscient narrators even when they are actors inside the setting of events. That is, although he or his wife are characters in the text, they are actually reporting the 'feelings, thoughts, reactions' of others as though seen from the inside. They thus take on the mask of 'internal focalizer,'[9] as though the others are representing their own feelings or motives, but never surrender control of the narrative. Only Mackenzie offers what appears to be a genuine internal focalization.

Thus each missionary's rendering of the 'feelings, thoughts and reactions' of convert Chou remains suspect. The controlling master narrative that is presented is heroic and accords with Joseph Campbell's analysis of the heroic myth. Both Goforth and Smith present an '*agon*' or struggle: 'A search to find treasure, rescue an endangered person, complete difficult labors with attendant rewards.'[10] All three narratives set up the obstacles to the missionary quest: the heathen, barbarous nature of Chinese society, its anti-foreignism, and the power of idolatry, most specifically the worship of the Great Goddess at the annual fair at Xun Xian, what the missionaries called the Mecca of China.[11] The missionary undergoes a trial – hostility or anti-foreign riot – and searches for treasure, the potential convert. The first section of the Goforths' *Miracle Lives* is entitled 'The Earliest Trophies of Grace,' even though 'first fruits' was the preferred agricultural metaphor. The soul is then rescued as conversion takes place, thus completing the difficult labour and bringing reward to missionary and convert alike.

Although the true hero of this narrative could be the convert, it is not. It is the missionary. The Goforths' *Miracle Lives* is, I maintain, actually a text of heroic 'muscular Christianity' fulfilling its imperial destiny. It is a colonizing text, as is Smith's. One sees this both in what is told and in how it is told, especially in the omissions. The Goforths' narrative emphasizes sin. While such an emphasis might be expected in a Christian narrative, the sins are those of the heathen inferior: idolatry and corruption, or what Westerners in China called 'squeeze.' The narrative is framed by a discourse that gives prominence to political power and

Chou's opportunities to 'squeeze' bribes from a corrupt legal system where abuses were endemic. The implicit comparison is to the Anglo-Saxon rule of law. Hence, the narrative begins with his title as chief of police of Xun county and a description of the 'system' and his corrupt power within it. This rendering of Chou's title stretches the *yamen* runner's job description into an ill-fitting Anglo-American mould; nonetheless, the description of his power is close to the mark. Chou's occupation does not get the same weight in the other tellings. Indeed, Smith omits it entirely and goes so far as to transform him into a scholar who could ask very intelligent questions about the gospels.[12]

Neither the Goforths nor Smith mention his opium addiction. Smith especially knew better as he was the attending physician and had described Chou's condition to his brother in an 1892 letter not intended for publication, but one that his brother sent to the *Presbyterian Record*.[13] Even after opium's physically addictive nature was finally understood by the medical profession, its use was still commonly described as a moral failing or sin.[14] But that particular sin was too closely associated with Western, especially British, imperialism in China to find a place in these colonizing discourses.

After locating Old Chou within the corrupt Chinese imperial system, the Goforths then narrate the story of the blindness, cure, and conversion in the form of three invented monologues or testimonies: Old Chou's, Jonathan Goforth's, and the 'mayor's' (actually village head), who is converted by the preaching of the first two. Without here elaborating on these embedded stories within the story, let me say that they present two themes central to the discourse of imperialism in China and found in all three narratives: Chinese anti-foreignism and idolatry. In the first, Goforth elaborates on the fact that Chou had to wait a year before his operation by having him go home and 'revile' the foreigners, the same term used by Smith in his narrative. In Mackenzie's narrative Chou returns disappointed and certain 'that the foreigners were humbugs.'[15] For all three, anti-foreignism was an obstacle for the heroic missionaries to overcome, and for some, as we will see below, it is more than that. The second theme is the power of God and/or Jesus against the false power of idols and the futility of idol worship. Whether the worshiper seeks a cure for blindness or the birth of sons, only the true Sovereign can answer prayer and determine one's fate. Thus all elements of the narrative have been chosen to focus on the heathen character of Chinese culture and the redeeming power of Western Christian culture.

While the testamentary form of the Goforths' narratives reflects their evangelistic preoccupations with sin, Smith's narrative stresses the medical aspects of the work, with the heroic 'I' drama focused on the cataract operation. When Chou's fellow villagers came armed with cudgels fearing the 'foreign devil had gouged out the eyes' – which were to be used for medicine according to common anti-foreign statements – they 'quietly slipped away much ashamed of themselves' when they heard he could see.[16]

It is Smith who maintains that as a preacher, Chou's 'great text was, "one thing I know, whereas I was blind, now I can see."'[17] That phrase is a commonplace in many gospel songs, for instance, the last line of the first verse of 'Amazing Grace,' written by a converted slaver, John Newton (1725–1807). An even more likely source was the hymn 'The Light of the World Is Jesus' by Philip P. Bliss (1838–76), whose chorus rises to a crescendo with the words, 'Once I was blind, But now I can see: The light of the world is Jesus!'[18] And one thing that Chou could clearly 'see' according to Smith, and to Mackenzie, was that Christianity was a universal not a foreign faith and that foreigners were not enemies of China.[19]

As a medical scientist, Smith wished to emphasize the ability of medicine not only to win converts but to overcome anti-foreignism. From his own preface, we know that Smith wrote his book hoping to encourage young students to take up the missionary cause in an era of growing secularism and even hostility to Christianity, and especially in light of the anti-imperialist, anti-Christian ideas of many Chinese intellectuals of the late twenties and early thirties.[20] Winning over a member of the scholar class, as opposed to a corrupt peasant *yamen* runner, through the power of science redraws the narrative for a new purpose. Indeed, the Rev. John MacVicar's foreword to the book cites it as a rebuttal to the future University of Toronto President Sidney Smith's critique of the missionary enterprise as 'the dreams of a dreamer' – hence the title, *Life's Waking Part.*

Murdoch Mackenzie presents what is, in my opinion, the closest we have to an internally focalized account that, while not verbatim, is probably a record of an oral interview he conducted in preparation for this twenty-fifth anniversary volume. In the section devoted to what he calls 'typical' Henan Christians, he says that he presents their stories 'wherever possible ... in their own words.'[21] Like most others of the mission, Mackenzie was of Scots Presbyterian background. An inveterate maker of lists, whose annual records in his diaries are the nearest thing we have to parish records, Mackenzie was what I like to think of as 'the Accountant of Souls.' That he would collect such oral stories does not surprise me. More telling, alone of all our storytellers, Mackenzie, in his published account, is internally consistent with what he recounted in an unpublished 1892 letter to the deacon of his sponsoring church concerning the baptism of Chou and his son Te-wen. Recounting Chou's cataract operation and his subsequent study of Christianity, Mackenzie noted that Chou's application to join the church was made more than a year earlier: 'As the old man had used opium up to that time it was deemed advisable to defer baptism until it was completely given up. That he has had the grace given him to do.'[22]

Mackenzie's 'I' narrative, given in direct quotes as a verbatim record of Chou's words, begins with blindness and the failure of Chinese doctors and idols to bring a cure. Despite his fear that foreigners might gouge out his eyes, he goes to see Dr McClure but is disappointed that he must wait for the doctor's return and fears he is a 'humbug.' But Dr Smith comes the following year and Chou accepts his terms: he will agree to be cut by the knife and will stay with them at the inn for ten days. While waiting for the bandages to come off he listens 'without interest' to the preaching – a clear refutation of Smith's version of the scholar asking intelligent questions. Chou begins to pay attention to the preaching only after the cure, when Dr Smith asks for no payment but that he 'Believe in my Saviour' who sent him to China so that he could cure illness. Chou then acknowledges his former sinful life as a corrupt 'Yamen constable' and an 'opium fiend' for over twenty-five years. He thus began to study and became a believer. He was a preacher and faithful servant of the church 'from my 54th year to this my 75th year' and his life was proof of the 'Lord's great power.'[23]

Several features of this narrative are noteworthy, aside from its obvious veracity. First, Mackenzie does control language, using such mild terms as 'humbug' or the stereotypical 'opium fiend,' neither of which seem likely from Chou's lips. Furthermore, he twice has Chou use direct speech to refute the charge that he unquestioningly follows foreigners. In the first instance, he speaks of the fear that the foreigners would not return: 'But mark my words, friends, when one of these people makes a promise, he always keeps it.'[24]

Again at the end, there is a long coda to the narrative in which Chou refutes the charge that he is a dupe of the foreigners: 'But I want to tell you, and tell you ever so earnestly that it is not the Saviour of the British people that I follow, but the Saviour of the world. Just as truly as there is only one sun in that sky, so truly is there only one Saviour in the universe ... whom I know to be the Light of the World.'[25]

This refutation of the 'foreign' character of Christianity was clearly of importance to the missionaries. It appears in all the accounts, and Smith even quoted this entire passage from Mackenzie's narrative. But it was not without significance for the converts, for that was the most often heard charge levied against them, and Chou refutes it using the most common of Chinese sayings, 'Just as there is only one sun in the sky, so there is only one Emperor under Heaven.'

Most significant of all is the final confession of faith that ends the coda: 'He that follows Jesus shall not walk in darkness, but shall have the light of life.'[26] These words derive from John 8:12. In the gospel text, this declaration occurs after a woman taken in adultery has her sins forgiven, but in this text it is the confession of a blind man. The focalizer, whether Chou himself or Mackenzie, draws us to the physical and spiritual blindness.

Whereas it was the gaps that were often telling in the other narratives, here it is the chronology of the telling that is revealing. The corruption and addiction are included but only after the chronology of blindness and cure. The recognition of sinfulness follows rather than precedes the cure. The Goforths began with the sinfulness of the constable and then proceeded to illustrate the futility of idol worship. Smith omits sinfulness altogether. What was most important to Mackenzie was the cure and the futility of idolatry, a major obstacle to the missionary's *agon*, or spiritual quest. In his coda at the end Mackenzie points to the transformation in Chou's life effected by his new faith: 'As we compare the blind, helpless heathen worshiping his idols.'[27]

I would suggest that Mackenzie's chronology of the story, his narrative, has got it right. For Old Chou the central fact of his life was that for six years he had been blind. Since the sectarian tradition in this region of North China linked sect teachings to medical treatments or cures,[28] it was not surprising that Chou interested himself in the teachings of the Jesus sect after so spectacular a cure. Only after he studied did he come to a recognition of the sinfulness of his previous life. This sequence would be consistent with the scholarly view that China is a culture of shame that does not take easily to the idea of sin and original sin especially.[29] Mackenzie understood this problem quite well even if the Goforths did not.[30] Alienated from the norms of Confucian village society by his hated position as *yamen* runner, his opium addiction, and finally his blindness, Chou could translate his shame, his loss of face, into sin through the gospel message. He could redeem himself through the new community of the church he helped to build. He could show proper respect for the sect teacher who had cured him by joining his sect. His teacher had come from afar, and asked for no payment except that. He could truly believe that 'once I was blind, but now I can see.'

In the final analysis, then, the secular language of postmodern discourse analysis, joined to more traditional forms of historical criticism, has enabled me to sort through these convert narratives and reconstruct not only the 'facts' about the life of Old Chou and the circumstances of his conversion but also the meaning of the 'Jesus sect' for him. So it may indeed be possible to glimpse the sacred in these narratives. This analysis suggests that not only can we accept his assertion that after the cure 'I began to listen carefully and to ask questions, and now I know,' but also that despite barriers of time and language, we can comprehend what it was he knew.

Naming Women

As noted previously, the first female convert was Old Chou's wife, the Sarah to her husband's Abraham, yet no narrative of her life exists. In *Miracle Lives of China*, Jonathan and Rosalind Goforth narrate Old Chou's life and say of Mrs Chou: 'Mrs. Chou was as forceful a character as her husband. Before conversion, when aroused, her tongue was a terror to her opponents. She, too, became a humble follower of our Lord and Saviour. The two became earnest evangelists and preached the gospel for many years.'[31] This description, undoubtedly written by Rosalind Goforth, is one of the few references to women in this entire volume, in which Rosalind herself narrated only one woman in any detail, the story of 'Old Autocrat Wang.' In his twenty-fifth anniversary volume, Rev. Murdoch Mackenzie includes no women at all. Mackenzie regretted that no women were 'named,' and although many were 'worthy of mention' he claimed not to know 'the details' well enough to do so.[32]

Dr James Frazer Smith's 1931 memoir does contain some narration concerning Mrs Chou. In this externally focalized account, Smith presents Old Chou as the heroic central figure who is 'reviled' by the women of his household, and other villagers, after he and his son convert. The women include Mrs Chou and her mother-in-law, who is the actual focus of this part of the narrative. It is only after Old Chou persuades his mother of the errors of her ways, and cures her of an illness through prayer, that his wife, 'impressed by what had happened to the mother-in-law, and the great transformation that followed,' became a follower of the new faith.[33] According to Smith, she is taught to read by her husband and son, although he does acknowledge that before being baptized she spent two weeks in study at the Mission compound in Xinzhen with 'Mrs. Wu, the saintly Bible woman, loaned to us by our American friends' (from the neighbouring Shandong Presbyterian Mission). 'The mission ladies assisted all they could,' concludes Smith, and, eventually able to read well enough, Mrs Chou is baptized.[34]

Dr Smith's account contains several interesting features. Mrs Chou's terrible tongue is muted to take second place to her mother-in-law's reviling and 'paroxysm of rage.'[35] This version has the effect of reducing Mrs Chou to a pale shadow of her seventy-five-year-old mother-in-law as the filial relation between Old Chou and his mother becomes the narrative focus. In Chinese Confucian social theory and norms of practice, that was his primary relation of filial piety. By stressing that relation, Smith serves to enhance Old Chou's heroic stature as his Christian faith withstood the test of filial obligation. Setting aside household or village gods and defying filial piety were among the most serious obstacles for new Christians, and Old Chou overcomes both obstacles in this heroic *agon* or quest narrative.

Although Mrs Chou and Bible woman Wu are both named in this narrative, neither is given heroic stature in what remains a narrative of androcentric 'muscular Christianity.' However, their naming is partial as only the surname is given, unlike the full name for male convert narratives. Thus, women are identified by status, as wife, mother, daughter, or Bible woman, but never as persons in their own right.

An 1894 letter to the WMS monthly magazine, the *Letter Leaflet*, from the Rev. W. Harvey Grant, the mission secretary, recounted the close escape from death of Bible woman Wu when her house collapsed following torrential rains. This letter suggests one explanation for the marginalization of their Chinese co-workers in the published accounts. My title quotation is drawn from this letter. In his preamble, Grant notes that the readers' interest 'naturally centres in those missionaries whom you have seen and known, and have sent out to foreign lands,' but he was sure that they would also be interested 'to no small degree in those native Christians who, while their names may not shine so frequently in print as the missionaries whom they assist, still faithfully

Country women at a Bible class, North Henan, early 1900s. This photo was likely taken in Ho-tao village at the Chou family courtyard, since it appears that old Chou is standing second from left, with Mrs Chou seated in front of him.

perform their part, which ... is so necessary to success in evangelizing heathen lands.'[36]

In Smith's narrative, not only does Bible woman Wu's name not shine, but the 'mission ladies' who 'assisted all they could' with Mrs Chou's education were not named at all. Female agency is further diminished as her son and husband are cited as primary, except for a brief stay at the Mission compound, assisted by the unnamed 'mission ladies.' A somewhat different picture emerges from a letter by nurse Margaret McIntosh published in the *Letter Leaflet*. Miss McIntosh records that Ho-tao, the home village of the Chou family, had twice been visited in 1893, and that in April of that year she, Mrs Murdoch Mackenzie, and Bible woman Wu spent three days there, and that another nearby village was visited six times. This was in addition to the several weeks Mrs Chou spent learning Bible and catechism at the mission station with these same ladies. After she returned home, her daughter-in-law came and did the same.[37]

It is clear from Miss McIntosh's account that Mrs Wu played an essential role both at the station and at rural itineration, especially as the Canadian women were themselves still learning the language. Once the regular Sunday Station Bible class for women was established in 1893, she visited the eight to ten students in their homes as well as doing regular village itineration. She was said to give instruction 'whenever and wherever there is an opening.'[38]

It is also significant that Mrs Murdoch Mackenzie was one of the unnamed 'mission ladies' whose agency in Mrs Chou's conversion has here been restored. Her role raises the question of why her husband professed to be so ignorant of the 'details' of the lives of the women converts that he omitted them entirely. This is all the more puzzling when we learn from Mrs Mackenzie's account that Murdoch Mackenzie and Donald MacGillivray performed the baptism. They spent the weekend of 22 March 1894 in Ho-tao village and Mackenzie questioned the two women. The 'answers given by the elder woman were very good indeed and quite surprised him,' whereas the younger woman 'naturally rather shy and nervous, did not answer so well but probably understands quite as much as her mother-in-law.'[39]

Mackenzie knew, or should have known, the details of these stories, but, like Smith and even the Goforths, did not 'name' the women. Surprisingly, neither did Mrs Mackenzie in her letter to the *Letter Leaflet*. Feminist scholars have long recognized the power of naming both as a tool of hegemonic discourse and as a feminist revision of androcentric historical narratives. Elisabeth Schüssler Fiorenza has called such a revision a 'hermeneutics of suspicion,' in which 'We are still able to disclose and unravel "the politics of Otherness" inscribed in and constructed by the androcentric text because feminists experience and theorize about a historical reality in which "the others" are present and active.'[40] My work is based on such a hermeneutic. I assume, and demonstrate, that the 'Others' are active and present.

Chinese women converts were at the bottom of a pyramid whose apex was the male missionary. The discourse concerning the women converts, very few of whom are ever named in the pre-1900 period, should, in my view, be seen as part of a larger discourse about women in China in this period. Much recent feminist scholarship has argued that women were signifiers of China's backwardness and that their elevation was necessary for the modernization of the Chinese nation. Such 'sexing of modernity' was a commonplace of nationalist discourse and politics in China as part of 'urgent public discussions about what kind of sex and gender relations could help constitute a modern nation in a threatening semicolonial situation.'[41] In discussions of literacy, footbinding, prostitution, or female infanticide, elements within the Chinese male intellectual class, beginning in the 1830s, created a new language to theorize 'the universal sign of woman' as part of anti-Confucian discourse that sought to create a modern Chinese culture.[42]

Christian missionary discourse about Chinese women had its own variant on this theme. In their writings, women became a signifier of Chinese heathenism and their status could never be as high as in a Christian country. Only the spread of Christianity, and the construction of Christian gender relations – the 'Christian home and family' – could alleviate their suffering.[43] Donald MacGillivray's 1898 pamphlet on the conditions of Chinese women, prepared as a study guide for the WMS, exemplifies this 'disease trope' for China's weakness and deformity, its heathenness.[44]

Narrating Chinese women as signifiers of the heathen 'Other' obscures and silences women as persons. Unlike male converts such as Old Chou, they are not the 'pillars' upon which the new church will be built. Success among them 'required the refashioning of the Other in a culturally familiar image.'[45] For the Canadian women in rural North Henan, there was also a class element in this cultural refashioning. References abound to the slow and difficult labour of literacy work among peasant women, who are often described as 'stupid.'[46] As the missionaries moved into the prefectural cities and encountered the 'better classes,' the descriptions are more glowing, such as this of Mrs Chang from the Nei-huang county magistrate's yamen: 'We do not often come across one so bright, intelligent, lady-like and thoroughly earnest as this woman is.'[47]

From my research into the writings of women missionaries in which this complex encoding of Chinese 'otherness' takes place, it is evident that women can write 'androcentric' texts when their gaze encounters only the 'heathen' and culturally unfamiliar 'other.' A feminist reading of these texts must acknowledge the unequal power relations inherent in them as well as their culturally imperialist assumptions that equated Christianity with Westernization and modernity. But women missionaries were not simply 'cultural imperialists' who moulded 'passive recipients of their religious and social work into their own perfect mirror image.'[48] Nor were their Chinese assistants and converts mere collaborators in the 'colonial enterprise, of which the task of religious conversion constituted a major facet.'[49] If we can treat their relationship 'dialectically and dynamically,' then our understanding will be enriched.[50] Years of intimate contact changed both sides. As Minnie Pyke, who went to China in 1896 and stayed until 1922, wrote in January 1900: 'As I am becoming more familiar with the language, I am also more and more attracted to the women among whom we labour.'[51]

NOTES

1 See, for example, an account of the travails of the first family of converts in their home village, in *Presbyterian Record* 17, no. 7 (July 1892): 181.

2 For a more detailed discussion see my essay, 'The "Jesus Sect" and "Jesus Opium": Creating a Christian Community in Rural North Honan, 1890–1912,' in Roman Malek, ed., *The Chinese Face of Jesus Christ*, vol. 2 (Sankt Augustin, Germany: Monumenta Serica, 2003), 685–706.

3 Because I lack the Chinese characters for the convert names, I use the old Romanization used in the documents, but otherwise employ modern *pinyin* for Chinese terms and place names (except in quotations).

4 For *yamen* runners and policemen, see Ch'u T'ung-Tsu, *Local Government in China under the Ch'ing* (Cambridge: Harvard University Press, 1962), 56–73; and John Watt, *The District Magistrate in Late Imperial China* (New York: Columbia University Press, 1972).

5 Mrs Murdoch Mackenzie, 'The Baptism of Two Women,' *Monthly Letter Leaflet* 11, no. 4 (August 1894): 97–9. Publication of the Woman's Missionary

Society (WMS) in the United Church of Canada Archives, Victoria University, University of Toronto (hereafter UCA).

6 Seymour Chatman, *Story and Discourse* (Ithaca: Cornell University Press, 1978), 19. Limiting 'story' to 'histoire' follows Gérard Genette, *Narrative Discourse Revisited*, translated by Jane E. Lewin (Ithaca: Cornell University Press, 1988).

7 Marie-Laure Ryan and Ernst Van Alphen, 'Narratology,' in Irena R. Makaryk, ed., *Encyclopedia of Contemporary Literary Theory* (Toronto: University of Toronto Press, 1993), 114–16.

8 'Monologic narrative: A narrative characterized by a unifying voice or consciousness superior to other voices or consciousnesses in that narrative ... in monologic narrative ... the narrator's views, judgments, and knowledge constitutes the ultimate authority with respect to the world represented.' Gerald Prince, *A Dictionary of Narratology* (Lincoln: University of Nebraska Press, 1987), 54.

9 Ryan and Alphen, 'Narratology,' on focalization.

10 Ibid.

11 See the descriptions in Jonathan Goforth's *Diaries*, 1892, which are in the Archives of the Billy Graham Center, Wheaton College, Wheaton, Illinois.

12 James Fraser Smith, *Life's Waking Part* (Toronto: United Church of Canada, 1937), 141.

13 *Presbyterian Record* 18, no. 7 (July 1893): 184.

14 Kathleen L. Lodwick, *Crusaders against Opium: Protestant Missionaries in China, 1874–1917* (Lexington: University of Kentucky Press, 1996).

15 Murdoch Mackenzie, *Twenty-Five Years in Honan* (Toronto: Presbyterian Church in Canada, 1913), 185.

16 Smith, *Life's Waking Part*, 142.

17 Ibid., 143.

18 I am grateful to my colleague at York University, William Whitla, for bringing these sources to my attention.

19 See Smith, *Life's Waking Part*, and Mackenzie, *Twenty-Five Years*.

20 See Jessie G. Lutz, *China and the Christian Colleges, 1850–1950* (Ithaca: Cornell University Press, 1971).

21 Mackenzie, *Twenty-Five Years*, 183.

22 Murdoch Mackenzie, Hsin Chen (now Xinzhen), letter to Mr Yuile, 15 July 1892, in Donald MacGillivray, *Memoirs* (unpublished typescript in UCA), 202–3. MacGillivray's own letter records that Old Chou helped to preach at the Xun Xian Fair, and that the family was the 'first unto Christ in Honan. We are keeping them on probation but they will soon be baptized' (183). MacGillivray's hostility to opium addicts as unsuitable converts and his

scepticism regarding the ability of the doctors to effect a cure is noted in several letters: see *Memoirs*, 171. That hostility may explain his failure to indicate the reason for the 'probation.'

23 Mackenzie, *Twenty-Five Years*, 188.

24 Ibid., 185.

25 Ibid., 189. His use of the phrase 'Light of the World' reinforces the view that Bliss's hymn is the source text for Chou's speech.

26 Ibid., 189.

27 Ibid.

28 See Susan Naquin, *Millenarian Rebellion in China: The Eight Trigrams Uprising of 1813* (New Haven: Yale University Press, 1976). This sect took hold in the same region of North China where the Canadian mission was established eighty-five years later.

29 See Wolfram Eberhard, *Guilt and Sin in Traditional China* (Berkeley: University of California Press, 1967).

30 See Mackenzie's discussion in MacGillivray's *Memoirs*, 196–8.

31 Jonathan and Rosalind Goforth, *Miracle Lives of China* (Grand Rapids: Zondervan, 1933), 5.

32 Mackenzie, *Twenty-Five Years*, 240–1.

33 Smith, *Life's Waking Part*, 218.

34 Ibid., 219.

35 Ibid., 217.

36 W.H. Grant, Chu Wang, 3 October 1894, in *Letter Leaflet* 11, no. 10 (February 1895): 259–61.

37 Margaret McIntosh, 'Report of the Woman's Work for 1893,' in *Letter Leaflet* 11, no. 3 (July 1894): 69–71. See also Woman's Missionary Society (Western Division), *Annual Report*, 1893–4, 28–9.

38 WMS *Annual Report*, 1893–4, 29; and McIntosh 'Report,' 70. See also *Letter Leaflet* 11, no. 10 (February 1895): 261.

39 Mrs Murdoch Mackenzie, 'The Baptism of Two Women,' letter from Hsin Chen, 29 March 1894, in *Letter Leaflet* 11, no. 4 (August 1894): 97–9.

40 Elisabeth Schüssler Fiorenza, *But She Said: Feminist Practices of Biblical Interpretation* (Boston: Beacon Press, 1992), 90.

41 Gail Hershatter, 'Modernizing Sex, Sexing Modernity: Prostitution in Early Twentieth-Century Shanghai,' in Christina K. Gilmartin et al., eds, *Engendering China* (Cambridge: Harvard University Press, 1994), 147–8.

42 Tani Barlow, 'Theorizing Woman: *Funü, Guojia, Jiating* – "Chinese woman, Chinese state, Chinese family,"' in Angela Zito and Tani E. Barlow, eds, *Body, Subject and Power in China* (Chicago: University of Chicago Press, 1994), 262–7.

43 For a review of this attitude as it pertains to writings about footbinding, see Patricia Ebrey, 'Gender and Sinology: Shifting Western Interpretations of Footbinding, 1300–1890,' *Late Imperial China* 20, no. 2 (December 1999): 1–34.
44 Donald MacGillivray, *The Condition of Women in China* (Toronto: Presbyterian Church in Canada, 1898), in York University Archives and Special Collections.
45 Maria Jaschok, 'Chinese "Slave" Girls in Yunnan Fu: Saving Chinese Womanhood and (Western) Souls, 1930–91,' in Maria Jaschok and Suzanne Miers, eds, *Women and Chinese Patriarchy: Submission, Servitude and Escape* (Hong Kong: Hong Kong University Press, 1994), 186.
46 Re the classes for women, see Margaret McIntosh, Chu Wang, 10 July 1896, in *Letter Leaflet* 14, no. 7 (November 1896): 184–6.
47 Margaret McIntosh, Changte Fu, 15 January 1903, in *Foreign Missionary Tidings* 19, no. 2 (April 1903): 275.
48 Maria Jaschok and Suzanne Miers, 'Introduction' to *Women and Chinese Patriarchy,* 16.
49 Jaschok, 'Chinese "Slave" Girls,' 191.
50 Ibid.
51 *Foreign Missionary Tidings* 17, no. 1 (May 1900).

Chapter 7

Shifts in the Salience of Gender in the International Missionary Enterprise during the Interwar Years

RUTH COMPTON BROUWER

In 1934 an article called 'Ideals of the Missionary Enterprise' appeared in the *Indian Social Reformer,* a nationalist weekly whose editor provided considerable space for exponents of Christian missions even as he subjected them to his critical gaze. Based on a sermon preached at Cambridge by former missionary Paul Gibson, the article dealt with the challenges that had confronted the missionary enterprise since the First World War. The war, Gibson wrote, had demonstrated to the rest of the world the lack of real Christianity in the so-called Christian nations, while the International Missionary Council's Jerusalem Conference a decade later had rightly acknowledged 'that the imminent danger lay not in non-Christian religions but in the rapid spread of secularism.' With nationalism also on the rise, missionaries could no longer afford to arrive from the West with a complacent sense of superiority. Instead, they must demonstrate a willingness to be co-workers with increasingly vigorous indigenous churches. As for the other great world religions, now that the sophistication of their texts was known, their adherents could no longer be regarded as benighted victims, dependent for salvation on missionary preaching. The central challenge of missionary work had passed 'from enunciation of doctrine to the compelling power of the Christian life.' Yes, Christ offered something unique and 'universally needed in the personal link He provided between God and man.' Nonetheless, what was required of the modern missionary was a 'life lived and not a message delivered.'[1]

As anyone familiar with this period in the history of the mainline Protestant missionary movement can attest, observations such as those made by Gibson were the stock in trade of missions-minded men and women of a moderate to liberal bent at the 'home base' and in many 'foreign fields.'[2] (Even these once-routine geographic signifiers were now under scrutiny.) Writing a decade earlier, Joseph Oldham, the London-based secretary of the International Missionary Council (IMC) and a towering figure in colonial as well as mission politics, had urged that, in the changing circumstances of the postwar world, missions would have to do nothing less than reinvent themselves if they were to be 'adequate to the demands of the hour.'[3]

Like Gibson, Oldham had in mind such challenges as those arising from secularization in the West and increased nationalism in the colonized and missionized societies of Asia and Africa. Though Gibson may not have been aware of it and though Oldham did not write about it in the way I shall do here, one of the strategies used by mainstream Protestant missions to meet the challenges of the interwar era was the deployment of professional women in situations that took them beyond the separate-spheres approach of an earlier era. That change, in turn, was linked to another, larger, development designed to address 'the demands of the hour': an increased emphasis on social and educational services, especially in the areas of medicine and higher academic and technical education, and the increasing disengagement of such services from aggressive proselytization.

It has been customary to attribute these changes to the influence overseas of Western (and, more particularly, North American) liberal theology and the Protestant social gospel. Certainly, conservative and fundamentalist missions spokesmen made this linkage when they decried the increasing emphasis on 'civilizing' rather than 'evangelizing.'[4] Yet, arguably, increases in the number and the quality of mission institutions offering advanced educational and medical work and a decline in their links to proselytization did not come about only, or perhaps even mainly, from the influence of Western liberal theology and the social gospel. Modernizing young men in colonial Asia and Africa who looked to mission institutions (and to such related organizations as YMCAs) to further their personal and/or nationalist goals created strong pressures on missions to improve the quality and range of their services. This was the case even if they were themselves Christians and inspired by Christian idealism. Those who were not Christians often expressed resentment when educational and other services came with religious strings attached.[5] Meanwhile, in the case of missionaries with training in the professions, many were newcomers to mission work in the postwar era. They brought with them a new understanding of what it meant to be a professional and a consequent unwillingness to have their professional ideals subverted to serve older evangelistic and gender norms.[6] These newcomers included women. One outcome of these diverse new ambitions and of the other challenges facing inter-war missions was that some Western professional women became colleagues of their male counterparts, and mentors and colleagues of modernizing, non-Western men.

In suggesting that a new gender pattern was emerging in mainstream Protestant missions in the interwar years, one that took some professional women beyond the discourse and the practice of 'women's work for women,' I am drawing on research on three Canadian women, United Church of Canada medical missionaries Dr Belle Choné Oliver and Dr Florence Murray, both originally Presbyterians, and literature specialist Margaret Wrong, who was not, strictly speaking, a missionary. In the pages that follow, I outline the careers of the three women and then deal briefly with one aspect of the larger context in which they worked: national and international missions bureaucracies. The last part of the chapter refers to some analogous patterns among secular professionals that lend support to my argument for a new gender paradigm in missions. But I also acknowledge the tentativeness of my argument and caution against seeing these 'modern' women either as fully liberated from conventional assumptions about gender roles or wholly unsisterly in their outlook.

Modern Women Modernizing Men: Three Canadian Examples

Dr Belle Choné Oliver

Because the India career of Dr Belle Choné Oliver (1875–1947) began well before the period on which I am focusing, she is a good exemplar of transitions in the missionary movement in the first half of the twentieth century. The daughter of an Ingersoll, Ontario, businessman and politician, Oliver studied medicine at the Woman's Medical College, Toronto, and interned for some ten months at the Woman's Hospital of Philadelphia, before sailing for India and the work awaiting her in the Presbyterian Church in Canada's mission in princely Central India, established in 1877.[7] Especially during her first term, 1902–7, the emotionally vulnerable Oliver suffered serious depression over her failure to win converts to Christianity. Except for a brief period during her second term, when she was put in charge of a girls' orphanage, she worked in women's hospitals and dispensaries until 1915. Then she

Dr Belle Choné Oliver in 1900, two years before she began her career as a medical missionary in India.

became responsible for a new general hospital for a mainly tribal and largely un-Hinduized population. The lack of rigid sex segregation in her new work in remote Banswara – it was sixty miles from the nearest railway – was a pragmatic reflection of what was locally feasible. But it was also a good fit with Oliver's approach to matters of gender in mission work. A feminist when it came to asserting women's abilities and forwarding their interests when they appeared to be neglected, she had no taste for perpetuating unnecessary gender separatism in mission work. The fractious gender politics that had plagued the first decades of the Presbyterian Church's India mission had led to the establishment of separate men's and women's councils to administer the work. It was a division that Oliver disliked and one from which she could briefly escape when she attended conferences of the All-India Medical Missionary Association, an organization that was both ecumenical and open to medical missionaries of both sexes.[8] It was because of this larger contact and her own avid reading in contemporary mission literature that Oliver's career took a wholly new direction, beginning in the 1920s.

Oliver would later recall that a reprinted address by J.H. Oldham came to her attention about 1923, stressing 'the need for missions to survey their work, deal ruthlessly with what was ineffective, and plan for at least ten years ahead.' A subsequent conversation on this subject with William Paton, then the secretary of the interracial National Christian Council of India (NCC), specifically with regard to medical missions, led to her paper in 1924 before the Medical Missionary Association conference in Calcutta on the topic 'Do We Need a Survey of Medical Missions?'[9] During the next two years, along with an American male colleague, Oliver became the key figure on the Association's Survey, Efficiency, and Co-operation Committee, whose report, published in 1928, reflected its critical investigation of medical mission work. By the time the Survey of Medical Missions in India was published,[10] the Medical Missionary Association had transformed itself into the Christian Medical Association of India (CMAI), thereby opening its doors to Indian Christian doctors and other nonmissionary doctors in sympathy with the organization's goals.[11] It was as a member of this organization that Oliver was sent as an NCC delegate from India to the IMC's conference in Jerusalem along with a Danish medical missionary, Christian Frimodt-Möller. At Jerusalem, Oliver and Frimodt-Möller not only drew insights from the Survey to the attention of an international audience; they also presented a rationale for Christian medical work that officially moved beyond the old view that its function was simply to open doors for the preaching of Christianity.[12]

In moving beyond this 'old view' they were by no means disavowing the ultimate desirability of winning converts to Christianity. They were, however, taking the position that medical missionaries could be true disciples of Jesus, 'the Great Physician,' without proselytizing. They were also distancing themselves from older instructions such as those which stressed 'the importance of giving constant attention to the spiritual part of their work and not allowing their medical duties unduly to absorb their time and energies.' Such instructions – still in at least one society's regulations in the 1920s – could now be recognized for what they were: professionally insulting and potentially dangerous.[13] Not surprisingly, many mission doctors had quietly moved away from such an approach well before the new theology of medical missions was presented at Jerusalem in 1928.

For Oliver personally, the working out of a new theological rationale for medical missions was a spiritually liberating experience.[14] Meanwhile, through her role on the Survey of Medical Missions and at the Jerusalem conference she had become associated in a public way with the task of rethinking Christian medical work in India in order to make it viable in a rapidly changing political and professional environment. It was this background that the NCC and the CMAI were drawing upon when in 1929 they asked the United Church of Canada for her services. The arrangement was initially an interim one, and she was to serve simultaneously as the NCC's secretary for medical work and as secretary-treasurer of the CMAI. In 1933, when her role with the CMAI became permanent, she remained on the NCC as its honorary secretary for medical work, sharing office space at its headquarters in Nagpur, the bureaucratic centre of Christian ecumenism in India. In one or both of these roles, she would initiate or advance such diverse undertakings as a nurses' auxiliary linked to the CMAI, a hospital supplies agency for coordinating purchases for medical missions, social hygiene work, and a prayer cycle for medical personnel. She contributed to and oversaw production of the CMAI's bimonthly *Journal*, and she represented and publicized the Association's causes as she travelled through India to inspect medical work and attend regional gatherings.[15] As past CMAI president Sir Henry Holland would observe when she was about to retire in 1944, 'To all intents and purposes ... Dr. Oliver is and has been the C.M.A.I.'[16]

While Oliver threw herself into all the Association's projects, the one that most fully absorbed her was the struggle to create a fully professional co-educational Christian medical college such as would enable Indian Christian men and women to become, in her words, 'colleagues and eventually successors' to the medical missionaries, rather than their assistants, as in the past.[17] What is most relevant about that struggle for purposes of this chapter can be stated briefly. First, it reflected concerns about the quality and reputation of mission medical work that had emerged from the 1928 survey, and a related point strongly emphasized by Frimodt-Möller at the Jerusalem conference. If Christian medical work was to function as an effective testament to applied

Christianity, rather than as simply a tool for proselytizing, he had argued, it should be continued even as the state came to play a larger role in the provision of Western-style medical services, *but* at a level of professionalism that would showcase rather than embarrass its Christian practitioners.

Frimodt-Möller's point was particularly important in the context of an interwar, nationalizing India where, on the one hand, secular and nationalist-minded elites (including elite medical professionals) were seeking to establish standards of Western medical professionalism on a par with those in the West, and, on the other, Indian Christians of all backgrounds and occupations suffered from an image of being denationalized as a result of having adopted the religious faith of the colonizer.[18] In the face of these twin challenges, CMAI leaders like Oliver and Indian Christian medical personnel who shared their fear of an impending beleaguered status sought to meet the dilemma by creating a medical training institution so strong that even its Christian identity would not be a barrier to acceptance in an eventual postcolonial India.

Furthermore, establishing a full-fledged medical college was, comparatively, an exceedingly expensive mission project. Put forward in Britain and North America just as the Great Depression was wreaking havoc on mission fundraising, the medical college plan came into conflict with other projects and, thus, after initially receiving their backing, encountered opposition from the leaders of the international and ecumenical missions bureaucracy in London and New York on whom it crucially depended for support, especially in its strategic fundraising goal of identifying and contacting 'men of large means.'[19]

The third and related point is that the struggle to establish a coeducational Christian medical college met resistance from women who were prominent practitioners and supporters of the older, separate-spheres, approach to missionary medicine and who were themselves seeking funds in the West to upgrade the training of Indian medical women. This resistance was centred at the Missionary Medical School for Women in Vellore, near Madras (Chennai), established in 1918 by a well-known American doctor, Ida Sophia Scudder. Like the two older mission medical schools in India (and many nonmission schools), the one at Vellore offered only licentiate-level training. As a result, its graduates were not recognized as fully professional. In the late 1930s the popularly controlled government of the Madras Presidency announced its intention to end recognition of such schools. Even then, Scudder's institution held out against the CMAI's proposal that it become the site of a fully professional, co-educational, medical training complex. It agreed to cooperate only when its efforts to raise funds to upgrade on its own failed to win support from powerful mission bureaucrats in Britain and North America. In their campaign of resistance, Dr Scudder and her supporters had continued to identify the medical college project begun by the CMAI as a project undertaken by and for men despite the fact that it was headed by a woman and officially co-educational in intent from 1932 onward.

In heading up this modernizing project, Oliver had clearly broken with an older gender pattern in missions. She had not, however, succeeded in making a name for herself as either a pathbreaker or an institution-builder. Working as an ecumenical missions bureaucrat and lacking the charisma and personal support possessed by Dr Scudder, she utterly failed to establish herself in the institutional memory of what became known as CMC (Christian Medical College), Vellore. From the mid-twentieth century, CMC, Vellore, would go on to establish a name for itself within and beyond India as a multifaceted medical complex practising both pioneering high-tech surgery and village-oriented medicine. Even in postcolonial, twenty-first-century India, one Western name does loom large in its institutional memory, but it is that of Scudder rather than Oliver. Few beyond Oliver's former CMAI associates acknowledged and paid tribute to her large role in establishing CMC, Vellore, when she died in Canada in May 1947, just months after her final return from India.[20]

Dr Florence Jessie Murray

If the trajectory of Oliver's career as a medical missions modernizer working mainly among men owed most to the particularities of the India context in which she had lived since 1902, that of Dr Florence Jessie Murray (1894–1975) had its roots in the circumstances of her professional training in North America. The Japanese colony of Korea, where her missionary career began in 1921, provided a congenial setting for her professional ambitions, offering challenges – but also, ironically, opportunities – unavailable to missionaries in the British Empire, as is evident from Hamish Ion's chapter 8 in this volume. Missionaries in Korea were both free from the stigma of being cultural kin of the colonizers and in a position to provide educational and other opportunities that were in high demand and short supply under Japanese colonialism.

This photograph of Dr Florence Jessie Murray and the staff of Korean doctors at the United Church of Canada's medical hospital at Hamhung appeared in the *Korean Mission Field* in May 1941, a year before Murray returned to Canada in an exchange of wartime internees.

The eldest of six children, four of whom became doctors, Murray was born in rural Nova Scotia, the daughter of a Presbyterian minister. A student from 1914 to 1919 at the co-educational medical school affiliated with Dalhousie University in Halifax, she would sail to Korea heavily imbued with the ideals of scientific Western medical professionalism then in the air. These ideals emphasized, among other things, university-based medical training and opportunities for extensive clinical experience supported by laboratory research. This new orthodoxy was at odds with the kind of holistic, personal approach associated with the late nineteenth-century women's medical schools and some proprietorial schools. For a novice medical missionary Murray was also well equipped in terms of hands-on experience outside an institutional setting. Unlike earlier medical missionaries of both sexes, who often began their overseas careers with little or no clinical experience, Murray had sought and found diverse opportunities to practise medicine both during and immediately after her classroom years. These opportunities included the Halifax explosion, the postwar influenza epidemic, a short stint in a hospital for indigents outside Boston, and a valuable period as an assistant to a prominent Halifax surgeon.[21]

In Hamhung, northern Korea, Murray became the superintendent of a small general hospital founded by her much-loved predecessor, Dr Kate McMillan, following the latter's sudden death in 1922. Until June 1942, when she was returned by Japan to Canada in an exchange of wartime detainees, Murray made it her mission to improve the hospital and its staff so as to 'transform ... [it] from what it was into one of the best and most flourishing institutions in Korea and incidentally demonstrate to the missionary community that women doctors are not necessarily cantankerous and inefficient.'[22] While there were many humbling setbacks, especially in the early years, some of them caused by her own outspokenness and her need to unlearn racial prejudice, Murray eventually succeeded in achieving her goal of making the hospital a model of its type. As for her attitude to women doctors, soon after her arrival in Korea she had concluded that female medical missionaries had made the term 'woman doctor' a byword for inferior standards. Murray's conclusion was based not only on the unsanitary condition and relaxed standards prevalent in the mission hospital under Dr McMillan (much of whose career had been devoted to a combination of medicine and evangelism outside a hospital setting), but also on medical work conducted by some American women missionaries in Seoul, which she inspected closely prior to attempting to upgrade the work in Hamhung. She was critical, among other things, of the limited scope of the American women's practice and their failure to keep abreast of new medical developments in the West, and of what she regarded as their inefficient use of ample physical and staff resources and their allegiance to an impractical policy of gender separatism in medical matters.

Especially in rural areas and in the north, where Murray worked, the influence of the *yangban* (the hereditary elite) was not sufficiently strong to require as strict a separation of the sexes as prevailed in the south. Given this fact and her observation that contemporary Korea had few women with the educational background and commitment to enter and remain lifelong in the medical profession (marriage in Korea was a near universal phenomenon),[23] Murray resisted pressures from some older women missionaries to concentrate exclusively on training and treating women. During her years as superintendent of the general mission hospital in Hamhung, all but one of her interns and colleagues were men.

Communist occupation of North Korea after the Second World War precluded the return of Canadian missionaries to their former field of work. In these circumstances, Murray reluctantly accepted an invitation from Helen Kim, president of Ewha Womans University in Seoul (then newly raised from college status), to assist in establishing a medical department there. Convinced that the impoverished circumstances of war-ravaged South Korea made it advisable to consolidate Christian medical training and treatment in a single co-educational college and hospital whose infrastructure and personnel could be built up with strong ecumenical support from abroad, and that Ewha's fledgling medical department was giving its female graduates the illusion rather than the reality of proper professional training, Murray had no heart in remaining at Ewha. After briefly serving on a government-appointed committee to investigate difficulties at the new Seoul National University Hospital, she became part of the more promising professional environment at Severance Union Medical College and Hospital in Seoul, where, among other roles, she was to teach in the College and serve as assistant superintendent of the hospital. Like Ewha's, Severance's infrastructure and staff had suffered severely under Japanese control during the Second World War years, and it would be reduced almost to rubble during the Korean War, but it had roots in a tradition of striving for Western-style medical excellence that went back to the early twentieth century, and a broader base than Ewha of ecumenical support in North America. In these circumstances, Severance was a more congenial professional environment for Murray than Ewha could be, especially given its strong allegiance to the 'women's work for women' tradition of its U.S. Methodist founders.

Inevitably, Murray would at times chafe at the sexism of her mainly male colleagues at Severance, most of whom were Korean in the new postwar era. But she accommodated herself remarkably well to the new racial and professional order, an order in which not a few of the younger physicians had medical specialities that she as a generalist (albeit with extensive surgical experience) did not possess. In the years after the Second World War and the Korean War, she would make her strongest contribution to Severance as its conduit to the New York–based ecumenical board that supported its work, seeking funds and personnel to upgrade its plant and personnel and opportunities for its staff and students to go abroad for further training and experience. Both she and the Woman's Missionary Society of the United Church of Canada, whose salaried employee she was, would remain on friendly terms with Ewha Womans University (which would go on to become the largest women's university in the world, even while remaining, like Severance, a Christian institution). But in the years that remained in her Korea career – it lasted eight years after her official retirement in 1961 – Murray showed no regret at having remained outside the separate-spheres paradigm.[24]

Margaret Christian Wrong

The personal and professional background of Margaret Christian Wrong (1887–1948) differed significantly from that of Oliver and Murray. Yet as the first secretary of the International Committee on Christian Literature for Africa, she, too, had a career in missions that took her beyond the older pattern of women's work for women. The daughter of University of Toronto historian and imperial enthusiast George Wrong, and the granddaughter of a former Ontario premier, Margaret Wrong left Canada in 1911 for England in the company of her brother Murray and their friend Vincent Massey, all of them bound for Oxford University. Following three years at Somerville College, Wrong returned home and for the next six years was associated with the University of Toronto, first as a YWCA secretary and then as an MA history student and part-time instructor and an organizer of residential and social facilities for women students. From 1921 to 1925 she worked out

Margaret Wrong, a few years after her appointment in 1929 as secretary of the London-based International Committee on Christian Literature for Africa.

of Geneva, Switzerland, as travelling secretary of the World Student Christian Federation (WSCF, the international link for national Student Christian Movements), and from 1926 to 1929 out of London, as a missions secretary for the British Student Christian Movement.[25] Her role as catalyst for the British SCM's 'Africa Group' reflected the fact that that continent had become an abiding interest, following a six-month tour of sub-Saharan Africa in 1926 with Mabel Carney of Teachers College, Columbia University. On the 1926 tour, as in her earlier work with the WSCF, Wrong demonstrated adaptability and enthusiasm, and liberal tendencies on race questions, qualities that made her a congenial figure for the reform-minded mission bureaucrats within the IMC who were engaged during the 1920s in efforts at restructuring the educational work of missions in Africa. Joseph Oldham, the leading figure in this restructuring process, was the person responsible for recruiting Wrong, in 1929, to take on responsibility for the International Committee on Christian Literature for Africa (ICCLA), newly created as a subcommittee of the IMC.[26]

For the rest of her life Wrong worked for the ICCLA, whose official mandate was to foster 'the preparation, publication, and distribution of literature for use in connection with missionary work in Africa.'[27] In the process she became so thoroughly identified with the Committee that the same kind of remark a male colleague had made about Oliver was also made in reference to her: 'The ICCLA was Margaret Wrong.'[28] From her base in London, England, Wrong built up essential contacts with publishers, authors, and missionary societies, and, increasingly in later years, with the Colonial Office, resident Africans, and such organizations as the Fabian Colonial Bureau. In London, too, she prepared the ICCLA's two periodicals. In sub-Saharan Africa she travelled so extensively and enthusiastically for the ICCLA – she was on her fifth major tour when she died suddenly in Uganda in 1948 – that her knowledge of Africa probably was almost 'unique in its depth, range, and sympathy,' as those who established a posthumous literary prize for African writers in her name wrote in the *Times* of London.[29]

Interpreting her mandate broadly and creatively, Wrong played an important role in many activities affecting the development of education and literature in Africa and, by the time of her 1936 tour, was strongly concerned with the development of written literature by Africans. The strategies implemented by Wrong and the ICCLA to encourage the development of literature for and within Africa, however, effectively privileged males. Such a pattern emerged despite the fact that Wrong was sympathetically attuned to issues involving African women's needs and rights. She was, of course, constrained by indigenous and colonial values and structures that favoured and facilitated the modernization of men. Yet she also had concerns and priorities of her own that ultimately had a similar effect. She was intensely interested, for instance, in the 'big' economic and political questions animating interwar Africa; concerned with types and instances of racial injustice that, in practice, impinged mainly on male elites; and, as a would-be cultural gatekeeper, anxious to shield African societies from what she deemed to be destructive or inappropriate Western influences, including those that seemed to her likely to bring about a premature destruction of existing gender systems.[30]

What also needs to be taken into account is the symbiotic relationship that developed between modernizing African men and the ICCLA as it sought to promote the development of literature for and by Africans. Like other instruments of liberal missionary reformism, the ICCLA both needed and could assist upwardly mobile young men. In its goal of developing 'suitable' reading material for Africans (material that was secular as well as religious), the ICCLA came to recognize the importance, indeed the necessity, of seeking out and supporting African talent. The mission-educated young men who were the most likely sources of such talent would in many cases reject their mission ties in later years as they grew to resent even the humane and serviceable aspects of missionary paternalism and turned in new literary and political directions. Still, the ICCLA and the cluster of initiatives for promoting literacy and literature with which it was linked were an important part of the heritage of many such men. As in Oliver's and Murray's medical missions work in India and Korea, so, too, in Wrong's work for literature through the ICCLA: symbiotic relationships across 'race' lines could simultaneously undermine traditional gender boundaries. Both developments reflected changes in the larger mission context.

The Larger Mission Context: Emerging Ecumenical and International Bureaucracies

The changing nature of race and gender relationships in mission work in the three cases just described was part of a larger pattern found in and facilitated by the ecumenical national and international bureaucracies that emerged after the First World War. Murray's links to these bureaucracies were mainly indirect even after the Second World War, but the organizations headed by Oliver and Wrong were very much a part of them.

Established in 1921 to facilitate the achievement of the shared mission goals of liberal Protestant missions from Britain and North America (and to a lesser extent continental Europe), the International Missionary Council (IMC) had as its chairman a dynamic American layman, John R. Mott, but its key figure for many years was Joseph Oldham, who had worked for its establishment on a salaried basis since 1910 and, since 1912, been editor of the *International Review of Missions* (*IRM*), a journal in which broad lines of mission policy were explored and debated and where missionary intelligence was disseminated. IMC 'members' were national or regional organizations of mission boards or churches. The Conference of British Missionary Societies (CBMS) and the Foreign Missions Conference of North America (FMCNA) were by far the largest of these organizations. Under IMC leadership, a series of ecumenical and interracial National Christian Councils were also developed in the non-Western world. Between 1921 and 1948 these increased from just four, out of a total of seventeen, to eighteen out of thirty. Both Mott and Oldham made it an early priority to establish such organizations and to encourage in them a strong indigenous presence rather than a mere token representation of nationals in mission-dominated bodies. The National Christian Councils established in the early 1920s in China, Japan, and India were notably successful in this respect. As specific challenges came to the fore, task- or institution-specific committees were also established as adjuncts to the IMC, the CBMS, the FMCNA, and the various national Christian councils. The CMAI, the ICCLA, and the New York–based boards that supported the work of Severance and Ewha were examples of such committees.

While the IMC did not interfere with the doctrines and faith practices of the denominations in its member organizations and had no formal say over their specific policies, it had immense influence. One reason was its Jerusalem and Tambaram (Madras) conferences (held in 1928 and 1938, respectively).[31] Another was the international stature of men like Mott and Oldham, whose influence extended into secular politics. A third was the IMC's ability to apply pressure on behalf of mission causes it favoured while denying support to those deemed retrograde. The IMC's legacy of ecumenism and world-mindedness would live on in the World Council of Churches, which it effectively brought into being in 1948.[32]

In his history of the IMC, William Richey Hogg, who was something of an insider, documented, but evidently did not feel a need to explain, a pattern whereby women came to play important roles in the organization and some of its ancillary bodies. One can speculate that the combination of the lower salaries for which they worked – a few were volunteers – and the extraordinary educational background and talents that they brought to their tasks made this group of women attractive to cash-starved organizations such as the IMC. Hogg acknowledges the latter qualities in a matter-of-fact way in introducing IMC staff. While the chairman and the three secretaries appointed in the 1920s were men (two in London; one in New York), women held important secondary roles. Thus, Georgina Gollock was from 1921 to

1927 Oldham's co-editor at the *IRM*, while Betty Gibson was associated with him as a translator, researcher, and, later, author, officially receiving the title of assistant IMC secretary in 1925. Four years later, as noted above, Wrong and Oliver were appointed to their specialized committee work, in London and India respectively. For many years Alice Van Doren was Oliver's colleague within the National Christian Council of India, with responsibility for facilitating rural education.[33] All these women seem to have maintained a strong interest in developments affecting their own sex, and yet, as with the three Canadians discussed above, all seem to have found great satisfaction in roles that took them beyond the separate-spheres approach of an earlier era. Some would work mainly with and for men and eventually be succeeded by men.

The working relationships in these ecumenical organizations could not be described as egalitarian. Even in 1936, in the context of discussing a new secretarial appointment, which they wanted to go to a woman, some of Oliver's women colleagues spoke of Oldham as having a problem in remembering that 'Half the people in the world are women.'[34] Yet over time the relationships in the ecumenical bureaucracies do seem to have evolved in the direction of greater formal acknowledgment of women's contributions. It was Oldham himself who suggested in 1921 that Gollock's position at the *IRM* should be upgraded from assistant editor to co-editor. As for Gibson, in a self-mocking letter to her family written the same year, she declared that at work she sat 'like a mouse and listen[ed] to the words of wisdom' of her seniors. In the course of the 1920s, though, as Oldham took on ever more tasks, he came to rely more heavily on her expertise, particularly with regard to African matters, and acknowledged that fact. It was he who suggested in 1925 that she be officially appointed to the IMC secretariat, and when their much-discussed *The Remaking of Man in Africa* was published in 1931 both Oldham and Gibson were credited, and recognized by colleagues, as its co-authors.[35] William Paton, who joined Oldham in London in 1927 as associate IMC secretary, was evidently somewhat less ready to acknowledge the contributions of female colleagues: even Eleanor Jackson's seldom-critical biography reports that Margaret Sinclair, Paton's able associate at the *IRM*, was 'annoyed ... that he would pirate her ideas without acknowledging them.'[36] Yet there was no denying that the new ecumenical structures had given rise to a need and opportunity for able men and women to work collegially.

How Dominant a Paradigm, and How Sharp a Break?

Changes in the gender organization of interwar mission work were certainly not confined to the international bureaucracies or to the specific cases I have described. As mission institutions strove to be more efficient and up-to-date in response to Western and non-Western pressures, there was a growing tendency to favour gender-integrated work as an aspect of consolidation, especially in medicine and higher academic and professional education, wherever local circumstances made it feasible. The comparatively high cost of such work as it aspired to transplant Western standards and the need for economies fostered by the Depression were powerful incentives. The important, if controversial, volume *Re-Thinking Missions* recommended not only more devolution in women's mission work to make use of the talents of indigenous Christian women but also 'a closer relationship with the general program.'[37]

Women missionaries' own inclinations when they took up overseas work were also a factor. By the 1920s, once-familiar tropes about degraded heathen womanhood were becoming less common, and a more gender-neutral vocabulary of Christian internationalism was coming into vogue.[38] There was also the matter of women missionaries' professional backgrounds: a substantial body of scholarship now depicts a pattern, particularly after the First World War, of Western professional women rejecting the notion of a 'woman's sphere' and identifying instead with the values and goals of their particular profession.[39] Furthermore, during this period specific circumstances as well as personal inclination and background preparation led other women, in addition to missionaries, into work that transgressed women's sphere in careers in, or involving, Asia and Africa in this period.[40]

But if the phenomenon of moving beyond 'women's work for women' was becoming a new and attractive possibility for Western professional women employed in mission institutional work, and for others in analogous careers in Asia and Africa in this period, it is too soon to assume that it became a pattern in more ordinary kinds of mission work. So few scholarly case studies of missionary activity in the years after the First World War have been published that generalizations about wholesale shifts in gender (and race) roles and relations are premature. Missionaries who worked with rural and illiterate communities – still the norm in much of Asia and Africa – were restricted by local norms and needs in the kinds of work they could do. Among the most marginalized, there might be few restrictions on the kinds of services and interventions that outsiders could offer. But that could not be taken for granted.

Meanwhile, in the lives of the three women featured in this chapter, the experience of working with and sometimes mentoring men did not necessarily signify the emergence of nonconventional ideas about gender roles generally. Like single career women in contemporary North America, Oliver, Murray, and Wrong took it for granted that most women would marry and that, in doing so, they would take on domestic responsibilities that would preclude outside occupations no matter what their previous work experience or educational background had been. Interestingly, this was as evident in Murray's and Wrong's expectations about their younger sisters' futures as married women in Canada as in their expectations regarding women in Asia and Africa. Murray's unwillingness to make a priority of helping women to become doctors during her years in northern Korea was, as noted, partly based on her assumption that marriage would take such women out of the profession.[41]

And yet if, through their work, the three women introduced here were, in practice, providing broader horizons for men than for women, they were nonetheless far from indifferent to problems and limitations in the lives of non-Western women. When, for instance, Wrong presented a report to the Gold Coast (Ghana) government in 1945 on the development of adult literacy programs, she rejected the idea that literacy should be regarded as a skill necessary only for 'certain vocations' and instead argued for it as a factor of the utmost importance in 'securing the participation of the people in the political, economic and social development of the country.' And 'the people,' she made clear, included women.[42] Wrong's efforts to promote women's literacy through the ICCLA itself and by pressing the colonial state to devote more resources to women's education were by no means insignificant even before the Second World War added a new urgency to the task. In doing this, however, she was not seeking to challenge fundamental gender roles. Literacy, she believed, should ideally make African women more effective at creating strong homes and communities, not turn them into mirror images of their literate male counterparts or encourage them to adopt inappropriate models of Western womanhood, whether as decorous chatelaines or in self-serving careers. In a society undergoing rapid changes in many other respects, Wrong believed that the maintenance of a strong family life was especially crucial as a source of stability. Nor was placing the responsibility for that task on women necessarily to sentence them to permanent subserviency. 'Diversity of function of [African] men and women,' she wrote in 1940, 'must not imply servility of status for women.'[43] Wrong may seem to us now to have been naive in thinking and writing this, but she was probably not being disingenuous.

As for Oliver and Murray, both were undeniably more concerned with the professional qualifications of doctors in the countries where they served than with their gender. In taking this position Murray was reflecting both her own professional training in Canada and her assumption about Korea's great need for Western medical science. In India, Oliver's interwar crusade to establish a fully professional Christian medical college reflected not only her belief in the utility of first-rate Western medical practice in India but also the importance of quality to a Christian medical college concerned to secure its future at a time when a mainly Hindu-based nationalism was making its religious identity a liability. Yet 'standards' did not preclude a sense of 'sisterhood.' Murray, for instance, provided moral and practical support to Korean women doctors in Seoul in the difficult years following the Second World War and the Korean War, meeting monthly with a group to whom she lent medical books and journals.[44] And, like Oliver in India, she provided friendship and support to nurses, who, in Korea only slightly less than in India, experienced marginal status because of their background and their occupation.[45]

Oliver, Murray, and Wrong were participants in a multifaceted process of modernizing missions so as to make them responsive to the 'demands of the hour.' Moving beyond 'women's work for women' in mission work did not automatically mean moving beyond older styles of missionary evangelism. Nonetheless, the gender shift was part was of a larger pattern that ultimately had that effect. Were my subjects unwitting participants in a process of secularizing missions? It has not been the purpose of this chapter to deal with that question. But it does seem important to conclude by noting that all three women seem to have had rich (albeit very different) personal faith lives and that they were far from being indifferent to the future of Christianity in Asia and Africa. As to how to bring that goal about, they would probably have agreed with Gibson's view that the central challenge of missionary work had passed 'from enunciation of doctrine to the compelling power of the Christian life.'[46]

NOTES

My thanks to all those who commented on previous versions of this chapter. Its theme is developed more fully in my *Modern Women Modernizing Men: The Changing Missions of Three Professional Women in Asia and Africa, 1902–69* (Vancouver: UBC Press, 2002).

1 J. Paul S.R. Gibson, 'Ideals of the Missionary Enterprise,' *Indian Social Reformer* (18 August 1934), 807–8; see also 'The Message of Christianity,' 25 August 1934.
2 The one point raised by Gibson that was perhaps not as routinely made was that governments were now taking up the kinds of educational, medical, and agricultural work that missions had pioneered. Though he did not elaborate, the implication was that the latter would need to improve their performance in order to avoid redundancy.
3 Quoted in Keith Clements, *Faith on the Frontier: A Life of J.H. Oldham* (Edinburgh: T&T Clark, 1999), 255, writing to John R. Mott on 18 November 1924.
4 Richard Elpick, 'The Benevolent Empire and the Social Gospel: Missionaries and South African Christians in the Age of Segregation,' in Richard Elphick and Rodney Davenport, eds, *Christianity in South Africa: A Political, Social, and Cultural History* (Berkeley: University of California Press, 1997), 347–69; William R. Hutchison, *Errand to the World: American Protestant Thought and Foreign Missions* (Chicago: University of Chicago Press, 1987), 138–45; Torben Christensen and William R. Hutchison, eds, *Missionary Ideologies in the Imperialist Era: 1880–1920*, 2nd ed. (Aarhuis: Farlaget Aros, 1983), Introduction.
5 Lian Xi, *The Conversion of Missionaries: Liberalism in American Protestant Missions, 1907–32* (University Park: Pennsylvania State University Press, 1997), chap. 4; United Church of Canada/Victoria University Archives, Toronto (hereafter UCA), William Scott, 'Canadians in Korea: Brief Historical Sketch of Canadian Mission Work in Korea,' unpublished typescript, 1975, 93–5. Christians and non-Christians of both sexes used mission services, especially for education, but females were less inclined to be verbal and militant in expressing dissatisfaction and perhaps had less dissatisfaction to express. On this point, see Maina Chalwa Singh, *Gender, Religion, and 'Heathen Lands': American Missionary Women in South Asia, 1860s–1940s* (New York: Garland Press, 2000), Introduction.
6 The new pattern was especially evident in regard to medicine. See R. Fletcher Moorshead, *The Way of the Doctor: A Study in Medical Missions* (Lon-

don: Carey Press, 1926 [?]), 102–3; William Ernest Hocking, *Re-Thinking Missions: A Laymen's Inquiry after One Hundred Years* (New York: Harper & Brothers, 1932), chap. IX, esp. 201–6, 210–11.

7 On Dr Belle Choné Oliver's early years in the mission, see my *New Women for God: Canadian Presbyterian Women and India Missions, 1876–1914* (Toronto: University of Toronto Press, 1990). Like the mission work in Korea discussed below, the Presbyterians' India mission work was transferred in 1925 to the newly created United Church of Canada.

8 *New Women*, chap. 5, esp. 159–60.

9 UCA, Dr B.C. Oliver papers in Glenna Jamieson fonds, 3330, 88-029C, box/file 001-02, 'Dr B.C. Oliver,' autobiographical sketch.

10 No copies of the original Survey appear to have survived, but it was discussed in various issues of the *Journal of the Christian Medical Association of India, Burma and Ceylon* (hereafter *Journal*), incl. 4, 4 (September 1929): 155–6, and it came out in an updated and expanded edition as *The Ministry of Healing in India: Handbook of the Christian Medical Association of India* (Mysore: Wesleyan Mission Press, 1932), compiled and largely written by Oliver.

11 *Journal* 1, 3 (July 1926): 108.

12 Oliver, 'Medical Missions at the Jerusalem Council,' *Journal* 3, 3 (July 1928): 102–4; Christian Frimodt-Möller, 'Medical Work and the Church,' *Journal* 3, 4 (September 1928): 143–6.

13 Instructions quoted by Oliver in 'The Why of Medical Missions,' *Central India Torch* 6, 7 (December 1927): 1.

14 She would later refer on several occasions to having begun the journey to a more satisfying understanding of the purpose of medical missions as a result of reading Dugald Christie's *Thirty Years in Moukden, 1883–1913* in 1915: see 'Some Furlough Experiences,' *Journal* 4, 6 (January 1930): 254, and 'The Moukden Medical College,' *Journal* 9, 6 (November 1934): 397.

15 UCA, Jamieson fonds, B.C. Oliver, 'Medical Matters: Report to the National Christian Council, 1944.'

16 'Dr. B.C. Oliver,' *Journal* 19, 4 (July 1944): 163.

17 See my *Modern Women Modernizing Men,* chap. 2.

18 Roger Jeffery, *The Politics of Health Care in India* (Berkeley: University of California Press, 1988), 74, 86, and 'Recognizing India's Doctors: The Institutionalization of Medical Dependency, 1918–1939,' in *Modern Asian Studies* 13, 2 (1979): 301–6, esp. 314, 323; Judith Brown, 'Who Is an Indian? Dilemmas of National Identity at the End of the British Raj in India,' paper presented to 'Missions, Nationalism, and the End of Empire' conference, University of Cambridge, September 2000. As Brown points out, non-

Hindus had a problematic relationship to national identity, since 'increasingly being Indian and Hindu became intertwined' (11).

19 Yale University Divinity School Archives (YDS), microfiche of Joint International Missionary Council/Conference of British Missionary Societies Archives: India, National Christian Council and C.M.A.I. records (hereafter NCC-CMAI records), mf box 398, mf no.38, minutes of meeting of College Committee, 6 and 7 April 1931, and 'Concerning the Proposed Union Christian Medical College for Men' (quotation at 3).

20 'Dr. B.C. Oliver,' *Journal* 19, 4 (July 1944): 163, and 'In Loving Memory of Dr. B. Oliver,' *Journal* 22, 4–5 (July-September 1947): 187. In tracing the story of the CMAI's role in establishing what ultimately became CMC, Vellore, I drew heavily on issues of the CMAI's *Journal*, on Oliver's papers in the Jamieson fonds, UCA, and in NCC-CMAI records.

21 Murray's medical background is discussed more fully in *Modern Women Modernizing Men*, chap. 3. The first volume of Murray's memoirs, *At the Foot of Dragon Hill* (New York: Dutton, 1975), deals only briefly with her pre-Korea years.

22 Public Archives of Nova Scotia (PANS), Maritime Missionaries to Korea Collection, MG 1, vol. 2276, file 3, Murray to father, 27 December 1922.

23 Laurel Kendall, *Getting Married in Korea: Of Gender, Morality, and Modernity* (Berkeley: University of California Press, 1996).

24 Murray was writing a memoir of this period when she died following a short illness in 1975. It has been published unaltered as *Return to Korea* (Belleville, ON: Essence Publishing, 1999), with a Foreword by Robert K. Anderson.

25 'Wrong, George MacKinnon,' *Dictionary of National Biography, 1941–50* [sixth supplement], edited by L.G. Wickham Legg and E.T. Williams (London: Oxford University Press, 1959), 979–80; Collection of the late Agnes Wrong Armstrong (privately held), 'A Canadian Family,' unpublished manuscript, chap. 1 (cited as Armstrong Collection); Agnes Wrong Armstrong, '"There's Too Much Waiting to Be Done,"' *Food for Thought* 16 (March 1956); *Modern Women Modernizing Men*, chap. 4.

26 Armstrong Collection, Wrong to mother, 8 and 19 March 1929, and untitled posthumous tribute to Wrong by J.O. Dobson; Library of School of Oriental and African Studies, University of London, International Committee on Christian Literature for Africa (SOAS/ICCLA), box 500, 'Early Plans,' esp. file on 'Africa Literature Bureau: Papers, etc.'; William Richey Hogg, *Ecumenical Foundations: A History of the International Missionary Council and Its Nineteenth-Century Background* (New York: Harper & Brothers, 1952), 277–8.

27 *Books for Africa* (January 1931), 1.

28 J.W.C. Dougall, quoted in *Books for Africa* (July 1948), tribute issue.

29 'Miss Margaret Wrong,' *Times* (London), 6 May 1949.

30 Wrong's personal priorities and the broad range of her work are discussed more fully in my 'Margaret Wrong's Literary Work and the "Remaking of Woman" in Africa, 1929–48,' *Journal of Imperial and Commonwealth History* 23, no. 3 (September 1995): 427–52.

31 For the dramatic influence of the Tambaram conference on one African churchman see Terence Ranger, *Are We Not Also Men? The Samkange Family and African Politics in Zimbabwe, 1920–1964* (Harare: Baobab, 1995), esp. chap. 3, 'Tambaram: A Re-making.'

32 Hogg, *Ecumenical Foundations*, esp. chaps. 4, 5; Ruth Rouse and Stephen Charles Neill, eds, *A History of the Ecumenical Movement, 1517–1948* (London: Society for the Promotion of Christian Knowledge, 1954), 368 (for growth of National Christian Councils); C.H. Hopkins, *John R. Mott, 1865–1955* (Geneva: World Council of Churches, 1979); Keith Clements, *Faith on the Frontier: A Life of J.H. Oldham* (Edinburgh: T&T Clark, 1999).

33 Hogg, *Ecumenical Foundations*, 221–6, 263–5, 277–9, 322–5; K. Baago, *A History of the National Christian Council of India, 1914–1964* (Nagpur: National Christian Council, 1965), 46, 87.

34 UCA, Jamieson fonds, Oliver diaries, entry for 15 November 1936.

35 Hogg, *Ecumenical Foundations*, 224; New College Library, Edinburgh, J.H. Oldham Papers, box 2, ref. no. 2.6, Gibson to 'Dear Family,' from India, December 1921; box 4, ref. no. 4.9, Oldham to Dr Lerrigo, 1 January 1929; and box 6, ref. no 6.3, E. W. Thompson to Oldham, 2 October 1931, and Max Yergan to Gibson, 13 October 1931.

36 Eleanor M. Jackson, *Red Tape and the Gospel: A Study of the Significance of the Ecumenical Missionary Struggle of William Paton, 1866–1943* (Birmingham, UK: Phlogiston, 1980), 177; see also Introduction, 14, regarding Paton's unease with some women colleagues.

37 *Re-Thinking Missions*, 279–83 (quotation at 279).

38 Patricia R. Hill, *The World Their Household: The American Woman's Foreign Mission Movement and Cultural Transformation, 1870–1920* (Ann Arbor: University of Michigan Press, 1985), 168; Dana Robert, *American Women in Mission: A Social History of Their Thought and Practice* (Macon, GA: Mercer University Press, 1996), esp. 273, 304–5, 313.

39 Nancy Cott, *The Grounding of Modern Feminism* (New Haven: Yale University Press, 1987), esp. chap. 7; Rosalind Rosenberg, *Beyond Separate Spheres: Intellectual Roots of Modern Feminism* (New Haven: Yale University Press, 1982), 210. For the pattern among doctors see Ellen S. More, *Restoring the Balance: Women Physicians and the Profession of Medicine, 1850–1995* (Cam-

bridge: Harvard University Press, 1999). For the more complex identities and identity shifts among women who became professional historians around this time see Bonnie G. Smith, *The Gender of History: Men, Women and Historical Practice* (Cambridge: Harvard University Press, 1998), esp. chaps. 7 and 8.

40 See, for example, Margaret Prang, *A Heart at Leisure from Itself: Caroline Macdonald of Japan* (Vancouver: UBC Press, 1995); Barbara Bush, '"Britain's Conscience on Africa": White Women, Race and Imperial Politics in Interwar Britain,' in Clare Midgley, ed., *Gender and Imperialism* (Manchester: Manchester University Press, 1998): 200–23; Henrika Kuklick, *The Savage Within: The Social History of British Anthropology, 1885–1945* (Cambridge: Cambridge University Press, 1993), esp. 213, 268–9, 317–19. The Middle East also attracted such women; see H.V.F. Winstone, *Gertrude Bell* (London: Quartet Books, 1980).

41 Murray would eventually learn that, as in the case of her sister, Anna, Korean women doctors who married often remained actively involved in medicine. For Anna see Enid Johnson MacLeod, *Petticoat Doctors: The First Forty Years of Women in Medicine at Dalhousie University* (Porters Lake, NS: Pottersfield Press, 1990), 117–18. Regarding prominent early Korean women doctors who remained in practice after marriage see the entries for Moon Gyung Chang and Duck-Heung Bang in Leone McGregor Hellstedt, ed., *Women Physicians of the World: Autobiographies of Medical Pioneers* (Washington: Hemisphere Publishing, 1978), 267–9, and 361–3. These are not isolated examples.

42 National Archives of Ghana, RG 3/1/323, Wrong, 'Report on Literacy and Adult Education in the Gold Coast,' 1945, 11–12.

43 Wrong, 'The Education of African Women in a Changing World,' *Yearbook of Education*, 1940, 501.

44 UCA, United Church of Canada, Woman's Missionary Society, Korea Correspondence, box 3, file 51a, '1949 Annual Report'; author's conversation with Dr Park Jung Jai, Seoul, 15 May 1997.

45 Murray, *Dragon Hill*, 168–9; YDS, United Board for Christian Higher Education in Asia, RG 11A, box 148a, file 181A-2577, Murray to Dr Fenn, 1 April 1954. Oliver, as noted, founded the Nurses' Auxiliary within the CMAI. She also helped individual nurses to upgrade their professional qualifications in North America.

46 Gibson, 'Ideals of the Missionary Enterprise.'

Chapter 8

Missions and Empires: A Case Study of Canadians in the Japanese Empire, 1895–1941

A. HAMISH ION

In North America, Africa, the West Indies, the Pacific Islands, South Asia, Southeast Asia, where missions and empires joined, the missionaries were either nationals of the imperial power or working in territory belonging to an imperial power that was Christian.[1] There were exceptions, of course; the Ottoman and Persian empires before the Great War were two, but in those places the rights of missionaries were protected by Capitulations and by the active interest of the great powers in assuring the rights of the Christian minority. In China down to 1943, extraterritoriality and the ubiquitous gunboats protected missionaries. The only real exception was the Japanese Empire, neither European nor Christian, and unencumbered by Capitulations or extraterritoriality in terms of missions and empires. Elsewhere, I have looked at British and Canadian missionaries in the Japanese Empire and their relations with the colonial authorities.[2] In this chapter I want to do two things: first, to draw together some of the broad trends that were evident in the relations between Canadian Protestant missionaries and the Japanese colonial overlords; and second, to stress the importance of Japanese missionaries sent by the Japanese Christian movement to various colonies within the Empire and how they impinged on Japanese Christian attitudes toward not only Japanese imperialism but also Japan's relations with the Western missionary movement in East Asia, notably, Canadian missions in Taiwan and Korea.

Missions and the Japanese Authorities

While Japan no longer has any territorial footholds in continental East Asia, it must be remembered that the Japanese Empire in the first decades of the twentieth century was both extensive and expanding. Prior to the beginning of the war in Europe in 1939, the Japanese Empire had come to include not only metropolitan Japan itself, but also Taiwan (1895), Sakhalin (1905), the Liaotung Peninsula (1905), Korea (1910), the mandated Pacific Islands (1919), and Manchukuo (Manchuria, 1931), as well as much of north and coastal China.[3] By the summer of 1942 Japanese-controlled territory within the euphemistically named Greater East Asia Co-Prosperity Sphere also included Indochina, the Philippines, the Dutch East Indies, Malaya, and Burma. The Japanese Empire possessed a strong central imperial government in Tokyo and had powerful colonial administrations in its colonies or overwhelming influence in the affairs of puppet regimes like those in Manchukuo and North China.

In the Japanese Empire, the question of missions and empire was not only the concern of Western missionaries but also of very considerable significance to the Japanese Christian movement, which maintained overseas missionaries in its colonies and elsewhere. Indeed, a major motive behind the formation of the government-backed Union Japanese Protestant Church, the Nihon Kirisutokyōdan, in 1941 was to create a church strong enough to assume Japanese Christian leadership and control within the Japanese Empire, but also at the expense of Western missionary movements and indigenous Christian movements. However, the challenge of taking the leading role in the Christianization of East Asia was not something that emerged suddenly as a result of the crisis between Japan and the other Great Powers in the late 1930s. The empire and the expansion of Japanese Christian missionary work overseas in the path of Japanese imperial expansion, as well as trans-Pacific among Japanese immigrants to North America, was an important theme within the history of the Japanese Christian movement from the late nineteenth century onwards.

There was much to be applauded in this endeavour. Imai Judō, the leading Japanese Anglican priest in the late 1890s, wrote in January 1895 in the Anglican journal *Nichiyō Soshi* that he felt the Japanese had a mission of leadership in Asia as they guaranteed the rights of Korea and possessed Taiwan. In this national mission, the Nippon Seikōkai, the Anglican Church in Japan, had received a heaven-sent calling [*tenshoku*] to undertake new Christian mission work in Taiwan.[4] Imai, who died in 1919, was deeply committed to the idea that it was the calling of Japan to light up the hope of civilization in East Asia.[5]

The Japanese Anglicans began their mission in Taiwan in 1897 under

A confirmation service held at the Canadian Anglican mission in Takata, Japan, during the visit of Bishop Heber James Hamilton (centre) in 1929. Among the senior members of the church behind the bishop are Rev. P.S.C. Powles, priest-in-charge, and Rev. K. Tsukada, deacon. Cyril Powles, the future mission historian, is the boy at far right.

the jurisdiction of the Bishop of Osaka, and indeed, a Canadian Anglican, Narcissus Peter Yates, from the Montreal diocese, worked with the Japanese Anglican Church in Taiwan from 1915 to his death in the late 1930s. Japanese Presbyterians had arrived in Taiwan two years earlier than the Anglicans, and by the 1930s Congregationalists, the Holiness Church, the Salvation Army, and the Japan Methodists were all represented in Taiwan. So too was it with Korea, and later Manchuria, where there was a broad denominational spectrum of Japanese Christian missionaries at work. Initially the efforts of Japanese missionaries were directed to catering to the needs of the Japanese population in those areas, but quickly they were extended to the indigenous peoples. Given the size of the Japanese Christian movement, which was less than 1 per cent of the national population, the scope of its overseas missionary endeavour was quite significant, even before it substantially increased in the last decade before the Second World War.

The issue of the co-operation of the Japanese Christian leadership with the government in the war effort, and especially the role of the Japanese Christian movement in the empire and occupied territories, is also a controversial and sensitive subject as it has considerable bearing on the issue of *kirisutokyō no sensō sekinin* (the war responsibility of Christians). Some might take umbrage that the motives of Japanese Christian leaders closely identified with *tennō*-centred ('Emperor worship') nationalism in wanting to assume control of the various Christian movements in the Japanese Empire and occupied territories could be open to criticism.

It was through their support of empire and imperialism that Japanese Christians could decisively show their fellow citizens that they were loyal Japanese. In Japan, as Cyril Powles has pointed out, 'Christianity appealed mainly to members of the middle class and what Maruyama Masao called "quasi-intellectuals," both of which groups tended to identify with the establishment ... [and] by and large affirmed the country's nationalist aspirations'[6] Eager to be counted as patriotic citizens and members of a 'mainline' religion, Japanese Christians saw that by enthusiastically supporting Japanese imperialism they had the opportunity to demonstrate to non-Christian Japanese their support of Japanese goals and their loyalty to the state. Likewise, Buddhist organizations with few exceptions were strong supporters of the war against China during the 1930s as a means of showing their patriotism and loyalty.

In the colonies, the response of Korean and Taiwanese Christians was

different, for the class-consciousness of the underclass converts reinforced opposition to the Japanese colonial authorities. Just as Western
missionaries in Japan aligned themselves with their Japanese Christian
friends, so too in the colonies the stand of Korean and Taiwanese Christians was supported by their Western missionary mentors. Japanese
missionaries, however, supported the colonial authorities. As well as
sponsoring Shinto and Buddhist missionary activities, the Japanese
authorities supported the Japanese Christian foreign missionary endeavour in a real sense because it was seen as one means by which they
could strengthen their hold over the country, spread the use of Japanese
language, and inculcate the Koreans with Japanese ideas.

The problem, however, that Japanese Christian missionaries confronted in Korea was that they were identified with the much-hated
colonial power. The attraction of many Koreans to Christianity related
to Western missionaries serving as a bulwark of defence for Korean
language, culture, and supporters of Korean nationalism, which were
under attack from Japanese colonial policies designed to assimilate
Koreans and turn them into ersatz Japanese. Whereas many Western
missionary societies, including Canadian ones, met with considerable
success in Korea in the first two decades of the twentieth century, the
Japanese Christian societies fared badly in comparison in terms of
attracting large numbers of Koreans.

Canadian missionaries as British subjects were identified with British interests in East Asia. Britain was the major Western power in the
region up until 1941, and Canadian missionaries certainly benefited
from this identification during the days of the Anglo-Japanese Alliance
between 1902 and 1923. Equally, Canadian missionaries suffered from
this connection during the late 1930s, as Britain became the prime target of Japanese anti-Western feeling ultimately leading to the Anglo-
Japanese War directed toward the forcible taking over of British interests and colonial possessions in East and Southeast Asia, even though
this would bring the United States into conflict with Japan.

Christianity and Christian missions had always posed awkward
problems for the Japanese government and its colonial administration
in Korea. To understand why the Japanese authorities acted in the way
that they did toward Canadian missionaries, it is important to look in
some detail at Japanese perceptions of Christianity. This will also help
to underline the fact that policies toward Christianity must be seen in
the context of Japanese policies toward religion in general. The Japanese had clear views in regards to religion and Christianity, stemming

Dr Frank W. Schofield, a Canadian Presbyterian missionary, and an unidenti-
fied Korean Christian. Schofield, a professor at Severance Union Medical College, Seoul, is considered a national hero in Korea because he was one of the
most hostile missionary critics of Japanese rule in 1919.

from their first experience with Christianity and foreign missionaries
in the sixteenth and seventeenth centuries. The perception that Christianity threatened the state served to continue to hamper the development of the Japanese Christian movement long after the *sakoku* (Closed
Country) policy was rendered useless, the Tokugawa shogunate itself
destroyed, and religious freedom guaranteed under the Meiji Constitution of 1889. Even then the meaning of religious freedom in the Meiji
Constitution had still to be defined; this was especially true in terms of
the church–state relations at the governmental and bureaucratic levels,
but also applied to issues surrounding the relationship between Japa-

nese nationalism and patriotism and Christian faith at the personal level. The famous case of Uchimura Kanzō's refusal to bow to the Imperial Rescript on Education while a teacher at the First Higher Middle School is illustrative of this latter point.[7]

From the 1868 Restoration onwards, the Meiji oligarchy saw the importance of using autochthonic, quasi-religious rituals and ceremonies to reinforce its power and control. As early as 1869 state rituals commemorating the founding of the state by the mythical first emperor Jimmu were being performed and, two years later, commemorative national holidays instituted. The new political leaders saw the emphasis on Jimmu as an important device in helping to legitimize the modernization of the Japanese monarchy through linking the present with the mythical past.[8] By the 1890s, it is clear the Meiji government saw that the role of religion in society was to serve the interests of the state, and that administrative or legislative measures had to be taken to ensure that religious freedom did not compromise those interests particularly in the sphere of education.

The influence of Shinto's relationship with the Japanese state as it emerged after the Restoration, and its implications for other religions – for new ones like Tenrikyō and Kurozumikyō, for older ones like Buddhism, but particularly for Christianity – as well as its impact on religious freedom is debatable. However, Japanese Christians were persecuted well into the Meiji period despite the presence of Western missionaries. The persecution of Christians, of course, varied both in nature and in degree from imprisonment and deportation of the Urakami crypto-Christians at the end of the 1860s, to simple personal or familial harassment as in the case of some of the members of the Christian group, the so-called Kumamoto Band, formed in Kumamoto in the mid-1870s.[9] The persecution of Urakami crypto-Christians in 1868 caused the first major diplomatic crisis that the new Meiji government had to face. Likewise, in 1872, when foreign governments put pressure on the Iwakura Mission, then travelling in Europe, which resulted in the removal from public view of the proscription edicts against Christianity, the Meiji government's continued to curb the influence of Christianity in less obvious ways.

In dealing with Christianity bureaucratically, the obvious model for government policy was its long experience with Buddhism, another foreign religion that also suffered persecution during the Meiji era. For their part, many Japanese Christians wanted to see Christianity recognized, along with Shintoism and Buddhism, to form a trinity of religions in Japan. Moreover, Japanese nationalism had an impact on the desire of Japanese Christians for an independent Christianity in Japan free from foreign domination.

Other than theological and religious arguments against the acceptance of Christianity, the Achilles heel of Japanese Christians was the doubt that was cast into the minds of non-Christian Japanese about their loyalty to Japan, and even their Japaneseness when they became Christians.[10] The question of being both Japanese and Christian proved to be an extremely difficult one for many Japanese converts. This stands in contrast to Japanese Buddhists, who did not suffer from a similar conflict between their religion and their Japanese identity. Already, by the end of the Meiji era, this desire for an independent Christianity in Japan had begun to develop signs of the creation of a Japanese Christianity (*Nipponteki Kirisutokyō*) distinct from the Christianity propagated by foreign missionaries. The point to be made is that the nature of *Nipponteki Kirisutokyō* under the impact of ultranationalism and *tennōsei* in the late 1930s changed to be a new nationalistic religion not only distinct from but also devoid of Western influences.

During the late Meiji period, however, nationalism, coupled with the demands of patriotism, led the Japanese Christian movement to be identified as supporting Japan's expansionism overseas especially after the Russo-Japanese War. It was in their support of Japanese imperial and military ambitions in continental East Asia that Japanese Christians could demonstrate visibly their loyalty to Japan to counter the doubts about their Japaneseness raised by their adherence to a foreign religion identified with the West.

Just as academic attention has been paid to the relationship between Christianity and modernization in Meiji Japan,[11] so, too, we must address the relationship between Christianity and Japanese overseas expansionism in the years following the Sino-Japanese War of 1894–5. While they were advocates of religious imperialism in the form of a Japanese missionary movement overseas, many Japanese Christians also supported Japanese imperialism and colonialism. In this, of course, the reaction of Christians bore a striking resemblance to that of Japanese Buddhists, who suffered considerable persecution at the hands of the Meiji government. In his study of Buddhist persecution in Meiji Japan, James Edward Ketelaar points out that 'cooperation in the colonization of the northern territories, at great expense and loss of life to many sects, was the first extensive "proof of loyalty to the throne" for post persecution Buddhism. These efforts were followed by institutional Buddhism's active support of involvement in the Sino-Japanese War (1894–5) and, to a lesser extent, the Russo-Japanese War (1904–5) wars.'[12] What Ketelaar here applied to Buddhism was equally true of post-persecution Christianity, and suggests that the urge to regain respectability at home led to active support of Japan's overseas expansionism.

The difficulties that the Japanese authorities had with Christianity in Korea related not only to traditional Japanese attitudes toward Christianity but also to the different cultural response to Christianity found in its major colony Korea. In common with the Ottoman, Persian, and Chinese empires, Japan possessed a strong traditional culture (skillfully manipulated for the purposes of a modernizing state after 1868) that was largely resistant to the Christian message. While the traditional Chinese culture of colonial Taiwan and puppet Manchukuo (Manchuria) also proved resistant to the Christian message, Korean culture proved to be more responsive to Christianity than any other culture in East Asia. Despite the differing responses of the traditional Chinese or Korean cultures, the Japanese colonial regimes also imposed on these cultures Japanese imperatives in regards to religious toleration and the purposes of religious organizations that affected Christian work in the Japanese Empire. Given the attitudes of the Japanese toward Christianity, it is not surprising that there was the real possibility of a clash of interests between the colonial authorities and Western missionaries in the Japanese Empire.

As well as wanting to control religion and religious bodies, Japanese authorities in both metropolitan Japan and in the colonies considered government control of education and school curriculum to be vitally important. The Governments-General in Seoul and Taipeh (now Taipei) believed that loyalty and patriotism to Japan should be inculcated into the Korean and Taiwanese populations through education. The problem with mission schools was that Western missionaries unconsciously passed political ideas and sympathies on to their Korean pupils, which ran counter to those of the Japanese colonial administration that aimed for the assimilation of the Korean population. As a result of mission school education a type of Korean intensely distasteful to Japanese officials was being produced.[13] Despite the repeated assurances by Western missionaries that they were not anti-Japanese, it was from the graduates of mission schools that many of the leading opponents of the Japanese came and missionaries must take some responsibility for making them such. It was inevitable that there would be difficulties between the Japanese colonial authorities and missionaries over education.

Government regulations concerning curriculum content, language qualifications for teaching staff, and ownership of private schools had by the end of the 1930s wrested control of mission schools in Japan from Western mission societies, and barred all but the most linguistically proficient missionaries from teaching in secondary schools. By 1939 the point was quickly being reached where no missionaries would be involved in secondary education. Similar regulations were also applied to mission schools in the colonies as part of the government drive to rid education of foreign influence. Western missionaries still continued to teach at universities and specialty institutions, which were less tightly regulated than secondary schools. Indeed, Charles Bates, for instance, remained the president of the Kwansei Gakuin University in Nishinomiya, near Kobe, until his departure for Canada in 1940.

Canadian Presbyterians in Taiwan

Canadian missionary activity in the Japanese Empire in Taiwan and Korea pre-dated Japanese rule. Canadian Presbyterian work in north Taiwan had begun in 1872, under the redoubtable George Leslie Mackay, and constituted the first independent Canadian mission in East Asia. Mackay came out of the Presbyterian piety of Oxford County, Ontario, which a generation later produced the founder of the North Henan Mission in mainland China, Jonathan Goforth. Mackay learned the local Taiwanese dialect (a variant of the Fujianese dialect on the adjacent mainland) and married a Taiwanese wife, known as Minnie. An expert at pulling teeth, Mackay became famous throughout northern Taiwan for introducing Western medicine and education. By any standards, Mackay was phenomenally successful: by the time of his death in 1901, after thirty years in the field, he had established sixty self-supporting chapels, each with its own pastor, and 2000 converts. Unfortunately, his indigenous, Taiwanese-speaking church seemed to have no room for foreign missionaries, and Mackay never had more than one married couple as colleagues at any time, and no single women from the WMS. Mackay is now regarded as a national hero of the Taiwanese independence movement as a symbol of its own pre-Japanese history independent from the mainland.

Yet, it should be noted that in 1895, Mackay himself welcomed Japanese rule in Taiwan and saw it as being preferable to Imperial Chinese rule. What Japanese rule brought initially was law and order and the removal of a Chinese regime and a Chinese gentry class who were seen as anti-Christian. The Japanese were seen as efficient and progressive and sympathetic to Western missionaries. Relations between Canadian and their English Presbyterian colleagues with the Japanese Government-General in Taiwan were for the most part good until the mid-1930s. It is true to say that the ordered and moral lives of Canadian missionaries generally lived served as a model for the Government-General as to how Westerners should live and behave in Taiwan.

Certainly, in the early days of Japanese colonial rule as Japan wished to show the world that it was capable of efficiently ruling a colony, little was done to curtail Western missionary activities among the Chinese population. In terms of its provisions for public health, its development of roads and railways, and provision for public education at the elementary level, there was much that the Government-General was able to achieve. The response of the Taiwanese to Japanese rule was not as negative as it was in Korea, where nationalism was deeply rooted. In general, colonial rule in Taiwan was less harsh than it was in Korea.

In reading both the Canadian and English Presbyterian reports, it is evident that Western missionaries did not concern themselves with providing much information about events happening beyond the circumscribed bounds of their Christian constituencies. While Murray Walton, an Anglican missionary from Japan, did visit the mountain tribes in the 1920s, there is little to be found in Canadian writings about the plight of Taiwanese aborigines in the eastern part of the island, which the Japanese closed to Westerners except with special permission. In that respect Canadian and English Presbyterians did not publicize the negative aspects of colonial rule.

For much of its early history, the Canadian Presbyterian mission in north Taiwan was a shoestring operation whose Christian constituency, schools, and hospital posed little challenge to the Japanese colonial Government-General or its policies. The number of Taiwanese Christians was too small to act as an opposition to the Government-General as they did in Korea, and, similarly, the number of mission schools and hospitals was too limited to serve as a viable alternative to Government-General institutions. This does not mean to say that the Mackay Memorial Hospital in Taipeh did not serve an important function as a Christian hospital serving both Taiwanese as well as the small Western community. While it flourished in terms of attracting patients through much of this period, Mackay Memorial did not have the financial resources to compete in terms of equipment and specialized staff with the Government-General hospitals. What developed over long years was a small Canadian Presbyterian mission engaged in educational, evangelistic, medical, and specialized medical work for the treatment of leprosy, and catering to a Taiwanese-speaking Presbyterian community of approximately 10,000.

The existence of various Japanese Protestant missionaries in Taiwan helped to add numbers to the Christian community being nurtured by the English and Canadian Presbyterian missionaries. While cooperation existed between the Japanese and the foreign missionaries, it is quite clear that there was little contact between them. In the 1930s, however, the Japanese Christian churches in Taiwan and their home churches in Japan did take on a heightened importance for the foreign missionary presence on the island. The importance of the Japanese Christians rose as the need for Japanese language in education increased, and Government-General regulations concerning foreign influence in religion as well as education became a factor.

It would appear that the English Presbyterians were more adept at dealing with the Japanese question than their Canadian counterparts.[14] In part, this was due to personality and longevity. Thomas Barclay, Duncan Ferguson, and William Campbell were decorated by the Japanese and, after their experiences of Manchu rule in Taiwan, were sympathetic to the Japanese and their efforts to modernize Taiwan. Indeed, in 1895 Barclay clearly went out of his way to help Hosokawa and other Japanese Christians.[15] The English Presbyterians were perhaps quicker than their Canadian counterparts to realize the need to have Japanese-speaking missionaries on their staff and in Edward Band possessed a highly talented missionary who was fluent in both Japanese and Chinese.

In the mid-1930s the quiet backwater of missionary life, characteristic of the Canadian Presbyterian mission, was punctured by the mission's victimization by the Japanese authorities beginning with the conflict over Shinto shrine attendance by pupils at the Canadian Presbyterian mission schools in Tamsui. In the effort to rid Taiwan of foreign influence, missionaries were a ready target. The anti-British feeling in the colony also broke out in the Keelung incident, in which some British bluejackets on a fleet visit to Tamsui were arrested on trumped-up charges and severely beaten by Japanese gendarmeries. Taiwan was strategically important not only for Japanese military expansion to the south toward the Philippines or to the west, into mainland China, but also as a key outpost for the defence of metropolitan Japan itself. Taiwan's military importance meant that the Japanese authorities were especially sensitive to the presence of foreigners: as it was, much of the eastern part of the island was closed to foreigners because of aboriginal headhunters.

The old treaty port of Tamsui, where the Canadian Presbyterian missionaries had their extensive property and the main mission schools (the Tamsui Middle School for boys and the Tamsui Girls' School, together with the Theological College), also happened to be a base for the Imperial Japanese Navy. The problems faced by the Canadian Presbyterians in north Taiwan are illustrative of the pressures on foreign missionaries throughout the Japanese Empire in the latter part of the 1930s.

By early 1937 the Presbyterian difficulties in Taiwan were reported in the *Fukuin Shimpō*, the Japanese Presbyterian newspaper in Tokyo, which implied that the Taiwan missionaries looked to the Japanese Presbyterians in the Nippon Kirisutokyōkai (the Japanese Presbyterian Church) to help them.[16] Indeed, the Japanese did help, particularly with finding suitable principals for schools.[17] As well as helping the missionaries, the Japanese also detected Taiwanese Christian dissatisfaction with the leadership of Western missionaries in the Presbyterian Church in Taiwan. The *Fukuin Shimpō* felt that the Japanese colonial authorities were hoping for a Japanese-led church there.[18] It is probable that Japanese Christians saw a parallel between their desire to displace foreign missionaries in metropolitan Japan from their positions of leadership and the perceived discontent with the English and Canadian Presbyterians within the Taiwanese Presbyterian Church.

However, if the Japanese had aspirations to replace Canadian or English Presbyterians within the Taiwanese Presbyterian Church, they conveniently overlooked that they, the Japanese, were still outsiders to the vast majority of Taiwanese Christians, who were either aboriginals or ethnic Chinese. Nevertheless, as became evident at the annual conference of the North Formosa Presbytery in 1937, both missionaries and Taiwanese Christians recognized the need to develop close ties with the Japanese Presbyterian Church. It was decided by the seventy

Taiwanese ministers to send four Taiwanese ministers (two of whom spoke Japanese) to visit the Presbyterians in Japan.[19] Furthermore, much attention was given to the question of Taiwanese self-support after they learned that the Presbyterian Synod in Japan had announced its decision to become self-supporting in five years. Yet, given the small number of Taiwanese Presbyterians in north Taiwan, some 10,000 out of a total 15,000 Christians in an overall population of 1,500,000, this would seem unlikely. Indeed, the conference estimated that because of the poverty of the Taiwanese congregations it would take Taiwan another fifteen years to achieve self-support. Even though self-support might take a long time to achieve, in sharp contrast to the impression given in the *Fukuin Shimpō* about relations within the church, the Taiwanese ministers were in no way dissatisfied with their Western missionary colleagues.

By February 1941, the Canadian Presbyterian mission in north Taiwan had come to an end. In the increasingly hostile international climate, every missionary had to decide whether it was possible to continue the work on the island considering the hostility of the military and police toward foreigners. Further, they had to decide that even though it might be possible, 'would the missionary be serving the Church better by quietly withdrawing from the Island and thus relieving the Church of the constant suspicion directed toward it because of its being associated with foreigners?'[20] The missionaries in Taiwan reached the decision that it was better for them to leave.

To a far greater degree than their colleagues in metropolitan Japan, missionaries had found themselves the object of growing Japanese anti-foreign sentiment. It was reported that 'it was intimated everywhere that all foreigners were spies, or potential spies, and was announced in a government-sponsored radio program in the Formosan language that missionaries were the worst of all spies, and warned the people to have nothing to do with them.'[21] In those circumstances, it was obviously trying for missionaries to conduct evangelistic work, all the more so because Taiwan was a colony under military control. As they returned home to Canada, one year short of the seventieth anniversary of the founding of the Canadian Presbyterian mission, the missionaries tried to put the best face possible on what they had left behind. While the Canadians were attempting to create an independent Taiwanese Presbyterian Church, they could not have foreseen that the future of the Taiwanese Church during the Second World War in East Asia lay with the yet-to-be-formed Union Church in Japan.

Canadian Presbyterians/United Church of Canada Missionaries in Korea and Manchuria

The reaction of Canadian missionaries to Japanese colonialism in Korea was more mixed than it was in Taiwan. In part this was simply because the nature of Japanese colonialism in the peninsula was much harsher than it was in the island. Further, from the start Japanese annexation of Korea in 1910 was met by stiff resistance from a rising tide of Korean nationalism, a factor that was largely absent in the Taiwanese response to Japanese colonial rule. The much larger Christian movement in Korea with its national network of churches and schools became identified with Korean nationalism.

It is too simplistic, however, to see Canadian missionaries in Korea as being staunch supporters of Korean nationalism and actively anti-Japanese. It has to be borne in mind that Canadian missionaries were interested in protecting their Korean Christian constituents from harm. Thus, it was quite reasonable for Canadian missionaries in Korea to be among the most vocal critics of the Japanese actions in the wake of the 1 March 1919 independence demonstrations or during the Chientao Punitive Expedition of 1920 because they had reports of Japanese committing atrocities against Korean Christians. A decade later, Canadian missionaries could be supportive of Japanese actions against Korean partisans in Manchuria during the 1930s because it was the Korean partisans who were hurting Korean Christians. In other words, missionaries were not in favour of Korean nationalistic aspirations or opposed to Japanese imperialism but, rather, they were concerned above all about the physical welfare of those Korean Christians they served. It is important to note that the Presbyterian (after 1925 the United Church) mission was in northern Korea near the border of Manchuria. Further south, away from Manchuria, the more likely it was that they would condemn the actions of the Japanese. In P'yongyang, now the capital of North Korea, well away from the dangers of the borderland, the missionaries were less sympathetic to the Japanese because they lived safe in the ordered world of colonial Korea, where the only possible danger came from the Japanese gendarmerie.

The issue of Shinto shrine attendance, which came to a head in the 1930s, can be seen as a major issue that had a different impact in each of the colonies than it had in metropolitan Japan. Within the Japanese Empire, the Japanese authorities transferred to their colonies many of the religious policies and regulations already in place in Japan and accepted by Japanese Christians. Government-General sponsorship of the state Shinto shrines in Taiwan and Korea and its insistence on the compulsory attendance of schoolchildren at shrine ceremonies was first applied in metropolitan Japan, then extended to the colonies. Likewise, with a Confucian twist, the Manchukuo (Manchurian) authorities attempted to apply to religion and mission schools the same policies adopted by the Japanese in colonial Korea. The shrine question was a key issue for Christians in the Japanese Empire: Japanese Christians, keen to show their patriotism, accepted the government position that shrine attendance was not an act of worship but rather an expression of patriotism and loyalty. The response of Korean Christians, who were supported in their resistance by Western missionaries, was to see shrine attendance as a religious act.

The question of attendance at shrine ceremonies was complicated by the fact that in Japan, Korea, and Taiwan religious freedom was guaranteed under Article 28 of the 1889 Meiji Constitution. The interpretation of the meaning of religious freedom, however, might have been open to debate, except that the Japanese government held that its interpretation was the only correct one. What is clear is that the 'religious freedom' did not stop the authorities from persecuting any religionist of whom they did not approve. Sheldon Garon has pointed out that while communism was seen as 'the unquestioned pariah in Japanese society' in the interwar period, new religions 'ranked a not-too-distant second.'[22] During the 1930s new religions in Japan such as Hitonomichi Kyōdan, Ōmotokyō, and Tenrikyō were severely persecuted. Although the major Japanese Christian denominations with the exception of the Japanese Anglicans escaped direct persecution, smaller Japanese Christian groups such as the Holiness Church, the Seventh Day Adventists, and the Salvation Army were persecuted.[23] One might cynically suggest that the persecution of these Christian groups had much to do with the state policy of thought control employed as a bureaucratic imperative, rather than because there was any real or imagined threat from the Church. Be that as it may, the persecution of Christian groups largely appealed to the Japanese lower classes, which benefited the least and suffered the most from the expanding war in China.[24] Given the government persecution of religion in metropolitan Japan, it was not surprising that this also happened in Korea when Korean Christians defied the colonial authorities over the shrine question. It is no coincidence that those persecuted in both Japan and Korea belonged to the underclass.

The Korean resistance to the shrine issue resulted in widespread persecution of the Korean Christian leadership and the closure of a number of mission schools. Yet, while Korean Presbyterians and their American missionary mentors to the south protested vigorously and courageously against the shrine ceremonies, the United Church missionaries led by William Scott in northernmost Korea took a different approach. Scott, like his United Church colleagues in Japan, most notably Howard Outerbridge, accepted the official Japanese government position that the shrine ceremonies were not a religious issue but simply a manifestation of loyalty. Scott certainly did not believe that the shrine issue was of such significance that missionary societies should close their schools in protest, as did the American Methodist Episcopalians and American Presbyterian North missions. It was much more important for the well-being of the Christian movement to have those schools opened, and to provide a Christian alternative to Government-General schools and private, secular Korean institutions.

The United Church mission in Korea took a different stand on the shrine issue than the vast majority of other Western missions in Korea. This might also have been a manifestation of liberal theology which again set it apart from the mainstream of the Western Presbyterian missions in Korea as well as the majority of Korean Presbyterians who were theologically conservative. However, by not standing firm against shrine attendance – in other words, not standing up to the Japanese even if it resulted in martyrdom – it is probable that the United Church mission lost support for Korean nationalism that was so intertwined with Korean Christianity. The United Church mission was odd man out, but it had not started that way. Duncan Macrae, one of the pioneer Canadian Presbyterian missionaries, who retired from Korea in the mid-1930s, retained a conservative outlook and was highly incensed by the stand of Scott and the younger generation of missionaries in Korea over the shrine issue.

The Japanese Christian missionary movement did not fare well in Korea. The Anglo-Catholic Korean Anglican Church, which was alone in treating Koreans and Japanese as equals within the same church, did not achieve any great growth in part because it did not seek confrontation with the Japanese. Yet it was in the years immediately after 1910, however, that the Japanese Government-General in Korea gave the most financial support to missionaries. The Japanese gendarmerie told Koreans that if they were Christians they had to attend Kumiai (Japanese Congregational) churches. Likewise, if a Korean Christian belonged to a Japanese church, he or she was able to obtain special tax relief and receive favourable treatment from the gendarmerie. The Government-General also helped to finance Christian activity in Korea by funding an increase in the number of Japanese churches and mission schools.[25] The 1 March 1919 Independence Movement demonstrations throughout Korea saw the Japanese Christian press as largely supportive of the policies of the Government-General in Seoul.[26] While there was considerable debate in the Kumiai Church, the impact of the demonstrations was such that it cut back on its work among Koreans.[27] Following 1919, Japanese Christian missionaries made little headway in Korea.

The provision of public funds for the support of Japanese missionary work abroad was the rule rather than the exception. In 1920 the South Sea Island Missionary Association, founded shortly after Japan had received the League of Nations mandate over the former German Mandated Islands in the Pacific, was given a sizable grant by the navy department.[28] This level of support was later continued by the Japanese government itself. Clearly, through their support of Japanese missionary work in Korea and the South Sea islands, the Japanese colonial authorities were attempting to utilize Japanese Christianity as a means of controlling their colonial subjects. This was also seen in Japanese Christian missionary work in Manchuria, which rapidly expanded after 1931 as Japanese responsibilities for Manchukuo became apparent.[29] Nevertheless, despite the growing presence of Japanese Christian missionaries and the persecution after 1935 of Chinese Christians with links to Western missions in Manchuria, the Canadian Presbyterian mission and other Western missions still continued to grow until 1941.[30]

The Widening War, Spiritual Mobilization, and the Empire

The Japanese Empire was in crisis from the Mukden incident in 1931, but no one could have predicted that Japan would be embroiled with the Western powers in a world war within a decade. In 1931, no Canadian missionary could have foreseen that within the same ten-year period Canadian missionary work would stop and virtually all Western missionaries would be withdrawn. In a real sense, the Western missionary movement in the Japanese Empire was a victim of decisions and priorities outside of its control. To Britain and the Western powers, Japan and East Asia were always subordinate to European concerns. For Britain the possibility of a new Anglo-Japanese Alliance, which was much talked about in 1933 and 1934, was scotched because such a new alliance would have alienated the Soviet Union. Britain needed Soviet support in eastern Europe to counter the rising power of Germany under Hitler.

Likewise, as far as Christian movements in East Asia were concerned, the participation of the Archbishop of Canterbury, Cosmo Lang, at a meeting in the Royal Albert Hall in 1937 that protested Japanese actions in China signalled the fact that Western Christians were prepared to sacrifice the Christian movements within the Japanese Empire in order to protect the Christian movement in China.[31] Even after the Albert Hall meeting Archbishop Lang continued to protest the Japanese invasion of China. Japanese suspicions of him contributed directly to pressure being put on the Japanese Anglican and Salvation Army churches to purge themselves of foreign missionaries and to divorce themselves from British influence.

The Japanese government also wanted full control over religious organizations. After the Marco Polo Bridge incident, which marked the beginning of the Second Sino-Japanese War, the Japanese government fostered a Spiritual Mobilization Campaign to mobilize and to unite religions behind the war effort; religion was to serve the nation. The government passed a Religious Bodies law that gave it increased control over religious organizations. At the turn of the century successive governments had consistently failed to pass such legislation because of the united opposition of sect Shinto, Buddhists, and Christians. In light of the China war and the need for spiritual mobilization, however, the Religious Organizations law was passed in 1939. The government also aimed to streamline religions so that they would be bureaucratically easier to control.

Thus, the government pressed for the amalgamation of all Protestant denominations in Japan into a single church. From the Meiji period onwards, there was a movement for Church Union within the Japanese Christian movement. In the early 1930s this union movement, with the support of the National Council of Churches, enjoyed new life even though the Japanese Presbyterian Church and the Japanese Anglican Church viewed it with suspicion. This changed after 1939 and led within two years to the creation of the Nihon Kirisutokyōdan (Union Church), which took place in 1941 through the union of all Protestant denominations in Japan save for the rump of the Anglican Church and some small sectarian groups. In this amalgamation process, the Japanese Protestant movement was not singled out; rather, it was part of a broader policy of religious union that also involved the amalgamation of Japanese Buddhist sects. The carrot held out to Japanese Christians by the Ministry of Education, which was in charge of religious policy, was control of the Christian movements within the Japanese Empire and Japanese-controlled areas. Amalgamation would facilitate this overseas missionary effort that the Japanese Christian movement was called upon to fulfill. By taking over the leadership of the Christian movement in East Asia, Japanese Christians were demonstrating not only their patriotism and support of Japanese national wartime goals but also allowing Japanese Christianity to become the guiding beacon for a Christianity in East Asia that was devoid of Western control and influence. In this new Christian order in East Asia, of course, Canadian or other Western missionaries had no part.

One of the desired ends of Japanese religious policies after 1937 was to bring about the voluntary withdrawal of Western missionaries; this had largely been achieved by 1941. The desire to rid the Christian movement of foreign control and influence was not restricted, of course, to the Japanese, for many Chinese Christians clearly felt the same.

Yet, Christian missions could also be used to support national goals, something which the Japanese chose to ignore but the nationalists in China very astutely exploited after 1937. The importance of Christian missions lay not in what impact they had internally – within China or in the Japanese Empire – but rather their usefulness in garnering goodwill and support overseas in the West. In the struggle for Western public opinion, China won hands down – and clearly one reason was the overwhelming support they received from the Christian constituencies in North America and Europe. Among their most vociferous supporters were Christian statesmen like the Archbishop of Canterbury and, in Canada, A.E. Armstrong, secretary of the United Church of Canada's Board of Overseas Missions. The China missionaries themselves, such as Dr Robert McClure and James G. Endicott, were also vocal critics of Japan. After 1937 the Japanese government continued to attack foreign missions in order to show the Japanese and colonial subjects alike that it could act against Christian missions without retaliation, thus revealing Britain's weakness. In doing so, they overlooked the fact that they were undercutting the attempts of missionaries in Japan, who had been overwhelmingly sympathetic to Japan, as a way to counter the anti-Japanese sentiments of China missionaries in the public opinion debate in North America and the West.

This played into the hands of the Japanese Christian leadership, who were moved by an enflamed Japanese nationalism, swayed by government appeals for Church union, and afraid of retribution (perhaps even the destruction of the Christian movement itself) if they did not comply with the perceived wishes of the government and willingly cast off their links with foreign missionaries. They willingly threw over the missionaries in order to preserve the Christian movement and to facilitate the creation of a Union Protestant church that would take on the leading role throughout Greater East Asia. Some missionaries were deeply distressed by the opportunism and lack of theological concern displayed by Japanese Christian leaders as well as the ungracious manner in which they were cast off. Nowhere was this more evident than in the rejection of Canadian missionaries and their financial help by the Anglican diocese of Mid-Japan in November 1940 after fifty years of Canadian Anglican work in that diocese. By the spring of 1941, most Western missionaries had left Japan in order to prevent the Japanese Christian leadership and Japanese Christians any further embarrassment caused by their presence in Japan.

Although the quiet, pleasant, and measured world of the Canadian missionaries in Japan (divided for the lucky ones between school terms in the cities and long holidays in the cool of the hill stations) came to an abrupt end, they were the only ones who were evicted. This did not happen in the larger Japanese Empire, where the Western missionaries, to a greater or lesser extent, acted as a protective buffer between the indigenous Christian movements and the Japanese colonial authorities. Thus, the withdrawal of Western missionaries could have a devastating impact on the local Christian community, leaving it completely at the mercy of Japanese officials. In one case, the Korean Anglican Church, which had always catered to both the Japanese and Korean communities in Korea, was saved from extinction during the war years by the selfless work of its Japanese vicar-general, Father Kudō. Yet, that was the exception.

The Japanese tolerated Western Christian missions operating in the territories of their empire for many years. Despite occasions such as the aftermath of the 1 March 1919 independence demonstrations when Canadian missionaries were openly and virulently critical of Japanese policies, the Japanese government did not demand their withdrawal. Yet Japanese governmental goodwill toward these missions was very much dependent on Japan's international relations. The intense efforts to form the union church in Japan and to rid the Japanese Christian movement of foreign influence came in the late 1930s at a time when

Japanese public opinion was violently anti-British. None of the missionaries wanted to leave their work in the Japanese Empire, and their
unwillingness was supported by the ambivalent attitude of the indigenous Christians. On the one hand, old friendships made them feel
needed. On the other, the identification of church leaders with *tennō*-
centred nationalism meant that the Canadians represented a source of
suspicion on the part of police and government agents. In its turn the
Union Church was directed toward taking over the leadership of the
Christian movements in the empire and in newly liberated territories
from the foreign missionary movement. The war gave the Japanese
Protestant movement through its overseas missionary endeavour the
opportunity to show itself as the Christian light in the East.

   With the peace in 1945, Japan was shorn of its empire. This also
meant that the Japanese Christian movement was deprived of its overseas responsibilities. While the question of the war responsibility of
the Japanese Christian leadership would eventually emerge as a con-
tentious issue within the Christian movement in the late 1960s, Western missionaries on their return to Japan with the Occupation were
animated with the desire to bring about reconciliation between
themselves and Japanese Christians. Far from being condemned for
supporting Japanese ultranationalistic aims, the Japanese Christian
leadership was lauded for saving Christianity in Japan in the face of
persecution. As the bamboo curtain came down in East Asia, those
same Christian leaders saw themselves as helping to defend freedom
and democracy within Japan against the threats posed to it by another
corrupt empire to its north.

NOTES

1 For a classic study of the issue of colonialism and missions, see Stephen
   Neill, *Colonialism and Christian Mission* (London: Lutterworth Press, 1966).
   Also see Max Warren, *The Missionary Movement from Britain in Modern History* (London: Student Christian Movement, 1967). Two important articles
   on religion and empire from a British standpoint are Andrew Porter's 'Religion and Empire: British Expansion in the Long Nineteenth Century, 1780–
   1914,' *Journal of Imperial and Commonwealth History* 20, no. 3 (1992): 370–90,
   and 'Changing People, Changing Places,' in *International Review of Missions*
   88, no. 351 (October 1999): 390–8.
2 A. Hamish Ion, *The Cross and the Rising Sun*, vol. 1: *The Canadian Protestant*

Missionary Movement in the Japanese Empire 1872–1931 (Waterloo: Wilfrid Laurier University Press, 1990); *The Cross and the Rising Sun*, vol. 2: *The British Protestant Missionary Movement in Japan, Korea, and Taiwan 1865–1945* (Waterloo: Wilfrid Laurier University Press, 1993); and *The Cross in the Dark Valley: The Canadian Protestant Missionary Movement in the Japanese Empire, 1931–1945* (Waterloo: Wilfrid Laurier University Press, 1999). For a survey of British missionary work in Japan see my 'Jujika no Shōri no tame ni: Eikoku ni yoru tai-Nichi Fukyō Katsudō no Gaikan 1869-1945,' in Tsuzuki Chushichi, Gordon Daniels, and Kusamitsu Toshio, eds, *Nichiei Kōryū Shi*, vol. 5: *Shakai: Bunka* (Tokyo: Tokyo Daigaku Shuppankai, 2001), 318–38.

3 For a general survey of Japanese imperialism, see W.G. Beasley, *Japanese Imperialism 1894–1945* (Oxford: Clarendon Press, 1984).

4 Tsukada Osamu, *Shoki Nippon Seikōkai no Kaisei to Imai Judō* (Tokyo: Seikōkai Shuppan, 1992), 14. The need for a Taiwan mission was also stressed in an editorial in the *Nichiyō Soshi*, 75 (1 February 1896). For a survey of Japanese Christian overseas missionary work in the Meiji period, see my 'Japanese Christian Overseas Missionary Movement during the Meiji Period,' *Japanese Relations* 29, nos. 1 and 2 (January 2004): 109–26. See also my 'The Cross under an Imperial Sun: Imperialism, Nationalism, and Japanese Christianity, 1895–1945,' in Mark R. Mullins, ed., *Handbook of Christianity in Japan* (Leiden: Brill, 2003), 69–100.

5 Ibid, 107.

6 See Cyril Powles's review of Ion, *The Cross in the Dark Valley* to be published in *Pacific Affairs*.

7 Ebisawa Arimichi and Ōuchi Saburō, *Nihon Kirisutokyōshi* (Tokyo: Nihon Kirisutokyōdan Shuppansha, 1971), 282–3.

8 Review by John Breen of T. Fujitani, *Splendid Monarchy: Power and Pageantry in Modern Japan* (Berkeley: University of California Press, 1996), in *Monumenta Nipponica* 52, no. 2 (Summer 1997): 268–71; quotation on 269.

9 For the persecution of members of the Kumamoto band, see George Eagleton Moore, 'Kozaki Hiromichi and the Kumamoto Band: A Study of Samurai Reaction to the West' (PhD diss., University of California, Berkeley, 1966), 132–40.

10 These arguments are clearly shown in the first major Japanese history of Meiji Christianity, Yamaji Aizan, *Essays on the Modern Japanese Church: Christianity in Meiji Japan*, translated by Graham Squires with introductory essays by Graham Squires and A. Hamish Ion (Ann Arbor: University of Michigan, Center for Japanese Studies, 1999).

11 See, for instance, Irwin Scheiner, *Christian Converts and Social Protest in Meiji Japan* (Berkeley: University of California Press, 1970).

12 James Edward Ketelaar, *Of Heretics and Martyrs in Meiji Japan: Buddhism and Its Persecution* (Princeton: Princeton University Press, 1993), 133. It is important to note that Notto R. Thelle, in investigating Buddhism and Christianity in Japan during the late nineteenth century, did differentiate between Buddhist nationalism and Christian patriotism; see *Buddhism and Christianity in Japan: From Conflict to Dialogue, 1854–1899* (Honolulu: University of Hawaii Press, 1987), 163–6.

13 See, for instance, Public Records Office, London, England, Foreign Office, 371/6586 China 1921, C. Elliot to Lord Curzon, 2 July 1921.

14 For a fuller discussion of this, see Ion, *Cross and the Rising Sun*, 2: 243–5.

15 Ibid. See Saba Wateru, *Uemura Masahisa to Sono Jidai*, 8 vols. (Tokyo: Kyōbunkan, 1977 edition), 3: esp. 273–8, 288–95. For an interesting, brief study of the English Presbyterian mission in south Taiwan and its response to Taiwanese culture, see Komagome Takeshi, 'Bunka no Chitsujo to Mishon: Ingurando Chōrō Kyōkai to Jūkyū Seiki no Buritan. Chugoku. Nihon,' in Kindai Nihon Kenkyūkai, *Nenpō: Kindai Nihon Kenkyū*, vol. 19: *Chiiki Shi no Kanōsei: Chiiki. Nihon. Sekai* (Tokyo: Yamakawa Shuppansha, 1997), 1–43.

16 *Fukuin Shimpō* (21 January 1937), 1. For the difficulties of the English Presbyterians in south Taiwan in regards to education and the Shrine Question, see Komagome Takeshi, 'Tainan Chōrō Kyō Chūgakko Jinja Sanpai Mondai: Fumieteki no Kenryoku no Yōshiki,' in *Shisō* 9 (2000): 34–63.

17 Hollington K. Tong, *Christianity in Taiwan: A History* (Taipei: China Post, 1972), 73–4.

18 *Fukuin Shimpō* (21 January 1937), 6.

19 *Presbyterian Record*, 62, no. 7 (July 1937): 212.

20 *Presbyterian Record*, 66, no. 2 (February 1941): 36.

21 Ibid, 35.

22 Sheldon Garon. *Molding Japanese Minds: The State in Everyday Life* (Princeton: Princeton University Press, 1997), 70.

23 For a recent history of Japanese Protestant Christianity during the interwar period see Kaneta Ryōichi, *Showa Nihon Kirisutokyō Shi* (Tokyo: Shinkyō Shuppansha, 1996). For details of persecution of Japanese Christians during this period, see Doshisha Daigaku Jinbun Kagaku Kenkyūjo/Kirisutokyō Shakai Mondai Kenkyūkai. *Senjika no Kirisutokyō Undō: Tokkō Shiryō ni yoru*. 3 vols. (Tokyo: Shinkyō Shuppansha, 1972); *Doshisha Daigaku Jinbun Kagaku Kenkyūjo hen. Senjika Teikō no Kenkyū: Kirisutosha. Jiyūshugisha no baai*. 2 vols. (Tokyo: Misuzu Shobō, 1978).

24 Shunsuke Tsurumi, *An Intellectual History of Wartime Japan 1931–1945* (London: KPI, 1986), 50.

25 Ibid., 557–60.

26 A selection of reports from the Japanese Christian press concerning the 1 March 1919 Movement demonstrations can be found in Ōgawa Kanji and Jig Myron Cowan, eds, *Nihon Kirisutokyō Kane Shi Shiryō* (Tokyo: Shinkyō Shuppansha, 1984), 453–550.

27 See Iinuma Jirō and Soku Hi Kan, *Nihon Teikokushugika no Chōsen Dendō* (Tokyo: Nihon Kirisutokyōdan Shuppan Kyoku, 1985), esp. 111–25.

28 Kozaki Hiromichi, *Reminiscences of Seventy Years: The Autobiography of a Japanese Pastor* (Tokyo: Kyobunkwan, 1934), 282.

29 Dohi Akio, *Nihon Purotesutanto Kyōkai no Seiritsu to Tenkai* (Tokyo: Nippon Kirisutokyōdan Shuppan Kyoku, 1975), 173–4.

30 For an overview of Canadian Presbyterian work in Manchuria, see the relevant sections of Ion, *The Cross in the Dark Valley*, vol. 2.

31 See *Kirisutokyō Sekai* (7 October 1937), 1. See also *Fukuin Shimpō* (21 October 1937), 1, and Tsukada Osamu, *Tennōseika no Kirisutokyō: Nippon Seikōkai no Tatakai to Kunan* (Tokyo: Shinkyō Shuppansha, 1981), 184.

PART III

Bringing It All Back Home

Chapter 9

The Silent Eloquence of Things:
The Missionary Collections and Exhibitions
of the Society of Jesus in Quebec, 1843–1946

FRANCE LORD

The Things of the Church

In 1925 Pope Pius XI, known as 'the Pope of Missions,' dedicated the Holy Year to the Mission and the missions of the Roman Catholic Church. To promote them, he inaugurated the Vatican Missionary Exhibition, entitled *Lux in Tenebris* (The Light in the Midst of Darkness), which displayed objects sent to the Vatican from around the world. At the close of the exhibition, he issued one of the most significant encyclicals of his pontificate, *Rerum Ecclesiae* (The Things of the Church, 28 February 1926), in which he referred to the 'silent eloquence of things' in arousing mission interest among the faithful. He hoped to establish a permanent Vatican museum to display 'these proofs of divine grace and of the nobility and greatness of the missionaries,' so that the 'faithful who visit the Museum will, We believe, experience the self-same feelings as did those who attended the original Vatican Exhibition.'[1]

The simple mention of 'silent things' in his text on the development of Catholic missions was enough to demonstrate their importance in the eyes of the church. In the exhibit and the artifacts that furnished it, Pius XI had found a 'spectacular' visual way of teaching and moving the faithful. The Catholic Church had a long history of conversion by objects, using crucifixes, holy pictures, images, scapulars, and medals as teaching tools,[2] but the novelty of using objects collected abroad – these 'missionary things' – had become a preferred medium of propaganda to instruct the faithful at home.

This chapter is an attempt to define the strategies of Catholic mission propaganda using objects and artifacts, based on the mission collections and exhibitions of the Society of Jesus (Jesuits) in Quebec from 1843 to 1946. It will shed light on this neglected aspect of Canadian Catholic missions as well as the specifically 'providential missionary vocation of French Canada' to spread the gospel to the ends of the earth. Although there has been considerable study of exhibitions and museums in nineteenth-century Canada, the specific field of missionary exhibits has hardly been touched, by historians of either Canadian Catholicism or of visual media.[3] Yet, they constitute a convincing mirror of mission practices and attitudes. Moreover, the missionary exhibitions – vast mass spectacles that combined missionary exhibits, radio and newspaper publicity, dramas, and liturgical celebrations, and were attended by hundreds of thousands of people – were a unique manifestation of Quebec's presence abroad.[4]

Canadian Roman Catholic missions had a different trajectory from Canadian Protestant missions because the inspiration and direction came from Rome, but the expression and support were primarily directed from Quebec. From the 1840s, Catholic missions worldwide experienced an unprecedented expansion. Bishop Ignace Bourget, the ultramontane bishop of Montreal, invited French orders to establish missions in Canada. Prominent among these were the Oblates, who established missions across the Canadian north and later in Africa, and the Jesuits. The Society of Jesus, which had a glorious history in the days of New France, had been suppressed in the 1760s: the last Quebec Jesuit died in 1800. In 1842 Bourget invited the reestablished Society to return to Canada, and Bishop Michael Power of Toronto granted them their historic mission in Huronia.[5] As the French orders became Canadianized, and new ones were founded, French Canadians began to establish their own missions to Canada and overseas. From the mid-nineteenth century, at first tens, then hundreds, then thousands of religious men and women from Quebec started to disseminate to the four corners of the world to bring the 'light' of the gospel to the 'pagans.'

And from those faraway lands – South America, Haiti, Africa, India, China, Japan, and others – Quebec missionaries brought back objects to educate and edify the faithful at home, to inspire vocations, as well as to raise money. Some communities accumulated valuable collections of artifacts. These could be found in the halls of convents and congregations, and in their educational and missionary museums. The most important was the Musée d'art chinois – the 'Chinese Art Museum' – opened by the Jesuits in 1931 in Sainte-Foy, a suburb of Quebec City. Two years after the Vatican Missionary Exhibit, in 1927, the Semaine

Missionnaire of Joliette inaugurated a series of national missionary exhibitions, where dozens of congregations had kiosks to display their 'missionary things.' The use of exhibitions as a tool to promote missions reached its apogee in 1942, when the *Ville-Marie missionnaire 1642–1942* exhibition was held at St Joseph's Oratory for Montreal's tricentennial celebrations.

Original Sources for Unrecognized Practices

The collections of the Quebec Jesuits offer an exceptional perspective on the 'reification' of mission propaganda using objects. Their archives, distinguished by quality and continuity, demonstrate the evolution of objects for promotion of missions since 1843. The letters, studies, and stories written by the Jesuits themselves about their missions present the context of object acquisition, and sometimes the opinions of those 'in the field' regarding collecting for that type of propaganda. By contrast, other communities do not possess the same documentary records for a long period. The Oblate collections of Inuit art are famous, but other important collections have been dispersed, such as the Soeurs Missionnaires de l'Immaculée-Conception, the largest Quebec-based overseas mission society for women, and the White Fathers, which concentrated on Africa and the Holy Land. The Société des Missions-Étrangères, a Quebec-founded congregation of lay priests dedicated to foreign missions, did not organize its archives until the 1960s.

This study would be impossible without the existence of visual sources, as well as archives. For the nineteenth century, these are limited to photographs, paintings, and drawings; by the twentieth, there are numerous iconographic documents and physical objects to illustrate the missionary exhibits in Quebec. The souvenir books of the missionary exhibitions contain photographs and floor plans, as well as lists of workers involved in the undertaking of such an enormous enterprise. The contents of the Musée d'art chinois have been deposited at the Musée de la civilisation in Quebec City in 1990, as well as most of the supporting photographs and documentary materials.

The history of the Jesuit collections in Quebec can be divided into three periods, characterized by the field that was the focus of their missions at the time: their first Amerindian missions at Kahnawake (formerly spelled Caughnawaga) near Montreal, and in Huronia from the 1840s; Alaska, from 1907 to 1912; and the China mission from 1918 to

1950. Although the sources are fragmentary, the correspondence and inventories in the Archives of the Society of Jesus in Montreal allow us to recreate the Jesuit museums, first the 'cabinet de physique' of the Collège Sainte-Marie, the secondary school in Montreal, and then the Musée d'art chinois.[6]

The acquisition of objects may lead, among other things, to a collection. However, since there was little continuity from one rector to the next, the collections of the Jesuit pioneers were random rather than systematic. The collected objects lost their practical function but gained a new symbolic function. Brother Jennesseaux's dental instruments, used in the 1860s in Ontario and exhibited at Joliette in 1927, became not only an eloquent testimony to the merit of those who brought dental hygiene to the Natives, but also revealed the hardships of the apostolic vocation.

This haphazard collecting began to change at the end of the 1870s, when the Jesuit mission of Canada became independent of New York, and Father Arthur E. Jones was appointed archivist. At the beginning of the twentieth century, the departure of French-Canadian Jesuits to Alaska brought new ethnographic and artistic material. This was a trial period for collecting, preserving, and exhibiting objects and documents related to the Society's past and present missions. The documents remain more or less the same, but they give evidence of a deeper thought concerning the acquisition of artifacts and of frequent references to building a collection.

From 1918, the French-Canadian Jesuits expanded to their first overseas mission, in Xuzhou (formerly spelled Süchow or Hsü-chow), in Jiangsu (formerly spelled Kiangsu) province of eastern China. This led to an intensification of the circulation of objects to promote the work of missions; consequently, the relevant sources multiply. The Society asked its missionaries to send artifacts for the first expositions missionnaires, so that by 1931 it had enough to stock the Musée d'art chinois. Unlike the fragmentary sources for Ontario and Alaska, the sources concerning collecting in China permit us to understand the paths of the objects in missionary promotion. In addition, we have access to an important number of the objects themselves: the contents of the museum. The museum also had a 'curio' shop which sold 'souvenirs' such as ivory cigarette holders, fans, and back-scratchers, the stuff of a typical Chinatown.

Printed sources increase exponentially with the missionary exhibitions. The souvenir albums include rich and essential documentation for analysis of the displays in which the Society of Jesus was actively involved. They recount the process which preceded the exhibition – its initiation, implementation, and achievement – and showed the process of approval, design, and construction. In other words, they reveal the apparatus which supported the exhibition: the committees, religious ceremonies, conferences, theatre, radio shows, press releases, and so forth. Finally, they demonstrate how the 'missionized' were 'represented' through the mass exhibition.

Considering the novelty of the subject, the use of objects in Catholic mission propaganda, I will focus on the acquisition of objects in the mission fields and the purpose of those objects. This allows us to identify the acquisition agents, to define their motivations and their choices, as well as the locations and modes of acquisition. The Jesuit experience in Alaska and China shows how the missionaries in the field improvised: sometimes as enthusiastic amateurs, sometimes as reluctant buyers. Thus, Father Édouard Laflèche wrote in 1935, 'Many nights, I would prefer to have seen myself in Süchow, cramming the Chinese language, the prose, not the art.'[7] Many artifacts were acquired by donation, such as products of the industrial schools or gifts to the individual missionary that he in turn presented to his superior, or by purchase. Many more were purchased wholesale: the Jesuits in Quebec would send shopping lists for objects from Shanghai or mission orphanages. These inventories were sometimes huge, for example, 3000 fans sent in less than two years. These transactions rested on two fundamental economic bases: they financed the mission economy, which sold the craft productions from its industrial schools and orphanages, and the secular trade in 'curios,' which the mission took part in.

Collecting Canada

The Jesuits had a long history of establishing museums, going back to the famous 'cabinet' of Athanasius Kircher at the College of Rome, the Musaeum Kircherianum, which dated to the 1650s. Kircher 'used his position at the center of the world-wide Jesuit order to enlarge it with exotica from Egypt, the Far East and the Americas as well as with mechanical, optical and acoustic instruments of his own devising.'[8] By the eighteenth century most Jesuit colleges had a *'cabinet de physique,'* a scholarly version of the 'cabinets of curiosities' of wealthy collectors. In the missions, too, the Jesuits established museums, such as the famous Heude museum and observatory at Xujiahui (formerly spelled Ziccawei), the Catholic complex in Shanghai, where Father Teilhard de Chardin S.J. displayed his fossils of early humans.

When the French Jesuits returned to their ancient field of Huronia in 1843, everything had changed since they had departed almost a century earlier. During the second half of the seventeenth century, the Hurons, decimated and dispersed, had abandoned their lands to the Iroquois, who soon lost it to the Ojibwa. After the American Revolution, Upper Canada (Ontario) was opened to waves of settlers. Huronia had been transformed into farmland, and the Amerindians were restricted to 'reserves.' 'By resettling most of the southern Ontario Ojibwa bands into areas where they had little chance of participating in the emerging agricultural economy, the settler society pushed the Ojibwa to the economic and geographic margins of Canada West [Ontario] before Confederation.'[9] By 1920 the Jesuits had missions to the Ojibwa, Ottawa, and Iroquois from Huronia to Wawa, Manitoulin Island to Kahnawake.

There is little in the correspondence to indicate the missionaries were actively assembling a collection. Nevertheless, even though the objects sent from the Amerindian missions were varied, they were always associated with three interests: the direct work of the apostolate, the teaching of science to high school students in Quebec, and the history of the Jesuits in New France. For example, in 1844 Father Jean-Pierre Choné wrote from the mission at Sainte-Croix on Manitoulin Island that he was raising a 'lottery in France to build a church here. I have asked my Savages to make all sorts of objects in the way for the prizes of the lottery.' The typed version of Choné's diary reads (in English): 'First hint of a *new church* to be built, and first effort to raise money with a box of Indian bark work, which brought back from France $600.00.'[10] The question arises whether these objects, destined to be sold for a profit in France, were given as gifts or whether they were exchanged for useful goods by the Natives. Other missionaries noted the Ojibwa bartered handicrafts, such as birchbark, porcupine quills, baskets, and furs, in exchange for 'cloth and other small provisions.'[11]

During the nineteenth century, there was considerable interest in Europe for North American ethnographic material. The idea of the imminent extinction of the Native populations – the 'vanishing races' – was repeated by politicians, missionaries, artists, and collectors on both sides of the Atlantic. The multiplication of pictures and exhibits created a popular stereotype of Amerindians as romantic and exotic.

The objects the Jesuits sent to France were meant to show that the Natives were not just 'savages,' but were capable of producing useful, everyday objects, thus demonstrating their humanity and their capacity for conversion. On the other hand, they sent few objects to Quebec, where tomahawks and baskets might have been considered less exotic or rare.

Surviving ethnographic objects collected in North America are not numerous. One important collection, though, of quilled barkwork given to Father Edward Purbrick, an English Jesuit, on a tour of inspection of Amerindian missions in Ontario, is deposited at the Museum of Mankind, in London, England.[12] We can also rely on the few mentions in the *Lettres des Nouvelles missions du Canada*, the printed letters that circulated among the international Society. The objects that could be shipped to Europe had to be small and portable. Since it was impossible to send large objects such as tents or canoes, models were preferred as well as baskets or table mats. But nothing suggests a systematic collection intended to preserve the material culture of a dying race, or a regrouping of the trophies of conversion, pagan objects confiscated by the missionaries. Incidentally, examples of the destruction of convert 'idols' or ritual objects such as drums are few.

The choice of ethnographic objects was further restricted by the poverty of the Amerindians, who could not spare their essential implements such as bowls and weapons. Here is the description – and judgment – given by Father Choné of their meagre material universe. The savage, he wrote,

> takes care of the precautions for daily living, for food, clothing, habitation and work. He is a man who suffers the most difficult things when necessity commands, without being instructed by the experience not to fall into new necessities. When he has to eat, he eats and lies down in his lodge; when he has nothing, he hunts. The Indian's shirt, very long, a buffalo skin blanket that he wears like a shawl: that is the clothing of the savage. Those who have contact with white people make a *redingote* [frock coat] with wool blanket which they receive every year from the English government. In winter, they wear shoes of skins they prepare themselves. Their habitation is traditional. The savage cuts several branches in the shape of a cone, the foundation being several planks of wood: that's his house. Three planks form his bed and table; a lamp, a bow or rifle, a line for fishing: there is the furniture of his lodge in the middle of which is the fireplace.[13]

At the time this undirected collecting was taking place, the Collège Sainte-Marie in Montreal enriched its own museum, mainly a *'cabinet de physique'* that had been in existence since the 1850s. *'Physique'* or 'Natural Science' was taught in the final two years of the classical Jesuit education, under the rubric of Philosophy. The *cabinets de physique* were teaching museums, with diverse specimens of natural history, antiquities, ethnographic objects, works of art, coins, and medals, as well as scientific instruments such as electrical devices and microscopes. Early twentieth-century photographs of the Collège museum show armoires and glass cases filled with stuffed birds and mammals, a placard of butterflies from Europe and North America, albums of plants, shells, fossils, everything from 'the most humble minerals up to the most varied products of industry.'[14] The museum had to be a mirror of God's creation as well as an epitome of Canada's national resources. The latter notion was summed up by the history of the museum: 'Chosen for the purpose of education, these treasures speak also to our hearts as Canadians. They indicate that our beautiful country possesses the animals which provide the glory and the wealth, the plants which embellish it, the minerals which make it fascinating, the original artifacts and all the varied products which industry manufactures. We want to convince them [the students] gently to love the country in order to protect against foreign monopolies or illogical and even dangerous exports.'[15]

Without doubt, the Jesuit ideal of amateur naturalist, collector, and teacher was Father Edmond Rottot, who was stationed at Sudbury from 1882 to 1915. He collected specimens of local flora and fauna, classified and labelled them, and exchanged them with colleagues in Europe. He consulted experts, such as priest Léon Provancher, an experienced naturalist and editor of the *Naturaliste canadien*. Their correspondence confirms their mutual interest in the scientific life of the time. Another naturalist was Father Joseph Richard, a missionary in Ontario for seventy years, who assembled specimens of practically every plant which grew in northern Ontario. Yet, outside of Rottot's collection, references to systematic collecting in the Ontario missions are almost nonexistent. The 'meagre corpus' of the museum was reflected in its comparative value: in 1884 the collections of the Collège Sainte-Marie were valued at $4000, while those of the Redpath Museum at McGill University were worth $60,000.[16]

There was one area which the Jesuits did collect assiduously, 'to gather all the relics connected to the history of the former missions of the Company of Jesus in Canada.'[17] Since the Society had been dissolved for forty years, this interest in their own history was not surprising: 'The elderly members ... and their younger brethren had to look to the order's history in an attempt to rediscover their origins. It was not long before French Jesuits began to examine the triumphs and sacrifices of their missionary predecessors in the New World. The Jesuit martyrs, after all, remained heroes of the Church.'[18] Immediately after the Jesuits returned to Canada, Father Félix Martin went in quest of manuscripts, of every relic in fact, of this history. Taking advantage of his involvement in Montreal's cultural life, Martin met with the city's first mayor and learned collector, Jacques Viger. This friendship led to a serious collaboration and fruitful research trips. Thus the Hospitalières de l'Hôtel-Dieu de Québec loaned, and then donated, the manuscripts that had been entrusted to them by Father Joseph Casot, the surviving Quebec Jesuit who had died in 1800.

In 1857 Martin also made a trip to Europe, financed by the Canadian government, to procure documents from France and Rome. 'For several years, particularly since the two fires which had consumed the library of the Legislative Assembly, at Montreal in 1849 and Quebec City in 1855, the government had set out to reconstitute and also to research the documents relative to the history of the country.'[19] It was not just documents the Jesuits sought, but particularly relics of their martyrs of Huronia. Martin, and later the archivist Father Arthur E. Jones, undertook amateur excavations at Sainte-Marie-among-the-Hurons, near Midland, the fenced village where two Jesuit fathers, Jean de Brébeuf and Gabriel Lalemant, were martyred.[20] It is also worth mentioning the 'heritage collection' of the mission of Saint-François-Xavier de Kahnawake, strongly connected to the person of Kateri Tekakwitha: the Iroquois virgin who died in the odour of sanctity in 1680, was beatified in 1980.

The Jesuit archives became a repository of inestimable value for the religious history of Canada – the History of Canada, in fact – acquired through legacies and donations. One product of their labour was the contribution of archivist Father Jones to the publication of the multiple volumes of the *Jesuit Relations and Allied Documents* by American Jesuit Reuben G. Thwaites from 1896 to 1901. Martin's and Jones's collected material was also exhibited on various occasions in the United States and France. Thus, by assembling (and exhibiting) the history of their predecessors, the nineteenth-century Jesuits were creating 'a true cult of heroes, religious and lay, of New France.'[21] Moreover they were giving the New France martyrs an international visibility. In this endeavour they were working towards the recognition by Rome of the saintliness of the Jesuit heroes.

It is impossible to compare the quality and the quantity of the collections of primary sources to those of the few archaeological specimens related to the ancient Huronia missions. Though Martin and Jones were involved in early diggings at Sainte-Marie-among-the-Hurons, they remained historians. And thus the first object of their quest was the written document. Digging would only confirm the content of the letters and maps they had previously found. It would also justify their re-appropriation of the mission's site.

Collecting Alaska

In 1907, the Society of Jesus elevated the mission of Canada to a Province, and as a sign of its maturity, Rome confided its first 'foreign' mission, to Alaska. The first Jesuits in Alaska, which had been acquired by the United States from Russia in 1867, were two Italians from the Rocky Mountain mission. They were companions of Charles-Jean Seghers, the Belgian bishop of Vancouver Island, who sailed for Juneau in 1886. But Seghers was murdered by his servant, a paranoid schizophrenic, and was falsely considered a martyr, since he did not die for his faith. Alaska was at first confided to the Turin Jesuits, under whose auspices the first French Canadian, Father Jules Jetté, was sent in 1898, at the time of the gold rush. Thus, just as the nineteenth-century Jesuits followed the ghosts of New France, the twentieth-century priests were new pioneers among the Natives on a barren and faraway land that possessed the same potential for sacrifice and martyrdom as Huronia had. When a novice asked Father Jetté 'Why Alaska?' he responded, 'Because there, one can suffer more for our Saviour.'[22]

The Canadian mission to Alaska lasted only five years, from 1907 to 1912, when it was transferred to the California Jesuits, and counted a total of seventeen Canadian priests. Nevertheless it marked a period of expansion for the Society in Canada as well as a watershed in the 'museification' of its missionary experience. In 1908, the Provincial, Father Édouard Lecompte, and his assistant Father Albert Bellemare, made a pastoral visit to the stations in Alaska. At that time Bellemare wrote about the clear intention of his superior to create 'a special department for the things from Alaska'[23] in the museum at the Collège Sainte-Marie. This collection would be a prestigious memento of the newly acquired autonomy of the Jesuit Province as well as of its first truly Canadian mission abroad.

This Jesuit mission effort coincided with the world expansion of the Catholic mission under Pope Leo XIII (1878–1903). By the end of his pontificate, ethnology and anthropology had become components of Catholic mission theory – the 'science of missions' – in order to rival Protestant missiology. Following this new trend the Jesuits had participated in the International Congress of Americanists held in Montreal in 1906, which had the 'object of historical and scientific studies of the two Americas and their inhabitants.'[24] Father Jetté himself published an article, 'On the Medicine-Men of the Ten'a,' in the *Journal of the Royal Anthropological Institute of Great Britain and Ireland*.

The will to collect Alaskan artifacts came from the leaders of the Quebec Jesuits and had a double impact on the missionary collections. The example of the Ontario missions showed a general practice of selling objects to raise money that varied according to time and circumstances. Now, the strategy of collecting became more precise and the sort of objects diversified.

The Alaskan collection of the Collège Sainte-Marie has not survived, except for a few objects which are inaccessible to researchers. So we are forced to rely on the catalogue cards entitled 'Ouvrages des Esquimaux' ('Works of the Eskimos'). The majority of objects, fifty out of sixty-one cards, were collected by Lecompte and Bellemare in 1908. The inscription noted: 'Works of the Esquimaux, men, women, and children. Many were made by the little boys and girls of the industrial school, and given by the respective superiors, the Sisters of Sainte-Anne, brothers, etc.'[25] Offering gifts to a visiting superior was a well-proven practice. Just as the written account or the photograph, it witnessed the missionary work and progress by showing the ability and the 'humanity' of the converts. Certain of the given objects were the products made by Dena and Inuit children under the missionaries' care. Made for a useful purpose, to clothe a child or to pay the school fees, for example, these objects were therefore invested with a new function as propaganda: the missionaries in the field offered tangible evidence of their labours to their superior. Certainly, the practice of gifts did not allow Lecompte to discriminate between objects, but with this mode of acquisition he did receive objects preselected, approved by his subalterns.

Not all the objects were made by the schoolchildren. Others were received as gifts from the 'missionized' by the missionary. This offering, either a gesture of gratitude or barter, was taking place in the less formal context of the mission's everyday life. Jetté wrote to his mother, the wife of the lieutenant governor of Quebec, 'This winter I have received among other presents, a bear skin, a winter hat of beaver skin, two pairs of mittens, a pair of moccasins, a pair of slippers. Never do I buy these things: they are always given to me in abundance. I do not mention the less important objects, which I accept in order not to cause pain to the poor people who offer them from a good heart, but which I give away at the first occasion.'[26] But despite Jetté's scholarly interest in Dena culture, there is no evidence that he provided the Collège Saint-Marie's museum with Alaskan artifacts.

Finally, the Jesuits were not merely passive recipients of gifts: they were provided small sums to purchase articles. The correspondence of Father Bellarmin Lafortune, for example, shows that the Inuit perceived him as a potential buyer for their 'antiquities.' 'When they find objects [of superstition], they bring them to me and ask me if I do not want to buy a demon or two.'[27] At the time the Jesuits came to Alaska, the Inuit of the coast were already commonly trading with the Amerindian populations of the interior, the Asians of the Bering Strait, and Westerners such as whalers, merchants, and explorers. Therefore the missionaries entered into the commercial activities of the Natives. According to the biographer of Lafortune, when the whaling boats stopped at the Diomede Islands, 'In accordance with customary procedure of trading in the nineteenth century, the Eskimos usually came aboard with their fur products, meat, fish, old tools, walrus ivory tusks, and often vast quantities of baleen, the popular "whalebone" used for women's corset stays. At certain places, and Little Diomede Island was one of them, they also brought small ivory carvings to trade or sell.'[28]

The Alaskan collection of the Collège museum reflected in part this market: furs, ivories, tools, and utensils. Yet the catalogue cards, which would suggest a collection that was organized scientifically, contain very little information, usually one or two words. However, at times Lafortune did send short explanations about his artifacts and Bellemare tried to obtain maps and written documents related to Alaska. But this effort of contextualization does not show in the catalogue.

The collection brought together a few models of dog sleighs and canoes as well as a large number of fur parkas and snowshoes, which 'show the way which the missionary is obliged to dress to protect him from the intense cold in these glacial regions.'[29] These objects were strongly related to the missionaries' way of living. The Jesuits did not choose to collect adornments, ritual dresses, clothing for women and children, or even summer clothing: in other words, they collected what they themselves wore. They kept this extraordinary and exotic fur costume which they had to wear in order to withstand the hostile environment. The clothing collection appeared to be more a representation of the Jesuit missionaries themselves than one of the Dena or the Inuit populations. As for the ivory objects, they seem to have been inspired by the tastes of a tourist clientele, such as a figurine of a baseball player, serviette rings, inkwell, paperweight, paper cutter, and ladies' buttons.[30] Utensils, containers, wooden statuettes, sculpting, fishing, and hunting tools, as well as archaeological specimens, also figured in the catalogue.

Was this collection the embryo of a scientific project, systematically gathered? In the development of what anthropologists and historians call the 'museum period' of anthropology, this attempt fits into the mainstream of nineteenth-century museums, but at a much smaller scale. But we shall not compare the collecting of a handful of French-Canadian missionaries to the 'scramble for artifacts' launched by the large anthropological museums of Europe and United States.[31]

After the loss of Alaska by the Canadian Jesuits in 1912, their sudden disinterest for the 'things of Alaska' clearly demonstrates their lack of intention to pursue the ethnographic project at the Collège museum. Everything indicates that the collection of Alaskan artifacts was due principally to a personal interest of Father Édouard Lecompte. In fact, the Canadian fathers collected these objects to support the Alaskan mission, to increase the prestige of the Province of Canada, and to edify their students. Thus they were on the margin of learned ethnological research, and the collection of Alaskan Inuit became a showcase of a new Canadian mission product, and then disappeared.

Collecting China

Six years after the Alaska mission was transferred to the California Jesuits, in 1918, the first French Canadians went to China under the auspices of the French mission in Shanghai. In 1924, when the Canadian Province was divided into independent Provinces of Lower (Quebec) and Upper (Ontario) Canada, the Quebec Jesuits were granted their own field in Xuzhou, a rural district between Shanghai and Beijing, which they operated until their expulsion after the Chinese revolution of 1949. The French-Canadian Jesuits also sojourned in Shanghai and Beijing, where they established the Chabanel international language school.

Like Alaska, Xuzhou had its own mystic appeal and missionary challenge. A poor rural area – *la brousse* (the bush), the missionaries called it – Xuzhou proved to be a particularly tragic field. In the 1920s, it was the scene of the *beifa*, the punitive Northern Expedition launched by the Nationalist army of Chiang Kai-Shek against the warlords in central and northern China. Since the main railway line from Shanghai to Beijing passed through the district, in 1937 Xuzhou became a major battlefield during the Japanese invasion and remained in Japanese hands until the end of the Second World War. The Canadian Jesuits were interned by the Japanese during the war. Afterwards the mission's position did not grow brighter, leaving Xuzhou devastated by a decisive battle of the civil war between the Nationalists and the Communists. Densely populated, the area was also exposed to droughts, floods, and frequent brigandage.[32]

In Quebec, the founding of the Chinese mission was the occasion for deploying what the Xuzhou diocese historian Father Rosario Renaud (who spent forty years in China) called a *complexe apostolique*, a range of propagandist tools 'to vivify the vocations and to obtain the essential support of the Catholics' prayers and alms.'[33] The purpose was to create a *mentalité missionnaire* among the population:

> We wanted to penetrate every class of society, and the program which we embarked upon [at the Joliette exhibition of 1927] included all the media: preaching, catechisms, conferences, diffusion of the letters from our missionaries, photos, calendars, cinema, poetry, songs and plays, organization of circles and leagues, of sewing rooms and expositions, articles in newspapers, founding reviews, publication and sale of works on the Missions, etc. Within less than ten years, we had realized and more this imposing conception of missionary propaganda.[34]

Gathering artifacts from China became part of this offensive. The first objects were brought back by three scholastics (nonordained philosophy and theology students) in 1923: 'Everywhere they raised such astonishment and provoked so many questions about China and the Chinese that we dreamt of reassembling them in a place open to the public.'[35] It was clear from the beginning that objects were, on the one hand, to be collected for exhibition and, on the other, to be sold for a profit. Thus in 1926 the scholastic Georges Marin asked his colleagues in Shanghai: 'As for objects, send everything you can. Try to get presents from the students, etc. Nevertheless, nothing in bamboo because bamboo springs here from dryness. *Buy* things too. Everything can bring a profit five times or more, if you organize a euchre with these objects as prizes, as we are going to do this year.'[36] Marin's request recalls Father Choné sending a lottery from Manitoulin Island to Paris in 1844. Indeed, some requests from Canada were quite explicit that the objects, whether given or purchased, were destined to be sold at a profit for the mission. Four years later, Philippe Côté, then a language student at Xujiahui and future bishop of Xuzhou, reported that he had spent $3000 for a forthcoming missionary exhibition, and had sent thirty-three cases, including six hundred fans. 'Everything is pretty, and everything can be sold, I believe,' he wrote.[37]

Despite the stock market crash, the commerce in Chinese *bibelots* (knickknacks) continued to the point that in 1934 the procurator and founder of the Musée d'art chinois, Father Joseph-Louis Lavoie, opened a boutique attached to the museum. Lavoie, who managed the mission's financial affairs, wrote to a colleague in China that he had

> set about to organize a store that was not ordinary. I asked the Monsignor [Georges Marin] to advance me $1,000. Do not act extravagantly with it. But buy me knickknacks which are not foolish, but which are at a popular and reasonable price ... Make sure to find the object which will tempt, or the truly useful object ... Keep this in mind: for the store, of the articles which bring in a profit of 100% when sold for 25 cents to $1.00, you must send us the largest quantity. Then the articles for $2.00, and $3.00 to $10.00. In inverse proportion of the price, calculate the quantity.[38]

Father Lavoie did not discuss the authenticity of the object, or its rarity, antiquity, or even its aesthetic value: he was concerned with pleasing the buyers. The benefactors and visitors to the museum could leave with an object 'Made in China,' evidence not of a real visit to China but a visit to the Chinese museum. Moreover the exotic souvenir or the useful object became a personal material proof of a contribution to the Jesuits' missionary work.

All the Chinese artifacts bought by the Jesuits did not finish their journey in someone's living room. The missionaries wanted to show China to the public – at least their interpretation of China. They wanted to gather a collection to be exhibited within the Society or at missionary exhibitions. Most of that collection was acquired before the actual opening of the Musée d'art chinois in 1931. This corpus could not compare with the Chinese archaeological and artistic treasures of the Royal Ontario Museum in Toronto, much of which was collected by Protestant missionaries, such as Bishop W.C. White and Rev. Dr James M. Menzies, discussed by Linfu Dong in chapter 12.[39]

In fact, considered from the perspective of mission propaganda, the acquisition and collecting of Chinese objects by the French-Canadian Jesuits calls for an entirely different interpretation, distinct from the questionings of archaeology and history of art. These were not Chinese art in the conventional sense of fine art, but rather chinoiserie, things crafted in the Chinese style for Western markets.

The collection brought together furniture, handicrafts, and 'oriental madonnas,' mostly made in the large workshops and the sewing rooms of the French orphanages in Shanghai. Like the missionaries in Alaska, the Jesuits in China entered into existing commercial activities between the Chinese and the Europeans dating as far back as the six-teenth century. The art of Xujiahui expressed the capacity and the virtuosity of the converts to build furniture with taste. Within the mis-sionary context, the chinoiseries became material evidence of the civi-lizing accomplishment of the Catholic mission. For the Jesuits, as professional propagandists, collecting 'cross' furniture – Western style with Chinese wood and ornament – as well as liturgical objects al-lowed them to illustrate the conversion of their Chinese protégés and, at the same time, to offer the museum visitor exhibits with which they could easily identify.[40]

Unlike their French colleagues in China, the Quebec Jesuits could not count on experienced sinologists for collecting outside the orphan-ages' circuit. Some missionaries like Lavoie[41] or Renaud can be seen as amateurs with a genuine sensibility for Oriental culture, but mission charges claimed most of their time. Therefore collecting was often per-formed empirically if not in total ignorance of the value and the use of the objects. In general the Jesuits responsible for acquiring artifacts depended on the orders and advice of their colleagues at home. Young priests and language students were confused by the inventories they were expected to fill from Canada. Answering an order placed by tele-gram, Brother Émile Lord wrote to Lavoie: 'A telegram is always a difficult thing to correctly interpret and not knowing what those mer-chandises were for, I was in an awkward position to make a choice: hopefully this will slightly come up to your expectations.'[42] They were

The silent eloquence of things: Interior of the Musée d'art chinois, at 183 Grande Allée, Quebec City, about 1935. This museum was first opened on the Chemin Sainte-Foy in 1931 by the French-Canadian Jesuits to promote their missions and raise money. The contents are now in the Musée de la civilisation in Quebec City.

also torn by their desire to support the mission by buying products of the orphanages and industrial schools – thus demonstrating the high quality of the students' work – even though the cost was often more than in the street markets.[43] Yet the procurator's museum was rapidly perceived as a luxury by missionaries 'in the bush.' Animosity arose. For them, the maintenance of a building for the museum and the collecting expenses were a burden a poor mission like Xuzhou could not afford.[44]

The Permanent Show at the Musée d'art chinois

Although the idea of a 'little museum' of Chinese artifacts went back to 1923, the immediate trigger was the missionary exhibition at Montreal in 1930, where the Jesuits and other communities displayed hundreds of objects from China and from around the world. Since 1929, a Chinese collection, including a rickshaw, had been housed temporarily in the Kateri Tekakwitha Hall at Kahnawake, an incongruous juxtaposition of Chinese and Iroquoian artifacts under the responsibility of the Saint Francis Xavier Jesuit mission. But as soon as the Montreal show closed, the artifacts were taken to Quebec City, where Father Joseph-Louis Lavoie shortly inaugurated his Chinese art museum. It was inspired by the Vatican Missionary Exhibition of 1925, as well as the museum at the University of Louvain, Belgium, which displayed objects from the Belgian Congo. More ambitiously, Lavoie even suggested the province should 'purchase' the contents of the Heude museum at Xujiahui, a renowned encyclopedic institution founded by the French Jesuits.

The Musée d'art chinois, as Lavoie named it, was located beyond a Chinese-style gate in a mansard mansion at 653 chemin Sainte-Foy, a prestigious address on the main boulevard, next door to the Procure des Missions. In 1934, it was moved to more spacious grounds on the Grande Allée, an elite street in the Upper Town. 'But why should a Chinese Museum be annexed to the Procure des missions of China?' wrote Father Lavoie – who described himself as a 'beggar by profession' – when the museum opened. 'Let us say quite frankly: we have to sustain and develop our Mission which needs a lot of money. A Museum has a better chance of attracting visitors than the procurator's office alone, don't you think? And among the visitors, it could join an excellent heart with a large purse.'[45] In other words, the procurator was convinced that the Chinese mission bureau would be more 'attrac-

Xiujiahui art. This collection of 'Chinese things' was made by the orphans and schoolchildren at the Jesuit complex in Shanghai. They were displayed in Quebec to convey 'the beautiful face of China' at a time when the Jesuit mission was occupied by the Japanese.

tive' for the visitor-benefactor if it were coupled to a museum, reinforcing the economic function of the object. For the museum director, the museum also had a less prosaic, but just as apostolic, value: to provide an educational and aesthetic experience for the visitor. The collection would convey a positive narrative of Chinese civilization which would reveal a different but valuable culture. Thus benefactors would contribute to the mission in an enlightened way.

The museum exhibited its collection and photographs in a cozy setting: mostly rooms arranged in a bourgeois atmosphere with glass cases and furniture of a mixed cultural influence – 'Chinese but not too much.' The most spectacular object was an 'imperial bed,' an ornately carved baldachin that supposedly was looted from the imperial Summer Palace in 1859 and found its way to the Quebec harbour.[46] Yet, the museum did shelter some ethnographic material, such as cult objects, figurines, games, pipes, and musical instruments. All were symbolically locked in glass cases illustrating the spiritual power of the Society over the 'superstitious' Chinese they wanted to convert.

One order list drawn up by Georges Marin in 1927 gives a hint about artifacts he wanted:

a) A complete winter costume for a man: gown, *gilet* [waistcoat], and pants. Nothing extraordinary, but to the contrary, very common such as the majority wear at Siu-tcheou [Xuzhou]: a wadded outfit. The same thing for a little girl.

b) A winter hat or head-gear of Siu-tcheou. Always the very common style worn by the people. We don't want to give them false ideas.

c) Straw shoes for winter.

d) The equivalent of our rubbers for winter.

e) A complete table service for four people: bowls, chopsticks, little plates, a large earthenware tea pot, a bucket for rice, etc.

f) Fans of diverse sorts for men and women; a series of pipes of different lengths and types; a variety of lanterns, etc.

g) Objects of superstition and cults: 2 or 3 gods, one of considerable dimensions, let us say one and a half feet tall; red candles (2); a print of the god of the hearth; two vertical and one horizontal inscriptions suitable for the decoration of an altar with the two gods you are sending; sticks of incense; an incense burner; and paper money which they burn at the graves; etc.[47]

It seems objects 'from the bush' were only incorporated into the museum exhibit in 1935, a suggestion made by the Father Provincial Adélard Dugré, back from an official trip to China. At that time, Lavoie had grand ambitions for his museum. He had put up a catalogue in order to obtain a government grant and wanted to buy Chinese antiquities. Should Lavoie not please his superior, in order to fulfill his goals, by adding an exhibit depicting the missionary realities of Xuzhou? Yet in spite of this 'missiologic' effort, the Jesuit museum remained the 'Musée d'*art* chinois' of Father Lavoie.

Lavoie kept banking on the rich-looking building of the museum and its bourgeois interior. By exhibiting Chinese Christian art, hybrid furniture with familiar forms, and exotic furniture in a familiar setting, the Jesuits defined China according to Western terms, common to the members of the Society and the visiting public. Moreover this scenography celebrated civilized China. 'To conceive of and to achieve art works you must be civilized.'[48] wrote Lavoie in the visitor's guide. Above all, China was a world capable of becoming Christian. Although the museum was built to shatter prejudices against Chinese people, the image of China given by Lavoie was a distorted one, far from the daily life of workers and peasants from Xuzhou.

Over the years, the Procure des missions and its museum did not attract crowds: one day, fifteen, another day, ten visitors. Yet this modest but constant flow of visitors from Quebec and the United States was enough to clear all the stock of Chinese curios from the boutique of the museum. It brought thousands of people to subscribe to the Jesuit missionary review, *Le Brigand*. Finally the museum 'seduction' also led elderly visitors to bequeath their property to the Society.

Exhibiting the Missions

The Vatican Missionary Exhibition of 1925 inaugurated a 'powerful means of propaganda,' the mass missionary exhibition.[49] Two years later, the first exhibition in Quebec was held at Joliette, a small town near Montreal where the relevance of a missionary exhibition would be tested by the church. Joliette's success was conclusive. This was followed by 'missionary weeks' in Montreal in 1930; Trois-Rivières in 1935; Sherbrooke in 1941; Montreal again in 1942 for the tricentennial of the city; and Saint-Hyacinthe in 1951. They were also held outside Quebec: Ottawa in 1943; Gravelbourg, Saskatchewan, 1944; and Saint-Boniface, Manitoba, 1945. The efficacy of these exhibitions, which lasted only a week or two, was founded on their temporary nature. They fit the description of the world's fairs and mass expositions – what we would call blockbusters – 'spectacular gestures which briefly held the attention of the world before disappearing into abrupt oblivion, victims of their planned temporality.'[50] But during the time, the exhibition was accompanied by an all-encompassing barrage of propaganda in the media, making a deeper impression than a museum permanent exhibit. The *Ville-Marie missionnaire 1642–1942*, held at St Joseph's Oratory, Montreal, in the depths of the Second World War, was described as a 'city of a thousand architectures,' attended by over 400,000 people.[51]

The organization model of the missionary exhibits in Quebec was obviously clerical, but the laity was nevertheless present. The clergy called on reliable underlings, members of religious associations, students, and alumni. They also called upon professional artists and crafts workers to create a 'matchless spectacle.' The organization left no room for improvisation; everything was worked out, from publicity and fundraising to the visual sightlines of each kiosk. Like many other aspects of the Catholic life (the Eucharist, saints calendar, jubilees, etc.), the exhibitions were often associated with commemorative events. In Quebec, these commemorations blended the apostolic ideal and the national pride together – for example, the 400th anniversary of the planting of the cross at Trois-Rivières. The exhibits were located in buildings large enough to hold the exhibit, its conferences, plays, and other related activities: seminaries, military bases, or churches. These places strongly recall the conquering power of the church and the army – the notions of recruiting, educating, as well as mobilizing – notions all perfectly adapted to the discourse of the exhibition.

The organizers saw the exhibitions as a true illustration of the 'providential missionary vocation' of French Canada. They brought together dozens of religious communities to promote their mission works, past and present. This celebration of the missionary vocation led to a hagiographic approach to the individual exhibits. Consequently, the missionary exhibition in Quebec departed from the scientific and missiological aspects of the Vatican exhibition. In Quebec, the missionary exhibition remained a popular manifestation in which the desire of the clergy to communicate missionary history and events took the shape of an exotic, edifying, and often colourful spectacle.

However the Quebec shows were not untrue to their European model. Designed for the Catholic masses, the Vatican exhibition also relied on edification. The spectacle of the 'poor pagan nations' was supposed to arouse a feeling of pity and indignation. As one Jesuit described it,

Enter for example the pavilions of Africa and Oceania, contemplate the scenes of cannibalism and the tableaux of martyrs. Study the photographs, these images of cannibals wearing barely any clothes, armed with arrows and poisoned lances, with bestial faces, their bodies deformed by hideous ornaments, with unbelievable dresses, all their collections of ridiculous amulets; of grinning idols and monstrous fetishes. In the face of these testimonies of sacrifice, stop and look and think of these seats tainted with human blood, and listen for a few minutes while the guide tells of the horror of these massacres of slaves which date back several years.'

The emphasis here, it is worth noting, was on the pre-missionary past. Suddenly, in the same space – the same kiosk – the visitor would witness the conversion through the powerful efficiency of artifacts and photography. Now, he concluded, the visitor could 'turn in the same place towards these portraits of Christians, metamorphosed in their faces, their posture and clothing.'[52]

What were the exhibiting strategies of the Society of Jesus? How, at the end of their journey, were 'the things of the Church' represented to the public? The Quebec Jesuits participated energetically in every exhibition. They always had the largest booth – competing with the Franciscans – prominently located on the main axis. 'Their large booth, at the centre of the building ... had the look of a grand salon where one would not dare sit.'[53] The design and contents of their booths grew more refined at each exhibition, depending on the selection of objects amassed by the *broussards* – the missionaries in the field. Yet the message was always the same: the unchanging nature of the Society of Jesus, and the connection between the Jesuit missions to New France in the 1600s and the present-day mission to China.

At Joliette – at a time when China was engaged in a civil war – the emphasis was on 'All the Jesuit Missions,' with representations of missions to Xuzhou, Zambezi (where some members worked under the English Jesuits), Alaska (which they had given up fifteen years earlier), Ontario (relinquished in 1924), and Kahnawake. Three years later, at Montreal, the emphasis had shifted, to reveal the contrast between 'the beautiful face of China, the learned and patient art, the wealth and the good taste'[54] and a simple evocation of the vanishing Amerindian. The highlights were the Chinese furniture (screens, chests, tables, chairs, etc.) made in the French Jesuit orphanages, silk embroideries, and Christian art. Taking into account the mitigated success – and the lack of glamour – of its contemporary works with Amerindians, the Society preferred a hagiographic visual discourse, focused on the past, on New France and its Holy martyrs.[55]

By 1942, when *Ville-Marie missionnaire* was held, Canada was at war. Xuzhou had been invaded with a bloody massacre, and in an unfortunate incident three Jesuits were killed by Japanese soldiers. After Pearl Harbor, the Canadian Jesuits and other Catholic missionaries were interned by the Japanese in concentration camps in Shanghai and

Beijing.[56] In Montreal, to counter this dark news and to inform the people about the world outside Canada, Father Lavoie emptied the museum to fill the exhibit.

Thematically the booth was no different from the earlier exhibitions: New France, illustrated by a central sculpture of its martyrs as well as manuscripts from the first Jesuits, and China, projected in the beauty of its arts and crafts. In 'this abundance of kiosks, of coloured pagodas, white mosques, of minarets, temples and cupolas, of huts and tents and igloos,'[57] the Jesuit pavilion combined exotic appeal and historical perspective with a large-scale monochromatic décor. 'In this multi-coloured fête, the kiosk of the Jesuits relaxes the eye: a huge blue map of the world on which show in white relief the five parts of the world.'[58] The exhibit was dominated by a huge statue, perhaps ten feet high, of a muscular Atlas holding up the globe, in recognition that the Jesuits made up one-seventh of all Roman Catholic missions throughout the world.

From 1930, unlike some mission societies, which concentrated on the more sordid aspects of missions – the small items of daily life, the primitive existence and painful conditions imposed on bodies and souls – the Jesuit booth showed a positive image of Chinese civilization through the works of Xujiahui orphans. If the Jesuits had held to 'realism,' they would have had to lay out a gallery of ragged people and poorly fed paupers, especially since floods had recently destroyed everything in their mission. Their strategy, based on exotic and aesthetic appeal, rejected the ethnographic discourse and sacrificed the 'reality' of their works in a troubled country at war, thus echoing the permanent exhibit at the Musée d'art chinois. The representation of the New France martyrs placed in an all-Chinese kiosk only symbolically referred to the hardship of mission.

The Jesuits – and the popular press – always described their Musée d'art chinois in glowing terms as 'inestimable artistic treasures,' 'a veritable Chinese museum, artistically arranged,' a 'veritable fairy land.'[59] Combined with missionary literature (books, reviews, etc.), circles, conferences, radio shows, and congresses, the exhibit allowed the Quebec Jesuits missionary propaganda to go beyond words into the popular universe of spectacle. These spectacular spaces – the museum and the exhibition – suggestive of power and thoughtfully arranged, offered the masses the 'weight of truth' of the artifacts and the missionary actors themselves, present as docent or animator. By winning over this form of modern education and leisure activity, the church turned

Part of the Jesuits' kiosk at the *Ville-Marie missionnaire, 1642–1942* exhibition, held at St Joseph's Oratory to celebrate the three hundredth anniversary of the founding of Montreal. The Atlas figure represents the Jesuit order, which made up one-seventh of the Roman Catholic foreign missionaries worldwide. The little figures represent the growth of Jesuit missions from 1500 missionaries in 1916 to 4000 in 1941.

this propagandist practice into a pious entertainment presented as an edifying journey through Catholicity.

Nevertheless the collection of 'things' for missionary propaganda had its own limits, for both the community and the material well-being of the mission. It was also restricted by the personal motivations of the collecting agents. Neither the Collège Sainte-Marie nor the Musée d'art chinois was a priority for the authorities of the Jesuit Province of Lower Canada. The propaganda by objects was certainly the order of the day, but they hoped to achieve it without a large investment while expecting to make an immediate profit. After the war, the Society decided it needed more muscular propaganda than a Chinese art museum, which was closed in 1947 and shipped to Montreal, where it was scattered among the Jesuit houses.

The missionary exhibitions continued after the Second World War, until they ran out of steam in the 1960s. No longer could the Jesuits pretend to display the 'real' China when the communist People's Republic was moving towards the Cultural Revolution. Besides, by then Quebec was no longer interested. The 'Quiet Revolution' had transformed Quebec by removing the Catholic Church from its pre-eminent position. The Chinese museum and the missionary exhibitions fell into disuse.[60]

NOTES

I would like to thank the Fonds pour les chercheurs et l'aide à la recherche du Québec and the Social Sciences and Humanities Research Council of Canada, whose research grants funded most of the research for this chapter based on my doctoral dissertation, 'La muette éloquence des choses: collections et expositions missionnaires de la Compagnie de Jésus au Québec, de 1843 à 1946' (PhD diss., Université de Montréal, 1999).

1 *Rerum Ecclesiae* (The Things of the Church), 'Lettre encyclique aux patriarches, primats, archevêques, évêques et autres ordinaires de lieu, en paix et communion avec le siège apostolique sur le développement des missions (28 février 1926),' in *Actes de S.S. Pie XI: Encycliques, motu proprio, brefs, allocutions, actes des dicastères, etc ...* , tome III, *Années 1925 à 1926* (Paris: Maison de la Bonne Presse, n.d.), 146.
2 François-Marc Gagnon, *La conversion par l'image: Un aspect de la mission des Jésuites auprès des Indiens du Canada au XVIIe siècle* (Montreal: Bellarmin, 1975).

3 For Protestant exhibitions see Alvyn J. Austin, *Saving China: Canadian Missionaries in the Middle Kingdom, 1888–1959* (Toronto: University of Toronto Press, 1986), 94–8.

4 One of the few studies mentioning Quebec missionary visual propaganda is the short essay by Sophie Lamontagne, 'La mission sans frontière,' in *Le Grand Héritage*, tome 2: *L'Église catholique et la société du Québec* (Quebec: Gouvernement du Québec, 1984).

5 Georges-Émile Giguère, 'La restauration de la Compagnie de Jésus au Canada, 1839–1957' (PhD diss., Université de Montréal, 1965), 287.

6 The Archives de la Société de Jésus du Canada français (ASJCF) in St Jerome, Quebec, contains the main primary sources, including those of the Collège Sainte-Marie and the Procure des missions correspondence. The Musée de la civilisation in Quebec City contains the contents of the Musée d'art chinois and the relevant documents and photographs.

7 Letter from Édouard Laflèche, Shanghai, to Joseph-Louis Lavoie, Montreal, 2 May 1935, in ASJCF, M-7-3L, file 'I Laflèche.' All translations by the author.

8 William Schupbach, 'Some Cabinets of Curiosities in European Academic Institutions,' in Arthur MacGregor and Oliver Impey, eds, *The Origins of the Museums: The Cabinet of Curiosities in Sixteenth- and Seventeenth-Century Europe* (Oxford: Clarendon Press, 1985), 174.

9 Arthur J. Ray, *I Have Lived Here since the World Began* (Toronto: Lester/Key Porter Books, 1996), 159.

10 Letter from J.-P. Choné to P. Chazelle, 5 January 1845, in ASJCF, A-3-3, 43; and 'Diarum de Wikwemikong, 1836 à 1937,' ASJFC, S-1-9.

11 Letter from 'Le père Dominique du Ranquet, missionnaire de la Compagnie de Jésus dans le Haut-Canada, au R.P. Provincial à Paris,' 1 December 1847, in Lorenzo Cadieux, ed., *Lettres des nouvelles missions du Canada, 1843–1952* [*LNMC*] (Montreal: Bellarmin, 1973), 435.

12 See Ruth B. Phillips, *Trading Identities: The Souvenir in Native North American Art from the Northeast, 1700–1900* (Montreal/Kingston: McGill-Queen's University Press, 1998), 182–3, for samples of that collection.

13 'Lettre du père J.-P. Choné à un père de la Compagnie,' 22 January 1845, in *LNMC*, 241.

14 Philippe Lesage, 'Le Musée,' in *Collège Sainte-Marie: Troisième souvenir annuel, 1918* (Montreal: Imprimerie du Messager, 1918), 30–2.

15 Ibid., 32.

16 ASJCF, C1-165, Fonds du Collège Sainte-Marie, 'Rapport annuel du recteur du Collège Sainte-Marie à Montréal au Surintendant des écoles en vertu de l'Acte pour l'encouragement de l'éducation supérieure,' 1887. Susan

Sheets-Pyenson, *Cathedrals of Science: The Development of Colonial Natural History Museums during the Late Nineteenth Century* (Montreal/Kingston: McGill-Queen's University Press, 1988), 91.

17 Paul Desjardins, 'Les trésors historiques du collège Sainte-Marie: riche dépôt d'archives sur le régime français,' *La Presse*, 15 October 1960, 24.

18 Paul J. Delany and Andrew D. Nicholls, *After the Fire: Sainte-Marie-Among-the-Hurons since 1649* (Elmvale, ON: East Georgian Bay Historical Foundation, 1989), 6.

19 Paul Desjardins, *Le Collège Sainte-Marie de Montréal*, tome 1: *La Fondation: Le fondateur* (Montreal: Collège Sainte-Marie, 1940), 224–5.

20 Sainte-Marie had to wait until the 1940s, when it was scientifically excavated by the Royal Ontario Museum. The pilgrimage church and reconstructed village are now a major tourist attraction near Midland, Ontario.

21 Denis Martin, *Portraits des héros de la Nouvelle-France. Images d'un culte historique* (Montreal: Hurtubise HMH, 1988), 1.

22 Antonio Dragon, *Enseveli dans les neiges: Le Père Jules Jetté* (Montreal: Fides, 1962), 78.

23 Letter from Albert Bellemare to a brother (probably the procurator or rector), 4 August 1908, ASJCF, D-7, 'Bellemare, Albert, 1859–1929'.

24 *Congrès international des Américanistes, XVe session tenue à Québec en 1906*, vol. 1 (Quebec: Dussault & Proulx, 1907), xxxviii.

25 'Curiosités. Souvenir historiques: Alaska/Antiquités romaines et grecques, 500 A. J.-C.' This is the catalogue. ASJCF, Fonds du collège Sainte-Marie, not classified, Catalogue B. No. 1-700.

26 Letter from Jules Jetté to his mother, Berthe Jetté, 6 March 1909, in ASJCF, BO-44-5, 2.

27 Letter from Bellarmin Lafortune to Bellemare, 3 October 1911, 'Bellemare, Albert,' in ASJCF, D-7.

28 Dorothy Jean Ray, *Artists of the Tundra and Sea* (Seattle: University of Washington Press, 1980), 3. See also Louis S. Renner and Dorothy J. Ray, *Pioneer Missionary to the Bering Strait Eskimos: Bellarmine Lafortune, S.J.* (Portland, OR: Binford & Mort, 1979).

29 *La semaine missionnaire de Joliette, 4 au 10 juillet 1927*, souvenir volume (Quebec: Charrier et Dugal, 1928), 242.

30 ASJCF catalogue.

31 Douglas Cole, *Captured Heritage: The Scramble for Northwest Coast Artifacts* (Seattle/London: University of Washington Press, 1985).

32 The only history of the Jesuit mission in English is Austin, *Saving China*, 143–58, 255–7, and 285–7. For a history of the mission during the Japanese

invasion, see Diana Lary, 'A Ravaged Place: The Devastation of the Xuzhou Region, 1938,' in Diana Lary and Stephen MacKinnon, eds, *The Scars of War: The Impact of Warfare on Modern China* (Vancouver: UBC Press, 2001).

33 Rosario Renaud, *Le diocèse de Süchow*, tome 1: *1882–1931* (Montreal: Bellarmin, 1955), 18.

34 Ibid., 1: 20.

35 Ibid., 1: 29.

36 Académie des missions, letter from Georges Marin to Armand Proulx, 5 February 1926, ASJCF, M-7, Cl. 7, 61.

37 'Côté, Philippe,' 1, 1929–33, letter from Côté to J.-L. Lavoie, 7 March 1930, ASJCF, M-7-2C.

38 Letter from Lavoie to Laflèche, 1 November 1934, ASJCF, M-7-3L, 1.

39 See also Alvyn Austin, 'Scholars, Archaeologists and Diplomats: China Missions and Canadian Public Life,' in Marguerite Van Die, ed., *Religion and Public Life in Canada: Historical and Comparative Perspectives* (Toronto: University of Toronto Press, 2001).

40 On the subject of 'cross' artifacts and souvenir art, see Phillips, *Trading Identities*. See also articles by Nelson H. H. Graburn, ed., *Ethnic and Tourist Arts: Cultural Expressions from the Fourth World* (Berkeley and Los Angeles: University of California Press, 1976); 'Art, Ethno-Aesthetics and the Contemporary Scene', in Sidney M. Mead and Bernie Kernot, eds, *Art and Artists of Oceania* (Palmerston North, New Zealand/Mill Valley, CA: Dunmore Press/Ethnographic Arts Publications, 1983), 70–9; and 'The Evolution of Tourist Arts,' *Annals of Tourism Research* 11 (1984): 396–409.

41 Joseph-Louis Lavoie did spend almost four years in Xuzhou, in the 1920s.

42 Letter from É. Lord to Lavoie, 10 August 1931, ASJCF, M-7-4L, 1930–6.

43 Letter from Laflèche to Lavoie, 2 May 1935, ASJCF, M-7-3L, 1.

44 See, among others, ASJCF, P-2-27, letter from J. d'Orsonnens to A. Dugré, 5 November 1934; M-7-3G, II, 1932–46, letter from A. Gagnon to Dugré, 7 February 1936; M-7-5R, II, 1936–47, letter from R. Renaud to Lavoie, 31 March 1936; M-7-2C, II, 'Dossier-Récits-Corr., 1935–51 (Côté),' letter from P. Côté to Lavoie, 3 November 1935.

45 J.-L. Lavoie, 'Musée chinois,' *Le Brigand* 6 (February 1931): 6.

46 Jean-Claude Drolet, 'Un lit impérial chinois au Québec depuis la fin du XIXe siècle,' typescript dated 'Chicoutimi: Université de Québec à Chicoutimi, 8 November 1971,' deposited in the Musée de la civilisation, Quebec City. This unreliable source states that the bed was sold to the Jesuits in 1937 by a businessman for $2000; the only record of an important payment is $350 in 1944.

47 Académie des missions, letters from Marin to Proulx, 18 January 1931, and

to Asa Souligny, same date, ASJCF, M-7-Cl. 7, 61. These kinds of artifacts can be identified on photographs of the Jesuits kiosk at missionary exhibits and of the interior of the museum on chemin Sainte-Foy. For example, *La semaine missionnaire de Joliette*, 238; Maison Bellarmin, Bureau des Missions, *Musée d'art chinois. Catalogue* (Procure des Missions de Chine, 653, chemin Sainte-Foy, Quebec, n.d.).

48 'Varia – Propagande, Joseph-Louis Lavoie,' *Guide pratique (gratuit)* (1930), ASJCF, M-7-3L, II.

49 Antonio Poulin and Horace Labranche, *Expositions missionnaires* (Montreal: Secrétariat de la Ligue missionnaire des étudiants, 1939), 21.

50 Paul Greenhalgh, *Ephemeral Vistas: The Expositions universelles, Great Exhibitions and World's Fairs, 1851–1939* (Manchester: Manchester University Press, 1988), 1.

51 'L'exposition du IIIe Centenaire,' *La Presse*, 5 September 1942, 38.

52 H.-M. Dubois, 'L'Oeuvre civilisatrice et scientifique des missions catholiques,' *Revue d'histoire des missions* 2, no. 3 (1 September 1925): 403–28.

53 Alexandre Dugré, s.j., 'Compagnie de Jésus en Chine,' in Paul-Eugène Trudel, *IVe Centenaire de la plantation de la Croix aux Trois-Rivières; célébré par une exposition missionnaire, du 31 août au 8 septembre 1935*, souvenir volume (Trois-Rivières: Imprimerie Saint-Joseph, 1936), 223.

54 Ibid.

55 The Jesuit martyrs of New France were canonized in 1930 and from then were called saints.

56 Austin, *Saving China*, 255–7; Lary, 'A Ravaged Place.'

57 *Ville-Marie missionnaire, 1642–1942. Exposition du IIIe Centenaire de Montréal tenue à l'Oratoire Saint-Joseph du 17 septembre au 4 octobre 1942* (Montreal: Secrétariat du Comité missionnaire, 1943), 220–1.

58 Ibid., 251.

59 'Fondation d'un musée chinois chez les Rev. Pères jésuites,' *Le Soleil*, 7 March 1931, 28. *Musée d'art chinois: Catalogue* (Montreal: Bellarmin, n.d.).

60 The collection of the Musée d'art chinois was given by the Jesuits of the French Canadian Province in 1990 to the Musée de la civilisation, Quebec City, announcing a new phase of diffusion for the missionary artifacts.

Chapter 10

Collecting Cultures: Canadian Missionaries, Pacific Islanders, and Museums

BARBARA LAWSON

Introduction

Ethnographic objects sit uneasily in storage or on display in museums around the world; many with stories long forgotten, others with shameful collection histories remembered. Along with the emergence of colonial realms as fertile ground for investigation,[1] there has been an efflorescence of works dealing with the colonial context of ethnographic collecting, bringing new interest to museum-bound artifacts.[2] One obstacle to this development has been the potential of negatively charged colonial baggage to eclipse all other meanings and contexts as evidenced in the public reaction to the Royal Ontario Museum's (ROM) exhibit *Into the Heart of Africa*.[3]

A contrasting response has occurred in the case of several exhibits in Nova Scotia that featured local missionary hero John Geddie, the most recent of which, *John and Charlotte Geddie: Mission in the South Seas*, was shown in many venues throughout the province from 1996 to 1998. This exhibit highlighted the work of both Geddies and was among the first exhibits anywhere acknowledging contributions by a missionary wife. The exhibit narrative provided useful cultural context for the objects presented, but clearly the focus was on the missionary couple, an emphasis which was well received and indeed expected by the exhibit audience. The Nova Scotian response presents a case very different from the community reaction to the ROM exhibit. Regardless of how these historical spectres confront their present-day publics, the virtue of considering colonial pasts lies in what they reveal of the historically contingent, intercultural relations that made ethnographic collecting possible. These contexts also yield valuable information about the manufacture and use of objects and the relation between local and introduced material culture.

Given the many particular features of the missionary enterprise, it is not surprising to see the subject of missionary collecting gain scholarly attention as a distinct domain of investigation.[4] Such critical consideration reveals numerous intercultural processes and subtleties that are lost when one looks merely to objects for tangible evidence of an unnegotiated cultural past. A cross-section of missionary 'souvenirs' brings forth objects that were discarded as they were being replaced by nonindigenous materials, goods that were sold or exchanged to enable participation in an increasingly cash-oriented economy, or items intentionally rooted out by those with plans to alter local behaviour. Included also would be gifts that had been presented by islanders to missionaries and their families upon their arrival, departure, or other special occasions according to customary protocol. The interest here is to examine the dynamics of Canadian missionary collecting in the South Pacific islands to determine how such collections might contribute to an understanding of the past and to see where their potential for continuing usefulness might lie.

Missionaries on Erromango and the Nova Scotia Mission to the New Hebrides

Erromango is the third-largest island in the Republic of Vanuatu, which is located 2445 km north of Sydney (Australia) and 800 km west of Fiji. This archipelago was designated the New Hebrides by Captain James Cook, and that name persisted until the nation's independence in 1980. The first documented European visit to Erromango (then spelled Erromanga) was during Cook's second voyage in 1774, when his vessel attempted to land in search of food and water. The stay was made very brief, its intention thwarted by misunderstandings and violence from both sides in a pattern that would be typical of encounters that followed into the next century. The impression of Erromangans passed on to posterity by Cook was that of an untrustworthy and hostile people, and the island was avoided by European ships for the next fifty years until the promise of sandalwood lured fortune seekers to its shores. A vigorous exploitation of sandalwood resources in the Pacific developed during the early nineteenth century as a result of the demand for tea by Australian settlers and the Chinese monopoly of that commodity.

There were two periods during which the island of Erromango was subject to intensive sandalwood trading activity in the nineteenth century, from the late 1820s until 1830, then beginning in 1841 and continuing to the mid-1860s. In November 1839, between these periods, John Williams led the first missionary expedition into the southwestern Pacific. Williams, a well-respected representative of the London Missionary Society (LMS), was killed with his assistant James Harris within hours of setting foot on Erromango. Before long, the Christian world came to perceive the island as the nadir of human spirituality. At about the same period, the Presbyterian Church in Nova Scotia was deliberating about the possibility of establishing its own foreign mission, led by John Geddie and the First Presbyterian Church in Pictou. Pictou native John William Dawson, who would later become McGill University's fifth principal, as well as founder and first director of the university's Redpath Museum, was also an active member of the group.[5] When the Nova Scotians sought counsel in Britain regarding potential sites for their activities, the London Missionary Society vigorously suggested the New Hebrides, a location the LMS was only too ready to abandon after Williams's unsavoury demise. With the settlement of John Geddie on Aneityum in 1848, the Presbyterian Church in Nova Scotia became the first colonial church to establish its own foreign mission. Canadian missionary activities in the New Hebrides continued until the early twentieth century with a total of thirteen missionaries sent forth. Four of these emissaries served on Erromango, the site where the following discussions of missionaries, islanders, and objects converge.

Missionary settlement on Erromango varied with local politics, foreign trading activities, and the temperament and physical constitution of the individuals involved. In spite of these variables, there was a discernible order of priorities common to all missionary endeavours on the island: establishing a residence, training teachers and holding classes, visiting villages and settling teachers, and building mission stations, churches, and schools. Missionary wives directed their attention to holding classes and also had considerable involvement with women engaged to work at the mission station. The presence of missionary wives and the fact that missionary families were long-term residents on the island provided an opportunity for women and children to interact with foreigners to an unprecedented degree.[6] Although missionary strategies varied in their emphases and efficacy, there was consensus that the physical appearance of traditional Erromangans and

Three Nova Scotia Presbyterian pioneer couples in the New Hebrides. Mr and Mrs J.W. McKenzie (left) arrived at Erromango in 1872. Rev. Joseph and Alice Annand (centre) arrived at Santo in 1873. Rev. Hugh and Christina Robertson (right) arrived at Erromango in 1863, and remained for forty years. Annand collected 'curios' for the Normal School Museum in Toronto, now in the Royal Ontario Museum, while the Robertsons made collections that were distributed to numerous museums, including the Redpath Museum in Montreal.

their warfare, cannibalism, feasting, treatment of women, infanticide, idolatry, and belief in sorcery had to be changed. One certainty is that missionary endeavour would not have been possible without the support of local chiefs and the guidance and assistance of native teachers. Among the latter group the names of Joe, Mana, Soso, Novolu, Navusia, and Yomot are well remembered in missionary texts and by contemporary Erromangans.

The Rev. Hugh Robertson and his wife Christina settled at Dillon's Bay in June 1872. Robertson was familiar with the region, having spent over four years (1864–8) as a cotton agent on the neighbouring island of Aneityum. A mission-sponsored company had employed him to buy cotton from the island's Christian population and ship it to Scotland, and as a result, he had become familiar with the local language and customs. In 1870 he went home to Nova Scotia to prepare for a missionary post. When he returned, he was told of the death of the missionary James Gordon on Erromango and offered to fill the vacancy. Robertson's published work *Erromanga: The Martyr Isle* (1902) was based on extensive contact with the local population during the first twelve years of what would be a residence of over forty years. Although solidly framed within the pious aspirations of nineteenth-century missionization, it is a valuable source of information about Erromangans and their way of life.[7] By the end of their sojourn, it would not be exaggeration to claim that Robertson and his wife knew Erromango better than any other Europeans alive during the nineteenth century.

Robertson relied heavily on Erromangan teachers for his missionary activities and worked diligently to establish a network over the island. His strategy was therefore strongly tempered by a belief that missionaries had to fit themselves into roles cast by Erromangan society, such as that of ritual specialist or chief. The former was largely determined by the missionary's ability to cure illness and ward off misfortune. With regard to the latter, although his predecessors had been aware of local politics and the influence of important chiefs, Robertson's understanding of the active role expected from missionaries was unique. The Christians and mission supporters on the island constituted a distinct 'Christian party' that had definite allies and enemies, suffered injuries, and occasionally had to seek revenge. In addition to party politics, efforts were made to fit mission activities into patterns established by traditional chieftainship and feasting practices, and also to keep disruptions of local activities at a minimum.

During the nineteenth century, missionary transformations were most successfully realized within the domain of material culture and figured as prominently in the strategies of other denominations as it did in those of the Presbyterians.[8] Numerous examples exist of Robertson's belief in the necessity and utility of trade goods for survival and for mission activities, knowledge perhaps gained from his earlier business experience as a cotton agent on Aneityum. His actions conformed to a well-established pattern of exchange that had served as the primary language of contact between European and island cultures from the time of the earliest encounters. He was less conservative and more active than his predecessors on Erromango were, and his dexterity in handling practical matters provided the necessary means for the religious concerns of the mission.

Although Robertson was far more sensitive to local custom than those before him had been, he remained true to missionary policy in his attitudes. He discouraged polygamy whenever possible and frequently used his influence to undermine traditional marriage. Other traditional activities, although not actively suppressed, were not considered appropriate for 'true' Christians. These included kava drinking and the veneration of sacred stones.[9] In spite of Robertson's flexibility regarding many aspects of traditional culture, he was fairly rigorous when it came to matters of physical appearance. The Robertsons distributed clothing to mission supporters and had very definite ideas as to proper grooming. The enormous efforts made to clothe local populations 'decently' and the proportion of goods presented or exchanged to this end testify to the importance missionaries invested in this conversion strategy, which became the symbolic representation of their accomplishment.[10]

Erromango was proclaimed 'a Christian island' in 1910, and three years later the missionary endeavour subsided with the departure of Hugh Robertson and his family. With their leaving, the export of local objects diminished and also a major source of desired introduced objects was gone.[11] In considering Robertson's collecting activities, it is important to recognize that they were influenced by particular contact experiences and were subsidiary to his missionary duties. They were mediated both by access to local materials and by a material culture repertoire that was accommodating to local innovations and changing interests. It is therefore essential to determine those historical, geographical, and professional factors that affected what he collected and especially the role of Erromangan desire and agency in determining what objects were made available. Attention to these latter concerns will allow reconsideration of my earlier work,[12] which acknowledges missionary collecting as one side of a two-way process, but does not attempt to examine in detail the contending forces of this symbiotic relationship.

Erromangan Desire and European Objects

Erromango's reputation for hostility and violence towards intruders was influenced by decades of exploitative campaigns by disease-

Group of teachers and Erromangan Christians at the mission station, circa 1890.

bringing sandalwood traders, visits by well-intentioned but poorly advised missionaries, and the disruptive actions of aggressive labour recruiters. The outcome of these early encounters was that local men aggressively discouraged infiltration by traders and successfully thwarted early missionary intrusions for two-thirds of the nineteenth century. Trading activities beginning in the late 1820s made a considerable quantity and variety of European goods available to Erromangan society. These were offered in exchange by traders, missionaries, and la-bour recruiters in order to establish contact, obtain food, and procure services from local populations. The requirements of these visitors were manifold; they were certainly more dependent on islanders for their survival and enterprise than islanders were on them or their manufactures. Although Erromangans were long indifferent to their 'exotic' offerings, once local interest developed, material incentives became a necessity for participation in the varied outsider concerns. As Dorothy Shineberg notes, that Pacific island populations were anxious for worldly barter and not simply passive subjects of European exploitation makes much difference to the interpretation of events.[13]

Iron tools, beads, cloth, firearms, and tobacco were common items of barter wanted from sandalwood traders. The types of goods sought by local populations, with the exception of tobacco, were mostly substitutes for items already belonging to the local material culture repertoire, and were employed for traditional activities such as warfare, competitive display, fishing, and subsistence agriculture. As islanders came to know the value of their goods and labour to the European trade, they made great efforts to get their fair share and also to have their preferences catered to in terms of what was offered for exchange. In spite of Erromangan success at limiting physical intrusion by foreigners, desire for, and increasing dependence on, foreign goods eventually modified some local priorities in order to accommodate European demands for year-round trading, mission-related activities, and labour contracts that conflicted with seasonal cycles of planting, harvesting, feasting, and fighting.

It is important to remember here that in spite of impressions of triumph and control that pervade the pages of missionary writings read by numerous enthusiastic home country audiences, missionaries were usually few in number relative to their resident communities. Their influence was often severely limited, while they preoccupied themselves with securing food and shelter, maintaining health, and sometimes life itself. Although the level of missionary dependence on the kindness of islanders varied from situation to situation, it was no doubt great on Erromango. Throughout the nineteenth century, there was never more than one missionary or missionary family on the island, with the brief exception of an intermittent four-year co-residence by James Gordon and the Macnairs, who in fact spent much of that time on opposite sides of Erromango. There were few, if any, other foreign residents to provide material or moral support. Missionary triumphs were therefore tempered and often determined by local needs and interests. They required trade goods to establish themselves and to carry out their basic activities, but at the same time were always limited in the quantities and types of materials available for distribution. Food, assorted household items, and tools were regularly given to islanders as payment for maintaining the mission premises and various construction projects. Other materials, such as medicine, clothing, and religious texts were introduced and later required to meet local demands as supplements or substitutes for traditional practices and objects.

Those Erromangans interested in increasing their involvement with the mission often had to make choices that distanced themselves both physically and mentally from traditional ways. As a result of moving to the mission premises, which would facilitate participation in mission activities, gardens might be abandoned, along with many village-oriented pursuits and traditions. Opportunities for engaging in local politics and warfare were reduced, these activities being disparaged both in principle and for their time-consuming nature. Christian marriages, if sought, separated people from their communities, thereby disrupting various obligations of exchange of traditional forms of wealth. Attachment to the mission precluded partaking in traditional feasting activities noted for their particularly 'un-Christian' behaviour, and also eliminated an important venue of traditional exchange.

European items were highly valued by local populations, because they were often more effective than the stone, wood, and other materials that they replaced. Metal tools, in particular, lessened the labour required for subsistence agriculture, fishing, house construction, canoe building, and toolmaking. Even where technological benefits were negligible, there were vast savings in labour over obtaining suitable raw materials and producing the local equivalent. The introduction of cloth, for example, relieved women of the arduous manufacture of barkcloth and leaf skirts. Time saved by introduced technologies, however, was frequently offset by European demands for wage labourers and participation in mission activities. In some instances, foreign items were desirable because their material substance was believed to convey spiritual power and status to those possessing them. This might be in addition to an object's functional qualities as in the case of cloth, axes, and even guns, or solely in relation to the material itself as with religious texts.[14] In the latter instance, initially missionary tracts and Bibles often were perceived as sacred objects or charms. Local leaders vigorously sought materials offered by traders, missionaries, or labour recruiters as a means of aggrandizing their status and political influence. Although women were limited in their contact with most foreign visitors, involvement with the mission as well as access to the goods missionaries provided would have enhanced the prestige of high-status individuals. Occasionally, situations arose which allowed previously powerless individuals to upset the established order as a result of their access to foreign-introduced wealth.

Islander preferences, rather than those of foreigners, orchestrated the abandonment of local manufactures and the selection or rejection of introduced objects. Stone axes were largely dispensed with during the sandalwood trade with the introduction of large numbers of metal axes, which provided a more versatile cutting edge and eliminated the labour-intensive manufacture of their stone predecessors. Erromangans held fast to their weapons, in spite of continued cajoling by the mission to relinquish them and stop the persistent fighting that was consuming the island. On the rare occasions when spears and clubs were cast aside, it was usually to replace them with metal axes and firearms, a decision that challenged missionary attempts at pacification. As islanders increasingly chose to embrace Christianity, warfare lessened in importance. This change of circumstance brought with it a reversal of missionary favour towards local weaponry, but again islander design prevailed. Missionary Hugh A. Robertson was keen to have Erromangans continue making war clubs because they were much sought after by European visitors to the island, but he observed that local interest in their production waned as the significance of warfare and clubs as status-bearing objects diminished.[15]

Once Erromangans had embraced aspects of European material culture and religion, the sale of traditional items as 'curios' became a way of acquiring additional goods, gaining influence in both Erromangan and European contexts, and a means of contributing to the mission effort. The missionaries, who often served as middlemen in these transactions, further encouraged the divestment of traditional objects.

Christian islanders, influenced by the Protestant inclination to frown upon anything from the past as heathen, were also motivated to sell old and treasured pieces to travellers on passing trading, whaling, or naval vessels. Imported items such as metal fishhooks, trade axes, guns, glass, beads, and trade cloth were probably held dearly by Erromangans and were therefore less likely to be surrendered than locally produced items. Local willingness to trade or sell objects is an issue of importance in considering items which were not included in collections made by outsiders. Objects requiring considerable effort to manufacture, especially those in daily use, such as fishnets, were probably rarely given up, unless trade substitutes were available.

Islanders introduced foreign goods into their material culture repertoire based on object efficacy, attractiveness, exoticism, perceived spiritual power, and according to locally changing needs and desires. These innovations made certain traditional objects obsolete or changed their forms into hybrid manufactures (e.g., clubs used as handles for metal axe blades, trade cloth bindings endowing traditional weapons with spiritual power, Christian vestments made from barkcloth, designs incorporating introduced imagery).[16] In numerous cases, local objects continued to be preferred because of their easy availability (e.g., baskets, mats, fans, digging sticks) or because there were no foreign equivalents. Among the latter were those valued for ceremonial use and exchange or having spiritual significance. In this regard, Erromangans' resistance to parting with their sacred stones until Christian belief predominated on the island is noted.[17] With islander criteria for keeping, modifying, or discarding local objects in mind as determinants of what might be available for outsiders to collect, the discussion now turns to another type of connoisseur, the missionary collector.

Erromango Collections in Museums

The Rev. Hugh Angus Robertson presented approximately 125 objects from the New Hebrides to McGill University's Redpath Museum in the last decades of the nineteenth century. The museum had been founded in 1882 by well-known palaeontologist John William Dawson, John Geddie's friend from Pictou and now principal of McGill University. The museum included holdings in palaeontology, mineralogy, zoology, and archaeology/ethnology. A close examination of donations to the latter collection reveals a virtually undisturbed pattern of Canadian contact with 'exotic' peoples that is global in scope and

reflects Canadian national and commercial endeavours of the late nineteenth and early twentieth centuries. These artifacts have endured
their own particular history of isolation and obfuscation, but very few
alterations to the original corpus have occurred. Doctors, missionaries,
geologists, and travellers, many of whom had been enlisted to participate in various British imperial or commercial endeavours in different
regions of the world, were among the museum's early donors.
Although most of these early supporters were affiliated with McGill
University, the Redpath's archaeological and ethnological collections,
being neither systematic nor the work of professional anthropologists,
were not acquired or displayed in a manner that accorded with the
museological principles of the emergent discipline of anthropology.[18]

Robertson's donation was probably encouraged by Dawson, a Pictou native who had been involved with the development of the Nova
Scotia foreign mission before coming to Montreal. Robertson presented
material to the Redpath in three separate donations that included barkcloth, clubs, bows, arrows, spears, skirts, and ornaments. Although
this material belongs to the genre of idiosyncratic rather than systematic collections, it appears to represent a reasonable cross-section of
utilitarian and ritual objects used throughout Erromangan society. The
museum's register is vague as to the specifics of each donation. It
appears that objects given in September 1883 (spears, arrows, clubs,
and matting) were from islands north of Erromango, while those
donated in March 1896 were mostly from Erromango; objects from the
middle donation (January 1890) are without attribution to specific
islands. Robertson, who visited Canada in 1883 during his two-year
leave of absence from the New Hebrides, probably made the first
donation in person. Erromango is the island most strongly represented
in the material donated by Robertson as this is where he was actively
engaged during his long career; it is only this part of the collection that
will be considered here.

In spite of Erromango's dramatic contact history, the island has been
little known for its production of objects. Although recent works have
discussed Erromango artifacts,[19] much recognition of these historical
productions has been downplayed in Vanuatu and especially on the
island itself. In the latter case, regard for past manufactures is muted
because of local Christian anxieties about the nineteenth-century
martyrdoms.[20] Robertson's Erromango collection is distinctive because
it gives evidence of specific intercultural relations during a period
marked at one end by intensive but very limited contact and at

the other by considerable depopulation from introduced disease and large-scale conversion to Christianity.

Artifacts from Erromango are scattered in museums around the world, usually in very small numbers, as single donations, or as part of larger collections, and consistently without documentation. One important collection is found at the Australian Museum (Sydney), which is also from Robertson and members of his family. Another smaller but still significant one is at the Nova Scotia Museum (Halifax) and is probably from the same source. Most of the Nova Scotia Museum's Vanuatu collection was transferred from Pine Hill Divinity Hall in 1971 and is attributed to John Geddie.[21] The Nova Scotia Museum's records, based on the attribution of this material to Geddie, presume that the material was collected between 1848 and 1864. Research of Pine Hill archival material, the large proportion of Erromango artifacts in the collection, and the presence of certain artifacts which would not have been available during the 'Geddie collection' dates suggest that most of the material was collected and donated not by Geddie, but by Robertson between 1883 and 1900.[22] Other Canadian institutions having a few Erromango items include the Royal Ontario Museum and the Agnes Etherington Art Centre.

Vanuatu's National Museum in Port Vila on the island of Efate has about twenty-four Erromango objects, while present-day Erromangans have very few examples from times past. During visits to Erromango in 1995 and 1998, I found many types of artifacts typically found in museum collections gone from memory, but for a few older individuals who recalled hearing about the manufacture or use of particular items. Cultural fieldworkers Jerry Taki and Sophie Nempan Sie are actively engaged in collecting this knowledge and disseminating it to younger Erromangans. With the exception of material in Vanuatu and twenty-one objects at Cambridge University's museum collected by anthropologist C.B. Humphreys, who did fieldwork in the southern New Hebrides in 1920, most of these collections, large and small, were assembled during the period of missionary residence on Erromango and all but a few directly or indirectly collected by Robertson and his family. Indirect collections of Erromango objects observed in a number of museums would include those by other Presbyterian missionaries such as Annand, Lawrie, and Paton, and by Captain Braithwaite of the mission vessel *Dayspring* and by visitors to the island such as C.F. Wood. This material might have been passed on to colleagues at mis-

Presbyterian missionaries bound for the New Hebrides (now Vanuatu) in the South Pacific on board the mission boat, the *Dayspring*, circa 1863–73. The *Dayspring* was built in Pictou, Nova Scotia.

sion synods, or, in the case of actual visits, would have been dependent on Robertson as intermediary and escort. Robertson's role as middleman is apparent in Wood's description of his Erromango visit.[23] Missionary James Gordon, Robertson's predecessor, also assisted in procuring objects, as is documented in the account of Julius Brenchley, a British naturalist and collector accompanying HMS *Curaçoa* during its 1865 cruise of the area.[24]

It is important to note here that although material at the Redpath Museum and in other institutions is attributed solely to H.A. Robertson in all documentation, it is more than likely that Mrs Robertson as well as other family members were involved in gathering objects for these collections. Acknowledgment of Christina Robertson's participation in collecting activities is absent from all published works consulted in this research as is her Christian name – 'Mrs Robertson' being used instead according to prevailing convention. However, based on her active role in the mission and the fact that her name is associated with some of the objects in the Australian Museum, one must assume her involvement whenever the 'H.A. Robertson' collection is noted. With a few exceptions, the literature of the day paid only the slightest notice to missionary wives and their works in the New Hebrides; the possibility of spousal and other contributions is worth considering when examining these texts and collections.[25]

Islander Innovations and Missionary Collecting

Robertson's donation to the Redpath Museum reflects an intersection between the primary targets of missionization and the areas of Erromangan desire. A parallel form of 'collection' favouring the accumulation of introduced European material culture defines the latter, although it must be sought within the historical record rather than from tangible holdings. In considering interactions between missionaries and islanders, the domains of greatest common concern appear to be personal appearance, warfare, feasting, and religion, but this does not imply that opinion and purpose were in accord on both sides of the divide within each of these categories.

The missionary emphasis regarding Erromangan appearance centred on establishing a dress code. Missionaries endowed the wearing of European dress with great significance, judging physical appearance that most closely approximated their own to be a measure of spirituality. They used clothing to mark distinctions among Christians, especially teachers and their wives, who received payments for their services in clothing and were therefore better dressed than the rest.[26] Although traditional Erromangan dress and ornaments were permitted and even admired in the case of women's garments, men's clothing, which was limited to a barkcloth girdle and leaf penis case was viewed with utmost distaste in missionary circles.[27]

Participation in mission activities and adaptation to dress codes were due less to missionary volition, however, than to local agency. With a single missionary family and a handful of native teachers on an island populated by over a thousand people, it would be unrealistic to ascribe changes in islander behaviour to the influence of so few. Erromangan men sought cloth and clothing from missionaries as gifts and as payment for services and food in much the same way they had done in previous exchange relations with Europeans. Many Erromangan women had extensive contact with missionaries and their wives and were in a position to have direct access to the cloth and clothing they offered. This was a significant departure from the limited opportunities afforded by previous male-oriented encounters with traders or labour-recruiters. Women's classes offered by the mission devoted considerable attention to teaching the advantages of garments made from imported cloth and their manufacture. Homespun cloth provided by home country supporters was industriously made into clothing on these occasions. Local interest in acquiring new skills and foreign materials (needles, thimbles, scissors, thread, cloth, and ribbons) provided impetus for sewing classes and ensured attendance.

Erromangan women did not generally need European clothing to attain the acceptable levels of Christian modesty that were required for participation in mission activities. The typical woman's ceremonial dress generously covered her figure from shoulder to ankle; nonetheless, it was relinquished in favour of print dresses for attending church. The wearing of imported clothing was a show of local support for the missionary presence. Leaf skirts with calico garments covering the upper torso were acceptable attire for Christian women in the 1890s.[28] Although there was growing pressure by colonizing forces to replace all traditional garments with European ones, there were many reasons why Christian islanders would choose to present themselves in Western attire.

Regardless of whether or not Erromangan women aspired to the same goals as the missionary program, the availability of manufactured cloth and clothing provided them with numerous tangible benefits which suited their own needs. It relieved some women of the arduous manufacture of barkcloth and leaf skirts and was highly desirable in its own right. The material properties of strength and durability, softness and washability, colour and design also made introduced fabric highly desirable for garments. Islanders involved in the mission were often those of status and influence, and association with the mission did provide opportunities for others to gain status and access to goods outside the bounds of the established social order. For Erromangan women, continuing engagement with the mission meant that barkcloth and leaf skirts, which had served as important indicators of status and exchange items for various rites of passage, were devalued. As these important forms of wealth lost prominence, the accessibility of a traditional iconography reflective of lineage, trade relations, religious belief, historical events, and other encoded meanings was increasingly diminished.

Imported material carried a prestige of its own, and its association with the perceived powerful spirituality of Christianity also potentially endowed it and its possessors with forces now seemingly waning from traditional religion. Even for those strongly confirmed in their ancestral religious beliefs, European artifacts (including cloth) held the promise of having greater power than local sacred objects and therefore were desired as a form of spiritual protection.[29] The practical and perhaps 'charismatic' advantages inherent in imported cloth assured prestige, influence, and also a valuable form of barter to its owners. Dress was the simplest way of approaching Christianity and potentially sharing the influence and spiritual power of its practitioners, who used clothing as a distinguishing feature of Christian identity. Thus, the barkcloths, leaf skirts, loincloths, neck ornaments, armbands, men's ornamental combs, and barkcloth beaters in museum collections would correspond to the cloth, dresses, skirts, blouses, trousers, shirts, head scarves, hats, and sewing implements that islanders chose in their stead.

Warfare was another area of mutual interest, although attitudes and innovations by missionaries and islanders were mostly discordant. All missionaries resident on Erromango were intent on the elimination of local warfare, an activity that proved fairly resistant to missionary interference. Erromangans were required to leave their weapons behind when attending mission activities, because missionaries feared islander aggression, both directed towards themselves and those Christians involved with the mission. Furthermore, the missionaries wanted to replace what they deemed a local obsession occupying an inordinate amount of time and energy, and potentially involving all members of the community, with activities and behaviour that befitted Christian belief and mission objectives. Missionaries were not alone in their fear and abhorrence of the Erromangan passion for fighting and ongoing engagement with intertribal conflict. Accounts of previous hostilities such as those witnessed by Captain Cook, sandalwood trader Peter Dillon, the *Sophia*'s naturalist/surgeon George Bennett, and HMS *Curaçoa*'s naturalist Julius Brenchley fuelled their strong views. Observers remarked not only upon the intense Erromangan involvement with

warfare, but also on the degree that islanders sought refuge from enemies or assistance in battle. The latter included an interest in procuring
the superior weapons possessed by the visitors.[30]

Warfare usually resulted from quarrels about women, ownership of
sacred stones, or raids on gardens. When aggression was thought necessary, it was instigated with a direct challenge such as burning a
house or cutting down banana trees. The weapons employed were
bows, arrows, spears, war axes, and clubs. Fighting was intermittent
and perfunctory. Although many were wounded during these battles,
prisoners were rarely taken and few individuals perished. When village chiefs were killed, their bodies might be carried away by the
enemy and eaten, a practice indulged in to give strength to the victor,
which was reportedly discontinued circa 1875.[31] In the event that no
one was killed in the first encounter, discussion ensued as to whether
the hostilities should be continued. It was common to offer a feast to
the aggressors and to make peace. However, if a killing had occurred,
the death would be avenged by taking the life of an opponent of equal
status before peace, or even a temporary suspension of hostilities,
could be considered. District chiefs joined one side or the other until
most of the island was embroiled in general conflict. These successions
of wars often continued for several months. This meant constant
movement and absence from home villages for considerable lengths of
time, although fighting was interrupted to tend gardens and also for
important feasts which required intensive preparation.

Missionaries tried to persuade local people to get rid of their traditional weapons and were frustrated by the fact that these were seldom
abandoned. On the rare occasions when they were cast aside, it was
usually to replace them with metal axes and firearms. Such imports
became readily available with the rise of labour recruiting activities
between 1860 and 1880. Metal knives, trade axes, and muskets super-
seded stone tools, clubs, bows, and arrows and affected the production
and utilization of locally manufactured weapons. It was observed on
the neighbouring island of Tanna that arms of native manufacture,
with the exception of spears, had almost disappeared by 1870.[32]
Although the demand for firearms was great, the effect of guns upon
traditional warfare was not as extensive as might be imagined. Guns
were desired for their psychological impact rather than for their killing
power; axes served the latter purpose more efficiently.[33] The active dis-
couragement of local warfare is reflected by the arrows, bows, and
clubs included in Robertson's collection. Museum collections of weap-

ons did arise from other circumstances, as is evidenced by the bows and arrows, slings, and spears gathered by Captain Cook during hostile encounters in the New Hebrides.[34] Missionaries also were subjected to aggression, and this would have provided them with a varied selection of arms. It is conceivable that they were anxious to collect weapons in an effort to remove them from local circulation. Weapons were also sought because their craftsmanship was admired.

Although traditional warfare had been removed from the repertoire of activities engaged in by mission supporters, it is interesting to note that during Robertson's residence, the carrying of metal axes and firearms became an acceptable practice for Christian Erromangans. He had gradually become sensitized to the need for members of the Christian party to be armed for protection from rival factions. Robertson's credo that Christian Erromangans had to 'fear God and keep their powder dry' was unmatched, however, among his colleagues.[35] That Christian islanders carried metal axes and guns for their self-defence indicates that they were the weapons of choice for islanders. Evidence of Erromangan desire for introduced weapons including metal knives, trade axes, and firearms is found in numerous accounts.[36] Although Erromangan collections of imported objects have not been preserved for posterity's gaze, one islander's interest in collecting and displaying weapons as 'trophies' is suggested by the following: 'As new and more modern guns were introduced, Yomot [a Christian Erromangan teacher] made every effort to possess one, and to the last I think he loved a first-rate rifle. His house was a kind of "Tower of London," for he kept all his firearms, from an old lumbering blunderbuss up to the modern expensive rifle, perfectly clean and in order.'[37]

The intense interest Erromangans had in warfare was matched only by the great local attention commanded by competitive feasts. These were held frequently and were prepared by one chief in honour of another. Whole seasons were reportedly given up to feasting, with participants travelling between villages and engaging in a thorough round of festivities. Preparations began several months before the actual feast and included the gathering of yams and taro in great numbers, which were attached to large scaffolding. The one aspect required was that the pigs, sacred stones, and other status gifts provided, equal or exceed those given at the previous feast in number and quality. Men and women adorned themselves with body paint and special dress for the occasion and were actively involved in singing, dancing, and feasting that lasted for several days or even weeks. Feasts were occasions celebrating indigenous religious beliefs and also were intertwined with intertribal politics and fighting. They involved displays of what missionaries considered 'heathen' customs including worship of sacred stones and the wearing of traditional dress. In addition to disapproving of religious practices and the type of personal display associated with these events, missionaries objected to the time spent preparing and engaging in feasting activities. They also disparaged the various excesses that typically accompanied feasts including fighting, dancing, and rampant sexual activity.[38] Participating in the displays, exchanges, and other feasting customs was contrary to what the mission considered acceptable behaviour. Missionaries eventually did develop the practice of holding Christian feasts, but these would have been very different from the traditional events. The status value of wearing customary clothing and displaying and exchanging traditional wealth forms (e.g., barkcloth, sacred stones, clubs, and pigs) would diminish, or possibly be inverted for islanders within the context of Christian feasts. Therefore objects related to traditional personal display and wealth would lose significance and be easily available to the missionary collector. This was especially so once European symbols of status gained primacy within the changed circumstances of feasting.

Finally, but not less significantly, both missionaries and islanders were preoccupied with traditional spiritual beliefs. In this domain, well beyond the diverse concerns with appearance, warfare, and feasting did the most profound oppositions lie. Erromangans recognized the great spirit Nobu as the maker of all things. Although he created the island, its people, and the surrounding seas, he was not considered to play an active role in human affairs. The spirits of departed ancestors, however, were believed to be actively engaged in causing harm to humans and were both venerated and feared. All death and illness were regarded as the work of evil spirits, rather than the result of natural causes. Ritual specialists were considered to have influence over these spirits, as well as over weather, gardens, health, and spiritual well-being. Their powers were exercised by the preparation of charms for which they received substantial fees and presents of food. Not surprisingly, these ritual specialists were viewed with hatred and dread.[39] From the arrival of the first resident missionaries, the battle between the efficacy of sorcerers' charms and Christian practices was watched with rapt attention. Missionaries offering medicine and claiming to have remedies for spiritual ills came to be regarded in the same manner as ritual specialists.[40]

Sacred stones and objects associated with sorcery were the material focus of traditional spiritual beliefs. Sacred stones known as *navilah* were kept as heirlooms by the families of chiefs who claimed exclusive possession, believing that they were made by spirits and had been directly given to the chief's first ancestor by Nobu. They were kept hidden and were passed on along hereditary lines upon their owner's death. *Navilah* were made of calcite and were found in a variety of sizes and shapes; each stone had its own distinguishing features, as well as its own name and history. They were used as brideprice and as presents at feasts. In the latter instance, a chief always expected a return in kind at the next feast.

Missionaries directly or indirectly discouraged the use of traditional objects that were viewed as opposing their teachings. They encouraged individuals to relinquish sacred stones and sorcery-related charms, as proof of their surrender to Christianity. It is likely that an increasing disregard for sacred stones was directly related to the introduction of missionary texts and bibles, which were initially perceived as sacred objects or charms. One missionary claimed that islanders feared books as objects capable of generating disease and death, but later came to regard them as charms to keep evil spirits away.[41] Both non-Christian Erromangans and missionaries recognized printed religious texts and sacred stones to be endowed with similar 'symbolic' capacities. When Erromangan traditionalists celebrated their periodic victories over Christian influence, they prohibited the use of religious texts and clothing, and in some cases destroyed them.[42] Alternately, Christian successes were marked by the removal of *navilah* from disease-ridden villages or when their owners abandoned them.[43] The local regard for the latter and the extensive negotiations required for their surrender suggest that they came to be regarded as trophies of missionary triumph.

As Erromangans chose to embrace Christianity, they increasingly adopted its symbols and charismatic objects. Not without significance, this period also corresponded with severe decimation of the island's population. Thus a surplus of traditional ceremonial items occurred as religious practices were altered and populations declined. Many of the ritual accessories collected by missionaries during this period had been supplied by recent converts to Christianity, although converts were also known to burn or otherwise destroy individually owned objects associated with their former religious beliefs. One of the reasons for the prolonged difficulty in obtaining *navilah* was that they were communal, rather than individual property.[44] The abrogation of their sanctity was presented symbolically as a spiritual victory both with regard to communities of Christian islanders and to home country mission supporters. Although the religious texts and mission-introduced garments that Erromangans sought and adopted in the nineteenth century have not been preserved, Erromangan language Bibles and hymnals and the omnipresent 'Mother Hubbard' as standard contemporary women's dress, bear witness to the persistence of Erromangan desire for these objects.

Concluding Remarks

Missionaries used objects to authenticate experiences in distant locales and to establish a visual impression of 'heathenism' more dramatic than could be achieved with the written word.[45] Their fascination with traditional objects may be explained perhaps by a romantic interest in salvaging material that was rapidly disappearing due to increasing use of imported goods and changing local practices. Many missionary collections were used in a practical effort to persuade home country supporters to assist in converting 'heathens' to Christianity. Hugh A. Robertson and his wife Christina, along with other of his colleagues, endeavoured to deepen interest in the New Hebrides mission by visiting various Canadian congregations and presenting examples of islander material culture. Many artifacts now in Canadian museums would have been found within the twelve cases of curiosities he brought on his return to Nova Scotia in 1883. These 'relics and curiosities from the South Seas' were exhibited for several days at the Halifax YMCA and subsequently 'distributed among the various colleges in the Dominion.'[46]

Political motives may have also influenced the selection of objects used to present Erromangans to the Canadian public. The unsettled political status of the area brought vigorous missionary agitation in favour of British annexation by those fearful that the Protestants would lose their ground in the New Hebrides if the French gained control.[47] The annexation argument was staged upon the belief that islanders needed protection, which was then convincingly confirmed with artifactual evidence. Displays of traditional material culture could be used to suggest an inability to adapt to a changing world, thus emphasizing past practices rather than islander capacities for innovation. Missionaries also may have supported nationalistic interests which strove to alter the Canadian self-image from that of a colonized nation to a colonizing one. It is likely that the presentation of objects that conveyed indigenous societies as static and undeveloped could be used to make a strong case for colonial paternalism. That missionary endeavour was linked with national progress was a frequently stated belief.[48]

This analysis is intended to demonstrate that missionary collections represent particular facets of contact history. Although they serve as important documents of cultural change, they may produce misleading results if used uncritically as a basis for reconstructing the past. Collecting is a tangential process to social encounter; in this instance, one between missionaries and islanders in the late nineteenth-century South Pacific. It also is not without its consequences: permanently transforming objects with certain cultural meanings into other ones, imposing interpretations on those that have none, and fixing contexts that are dynamic. Missionary endeavour concentrated on replacing certain material embodiments of Erromangan identity with those that signified a specifically Christian one. At the same time, Erromangan efforts concentrated on innovating traditional material culture, gaining skills, and altering local identities. The latter might include adopting aspects of Christian appearance, non-Christian European custom, or enhancing status by more traditional means such as displaying wealth. None of these were necessarily mutually exclusive adaptations.

Many traditional Erromangan objects were rendered obsolete as a result of the introduction of more efficacious materials, or because the situations in which they were used changed, or because they had been replaced with those that endowed greater status. As traditional manufactures filtered out of local use, they became increasingly available to visitors wishing to document their experiences of exotic culture in a form that was transportable to their home countries. Islanders made certain items available for outsiders to collect, and the very same objects spoke the narratives that missionaries and museums desired to tell. Collections of artifacts in the world's museums resonate with the actions of islanders domesticating their own selections of curios. These Erromangan collections have not been preserved in museums for present-day perusal, but recognition of their past existence encourages an investigation of relationships rather than a mere history of extractions by Europeans and other visitors.

NOTES

1 See, for example, James Clifford, *The Predicament of Culture* (Cambridge:

Harvard University Press, 1988); John Comaroff and Jean Comaroff, *Ethnog-raphy and the Historical Imagination* (Boulder: Westview Press, 1992); Nicholas Thomas, *Entangled Objects: Exchange, Material Culture and Colonialism in the Pacific* (Cambridge: Harvard University Press, 1991); and his *Colonialism's Culture: Anthropology, Travel, and Government* (Princeton: Princeton University Press, 1994).

2 Sally Price, *Primitive Art in Civilized Places* (Chicago and London: University of Chicago Press, 1989); Thomas, *Entangled Objects*, 151–61; Barbara Lawson, *Collected Curios: Missionary Tales from the South Seas* (Montreal: McGill University, 1994). The research for *Collected Curios* was based on my 1990 master's thesis in anthropology at McGill University, one chapter of which was published in *Museum Anthropology* 18, no. 1 (1994): 21–38.

3 Jean Cannizzo, *Into the Heart of Africa* (Toronto: Royal Ontario Museum [ROM], 1989); For a critical analysis of the controversy that developed around this exhibit, which showed in Toronto from November 1989 until August 1990, see Shelly Butler, *Contested Representations: Revisiting 'Into the Heart of Africa'* (Amsterdam: Gordon and Breach Publishers, 1999).

4 See, for example, Thomas, *Entangled Objects*, 151–61; Lawson, *Collected Curios*; Nick Stanley, 'Melanesian Artifacts as Cultural Markers: A Micro-anthropological Study,' in Stephen Riggins, ed., *The Socialness of Things* (New York: Mouton de Gruyter, 1994), 173–99; Jean Cannizzo, 'Gathering Souls and Objects: Missionary Collections,' in Tim Barringer and Tom Flynn, eds, *Colonialism and the Object: Empire, Material Culture and the Museum* (New York: Routledge, 1998), 153–66; Richard Eves, 'Missionary or Collector: The Case of George Brown,' *Museum Anthropology* 22, no. 1 (1998): 49–60; and his article, 'Dr. Brown's Study: Methodist Missionaries and the Collection of Material Culture in the Pacific,' *Museum Anthropology* 24, no. 1 (2000): 26–41; Molly Lee, 'Divine Intervention: Missionaries and Indigenous Art' (Introduction to special issue devoted to Missionaries and Indigenous Art), *Museum Anthropology* 24, no. 1 (2000): 3–4; Helen Gardner, 'Gathering for God: George Brown and the Christian Economy in the Collection of Artifacts,' in Michael O'Hanlon and Robert Welsch, eds, *Hunting the Gatherers: Ethnographic Collectors, Agents and Agency in Melanesia, 1870s–1930s* (New York: Berghahn Books, 2000), 35–54.

5 Dawson's participation foreshadows his lifelong religious commitment and later ambition to change Canada's status from colonial outpost to active participant in the world of scientific and cultural empire. See Susan Sheets-Pyenson, *Cathedrals of Science* (Montreal/Kingston: McGill-Queen's University Press, 1988); and Barbara Lawson, 'Exhibiting Agendas:

Anthropology at the Redpath Museum (1882–1899),' *Anthropologica* 61, no. 1 (1999): 53–65.

6 Although there had been some limited participation by women in the labour trade, Erromangan women and children had little contact with the earliest visitors until the missionaries arrived, usually accompanied by wives and often children.

7 Robertson's book *Erromanga: The Martyr Isle* (Toronto: Westminster Co.) was published in 1902, but cannot be assumed to represent the culmination of his experience to that date. It ends with the description of a trip to Canada in 1883, his return to Erromango in 1885 after a two-year leave, and a few sketchy comments regarding later events, especially those between 1886 and 1887. In all probability, the book is based on journal entries or letters written during this period.

8 See, for example Darrell Whiteman, *Melanesians and Missionaries* (Pasadena: William Carey Library, 1983), 99–169, regarding the Anglican Melanesian Mission.

9 Robertson, *Martyr Isle*, 359, 394.

10 See Barbara Lawson, '"Clothed and in their Right Mind": Women's Dress on Erromango, Vanuatu,' *Pacific Arts* 23/24 (2001): 69–86. This strategy is often highlighted in missionary tracts with illustrations showing the difference in attire between 'heathens' and 'Christians.' See Lawson, *Collected Curios*, 143.

11 The most dramatic changes occurred in local population levels, which had dwindled from an estimated 2500 in 1882, to 1500 in 1894 (excluding those engaged as labourers in Queensland or elsewhere), to 420 people in 1920. See Clarence B. Humphreys, *The Southern New Hebrides: An Ethnological Record* (Cambridge: Cambridge University Press, 1926), 128; and Lawson, *Collected Curios*, 94, 126.

12 Lawson, *Collected Curios*.

13 Dorothy Shineberg, *They Came for Sandalwood: A Study of the Sandalwood Trade in the South-West Pacific, 1830–1865* (Melbourne: Melbourne University Press, 1967), 15.

14 Lawson, *Collected Curios*, 78, 88, and 'Clothed and in Their Right Mind.'

15 Robertson, *Martyr Isle*, 372–3.

16 These particular hybrid objects have all been observed by the author in various museum collections.

17 Lawson, *Collected Curios*, 149–50.

18 The Redpath's Ethnology collections include over 16,000 ethnological and archaeological artifacts, with particular concentrations from central Africa,

Oceania, and ancient Egypt. For details regarding their history, see Lawson, *Collected Curios*, and Lawson, 'Exhibiting Agendas.'

19 Lawson, *Collected Curios*, and also 'Clothed and in their Right Mind.' See also Kirk Huffman, 'The "Decorated Cloth" from the "Island of Good Yams": Barkcloth in Vanuatu, with Special Reference to Erromango,' in Joël Bonnemaison et al., eds, *Arts of Vanuatu* (Bathurst: Crawford House, 1996), 129–40.

20 Barbara Lawson, 'From Curio to Cultural Document,' in Simon Knell, ed., *Museums and the Future of Collecting* (Aldershot, UK: Ashgate Publishing, 1999), 63–72; and Lawson, 'Clothed and in Their Right Mind.'

21 The transfer is documented in a letter dated 26 July 1971 at the Nova Scotia Museum from G.R. Smith, Secretary, Pine Hill Divinity Hall to the Nova Scotia Museum's Chief Curator of History, George MacLaren. This letter refers to the material being transferred as the 'Geddie Collection.'

22 In terms of the relative difficulty of acquiring sacred stones in the 1870s, see C.F. Wood, *Yachting Cruise in the South Seas* (London: Henry S. King and Company, 1875), 87; and Robertson, *Martyr Isle*, 359–60, 390.

23 Wood, *Yachting Cruise*, 84–90.

24 Julius L. Brenchley, *Jottings during the Cruise of H.M.S. 'Curaçoa' among the South Sea Islands in 1865* (London: Longmans, Green, and Company, 1873), 298, 300–5.

25 There are also a few donations from their daughter/s, 'Miss C. Robertson' and some from a 'Miss Robertson,' at the Bishop Museum in Hawaii.

26 Lawson, 'Clothed and in Their Right Mind.'

27 Robertson, *Martyr Isle*, 364.

28 Lawson, *Collected Curios*, 143–6.

29 This was true not only of cloth, but also of the medicines and printed texts offered by missionaries in competition with the cures and charms available from local ritual specialists. See Lawson, *Collected Curios*, 100–1, 107–8, 116, 136–8. See also Nicolas Thomas, 'The Case of the Misplaced Ponchos: Speculations Concerning the History of Cloth in Polynesia,' *Journal of Material Culture* 4, no. 1 (1999): 5–20, regarding Christian clothes in Polynesia as 'technologies' of empowerment.

30 James Cook, *The Journals of Captain James Cook on his Voyages of Discovery: The Voyage of the 'Resolution' and 'Adventure,' 1772–1775*, vol. 2, edited by John Beaglehole, Hakluyt Society extra series 35 (Cambridge: Cambridge University Press, 1961), 477–9; J.W. Davidson, 'Peter Dillon and the Discovery of Sandalwood in the New Hebrides,' *Journal de la société des Océanistes* 19 (1956): 99–105, esp. 102–3; George Bennett, 'Account of the Islands Erromanga and Tanna, New Hebrides Group,' *Asiatic Journal and Monthly Regis-*

ter for British and Foreign India, China, and Australasia, n.s., vol. 7 (1832): 119–31, esp. 123; Brenchley, Jottings during the Cruise, 300–1; Robertson, Martyr Isle, 25.

31 Robertson, Martyr Isle, 393.
32 William T. Wawn, The South Sea Islanders and the Queensland Labour Trade (London: Swan Sonnenschein & Company, 1893), 10, 21–2.
33 Dorothy Shineberg, 'Guns and Men in Melanesia,' Journal of Pacific History 6 (1971): 61–82.
34 Adrienne L. Kaeppler, Artificial Curiosities: An Exposition of Native Manufactures Collected on the Three Voyages of Captain James Cook, R.N. Bernice P. Bishop Museum Special Publication, no. 65 (Honolulu: Bishop Museum Press, 1978), 247.
35 Robertson, Martyr Isle, 209.
36 Bennett, 'Account of the Islands,' 123; Brenchley, Jottings during the Cruise, 300–1; Robertson, Martyr Isle, 202, 209, 216–19, 247, 269, 318, 351–2; Wawn, South Sea Islanders, 10, 21–2.
37 Robertson, Martyr Isle, 351.
38 Ibid., 391.
39 Ibid., 402.
40 Lawson, Collected Curios, 72–3, 80, 100–1, 106–8, 123, 138.
41 Ibid., 78.
42 James D. Gordon, The Last Martyrs of Erromanga, Being a Memoir of the Rev. George Gordon and his Wife (Halifax: McNab & Shaffer, 1863), 179; George Patterson, Missionary Life among Cannibals, Being the Life of Rev. J. Geddie (Toronto: James Campbell & Son, 1882), 448; Robertson, Martyr Isle, 157.
43 Robertson, Martyr Isle, 359–60, 390.
44 Ibid., 390.
45 See Lawson, Collected Curios, 151–2.
46 As reported in the Presbyterian Record 8, no. 8 (1883): 216, and in the Maritime Presbyterian 3, no. 9 (1883): 261.
47 Lawson, Collected Curios, 82–9, 153.
48 See, for example, J.W. Dawson's expansionist views regarding foreign missions in 'Foreign Missions,' Presbyterian Record 10 (1885): 20, and A.B. Dickie, 'The Commercial Value of Missions,' Maritime Presbyterian 1 (1881): 160, regarding the commercial potential of foreign missions.

Chapter 11

'Curios' from a Strange Land: The Oceania Collections of the Reverend Joseph Annand

ARTHUR M. SMITH

A number of Canadian museums are guardians to collections of artifacts acquired by Canadian missionaries during the nineteenth century. The Robertson collection at McGill University's Redpath Museum, described by Barbara Lawson in chapter 10, is one example, as well as another collection from Vanuatu, the Geddie collection at the Nova Scotia Museum. The Royal Ontario Museum (ROM) in Toronto has many missionary collections, such as the Walter T. Currie collection, which was featured in the ROM's *Into the Heart of Africa* exhibit (16 November 1989–29 July 1990), and the Richard W. Large collection of Pacific northwest coast Native art.

During the Victorian era ethnological material from Africa, Asia, Oceania, and Native America was highly sought after by private collectors and museums in North America and Europe. Canadian institutions were no exception. In the late 1800s Ontario archaeologist David Boyle established one of the first ethnological museums in Canada at the Toronto Normal School. Although his primary focus was on North American Native artifacts, Boyle wanted to expand the collection to incorporate material from other 'primitive' cultures. He enlisted the aid of Canadian missionaries in foreign mission fields to fulfill this goal.

Boyle's biographer Gerald Killan observed that Boyle's admiration for the ethnological collections in such major European museums as the Louvre and the British Museum strengthened his resolve to place considerably more emphasis on the anthropological side of his work. Upon returning to Toronto following a two-month tour to Liverpool, Paris, London, Edinburgh, and Glasgow in 1900, a stream of letters soliciting donations flowed out of his office to various museums and to religious missions all over the world. Within two years, missionaries in such far-flung outposts as the New Hebrides, Angola, Bella Bella, BC, and Herschell Island near the mouth of the Mackenzie River obliged him by sending crates full of samples of Native dress, ornaments, weapons, and utensils. By 1903 Boyle had gathered sufficient material to warrant the opening of a separate ethnological room in the provincial museum.[1]

Among those with whom Boyle cultivated a relationship was the Rev. Joseph Annand, a Presbyterian missionary from Nova Scotia who served in the New Hebrides mission (present-day Vanuatu) from 1873 until 1912. Annand left a substantial legacy of daily journals documenting the forty-year period he resided in the South Pacific,[2] which complement his artifact collections now housed at the Royal Ontario Museum,[3] and the Maritime Conference of the United Church of Canada Archives in Sackville, New Brunswick.[4] Annand was also a prolific writer of letters, both personal and corporate.

His written material is a rich source of information on his life and work in Vanuatu. They are particularly useful for determining Annand's perspective on Vanuatu culture and for recording his interaction with the native peoples, especially his encounters with traditional practices such as feasting, 'singsings' (dance ceremonies), infanticide, widow strangulation, treatment of the infirm, the ritual sacrifice of pigs, and the drinking of the narcotic *kava*. They also document his intense opposition to the labour trade (referred to as the 'slave trade' by the missionaries in the New Hebrides), which saw the islands depleted of a high percentage of the young male population for use on the British plantations in Queensland and the French plantations in New Caledonia. The missionaries maintained that most of the men were recruited using forceful and fraudulent means, and the conditions of the labour trade were so harsh that many *kanakas* (labourers) failed to survive their indenture and to return to their homeland.

Presbyterian religious zeal was the motivating factor for a number of missionaries to leave their homes in Nova Scotia and Prince Edward Island for the un-Westernized and un-Christianized islands of the South Pacific between 1845, when the Rev. John and Charlotte Geddie were the first Canadian missionaries sent overseas, and 1900. Their endeavour to Christianize the native peoples went hand in hand with their importation of Western culture and the destruction of traditional customs or *kastom*. The missionaries acted as agents of cultural change that was part and parcel of the Victorian era of colonialism and imperialism.

Joseph Annand was born 1 January 1844 at Gay's River, Nova Scotia, and raised on the family farm. After education at the grammar school in Shubenacadie, he received a bachelor of arts degree from Dalhousie University and taught for two years in rural Nova Scotia, prior to attending Princeton Theological Seminary in 1869. Annand retired from the New Hebrides mission in December 1912, settling in Hantsport, Nova Scotia, where he died 28 January 1932. His wife Alice predeceased him by two years.

Annand agonized over his decision to seek a foreign mission field while a theological student in 1869–70. He was committed to the Presbyterian theology of saving the 'perishing souls' of the 'heathen.' 'My highest aim in life is to live for my Redeemer to the conversion of lost souls.'[5] Princeton afforded Annand the opportunity to hear first-hand the accounts of missionary experiences. On 24 October 1869 he heard Dr Andrew P. Happer of the American Presbyterian mission in China mission speak of his work. Later that day Annand wrote in his journal: 'This day has almost decided my offering for a heathen land. Oh for light from on high to guide me aright. Wrote my brother for advice on this point. Feel quite a missionary spirit tonight. May it never die nor slumber in me.'[6]

He also noted reading a number of missionary biographies, including that of John Williams of the London Missionary Society, the first European missionary to visit the New Hebrides in 1839, who was 'martyred' on the island of Erromango by the 'cannibals.'[7] 'Read lives of several missionaries today, of [Jacob] Chamberlain, Gordon, Hall, S[amuel] Newell to India and that of John Williams to South Seas. Great success attended this last.'[8] Annand was so inspired by Williams and his 'martyrdom' that he felt called to volunteer for an overseas mission, ignoring the advice of his older brother, the Rev. Edward Annand, who counselled him to return to Nova Scotia where there was plenty of work for a newly ordained Presbyterian minister.[9]

Annand expressed his dilemma in his daily journal at the time: 'I feel that Jesus is my friend and I am safe for eternity. Oh that he would fit me for the work in heathen lands! I dread some things about leaving all that is near and dear to me but my commission says go into all the world. Some must go and others will not so I shall. God seems to be designing me for that work ... I feel some times that I could die for the gospel's spread and God's glory.'[10]

The Foreign Mission Board in Nova Scotia accepted Annand as a missionary in July 1870. By this time he had decided not to continue his studies at Princeton due to the expense. He returned instead to Halifax to complete his theological studies at the Presbyterian College and a master of arts degree from Dalhousie University, graduating with both his MA and Bachelor of Divinity in the spring of 1872. Following his ordination at Lunenburg, Nova Scotia, Annand did some supply preaching in Nova Scotia during the autumn of 1872. In the same year the Presbyterian Synod appointed him to its New Hebridean mission.

Annand did not wish to pursue his vocation as an overseas missionary alone. While a student he had courted one woman who rejected his offer of marriage because she was unwilling to accompany him overseas. He subsequently met Alice Mary Seville, a native of England teaching in Halifax, who shared Annand's passion for foreign missions. They were married on 3 July 1872, and embarked for the South Seas four months later on 5 November 1872. Having a wife set Annand apart from the single white traders and labour recruiters who were often feared by the native peoples for their exploitation and violence. Annand believed Alice's presence inspired the native peoples to trust him in ways they were unprepared to trust the other white men.

The Annands established their mission station on the tiny islet of Iririki during the summer of 1873, within close proximity to native villages on the islets of Fila and Meli, off the west coast of Efate (the current site of Port Vila, capital of Vanuatu). They brought with them hired native servants from the established Presbyterian mission station on the island of Aneityum. Annand's journals offer insight into the frustrations he experienced during his three-year tenure at Iririki. The inhabitants of Meli and Fila viewed the Annands' presence with great suspicion, limiting most of their contact to trading activity and medical assistance. His journals contain almost daily laments for his inability to carry out his mission, and are filled with petitions for God's intervention to make the natives receptive to his message of salvation. The Annands' early years were committed to establishing a mission station at Iririki, planting a garden, learning the language, and coping with debilitating illnesses (especially malaria and painful boils) that often laid low both of them. The mission station was erected at the top of the hill on Iririki. The Annands' house was a framed structure with a verandah, built on a foundation, using lumber brought with them from Australia and local coral for flooring. Construction began on 1 August 1873, and they occupied their new home eight days later. They then proceeded to erect a 'native house' for their servants. This was followed by a boat house and a road from the mission station to the landing, as well as a goat house and a bath house. Once established in their new abode, the Annands worked at making it more hospitable and attractive. A lime kiln was constructed to provide whitewash for painting the house. Some time was also given over to their garden, where they planted border grass and bananas (provided by their closest missionary neighbour, the Rev. James W. MacKenzie at Erakor) in addition to beans, corn, orange seeds, melons, pumpkins, tomatoes, taro, yams, and cedar.

Learning the native language proved to be an exacting task for Annand. The limited contact he had with the nearby inhabitants frustrated his efforts, and were compounded when he discovered they were deliberately giving him incorrect words. During their second year on Iririki, Annand engaged the services of a local youth named 'Kalivevi' to perform chores around the mission station. Annand referred to him as his 'pundit,' and was slowly able to build up his vocabulary through his interactions with him.

While en route to the South Pacific in 1872 the Annands had toured England and Scotland. Annand noted in his journal visits to the botanical gardens in Edinburgh and London. Victorian botanical gardens were noted for generating a personal interest in gardening and the transplanting of botanical specimens from one geographic locale to another. Annand was no exception, for he cultivated a Victorian-style garden around his mission station on Iririki with 'fancy shrubs and transplanted ... flowers' and walkways of local coral.[11] By 1875 he was boasting a hundred rose flowers in bloom, and when he departed in 1876, he wrote of leaving 'a lovely spot well in order and adorned. The garden is beautiful still.'[12]

Annand's gardening practices suggest the influence of the botanical gardens, rather than the utilitarian gardening with which he would have been familiar growing up in rural Nova Scotia. Later in his missionary career Annand mentioned visiting botanical gardens in Sydney (New South Wales), Hobart (Tasmania), Dunedin and Christchurch (New Zealand), and Kew Gardens (London). The botanical gardens are one clue to suggest the Victorian cultural forces that influenced Annand and his future collection practices.

By 1876 the Annands were forced to admit defeat in the missionary endeavour at Iririki, having failed to convert any of the native peoples of Meli and Fila. They abandoned the mission station at Iririki and relocated to the well-established mission at Anelgauhat on Aneityum, where there was more time for leisurely activities.[13] Now for the first time, his journals begin to record his collecting expeditions, often accompanied by Alice. Sometimes he would be joined by visiting seamen, such as Captain G. Braithwaite of the Presbyterian mission ship *Dayspring*, or touring naturalists such as the German botanist and explorer Baron Ferdinand von Müller.

Annand's natural history collecting was broad-ranging, encompassing both flora and fauna of the islands. His collection efforts were not casual in nature, but demonstrated a deliberate attempt to fully document the natural history of the region. In the tradition of Victorian naturalists, the Annands used their collecting excursions to combine 'the study of nature with the pleasures of the picnic and healthy outdoor exercise.'[14] Annand's collections embraced ferns, orchids, cowrie shells, mosses, seaweed, red coral, butterflies, beetles, silver weevil, mineral specimens, bats, and birds (including pigeons, plovers, and curlews). The bird and bat specimens were skinned and stuffed to preserve them. The ferns, mosses, and seaweed were pressed and mounted in books, usually with the assistance of Alice.

In addition to his personal collections, Annand sent specimens of ferns and coral to church women in Australia (including a Miss Gibson of Greenfield); a large array of butterflies to Levi Mengel (a schoolteacher in Reading, Pennsylvania, who had written Annand seeking specimens); plants for a Dr Marden; butterflies, flower seeds, and leaves of an acacia for Baron von Müller; shells for the Rev. Dr McGibbons of Sydney, NSW; and natural specimens to Dr Hubert Lyman Clark at Harvard University. In his collecting Annand demonstrated a passion for natural history that society expected of a well-educated Victorian.

Turning again to Annand's journals, we find clues to the Victorian institutions that would have moulded and informed his collecting practices. As early as 1869 while a student at Princeton, Annand commented on a trip to New York City and the wild animals he saw at the menagerie in Central Park. In Princeton he enjoyed several visits to the renowned Victorian gardens of Judge Richard Stockton Field.[15] During his stopover in England in 1872, Annand wrote of visiting the zoological gardens in London and seeing the many varieties of beasts and birds as well as reptiles and fishes to be seen in that place. 'We had a very pleasant day of it and got our money's worth certainly. The things of greatest interest to us were the seals, sea lions and hippopotami. The latter especially are something that cannot be seen elsewhere on this continent so far as I am aware and none of them have been taken as yet to America. The elephants are huge monsters and very tame and obedient to their masters. Came away home fully satisfied with the day's experiences.'[16]

Combined with the influence of the botanical gardens, the zoological gardens served to inspire Annand's evolution as a Victorian naturalist and collector of the highest order. Unfortunately, however, no remnants of Annand's natural history collections appear to have survived to the present.

Whereas numerous journal entries document Annand's passion for natural history, he did not confine his collecting solely to ferns and butterflies. As early as 1875, while at Iririki, he wrote of the purchase of ethnological artifacts, specifically a number of spears and clubs. In 1881 he noted the acquisition of a considerable number of 'curios' when visiting the Vanuatu island of Tongoa, including 'a spear, two clubs and some pudding carvers.'[17] On a trip to Meli on the island of Efate in 1897, he described the purchase of some armlets and beads.

The 'spirits' were represented in traditional Vanuatu culture (or 'kastom') by sacred objects referred to as *natmasses*. Jeanne Cannizzo uses the more generic term 'fetishes' in her work on the W.T. Currie missionary collection to refer to such sacred objects. These 'fetishes' were often surrendered by native peoples to the missionaries at the time of their conversion to Christianity. Although 'fetishes' figured prominently in a number of missionary collections,[18] they do not appear in the surviving collections of Annand, despite a journal entry of 1884 acknowledging the receipt of a 'stone of Jobe's called and used by him as a natmas. Had two but one was thrown away. Kaka sent it to me with explanatory note.'[19] Other *natmasses* noted in his possession included Mataro's 'Turtle eye' and 'the eye of the Sancho.' These were given to Annand by the converts to Christianity, and were considered by Annand to be relics of 'heathen' practices which he was determined to eliminate.

Annand acquired ethnological material for himself as well as for colleagues in the mission field. In 1892 he described 'putting up spears for Mrs. [Agnes C.P.] Watt and Mrs. [Hugh A.] Robertson.'[20] His most significant museum contribution was to the Ontario Archaeological Museum at the Toronto Normal School in 1896 at the behest of its curator, David Boyle, for which he sought no remuneration other than the costs of shipping.[21] Whereas masks and carvings were most sought after by museums, Boyle and Annand were more interested in domestic artifacts as examples of the concept of 'survivals' within the academic field of comparative ethnology. They believed these 'survivals' demonstrated the evolutionary nature of manners and customs from prehistoric times to the present. The study of domestic artifacts belonging to 'primitive' cultures such as those found in nineteenth-century Vanuatu was the means to understanding the superior culture of Western civilization and to interpreting the prehistoric era. Since Boyle wanted to expand the collections at the Toronto Normal School museum to include ethnological artifacts from other continents, he specifically appealed to Annand for 'a collection of things that might fully illustrate the life of the female from infancy to old age.'[22]

Although Annand was sympathetic to Boyle's request, he responded, 'Of course among these people the life of the two sexes are so interwoven in their work, and the things distinctively female are so few that I fear we can not do much to carry out your idea. However I will try and bear in mind your suggestion and possibly it may come to something substantial.'[23] Annand's response is indicative of the thought and consideration he gave to collecting native material culture, and his collecting was not undertaken lightly at another's behest.

The accessions book for the Toronto Normal School collections, now held by the ROM, documents the receipt of the Annand collection in 1897. The collection consisted of native dress for men and women, seven clubs, bows and arrows, spears (one believed by Annand to be tipped with human bones), stone adzes, a walking stick, mouth organ, fire drill kit, shell breastplate, spoon, cup made from coconut shell, combs, axes, boars' tusks, *kava* plates, 'pudding platter' and dishes with sticks for pounding cooked breadfruit, a figurehead from a canoe, strings of beads, belt girdle, baskets, mat, pot, and basin. Annand included a written description of each artifact and its traditional native functions. These descriptions were copied into the Normal School accessions book in some detail, in contrast to other donations such as the Dr T.W. Beeman collection from Perth, Ontario, which only had brief entries identifying the object and its geographical origins.

One example of Annand's descriptive detail is a club: 'The most highly valued club of Epi, Paama and Ambinu [*sic*], the loop is for carrying the club hung from the shoulder.' Greater elaboration is given for four boar's tusks, which were 'worn as bracelets, also hung from the neck both front and back. The social standing of chiefs in the north end of the group [Vanuatu] depends upon the number of boars with such tusks that the chiefs have killed and given in feasts. No man becomes a "Moli" (high chief) until he has killed a hundred of them and several hundred other pigs. The tusk is made to grow circularly by knocking out the corresponding upper teeth when the animal is young. In every chief's house the lower jaws are hung up as evidence of the owner's social position.' Annand devoted considerable effort to providing Boyle with full descriptions of the artifacts he sent, demonstrating his interest in the evolving field of ethnological studies.

A suggestion from the American teacher Levi Mengel that Annand send 'older anthropological material of the natives ... such things as the implements of warfare, &c' to the Academy of Natural Sciences in Philadelphia was very cooly received.[24] The Annands passed through San Francisco while on furlough in 1887, where they received an inquiry from the firm of Nathan Joseph & Co. for 'skulls, axes, any of their handiwork, not too large, but not weapons unless small, minerals, &c &c &c &c.'[25] Annand agreed to try to accommodate the request. However, there is no indication within his journals that he ever fulfilled the order.

It would appear from these two instances that Annand was principally interested in contributing ethnological artifacts to public collections in Toronto and Halifax, where he had personal knowledge of the institutions and their keepers. One exception was a collection of bows, arrows, and spears which he sent to the North Henan Mission museum in China, probably in response to an appeal from one of his Presbyterian missionary colleagues.[26]

When Annand first travelled beyond the borders of Nova Scotia to study at Princeton, he commented, 'Am getting new and enlarged ideas of the world by travelling in the States.'[27] Over the next fifty years he circled the globe a number of times, becoming an avid sightseer as well as a connoisseur of museums and galleries. He visited the Academy of Fine Art in Philadelphia in 1869, and later entries record his visits to the Museum of Antiquities in Edinburgh; the South Kensington (now the Victoria and Albert Museum) and British Museums in London;[28] museums and galleries in Sydney, Melbourne, and Hobart; and the Cairo Museum in Egypt. His journals offer brief glimpses of his reactions to these visits with such comments as 'our choice' and 'terribly grand.' Following his 27 March 1885 tour of the South Kensington Museum he wrote: 'We saw an immense variety of things of great interest but still we did not get over the whole. The Indian departments pleased us most of all. A gold chair took my eye.'

Annand attended such places with a critical eye, passing judgment on pieces which were of particular interest to him, such as 'The Queen of Sheba before Solomon' in the art gallery in Sydney, and the classical portrayal of Oberon and Titania by Paton in Edinburgh. We get a flavour of Annand's 'critical eye' from this journal entry of 27 March 1885, in which he described in considerable detail some paintings he had viewed at the Doré Gallery of Paintings in London:

> Enjoyed them very much indeed, especially 'Christ leaving the Practorium' 20x30 feet, made from 1867–72; 'Christ's entry in Jerusalem,' same size, 1876; 'The Vale of Tears' 14x21; 'Come unto me &c,' two 'Ecce Homo' and the 'Ascension' are very fine. Thence we went to see the New Spanish picture of Senor Echena called 'Arrival at Calvary.' Was a little disappointed in this picture. The figures in the foreground are very good but in the Saviour's features as well as in that of the women he fails.

From this account we get a strong sense of Annand's appreciation for the arts of the Victorian era.

Annand used the term 'curios' to refer to his collections, which served a basic function common to missionary collectors of the nineteenth century such as the Rev. Hugh A. Robertson. They were maintained to accompany Annand on his furloughs in Australia and Canada, when he sought to raise interest and funds from Presbyterian churches to support his missionary endeavour in Vanuatu.[29] They served to demonstrate to Western audiences the 'primitive' and 'exotic' nature of the native peoples who were being Christianized and civilized by their missionary effort. Nicholas Thomas has argued that by the end of the nineteenth century the term 'curio' was associated in the eyes of Westerners with symbols of idolatry and cannibalism in such a manner as to evoke strong moralistic responses.[30] Consequently, 'curios' were a valuable visual aide for Annand to use as he travelled on furlough, seeking financial and moral support for his mission work,[31] as illustrated by his diary entry of 15 October 1906 at Alberton, Prince Edward Island, when he recorded receipt of a 'thank offering' of '$14+.'

Creating a collection of 'curios' to take with him on furlough was not Annand's sole motivation for collecting native artifacts. In a letter to Boyle, he noted: 'Few people seem willing to contribute to Museums, while private collectors increase in number almost daily.'[32] Annand was committed to acquiring material for public institutions to preserve domestic remnants of a native culture he believed to be dying as a consequence of Westernization, in which he played an instrumental role as an agent of cultural change. A significant depopulation of the islands of Vanuatu occurred throughout the latter half of the nineteenth century due to imported diseases and loss of young males to the slave trade. Annand fully believed that whole islands would eventually see their populations wiped out. Among the surviving populace Annand was determined to stamp out traditional native practices, or 'kastom,' through the introduction of Western material culture, including European-style dress, meals and homes, church organ music, and English as the language of instruction at the Teacher Training Institution at Tangoa. While promoting the cause of 'salvation ethnography,' Annand firmly believed in the superiority of Western culture and Christianity, much to the detriment of local 'kastom.'

Several photographs of the Annand home on Tangoa survive and reside with family members in Nova Scotia. They vividly illustrate how the Annands created a Western culture in a foreign land. Though the furnishings are Victorian in style, Annand also indulged in the Victorian tradition of decorating his home with the 'exotic.' As he packed up his residence to retire to Nova Scotia in the autumn of 1912, he wrote of taking down the spears that had adorned his abode for a number of years, and of his provision for shipping home his personal collection of artifacts. 'This day I got our spears, clubs, bows and arrows and golf clubs (5) packed for shipping home.'[33] The whereabouts of his personal collections are unknown, though a few artifacts continue to reside with surviving family members in Canada.

Annand acquired his ethnological collections through barter with the native peoples of Vanuatu who were willing to trade their spears and clubs, baskets, and shells in exchange for fish hooks and lines, calico, tobacco, beads, hatchets, and knives. Trading their 'curios' was also one of the few means by which native peoples could acquire money, other than working for missionaries and traders, and selling yams and fowls.[34] In a letter to the Rev. Dr Peter M. Morrison published in 1896, Annand described the acquisition of a native male costume while on a sailing expedition around the island of Santo in August 1896 looking for prospective mission sites: 'Here we noticed a peculiar style of dress not seen elsewhere in the group. It consists of a block of wood worn across the upper part of the hips, with a lot of fancy strings with beads stretched across the front and fastened to the ends of the block. I secured one for the Ethnological Museum in Tor-

Interior of Joseph Annand's house in the New Hebrides in the 1890s, where he displayed his collections of 'native curios' in a Victorian bungalow before he brought them back to Canada.

onto.'[35] This particular artifact was sent to David Boyle with an accompanying note from Annand indicating that it had been purchased off a man's back. He had been reluctant to part with it as it would leave him 'nude,' but Annand 'induced him to part with it ... [for] twenty sticks of tobacco.'[36] The use of tobacco as a medium of exchange is ironic in light of Annand's disapproval of smoking, but it was commonly used for barter by the missionaries on Vanuatu.

Soon after retiring to Nova Scotia Annand assisted the Rev. Dr Clarence Mackinnon, principal of the Presbyterian College in Halifax, with labelling the ethnological artifacts he had donated to the college. This small collection currently resides in the Maritime Conference Archives in Sackville, New Brunswick, with some of Annand's original labels still attached. By labelling his collection of native artifacts as 'curios,' Annand decontextualized them. He adopted the prevailing European approach to artifacts, whereby objects were displayed in a symmetrical arrangement that totally ignored their function and value in traditional native culture. When Annand's collection at the Ontario Archaeological Museum was exhibited to the public in October 1897, domestic tools were placed beside traditional costumes, while all arms were labelled as 'weapons of warfare,' a highly suspect categorization since Annand himself identified many of the objects as used for hunting and ceremonial purposes. An article in the Toronto *Mail and Empire*, entitled, 'War Clubs and Axes; The New Hebrides Islanders' Terrible Weapons,' highlighted the use of human bones, and labelled a 'Santo war spear ... a truly hideous affair.'[37] The text deliberately portrayed a negative image of an 'uncivilized' and 'savage' culture from an exotic part of the world, thus allowing its Canadian audience to perceive itself as a superior or dominant culture.

The Annand journals and collections survive as a reminder of a Victorian culture fascinated by the 'exotic' and the 'primitive,' and dedicated to preserving remnants of a perceived 'vanishing' culture. Within the framework of the museum Annand believed his 'curios' from an 'uncivilized' culture could be forever preserved as a means of documenting the evolution of humankind. Annand's collecting activities may be considered an example of 'salvage ethnography' as defined by ethnologists such as Abraham Rosman and Paula G. Rubel only in so far that he helped to preserve 'survivals.' In their study of the collection practices of the Rev. George Brown in New Ireland, Rubel and Rosman acknowledge ethnographical salvaging as the primary motivation for Brown. They suggest Brown held a genuine interest in indigenous culture and language, and was committed to their preservation.[38] Annand, on the other hand, was not attempting to preserve *'kastom,'* but, as noted earlier, its eradication.

From another perspective Linda Hutcheon has argued that missionary collections must be viewed within the context of the history of imperialism, whereby they represent the spoils of colonial conquest.[39] Annand, the missionary, was very much a part of the colonial era. He was a promoter of not just Christianity, but British culture and values. His collections must be viewed within this context. Whether 'salvaged' artifacts or spoils of conquest, the challenge for ethnological museums in contemporary society is to create a new paradigm within which the integrity of native artifacts is maintained and the culture from which they were acquired is acknowledged, while respecting the multicultural diversity of the community in which they are exhibited. Hutcheon has articulated much of this discussion in her 1995 study of the ROM's *Into the Heart of Africa* exhibition. Museologists have begun to chart a new course when creating new ethnological exhibitions in light of these discussions. The most notable change has been the integration of community consultations with multicultural groups and First Nations into the exhibition planning process, as evidenced at institutions like the ROM and the Canadian Museum of Civilization. While it is important to recognize the cultural motivations of the Victorian missionary collector within the context of the imperial era, contemporary culture needs to acknowledge their role in preserving native material culture and history.

NOTES

1 Gerald Killan. *David Boyle: From Artisan to Archaeologist* (Toronto: University of Toronto Press, 1983), 203. Contrary to Killan's assertion, the Annand–Boyle relationship pre-dates the Boyles' European tour of 1900. The Annand Collection arrived in Toronto in 1897, and surviving correspondence between Annand and Boyle is dated as early as 1896. Annand's journals mention visiting the lyceum and museum at the Toronto Normal School while on furlough in 1895. In December 1895 Annand indicated that he had written to Boyle (Annand, 11 December 1895). The final contact between Annand and Boyle appears to have been in 1907, when Annand visited Boyle in Toronto and toured the museum. (Annand, 5 March 1907).

2 Annand's journals were donated by his nephew, Donald Annand, to the

Nova Scotia Archives and Records Management (NSA), Halifax, Nova
Scotia (cited as Annand, *Journals*). Several letters to his sister Bertha (Lynch)
Grant have survived, and may be found with the journals. Two letters writ-
ten to David Boyle reside with the Boyle papers at the Royal Ontario
Museum (ROM). Numerous letters by Annand were published in Presbyte-
rian newspapers in Canada, including the *Presbyterian Record* and the *Home
and Foreign Record* of the Presbyterian Church of the Lower Provinces of
British North America.

3 The collections of the Toronto Normal School (also referred to as the Provincial Museum, the Ontario Archaeological Museum, and the Ethnological Museum) were transferred to the ROM in 1933.

4 The small collection of artifacts in the Maritime Conference Archives were
originally presented by Annand to the Presbyterian College in Halifax.

5 Annand, *Journals*, 7 April 1870.

6 Annand, *Journals*, 24 October 1869.

7 Williams was murdered at Dillon's Bay on the island of Erromango when
he ventured inland to explore the island's interior. In later years the native
inhabitants explained that Williams was killed because they feared the
white man had come to steal their women and food. These were legitimate
fears, for shortly before Williams's arrival a chief's daughter had been
taken by white traders, in addition to pigs and yams. See Robert S. Miller,
ed., *Misi Gete, John Geddie: Pioneer Missionary to the New Hebrides* (Launces-
ton, Australia: Presbyterian Church of Tasmania, 1975), 6–7.

8 Annand, *Journals*, 21 November 1869.

9 Annand, *Journals*, 15 March 1870.

10 Annand, *Journals*, 7 April 1870.

11 Annand, *Journals*, 3 March 1874.

12 Annand, *Journals*, 12 July 1876.

13 The Presbyterian mission station at Anelgauhat on Aneityum was established in 1848 by the first Canadian missionary to Vanuatu, the Rev. John
Geddie. Geddie retired to Australia in 1872 and died later that year. When
the Annands arrived in 1876, they assumed responsibility for the mission
station recently vacated by the Rev. James D. Murray due to his wife Ellen's
blindness. The Annands resided at Anelgauhat until 1887, when they were
relocated to the isle of Tangoa, off the south coast of Santo. The Synod
approved the establishment of a teachers' training institution on Tangoa in
1887, naming Annand as its first principal. It opened with seven students
on 18 March 1895.

14 Carl Berger, *Science, God, and Nature in Victorian Canada* (Toronto: University
of Toronto Press, 1983), 17.

15 Annand, *Journals*, 4 and 25 September 1869.

16 Annand, *Journals*, 16 December 1872.

17 Annand, *Journals*, 4 October 1881.

18 The Rev. Walter T. Currie collection of African artifacts at the Royal Ontario Museum is one example of a missionary collection containing a number of 'fetishes.' It includes numerous animal horns still filled with beeswax and various herbal preparations, a small skin pouch labelled in Currie's hand as being 'full of poison powder to kill an enemy,' and a tortoise shell used in the treatment of goitre. Others acted to prevent miscarriage and infant death and as protection against gunshot wounds. Many of these objects are marked as being 'from a native converted by Reverend Currie.' See Jeanne Cannizzo, 'Gathering Souls and Objects: Missionary Collections,' in Tim Barringer and Tom Flynn, eds, *Colonialism and the Object: Empire, Material Culture and the Museum* (London: Routledge, 1998), 163.

19 Annand, *Journals*, 6 February 1884.

20 Annand, *Journals*, 18 May 1892.

21 The Annand collection was shipped to Sydney, Australia, in November 1896 by the Presbyterian mission ship *Dayspring*. The Rev. James Cosh acted as Annand's agent in Sydney for forwarding the collection on to David Boyle via the Huddart-Parker line to Vancouver, and by Canadian Pacific Railway to Toronto (*Archaeological Report*, 1896–7, 10).

22 Annand to Boyle, 8 June 1897, in Boyle Papers ROM.

23 Ibid.

24 Mengel to Annand, 6 November 1902, in NSA.

25 Annand, *Journals*, 8 February 1887.

26 Annand, *Journals*, 8 August 1908.

27 Annand, *Journals*, 27 August 1869.

28 After visiting the British Museum on 18 December 1872 Annand recorded: 'we ventured out to the British Museum and saw the wonderful things to be seen in that labrynth [*sic*]. Truly there is a very great collection of things yet we did not enjoy them so much as we did the Zoological Gard[ens] and Crystal Palace nor even as we did the National Gallery of Paintings.'

29 While on furlough to Canada in 1906, Annand mentioned the purchase in Sydney, Nova Scotia, of 'a cheap case to hold my curios' (Annand, *Journals*, 15 August 1906). Prior to his 1885 furlough, Annand wrote of packing cases containing shells and coral, which he referred to as 'curios' (Annand, *Journals*, 15 September 1884).

30 Nicholas Thomas, 'Licensed Curiosity: Cook's Pacific Voyages,' in John Elsner and Roger Cardinal, eds, *The Cultures of Collecting* (London: Reaktion Books, 1994), 122.

31 Annand's journal for 17 August 1906 mentioned showing 'the dresses, ornaments &c that I have with me' during a speaking engagement in Louisbourg, Nova Scotia. Subsequent entries mention exhibiting his 'curios' during stops at Presbyterian churches in Mabou, Saltsprings, and Scotsburn, Nova Scotia.
32 Annand to Boyle, 1 November 1897, in Boyle Papers ROM.
33 Annand, *Journals*, 2 October 1912.
34 Letter from the Rev. Hugh Angus Robertson to *Presbyterian Record* (November 1898), 291.
35 *Presbyterian Record* (December 1896).
36 'War Clubs and Axes: The New Hebridean Islanders' Terrible Weapons,' in Toronto *Mail and Empire* (4 October 1897).
37 Ibid.
38 Paula G. Rubel and Abraham Rosman, 'George Brown, Pioneer Missionary and Collector,' *Museum Anthropology* 20, no. 1 (1996): 60–8.
39 Linda Hutcheon, 'The Post Always Rings Twice: The Postmodern and the Postcolonial,' in *Material History Review* 41 (Spring 1995): 5.

Chapter 12

Finding God in Ancient China: James Mellon Menzies, Sinology, and Mission Policies

LINFU DONG

The Waste of Yin

Early in the spring of the year Chia Yin the writer was riding his old white horse along the south bank of the Huan River north of Changte City in the province of Honan. The ground had just been harrowed for cotton planting, and the farmers had thrown the freshly ploughed up potsherds and rubble to the edge of the fields. A number of potsherds of a very early date attracted the rider's attention, and led him on from sherd to sherd to a bend in the river ... This was the Waste of Yin.[1]

The young man on the old horse was a Canadian Presbyterian missionary named James Mellon Menzies, and the year was 1914, the third spring of the Republic of China. The place was a village named Xiao Tun (formerly spelled Hsiao-t'un) – literally 'Little Village' – on the broad North China Plain in North Henan (formerly spelled Honan). (This is the same mission discussed by Margo S. Gewurtz in chapter 6.) Menzies was a unique missionary, for he was a civil engineer and Dominion land surveyor who had spent his summers surveying the bush of northern Ontario. Although he had only been in China for three years and at Zhangde (which he spelled Changte) for a few months, he had heard of an ancient ruin nearby. As he made his evangelistic tours of the rural districts, he knew what he was looking for, and when he found it, with eyes trained to see signs on the earth as indicators of what lay below the surface, he understood its significance. He believed he was guided by providence that day, for as he reflected years later, 'God seemed to guide me when he placed in my hands the discovery of the "Oracle Bones," the actual relics of the ancient religious life of the Chinese at 1400–1200 B.C.'[2]

Rev. James Mellon Menzies beside a prehistoric dolmen in Shandong province, 1935. Menzies was an expert on the arcane study of oracle bones and a founder of scientific archaeology at Cheeloo University. He later earned his doctorate from the University of Toronto for his studies of ancient Chinese culture.

The discovery of the 'Waste of Yin' was as important to the archaeology of ancient China as Howard Carter's discovery of King Tut's tomb (1923) was to Egypt, or Leonard Woolley at Ur of the Chaldees. This was the site of the last capital city of the Shang dynasty (also known as Yin, revised dating 1200–1050 BCE), and its excavation by the Academia Sinica after 1928 was the first full-scale scientific archaeological dig in China. Indeed, it was as spectacular as the more recent discovery of the pottery army of the First Emperor, Qin Shihuangdi, at Xian – and a thousand years older. For fourteen years, from 1914 to 1927, James Menzies took upon himself the role of custodian of this ancient site, collecting the tiny fragments that came to the surface and trying to prevent looting.

James Menzies, a shy, almost self-effacing man, never claimed he was the discoverer of the Waste of Yin – the peasants had been gathering the bones for hundreds of years, which they ground up to make 'dragon bones' used in traditional medicine – but rather he claimed he was 'the *first foreign or Chinese archaeologist* to *visit* the Waste of Yin with a *purely scientific interest* in these objects.'[3] Shard by shard, he became one of the few non-Chinese experts on Bronze Age China, who helped decipher the oracle bone script, the earliest form of Chinese writing. What started as a hobby, collecting potsherds and fragments of bone – his colleagues nicknamed him affectionately 'Old Bones' – became his obsession. Working with Western and Chinese colleagues, he helped create the field of scientific archaeology and taught the first university course (in Chinese), at Cheeloo (pinyin Qilu) University in Jinan, Shandong province. (Menzies' professional, scientific qualities set him apart from nineteenth-century 'amateur anthropologists' such as those Barbara Lawson and Arthur Smith describe in their respective chapters.)

Above all, he became a collector. In the last hundred years, the Waste of Yin has yielded about 150,000 pieces of inscribed oracle bones. Excluding those which were destroyed by warlord soldiers, the extant inscribed oracle bones collected by James Menzies total 35,913 pieces, plus another 23,000 ancient artifacts. To put this in context, he gathered this, the largest private collection of oracle bones, on the meagre salary of an ordinary missionary with limited financial resources. It was mainly through his own economy that he helped collect and preserve these cultural treasures.

Unlike most collectors in China at the time, such as Bishop William Charles White of the Anglican diocese in Henan, Menzies was determined that he was not sending art and artifacts out of China to be 'preserved' in the West. With his strong religious motivation, he conducted his collecting activities according to a set of principles and ethical standards that set him apart from other collectors. He did not collect clandestinely. He bought from the peasants or simply picked up bits of bones from the fields. He collected in China, for China, and intended to leave his collection in China. Indeed, the bulk of his collections did in fact remain in China, where they have been divided among the Palace Museum in Beijing, the Nanjing Museum, and the Shandong Provincial Museum. Two smaller collections were deposited after his death in the Royal Ontario Museum and the Art Gallery of Greater Victoria.

Although Menzies became a recognized archaeologist, he did not feel that scholarship and Christian higher education were ends in themselves, but rather the means or components of a new evangelism: a living church led by educated Chinese Christians who were aided by an indigenized gospel. This was far different from the old evangelism imported by foreign missionaries and preached in terms of foreign religious concepts. He gradually came to the view that in order to survive Christianity must be inculturated within Chinese culture, as Buddhism had been 'sinicized' fifteen hundred years earlier. This was the path of accommodation or synthesis pioneered by the seventeenth-century Jesuits and Protestant missionaries such as W.A.P. Martin (1827–1916) and Timothy Richard (1845–1911).[4] It was also common among international missions in the interwar years, as Ruth Brouwer discusses in chapter 7: Menzies was the only one, though, to use archaeology to present the gospel.

In his studies of Shang religion, Menzies came to the conclusion that the ancient Shang people – living about the time of Moses in the Bible – had worshipped a god they called *Shangdi* (formerly spelled Shang-ti; usually translated as 'Lord on High'). This also happened to be the most common term used by Protestants for the name of Jehovah, God Almighty. As a scientist, he wanted to prove with scientific methods that God, the universal lord of creation, did not exclude the Chinese. In other words, he wanted to find how 'grace' operated in the Shang culture. Once he had identified the ancient ideograph of *di*, or god, he believed he had found the scientific evidence. This became his 'mission' in life: the search for Jehovah, God Almighty in ancient China.

Menzies' search for God was a tedious and painstaking process. For two decades he collected oracle bones and related archaeological artifacts, and spent his spare time identifying the archaic oracle bone graphs, which bore information about the religious concepts and practices of the Shang Chinese. Working in 'the still watches of the night,' he studied all periods of Chinese calligraphy and epigraphy to decipher the original meaning of each character. 'Some of us,' he wrote, have to 'school ourselves in Chinese thought, and ideas, so that we know something of the soul and mind of China as well as the outside form.'[5] After moving to Cheeloo University in 1932, he started to theorize his distinctive interpretation that the Shang were worshippers of 'God' or *Shangdi*, which had remained as a religious belief among the Chinese in one form or another.

Out of his experience in North Henan, Menzies concluded that the conversion of China could only be achieved by adapting the gospel to the Chinese reality. As he reflected in the early 1950s: 'While I have counted 1000 persons baptized and many more prepared for the catechumens, yet perhaps my work on the bones permeated deeper into Chinese life than my work among the schools and churches of North Honan ... When one starts from the premise that God is the God of the Chinese and was so recognized by them, Christianity no longer becomes a foreign religion in the eyes of the Chinese and you have a firm foundation for your Christian preaching.'[6]

James Menzies had a unique career and a unique legacy. He was quiet and modest, with a strong sense of humility. He suffered from constant migraines, brought on by his service in the First World War. At the same time, he was a man of commitment, determination, and principle. Physically, he was short and stocky; intellectually, he had a larger presence than most people of his times. He was a rigorous scholar, a scientist and a theologian, with a mind capable of deep philosophical thinking. These personal qualifications allowed Menzies to follow a unique career path by crossing gaps that seemed too huge for others. The most important gap was between Western culture/faith and Chinese culture/faith. Now we live in a world of rapid globalization, with barriers between different cultures and faiths being greatly reduced. James Menzies' world was very different, with peoples alienated from each other by cultures and faiths. Ethnocentrism was the order of the time, even among the missionary movement. In the process of pursuing his life's mission, Menzies successfully broke the yoke of ethnocentrism and became an advocate of intercultural and interreligious understanding. Shard by shard, he found God in *Shangdi*, and crossed the gap between two very different cultures.

The Student Activist

James Menzies was born on a bitterly cold day, 23 February 1885, at the comfortable home of David Redpath Menzies and his wife Jane McGee in Clinton, a small yellow-brick town in southwestern Ontario. The parents were overjoyed, for their second son was born twelve years after Robert. Four years later, Margaret was born. Of the three, James would be the brightest and best educated. Robert, like his father, was a worker not a scholar; he found farming and managing the family business more interesting than the schoolroom, and spent his life as a farmer and general store manager. Margaret graduated from the University of Toronto and married a fellow student of her brother James, Jack Judge, an engineer who became a prominent civil servant in Alberta, in charge of road building for the province. She had a special bond with James and played a helpful role in keeping the family ties together.

David Menzies, James's father, was born in 1837, within the sound of the guns of the Upper Canada rebellion. In fact, David's father Robert had become embroiled in the heated politics of the day, and had joined the Scottish revolutionary William Lyon Mackenzie against the oligarchy known as the Family Compact. Robert heard of his son's birth while he was fleeing with Mackenzie's band to an island in the Niagara River. David grew up on a farm near Milton, and became a cabinet maker, specializing in ornate desks and organs. He bought the farm at Clinton, where in 1872 he married Jane McGee, whose parents had come from County Antrim in Northern Ireland. He was co-owner of the Doherty Organ Factory, which turned out two to three hundred organs a month. By the time James was born, he had built a large house to provide his family with a gracious life.[7]

The Menzies family were Presbyterians, and the children were imbued with a spirit of sober devotion. They did not believe in dogmatic principles, but in faith exemplified in their daily lives. Yet theirs was a private faith, nurtured within the family, for they were not able to attend church regularly. As James explained in his application to the Foreign Mission Board in 1910, 'our home life was of the very best, but there was no Presbyterian church in the community. A Methodist Church was built by the community but was abandoned after a year or so. Sunday school was kept going. During my boyhood we organized a Boys Club and S.S. Class. In that I was trained. At high school, no opportunity afforded itself for the course in my life for I was at home part of the time.'[8]

The family moved to Staples, near Windsor, when James was nine, where David owned a general store and lumber company. He invested in land that became downtown Winnipeg, which he sold later at a good profit, enabling him to retire comfortably and send money to his poor missionary son. David was a practical man, and as a good Christian, he felt that making money honestly and diligently was God's reward for his 'stewardship' of money and resources. He never tired of telling James the importance of hard work.

After graduating from Leamington Collegiate in 1903, James Menzies entered the School of Practical Science at the University of Toronto, majoring in civil engineering. The idea of becoming a foreign missionary had not entered his mind. Rather, in the most secular of settings – the rowdy 'Skule of Engineering,' as it was nicknamed – Menzies was initiated to public religion, the modern piety expressed through student organizations such as the YMCA, Bible studies, and mass religious conventions. His decision to give up civil engineering for the ministry was not sparked by a sudden and emotional conversion, but by gradual, inexorable changes in his spiritual and intellectual life. They came so naturally that he did not have a traumatic spiritual experience. His first step toward China was his decision to join the Young Men's Christian Association, the largest and most prominent organization on campus.

By his second year, he was active in the YMCA and the Student Volunteer Movement (SVM). Founded under the direction of the American evangelist D.L. Moody, the SVM became the foremost recruiter of college-educated foreign missionaries. It did not send them on its own, but recruited students for denominational missions. With its slogan 'The Evangelization of the World in This Generation,' it was a powerful recruiting agency and sent 9000 North American college graduates to foreign missions by 1920.[9] Every four years, the SVM held an international student conference, attended by thousands of delegates, where they were encouraged to sign a pledge, 'I will, God willing, volunteer to go as a foreign missionary.'[10]

Menzies summarized his experience as a student activist in his application to the Foreign Mission Board (FMB) in 1910:

> I have been a member of the University YMCA Executive as Councillor, Recording Secretary, Bible Study Convenor and Student Volunteer Chairman. I have been closely associated with City Mission work, being an advisory member of the Committee. I am also an advisory member of the Canadian College Mission. Almost all my time has been spent on religious work in the University. I have done some work in the city in young people's work, city missions, street preaching, prison work, and personal work during Revivals. This last summer I spent on the mission field of Lake Joseph Muskoka ... I have been connected with the Laymen's Missionary Movement and Young People's Missionary Movement at their conferences, also Student Conferences. I have led normal Bible Study groups. In college I have led Bible Study and Missionary Classes.[11]

(His contemporary at Victoria College was Edward Wilson Wallace, the subject of Alvyn Austin's chapter 5.)

In 1907 Menzies graduated with a BSc Honours in Civil Engineering, and registered at Knox College to prepare himself as a foreign missionary. He was the first student in Knox's history to enter with a science degree. Knox was the largest of the five theological colleges maintained by the Presbyterian Church in Canada. Great changes had taken place in the college's theological perspective as the traditional confessional orthodoxy was replaced by the new progressive orthodoxy.[12] While Menzies was a student, seven of the eight faculty members were progressives or liberals. He recollected many years later: 'My training in Hebrew and Greek did not make me either a Hebrew scholar or a Greek expert, but they did provide the background of all my linguistic research in Chinese language.'[13] More importantly, the theological training at Knox was progressive, which equipped him with an open mind and an understanding heart to appreciate Chinese culture and develop a liberal perspective on mission policies.

The Rural Evangelist

In April 1910, the FMB appointed Menzies to North Henan, which had been pioneered by Jonathan Goforth and the 'Honan Seven' in 1888. With his sister he sailed to Britain, where he attended the World Missionary Conference in Edinburgh. This was the high point of ecumenical missions, where for the first time he was exposed intensively to the opportunities and problems of the missionary enterprise. From Britain, he continued by the Trans-Siberian Railway over the steppes of Russia and North China.

He arrived in China with fresh enthusiasm. He was assigned to language study at Wuan, a new station, where six months later, he brought his new bride, Annie Belle Sedgwick. She and her sister Maude were working in the adjacent Anglican diocese at Kaifeng, the capital of Henan province, under Bishop William C. White. They were grateful to Bishop White, who generously allowed Annie to marry James, and thus leave the Anglican mission for the Presbyterians. For two years, James and Annie led a generally peaceful and routine life at Wuan county, amidst the Revolution of 1911 and social disorder outside the mission compound. In addition to his struggle with the Chinese language, he also learned under the supervision of senior missionaries the skills needed for evangelical work among the farmers.

In 1914 Menzies was relocated to Zhangde (now called Anyang), where a few months later, he providentially 'discovered' the 'Waste of Yin.' Fifteen years earlier, in 1899, an antiquarian in Beijing named Wang Yirong had bought some 'dragon bone' medicine and recognized that the 'chicken scratches' were in fact ancient Chinese characters, the so-called *Jiagu Wen* or oracle bone script. Another scholar, Luo Zhenyu, learned that the bones came from Xiaotun, a couple of kilometres northwest of Anyang. But Menzies was, as he claimed, the first scientist to visit the site. His status as a leading scholar derived from his intimate knowledge of the site before it was 'carpet-rolled' by the archaeologists.[14]

For Menzies, the importance of his 'discovery' could never be overstated. He grasped the importance of these inscriptions not only for Chinese culture but also the Christian cause in China. A correct understanding of the root of the Chinese mind, he thought, would help find the appropriate way to approach the Chinese with the Christian gospel. It was with this end in mind that he devoted the rest of his life to the study of early Chinese culture. From this time until he left North Henan in 1932, Menzies was doing two men's work. As an evangelical missionary, he carried out his manifold mission duties, including annual evangelistic campaigns. At night he studied Chinese culture.

In 1917 Menzies published his first book, *Oracle Records from the Waste of Yin*, which contained line drawings of 2369 inscriptions. Unfortunately, just as the proofs came off the press, he was forced to leave China, which turned out to be a three-year interruption of his missionary career. In 1916, while officially neutral, the Chinese government surreptitiously agreed to a British scheme that brought it closer to the Allied side, hoping for better treatment after the war. This was the Chinese Labour Corps (CLC), also known as 'the coolie corps,' which eventually sent about 92,000 Chinese to France as noncombatant workers. This little-known episode was strategically important in the British war effort. As casualties escalated, the CLC released soldiers from manual labour such as digging trenches, building roads, and other logistical tasks. It was also a strange story of culture shock as these illiterate Chinese peasants – and their white officers – were taken across the Pacific in crowded troop ships, put into sealed trains from Vancouver to Halifax, and then dropped into war-torn France.

When the British Legation in Beijing issued a formal and urgent call to all missionaries to join the CLC, the Canadian Presbyterian mission in North Henan was particularly responsive. Eventually sixteen of thirty-two male missionaries – all the younger men – did join the CLC, thus decimating medical, educational, and evangelical work in the field. Murdoch Mackenzie, in a private letter to R.P. MacKay, secretary of the Foreign Mission Board (FMB), summed up the dilemma of 'our workers in Honan':

Years ago they had listened to the voice of the highest King, and in obedience to His command had come to China. They studied Chinese for the express purpose of making Christ and His great salvation known to the Chinese people in north Honan. In many spheres they had rendered whole hearted and cheerful service to their Divine Master. An opportunity, such as does not come often in an ordinary lifetime, has now led them to ask whether their lives, and all the knowledge they have gained of Chinese, may not be turned to account in the struggle now being waged. Britain is about to put forth its maximum effort. The weightiest issues for our Empire and the World depend on the result. No one worthy of the British name would shrink from considering the question of duty at such a time. It has been taken up seriously by all our brethren, and their response is only that which was expected of them.[15]

In March 1917 Menzies shipped out on the S.S. *Protesilaus*, which contained over 3000 labourers under ten British officers, under the command of a businessman who had supervised Chinese labourers in South Africa. As the only missionary, Menzies complained to Annie, 'It has been rather a shock getting back into the old life again. Of all the filthy language, the drinking and smoking, I will not attempt even to let you get the slightest intimation. Not even my old experience prepared me for this.'[16]

It is difficult to trace Menzies' life in the next two years because his letters were always written from 'somewhere in France.' By November 1917, when he was promoted to Captain, his company was building roads, prison camps, and military structures. Even though the war ended on 11 November 1918, the CLC were considered cheap labour and were held back to 'mop up' the mess. Consequently, Menzies was not discharged until February 1920, when he returned to Toronto. Considering they had served a full seven-year term in Henan before he joined the CLC, the FMB granted James and Annie an extended furlough, which lasted until August 1921. By this time, they had three children: Marion, born in 1913, Frances in 1915, and Arthur in 1916.

Chinese Nationalism

By September 1921, when Menzies returned to North Henan, the district was just recovering from the grip of the Great North China Famine of 1920–1, one of the worst in modern Chinese history. Altogether some twenty million people had perished across the North China plain. Reconstruction after the famine gave Menzies the opportunity to put his civil engineering skills to use. The China International Famine

Relief Commission had been established as a permanent organization for famine prevention, carrying out comprehensive conservancy projects on a national basis and supporting scientific agriculture and education.[17] As one of the few engineers in China, Menzies was called upon to supervise the digging of a canal in Shanxi and dikes along the Yangtze River.

He also used his mapmaking skills to draw up an evangelistic map of North Henan, with detailed information about each village, the population, churches, and number of converts. This was one of the first modern maps of North Henan. Since there were over 10,000 named villages in North Henan, it was a huge job to put all of them on one map. Although the complete map was never printed, smaller maps of particular districts were printed. Years later, Menzies managed to complete a draft of his map, which he mounted on six scrolls like Chinese paintings and hung on the walls of his study in Toronto, as a reminder of the villages he had visited and the churches he had helped found.[18]

Menzies' second term in China occurred against a backdrop of civil wars between contending warlords, who considered Henan a prime target, and rising Chinese nationalism among the students and intellectuals. For two decades, since the mass movement of 1905, the Chinese seemed to have been open to the Christian message. Missionaries had helped organize educational, medical, and social services, as they became a 'new gentry' in local society.[19] Ironically, their status proved to be a product of China's weakness and could not withstand the nationalist, anti-warlord, anti-foreign, anti-imperialist, and anti-Christian movements that started with the May Fourth Movement of 1919.

These anti-Christian campaigns, which brought a decline in religion among educated Chinese, had a great impact on the work of Christian missions. It became increasingly difficult to deliver the gospel to educated Chinese, who came to worship science and nationalism. Battered and disappointed, many 'old China hands' among the missionary force retired from China. Those who stayed believed they could meet the new challenges by adapting their gospel to changing China. James Menzies was one. Sympathetic to Chinese aspirations, yet confined to rural evangelism, he became increasingly restless with the conservative policies of his mission. He was no longer comfortable with the mission's paternalistic attitudes and felt drawn to progressive approaches to missions. He believed his own place was not among the peasants, but in a Christian university, where he could help train future Chinese Christian leaders.

But his missionary career was interrupted a second time by war. This time, in 1927–8, it was civil war, when Chiang Kai-shek and the Guomindang (old spelling Kuomintang, or Nationalist Party) launched the Northern Expedition to conquer the warlords and establish a national government. By the spring of 1927, the foreign governments ordered their nationals – including some 8000 missionaries – to evacuate from the interior to the coastal cities. Once again China teetered on the brink of war with the foreign powers.

After the Canadians evacuated from North Henan, the mission properties were occupied and looted by one army after another. When Menzies managed to return for a brief inspection a year later, he found everything in ruins. The tragedy was not the broken furniture and ravaged gardens, but the 'whole of one's lifetime of gathering together: books of which I had nearly 5,000 and into which I had put nearly all my spare money were wilfully destroyed.' Worse, the soldiers had dumped his precious archaeological artifacts into the courtyard and crushed thousands of fragile oracle bones underfoot. 'I was gathering materials for a description of ancient Chinese life and manners. I had a lot of pottery, true, much of it was broken, but then it was enough to show the shapes of old vases and sacrificial vessels. I had also a considerable amount of stone-age implements and then there was a great many fragments of oracle bones. All these were destroyed. One of the first things I saw as I was being led around by the soldier to see our house was a broken vase over 3000 years old, old as David in the Old Testament. It was smashed in a hundred pieces on the sidewalk.'[20]

The Scholar

During the evacuation, in September 1927, Menzies and his family were seconded to Beijing, where he taught in the North China Union Language School (NCULS). This was the largest and best language school in China, teaching the 'correct' Beijing accent. It had been founded by British and American missions, legations, and the Chamber of Commerce. By 1920 it had twenty foreign and eighty Chinese teachers, with 250 students representing twenty-four societies, five legations, and twelve business firms. Besides language study, it also offered classes on Chinese History, China's International Relations, the government system, educational work, social conditions, the 'Chinese Point of View,' and Work for Women and Girls.[21]

The year in Beijing was pivotal in Menzies' career, since it provided an opportunity for him to meet Chinese scholars and concentrate on his study of oracle bones. He had been working alone until this point, except through correspondence and books. In Beijing, he entered into the intellectual life, which included professors from the Harvard–Yenching Institute, American museum collectors, missionary ethnologists, Chinese antiquarians and epigraphers, and young nationalist Western-trained archaeologists. With an able Chinese assistant, Menzies completed most of his second book, *Additional Collection of Oracle Records from the Waste of Yin*, which unfortunately was not published until after his death, in 1972.

The principal of NCULS was William B. Pettus, one of the most gregarious people in Beijing, who was attracted by Menzies' mastery of the Chinese language and scholarly interests. He appealed to the North Henan mission (NHM) to appoint Menzies to the school after his furlough. Menzies was delighted by this recognition, and welcomed this invitation.[22] By this time, the Methodist, Congregationalist, and Presbyterian churches in Canada had merged into the United Church of Canada, except for the small Continuing Presbyterian Church. The Presbyterian missions in North Henan, Shanghai, and South China, as well as India and Korea, joined the Methodist West China and Japan missions, and the Congregational mission in Angola under the United Church and run by one corporate body, the Board of Overseas Missions (BOM). Taiwan remained Continuing Presbyterian.

Initially, the BOM supported Menzies' assignment to NCULS, but changed its position under pressure from the NHM. A.E. Armstrong, assistant secretary of the Board, had encouraged him to write a book on ancient Chinese culture. 'It was suggested that you collect material for a book that would add to knowledge concerning archaeology and other subjects. It might not be wise to issue it for a few years, but I hope you are storing up some material on which you can draw. In that connection, if you have time, I would like to hear from you as to whether you are following up the volume you did publish showing cuts of bones found in "the Waste of Yin."'[23]

The mission, however, was opposed to sending him to Beijing. It always ran a chronic deficit and could not afford the financial commitment of supporting missionaries working outside the field. Besides, some colleagues felt that 'archaeology' – however they understood the term – was not 'real' mission work, such as evangelistic campaigns. Menzies replied that he could do more in Beijing than in North Henan because the school's role in 'fitting new missionaries for the field' initiated them into study of the 'heritage of China.'

Since James and Annie Menzies were due for a furlough at the end of 1928, in order to prepare himself for his new duties, he took the family on a round-the-world trip. They sailed to India, where they toured for two months, and spent a month in Jerusalem and Nazareth. They visited every archaeological site and museum, where he sought out local experts, missionaries, museum directors, archaeologists, and native teachers who knew the ancient history. In particular, he wanted to comprehend the chronology of the Bronze Age, to gain an international perspective for his own studies. In Palestine, he was invited to join an excavation conducted by the American School of Oriental Studies, whose field surveyor had fallen sick. Since he was a Dominion Land Surveyor, this gave him 'hands on' experience in scientific archaeology with professionals who had the latest technology. He remained for four months while Annie took the children to Europe and Canada.[24]

By the time Menzies arrived in Toronto in late 1929, the Board had decided to cancel his appointment to the language school. Nevertheless, despite this bad news, he was treated as a respected scholar in the United States, where he gave a paper at the annual meeting of the American Archaeological Institute. He had offers from Dean Chase of Harvard to prepare a proposal to excavate the Waste of Yin, and from John Leighton Stuart to spend a year at Yenching University to publish some of his work. If Menzies had taken either opportunity, he would have become an internationally recognized scholar, but instead, bound by loyalty to his mission call, he refused a 'pure' academic appointment and returned to North Henan in 1930.[25]

Fortunately, while he had been absent from Henan, the Academia Sinica, a government scientific academy established to foster a national intellectual culture, had conducted three preliminary excavations at Anyang (the Waste of Yin). We do not know the exact nature of Menzies' involvement with Anyang excavations. The site was near his home, and he always took his evening walk around his 'adobe city' beneath the sands. The fourth season, in the spring of 1931, was the most ambitious. Li Chi (pinyin Li Ji), the chief archaeologist known as 'the father of Chinese archaeology,' made the decision 'to excavate the Hsiao-t'un (Xiaotun) site in its totality by the carpet rolling method,' that is by systemically digging down to the lowest strata, a depth of three metres or more, to trace the architectural foundations. This uncovered many treasures, such as the royal tombs and the state archives of oracle bones.[26]

The excavation of Anyang ('the Waste of Yin') by the Academic Sinica in the 1930s. J.M. Menzies was stationed at Zhangde in 1914, where he was the first foreign or Chinese scientist to visit this Bronze Age site. This photograph may depict the spring of 1931 season when the entire site was 'carpet-rolled' down to the mud-brick foundations. The trio in front seem to be a Chinese scholar and a missionary couple, perhaps James and Annie Menzies themselves.

Li Chi, one of Menzies' colleagues from Beijing, welcomed him as a resident expert – after all, certified Dominion Land Surveyors were a rare commodity in rural China – and consulted him on the Shang royal genealogy. When he came to write his history of the excavations, *Anyang*, which was not published until 1977, forty years after the last dig, he gave a gracious tribute:

> A pioneer in this field was the author of 'Oracle Records from the Waste of Yin,' Mr. James Mellon Menzies, the Canadian missionary. Menzies was first sent to Changte Fu in 1914, and after World War 1, was again stationed there from 1921 to 1927. He was thus in a position to learn, *in situ*, about the unearthing of oracle bones by the native diggers on his frequent visits to Hsiao-t'un. This fortunate combination of an appropriate appointment and an inborn instinct for archaeology prepared the way for his special contribution to the oracle bone studies among the small community of scholars.

In a footnote, Li Chi noted that although Menzies' lecture notes from Cheeloo University 'were never published, they were widely read and quoted.'[27]

As a more lasting tribute, a fossil animal discovered at Anyang was named after Menzies. The *Elaphurus Menziesianus* is an extinct form of water buffalo or elk with magnificent backward-turning antlers, which were sometimes used for oracles. (Its nearest living relative is the strange Père David's deer, which survives only in captivity.)

God in Ancient China

Menzies never doubted that his 'discovery' of the Waste of Yin was providential. He never doubted that the discovery was God's will to enable him to prove to the Chinese that they were also His children. With this religious reading of the event, it becomes understandable for him to be a devoted missionary and at the same time a fervent China scholar.

To carry out his god-given mission, the first task Menzies assigned to himself was to make a collection of all the oracle bones and other artifacts that came to the surface at the Waste of Yin. He did all his collecting between 1914–17 and 1921–8. Unlike Bishop White, who had been appointed the purchasing agent for the Royal Ontario Museum, Menzies did not have money to spend for large, beautiful pieces. The few dollars he squeezed from his missionary salary never allowed him to buy expensive curios. However, he overcame this disadvantage by following a different set of collection principles.

As an evangelistic missionary, Menzies travelled widely throughout North Henan, which gave him a knowledge of other ancient sites. In addition, his interest in '*gu dong*,' or old stuff, gradually became known inside and outside the church. With his amiable personality, he made friends with local people. His daughter recalled that it was not rare for him to be called away from the dining table to receive visitors with 'dragon bones' or other objects they found on their lands. On occasion, he was visited by country peddlers who had purchased some 'old stuff' on their buying and selling travels, and knew Ming Mushi (Pastor Ming) wanted broken objects.[28]

Menzies once said he had a 'lover's eye' for broken things.[29] 'To me a broken fragment which I personally found on a site was a fact to be trusted, while a valuable object purchased from a seller was almost certainly not excavated in the place where he stated it had been found.' He did not trust curio dealers who, he thought, never missed a chance to make money. Rather, he tried to buy from the first owners or discoverers, the poor but trustworthy peasants. They sold the best pieces to the curio dealers, and offered him what was left. The price was low because they knew he only purchased broken pieces.[30] For academic purposes a potsherd or bone fragment, seemingly useless, covered with the original dirt, had more scientific value than an intact vessel with no context. He collected what others thought were 'old trash' (*polan*), fingernail-sized fragments of bone with one or two characters.[31]

A survey of his collections, now dispersed in China and Canada, reveals they consisted mostly of pottery, oracle bones, stone implements and jade disks, and a few bronze vessels. The Cheeloo University collection, now at Shandong Provincial Museum, consists of 28,743 artifacts, including 8168 bone fragments; only 3668 had inscriptions.[32] By placing academic value over artistic value, Menzies built up his collections, though in the eyes of the world, his things were simply the waste from the Waste of Yin. But for serious scholars, they were treasures of humanity's past.[33]

As a self-taught archaeologist, Menzies was a scientist consciously assembling a scholar's collection for future generations. He was not satisfied with acquiring artifacts, but tried to secure as much information as possible. Whenever possible, he would personally visit the site and record detailed information on note cards that he attached to each artifact. He even tried to preserve the original earth attached to the artifact, which he hoped someday might be useful scientifically for dating and context.[34]

Finally, Menzies was sympathetic to the attitude of Chinese scholars towards the exporting or smuggling of cultural artifacts out of the country. Charles Trick Currelly of the Royal Ontario Museum approached Menzies several times to act as the museum's purchasing agent, but each time he refused. He wanted to keep his collection in China. He did, however, help Bishop White authenticate many objects that were destined for the ROM.

The most difficult task to which Menzies devoted his life was the search for the mind of ancient China by studying the archaeological artifacts he collected. Among the many subjects of Chinese archaeology, oracle bone studies are considered the most difficult, what the Chinese call 'jue xue,' arcane studies few can master. To be competent, he needed a foundation of the Chinese classics on which he could build the structure of the Chinese written language (epigraphy) that had developed over a thousand years. This called upon the specialized skills Menzies had brought from Canada, which had lain dormant in his mission work: his childhood on a farm, the hours spent in engineering drawing, the lessons in Hebrew at Knox.[35]

Menzies' first achievement as a scholar of oracle studies was drawing each artifact. After being buried underground for 3000 years, these bits of animal bones and turtle shells were so fragile that they broke into many pieces during the process of excavation, shipping, and selling, so pieces of one bone might end up in several collections. Their scientific value was thereby reduced. Ink drawings and rubbings were the usual methods used to reproduce bone inscriptions. By 1917, three years after he started collecting, Menzies published *Oracle Records from the Waste of Yin*, which was the first book authored by a foreigner in the field of oracle bone studies.[36]

As the price of Chinese antiquities soared in the 1920s, Menzies became an expert on detecting forgeries. This was a serious problem because some conservative scholars cited the forgeries as proof that 'all the so-called oracle bone inscriptions were pseudo-classic inscriptions, fabricated by a number of pretenders to scholarship to deceive the public at large.'[37] With his inborn instinct for engineering precision, only one of the 2369 inscriptions in *Oracle Records* is a forgery: an exceedingly rare achievement.

To restore the scientific value of these broken bones, he also became a pioneer in piecing together the scattered pieces to reconstruct large inscriptions.[38] In 1933 he published 'A Comparative Study of the New and Old Editions of Lo Chen-yu's *Earlier Compilation of Written Inscriptions from the Waste of Yin*, and the Resultant Newly Discovered Historical Materials.'[39] Under Menzies' influence, his research assistant Zeng Yigong specialized in matching broken oracle bones. In 1939 Zeng published his important work *Restored Oracle Bones*. In the introduction, he wrote, 'This book is the result of my teacher's [Menzies'] instruction and encouragement.'[40]

Fortunately, in 1932 the North Henan mission acknowledged Menzies' work by appointing him as Director of the Chinese Institute and Professor of Chinese Archaeology at Cheeloo University. He remained there for four years, the happiest and most productive of his career. Since archaeology was still a young subject in Chinese universities, Menzies had to write the textbooks. *Oracle Bone Studies*, printed in 1933, widely circulated among serious scholars, was Menzies' masterpiece. His history of the discovery of oracle bones is still regarded as 'the most correct, detailed, and authoritative history.'[41] The most important breakthrough was his ideas about Shang royal genealogy. He even had the courage to challenge Wang Guowei, the great master, pointing out that Wang misinterpreted one king's name and missed another.[42]

Menzies' most astounding publication was a small pamphlet called 'God in Ancient China,' in which he distilled a lifetime's scholarship as a missionary and an archaeologist. One of the debates among secular nationalist scholars declared that the Chinese – ancient and modern – were not a 'religious' people, but a 'philosophical' or Confucian culture. Menzies' argument fitted into this debate; if he could prove scientifically that the ancient Chinese had worshipped God, then Chinese scholars could no longer say that 'the Chinese are not religious and have never believed in God.'[43]

According to the oracle bone inscriptions, the ideograph for *Di* (or *Shangdi*) was written as 棗. It consisted of three parts. At the bottom is the ancient character for 'wood' 木, here pictured as three sticks or a 'faggot' 朿. In the middle is —, which is the ancient representation of 束, 'to bind.' Above this bound faggot is placed 二, the ancient version of 上, 'above.' The character *Di* may be used for the verb 'to offer the burnt offering of wood on the altar to God,' or the noun, to indicate the 'burnt offering.'

Based on this reading, Menzies thought that he had scientific, archaeological evidence to prove that the Shang people had worshipped a monotheist God, before they were corrupted by the ancestor worship of Confucianism and the magic of Daoism.[44] 'It is thus a term without anthropomorphic form or representation and simply means The One on High Above All.' He reflected that 'when one starts from the premise that God is the God of the Chinese and was so recognized by them, Christianity no longer becomes a foreign religion in the eyes of the Chinese and you have a firm foundation for your Christian preaching. God did not leave them out in the beginning.'[45]

Detained at Home

In 1936 James Menzies was granted his regular furlough; Annie had already returned to Toronto, where all three children were enrolled at Victoria College. Since he expected to return in a year, he left his collections and notes in storage, taking only the research material he needed. The largest collection was at Cheeloo University, particularly in the archaeological museum he founded; other collections were stored in the attic of the NHM's business office in Tianjin and in the safe at the NCULS in Beijing.

On 7 July 1937, just as James and Annie Menzies were in Toronto preparing to return to Cheeloo, with their luggage packed and tickets purchased, Japan launched a full-scale invasion of North China, the beginning of the eight-year Anti-Japanese War. This was among the most brutal atrocities of the twentieth century. By the end of 1937, both the North Henan mission and Cheeloo University were under Japanese control. Worried about their safety, the Board of Overseas Missions postponed the Menzies' return. Tragically, this delay turned out to be permanent. Menzies was 'detained at home' from 1936 to 1951, when he accepted retirement. He never returned to China.

Other missionaries managed to reincorporate themselves into Canadian life, but for him this seems to have been especially difficult. Deeply committed to his oracle studies, he only engaged in activities related to China: he wandered through North America, took a research position at the Royal Ontario Museum, obtained his doctorate from the University of Toronto, then became a China expert with the U.S. Office of War Information in San Francisco and the State Department in Washington, D.C. He had opportunities to settle down, but China was his home, and he did not want to become 'less useful' in Canada. Nevertheless, as one of Canada's best China scholars, he made important contributions to Chinese studies in Canada through his research at the ROM and the University of Toronto, even though he failed to see his work published in his own country.

One month after his arrival in Toronto, at the age of 51, with two decades' experience in Chinese archaeology and four years as a professor, he returned to his alma mater as a 'special student' in the Department of Art and Archaeology. In his application, Menzies stated his purpose was 'to make available in English work already done during the past 22 years in the culture, religion and language of early China based on the Oracle Bones and other archaeological material found at Anyang, Honan.'[46] During the 1920s and early 1930s, Bishop W.C. White had collected tens of thousands of objects for the Royal Ontario Museum, making it supposedly the best collection of Chinese art outside China. In 1934, when he retired as bishop in Henan, he was appointed Keeper of the Chinese Collection at the ROM and Professor of Archaeology in the School of Chinese Studies (more prestigious than a Department) at the University of Toronto. Bishop White was Menzies' doctoral supervisor, although Menzies was the greater scholar.

At first, Menzies' studies went well, because they served everyone's interests. It was an opportunity to use his exile in Canada to redeem the time, to gather the results of his studies while earning a doctoral degree. The ROM was pleased to have a recognized authority to catalogue its large collection of oracle bones, bronzes, and other artifacts from the Shang dynasties. Bishop White, who had come to rely on Menzies' expertise in authenticating artifacts in China, was able to have his assistance again. This time, however, their relationship was different: no longer between equals, but between supervisor and research assistant. This hierarchical relationship and personality differences would ruin their friendship and make Menzies' studies at the ROM extremely difficult.

It is remarkable that Menzies was able to carry on his work against so many odds. In April 1941, he completed the draft of his thesis, 'The Bronze Age Culture of China,' the result of five years' effort and the largest research project he had ever undertaken. The first part was a general study of Shang culture, which showed his special expertise on oracle bone inscriptions, and the second, a detailed study of *ge* (formerly spelled *ko*), the typical weapon of the Shang armies, a short, sickle-shaped sword with a long, thick handle, shaped like a tomahawk. His committee, headed by Bishop White, rejected it, supposedly because it was 'too broad.' He reconstructed the second part – on the

Shang *ge* not oracle bones, his speciality – which he defended in an oral examination on 10 November 1942.[47]

At the age of 57, James M. Menzies became a Doctor of Philosophy. What was he to do? The United Church, which had supported him all those years, urged him to take up employment as a local church minister, but that, he felt, would be a waste of his expertise.[48] He was not welcomed at the ROM or the University of Toronto. After Pearl Harbor, it was impossible to consider going to Cheeloo in exile in Sichuan. Moreover, he may have lost more than he gained. He failed to make his studies of Shang culture available in English as he had hoped. His draft thesis, 'The Bronze Age Culture of China,' was a strong piece of scholarship, but too academic for an ROM publication, the Museum Studies Series, which under White's control was intended 'to make available to the public, in popular form but without sacrificing scientific accuracy, an interpretation of the history, culture, and processes of development that lie behind the objects in the Museum collection.'[49]

In 1940, James Menzies' son, Arthur, age 24, joined the Department of External Affairs, the beginning of a long and distinguished career as a Canadian diplomat. (He served as Canada's third ambassador to the People's Republic of China in 1976–80.) Arthur took graduate studies in Far Eastern History at Harvard University, where he studied under the legendary John King Fairbank, completing his MA but not his PhD. After Pearl Harbor, the American government began to recruit 'Japan and China specialists, preferably male between twenty-one and thirty, field-experienced and fully fluent.'[50] Arthur, Third Secretary in Ottawa, passed this information on to his father, who was hired by the Office of War Information (OWI) for its Foreign Information Service.

After consulting the Board of Overseas Missions, James Menzies accepted the OWI job, even though it meant relocating to San Francisco, because it provided an opportunity to use his professional knowledge. In exchange, he had to give up the possibility of returning to China until the end of the war. The OWI was concerned mainly with radio propaganda on the Voice of America and monitoring the propaganda put out by the enemy. As Senior China Specialist, Menzies was concerned with policy and intelligence. In November 1944 he was 'borrowed' by the OWI headquarters in Washington, a temporary arrangement that became permanent until 1949. As his seniority increased, he received a salary of $5905, the highest he ever earned in his life.[51] (As a missionary on furlough, his stipend had been $800.)

In 1945, as the Pacific War drew to a close, James and Annie prepared again to return to China. Both Cheeloo and the North Henan mission – both in exile in Sichuan – invited him as soon as possible. But Menzies felt bound by his commitment to the OWI. Then in June 1946, he suffered two heart attacks, which incapacitated him for several years. By the time he recovered, the Board was not willing to take responsibility for sending him to China. James and Annie remained in Washington until June 1949, when they bought a house and moved to Toronto.

After all these years of waiting, in April 1951 James Menzies, a great missionary scholar, accepted 'honourable retirement.' In the letter to the Board, signed by James and Annie, they made the following statement:

> We do not regret that we went as missionaries to Honan and North China nor do we consider that the life effort we put into the work there is lost. Unless a corn of wheat fall into the ground and be buried, it cannot bring forth fruit. We have faith that there will be a Christian harvest in China in God's good time. We loved and tried to understand the Chinese people in Honan and at Cheeloo University and we believe that the Christian Church will survive even though the persecution may be as severe as it has ever been in China's history. The United Church of Canada must not abandon the Christian Church in China but must continue to believe that it is our Christian duty to extend the Kingdom of God and the Gospel of Jesus Christ to China by whatever means is possible.

Still they had hope: 'If it is ever possible in the future for me to return to China for a short period to arrange about books and archaeological collection at Cheeloo University, that can be considered when the time comes.'[52]

James Menzies died on 16 March 1957, aged 72, in his small house in Toronto, surrounded by a few pieces of his precious collections. Annie sold the house and moved to London to live with daughter Marion and her husband Jim Hummel, who was a United Church minister. She died on 18 October 1962, aged 80. She was buried beside her beloved husband – 'Old Bones' – in Mount Pleasant Cemetery, Toronto.

Conclusion

Among the modern missionary army in China, the Canadians formed a small but identifiable group. They did not lack their own stars. In order to save China, some turned red, some held up the flag of fundamentalism, while others used their pens to battle with Chinese conservatism and antagonism. Menzies broke a new way for himself. Following generations of missionary giants, he laboured to understand the mind and soul of the Chinese. He tried to find an intellectual basis for the Christian cause in China, not within the mission movement but within the culture to be converted. By linking Christianity with ancient Chinese culture, he sensed that Chinese culture and tradition, far from being obstacles to the Christian cause, could provide a rational basis for its propagation. Unfortunately, his ideas on mission policy, like his achievements in oracle bone studies, were not widely known. Nonetheless, they reflected the work of a great mind that exhausted itself for God's kingdom in China.

Perhaps we, half a century later, can gain inspiration from Menzies' life for his open and tolerant understanding of different cultures. His ideas on a Chinese Church deeply rooted in the Chinese social and cultural soil help explain the revival of the Christian faith in China. All these prove that Menzies was an extraordinary man, a man with vision.[53] He summed up his life in a letter to Sidney Smith, President of the University of Toronto:

> I have directed my life toward endeavouring to convince the peasants, students and scholars of North China that there is no contradiction involved in being a true Chinese, proud of his cultural tradition, a true scientist searching for truth wherever it may be found and a true Christian living a Christian life in his own Chinese society. This was but the expression of the three great passions of my life, my Sinophilia, my scientific bent, and my missionary purpose.[54]

NOTES

This chapter is adapted from my doctoral thesis at York University (2000). The thesis has been revised as *Cross Culture and Faith: The Life and Work of James Mellon Menzies* and is to be published by the University of Toronto Press in 2005.

1 James Mellon Menzies (JMM), *Yinxu Buci: Oracle Records from the Waste of Yin* (Shanghai: Yee Wen Publishing Co., 1917), Preface.
2 JMM to A.E. Armstrong (AEA), 9 December 1929, United Church Archives (UCA), United Church of Canada (UCC), Board of Overseas Missions

(BOM), North Henan Mission correspondence, box 3/file 48. (Cited as UCC/NHM correspondence.)

3 Ibid.; emphasis added.

4 W.A.P. Martin's thoughts on mission policies are expressed in his two books *A Cycle of Cathay* (republished Taipei: Ch'eng-Wen Publishing Company, 1966), and *Lore of Cathay* (New York: Fleming H. Revell, 1901). For Richard, see William E. Soothill, *Timothy Richard of China* (London: Seeley, Service & Co., 1924); and Paul Richard Bohr, *Famine in China and the Missionary* (Cambridge: Harvard University Press, 1972).

5 Soothill, *Timothy Richard*, 8.

6 JMM to Knox Classmates, undated but probably early 1950s, in Menzies Family Papers (cited as MF Papers). The MF Papers are in the possession of Arthur Menzies and are to be deposited in the National Archives of Canada.

7 Interview with Arthur Menzies (AM), 19 July 1997, York University, Toronto.

8 JMM to R.P. Mackay (RPM), secretary of Foreign Missionary Board (FMB), Presbyterian Church in Canada (PCC), January 1910, in MF Papers.

9 There has been considerable scholarly attention to the SVM. Valentin H. Rabe, *The Home Base of American China Missions, 1880–1920* (Cambridge: Harvard University, Council on East Asian Studies, 1978); Michael Parker, *The Kingdom of Character: The Student Volunteer Movement for Foreign Missions (1886–1926)* (Lanham, MD: University Press of America, 1998); and Nathan D. Showalter, *The End of a Crusade: The Student Volunteer Movement for Foreign Missions and the Great War* (Lanham, MD: Scarecrow Press, 1998).

10 Alvyn Austin, *Saving China: Candian Missionaries in the Middle Kingdom 1888–1959* (Toronto: University of Toronto Press, 1986), 96–7, for description of the 1902 SVM convention in Toronto.

11 JMM to RPM, January 1910, in MF Papers.

12 Brian J. Fraser, *Church, College, and Clergy: A History of Theological Education at Knox College, Toronto, 1844–1994* (Montreal/Kingston: McGill-Queen's University Press, 1995), chap. 4. See also Ruth Compton Brouwer, *New Women for God: Canadian Presbyterian Women and India Mission, 1876–1914* (Toronto: University of Toronto Press, 1990), chap. 2.

13 JMM to AM, 1947, in MF Papers.

14 In China there is no dispute that Luo Zhenyu was the 'discoverer' of the Waste of Yin, but in Canada Menzies has been regarded as the discoverer. This is largely due to a misreading of Menzies' introduction to his *Oracle Records*. His statement emphasized that he was the first trained scientist *to visit the place*, not that he *discovered* it. Four years earlier, Luo Zhenyu had

proved and publicized the provenance of oracle bones came from Xiao Tun, which he identified as the Waste of Yin.

15 UCA, PCC, FMB, North Henan Mission correspondence, Murdoch Mackenzie to RPM, 25 January 1917. (Cited as PCC/NHM correspondence.)
16 JMM to Annie Belle Menzies (ABM), 8 May 1917, in MF Papers.
17 Andrew J. Nathan, *A History of the China International Famine Relief Commission* (Cambridge: Harvard University Press, 1965).
18 JMM to ABM, 11 and 30 September 1916; and JMM to AM, 26 August 1951 and 2 March 1952, in MF Papers.
19 This idea of missionaries as 'new gentry' was developed by Margo S. Gewurtz, 'Famine Relief in China: North Henan in the 1920s,' University of Toronto–York University Joint Centre for Asia Pacific Studies, Working Paper no. 50, 1987.
20 Ibid.
21 PCC/NHM correspondence, 6/87, 'The North China Union Language School,' bulletin for the school year of 1919–20.
22 *Yin-Hsü P'u-Tz'u Hou Pien* (Additional Collection of Oracle Records from the Waste of Yin), edited by James Chin-hsiung Hsü (Taiwan: Yee Wen Publishing Co., 1972).
23 AEA to JMM, 26 December 1924, in PCC/NHM correspondence, 8/133.
24 Ibid.
25 Yale Divinity Library, R611 box 343 / 5264, JMM to John Livingstone Stuart, 20 February 1930.
26 JMM to AEA, 20 April 1930, in MF Papers.
27 Li Chi, *Anyang* (Seattle: University of Washington Press, 1977), 20, 267 n.6.
28 Interview with Marion Menzies Hummel, Ottawa, September 1996.
29 JMM, *Yinxu Buci*, Preface.
30 Interview with AM, September 1996.
31 This point is confirmed by many letters in both the Menzies Family Papers and the Bishop White Papers in the Thomas Fisher Rare Books Library, University of Toronto.
32 Shandong Provincial Museum, 'List of Menzies Collection.'
33 Royal Ontario Museum (ROM), Registrar Office files, JMM file, JMM to C.T. Currelly, March 1940.
34 Ibid.
35 My evaluation of Menzies' contribution to Chinese archaeology is shared by Dr Fang Hui, a Chinese archaeologist at Shandong University.
36 JMM, *Yinxu Buci*. The plates for this book were printed in Kaifeng in 1916 when JMM was seconded to the YMCA. The introduction was written

March 1917 in Shanghai, while JMM was sending his family to Canada and he was about to report to the CLC at Weihai Wei.

37 Li, *Anyang*, 20.

38 Ibid., 147.

39 See *Cheeloo Quarterly* (Tsinan [now Jinan], Shantung), no. 2 (1933): 119–32.

40 Zeng Yigong, *Restored Oracle Bones* (Tsinan: Sinological Study Institute of Cheeloo University, 1940). Zeng was a young Manchu scholar who met Menzies in Beijing in 1927 and was hired to make rubbings of oracle bone inscriptions while JMM was exiled from Henan. When JMM went to teach in Cheeloo, he insisted the university hire Zeng as his research assistant. Zeng learned from JMM about oracle bones and Shang history although he was not a formal student; a strong master–student bond developed between them.

41 Wang Yuxing, *Jiagu Yanjiu (Oracle Bone Studies)* (Beijing: China Social Science Press, 1989), 40.

42 JMM, *Jiagu Yanjiu (Oracle Bone Studies)*, edited by Fang Hui (Jinan: Qilu Press, 1995). At roughly the same time, Guo Muoruo reached similar conclusions in his *Buci Tongzuan* published in Japan. However, Guo's book was later reprinted several times while Menizes' book did not get published until 1995.

43 JMM to FMB, 1930, in MF Papers.

44 JMM, *God in Ancient China*. To support his philological reading of the ancient Chinese character *di* or *shangdi*, Menzies also made the following observation on local religious practice in Henan. 'There is in China today an ancient custom at China New Year of first binding a bundle of sesame stalks or cedar branches with a red cord. They are then stood up on end in the center of the open courtyard, and burnt in worship. This was the sacrifice of the burning faggot to God Above, although now they often call it a sacrifice to Heaven.' This was not a new idea. In fact it had been around since the seventeenth century, when the Jesuits laboured to construct their Confucian–Christianity synthesis. For reference, see David E. Mungello, *Curious Land: Jesuit Accommodation and the Origins of Sinology* (Honolulu: University of Hawaii Press, 1989). In the mid-nineteenth century this idea was used by the Taiping Rebellion, the largest peasant rebellion in Chinese history and the only one in which Christianity played an important role. The Taipings believed that ancient Chinese before the Zhou time were also worshippers of God and only later led astray by Confucius, the Chinese philosopher king. However, the negative impact of the rebellion on the Christian cause in China made the idea almost a taboo. It took a long time for open-minded missionaries to take it up again. Menzies was one of these

missionaries. For the Taiping ideology, see Vincent Y.C. Shih, *The Taiping Ideology: Its Resources, Interpretations, and Influences* (Seattle: University of Washington Press, 1967).

45 JMM to Class of 1910, Knox College, 1953, in MF Papers.

46 University of Toronto Archives, School of Graduate Studies, File A84-0011-068. For a complete examination of Menzies' relations with Bishop White, see my forthcoming monograph. White retained a copy of JMM's draft thesis, as well as the final version (1942), which he used as a basis for his own monographs, *Bone Culture of Ancient China: An Archaeological Study of Bone Material from Northern Honan, Dating about the Twelfth Century B.C.* (Toronto: University of Toronto Press, 1945), and *Bronze Culture of Ancient China: An Archaeological Study of Bronze Objects from Northern Honan, Dating about 1400 B.C.–771 B.C.* (Toronto: University of Toronto Press, 1956).

47 As was the custom, the abstract of the thesis was printed for the oral examination; a copy is in the UCA, JMM bio file, 'Programme of the Final Oral Examination for the Degree of Doctor of Philosophy of James Mellon Menzies.'

48 JMM to AM, 11 August 1943, in MF Papers.

49 C.T. Currelly, 'Foreword' to White's *Tomb Tile Pictures of Ancient China* (Toronto: University of Toronto Press, 1939).

50 John King Fairbank, *Chinabound: A Fifty-Year Memoir* (New York: Harper & Row Publishers, 1982), 182.

51 JMM to AM, 25 November 1945, in MF Papers.

52 UCC/NHM correspondence, 12/209, JMM to Jesse H. Arnup, 4 April 1951.

53 Menzies' ideas on building an authentic Chinese Church were appreciated by Chinese Christians in North Henan. In late 1943, while the Anti-Japanese War was still going on, the Chinese Church put Menzies at the top of the list of Canadian missionaries whom they wanted the most to assist their postwar rehabilitation work. He was regarded by Chinese church leaders as a man with wide vision who was ready to cooperate fully with them and trust them. See UCC/NHM correspondence, 11/184, Bruce Copland to JMM, 2 December 1943.

54 JMM to Sidney Smith, 22 March 1948, in MF Papers.

Contributors

Alvyn Austin received his doctorate in Canadian and Chinese studies from York University. He teaches Chinese history at Brock University. He is the author of *Saving China: Canadian Missionaries in the Middle Kingdom 1888–1959* (1986) and of the forthcoming *China's Millions: The China Inland Mission and Late Qing Society, 1832–1905*.

Ruth Compton Brouwer, professor of history at King's University College, at the University of Western Ontario, is the author of *New Women for God: Canadian Presbyterian Women and India Missions, 1876–1914* (1990) and *Modern Women Modernizing Men: The Changing Missions of Three Professional Women in Asia and Africa, 1902–1969* (2002).

Linfu Dong received his MBA from University of Toronto and his doctorate from York University. His book *Cross Culture and Faith: The Life and Work of James Mellon Menzies* is published by the University of Toronto Press, 2005. He teaches cross-cultural management and international business at the School of Management, Ocean University of China, Qingdao, China.

Gail Edwards holds a doctorate in Educational Studies from the University of British Columbia. She teaches Canadian, British Columbia, and Aboriginal history at the University of British Columbia and at Douglas College, and is the bibliographer for *BC Studies*. Her current research interests include Aboriginal history, mission history, and the history of print culture in British Columbia.

Margo S. Gewurtz is professor of humanities and master of Founders

College at York University. Her research focuses on the modern history of Sino-Western cultural contacts. She has published numerous essays on Canadian missionaries in China and their Chinese partners.

A. Hamish Ion is a professor in the History Department at the Royal Military College of Canada. He is a specialist in modern Japanese history, and is the author of the three-volume study *The Cross and the Rising Sun: The Canadian Protestant Missionary Movement in the Japanese Empire, 1872–1931* (1990); *The Cross and the Rising Sun: The British Protestant Missionary Movement in Japan, Korea and Taiwan, 1865–1945* (1993), and *The Cross in the Dark Valley: The Canadian Protestant Missionary Movement in the Japanese Empire, 1931–1945* (1999). Ion is currently writing a monograph on the American Protestant missionary movement in Japan in the early Meiji period.

Barbara Lawson is curator of ethnology at the Redpath Museum, McGill University. She has published a book entitled *Collected Curios: Missionary Tales from the South Seas* (1994) and has written extensively on museums and anthropology, the history of collecting, and material culture.

France Lord is a public historian and museologist for the firm she co-founded, Pirogue Communications. She holds a PhD in history from the Université de Montréal, where she examined the use of artifacts in Catholic home missionary propaganda in French Canada.

Susan Neylan is associate professor of History at Wilfrid Laurier University. She is author of *The Heavens Are Changing: Nineteenth-Century Protestant Missions and Tsimshian Christianity* (2003).

Myra Rutherdale is assistant professor of History at York University and the author of *Women and the White Man's God: Gender and Race in the Canadian Mission Field* (2002). She is currently researching the history of Western medicine in northern Canadian communities.

Jamie S. Scott is professor of humanities at York University, where he teaches Religion and Film, Religion and Television, and Religion and Postcolonial Literatures in the Religious Studies Program of the Division of Humanities. He is also appointed to the Graduate Programs in English, Geography, Humanities, and Interdisciplinary Studies. He is author of *Christians and Tyrants: The Prison Testimonies of Boethius, Thomas More, and Dietrich Bonhoeffer* (1995), editor of *'And the Birds Began to Sing': Religion, Literature, and Postcolonial Cultures*, and co-editor of *Mapping the Sacred: Religion, Geography, and Postcolonial Literatures* (with Paul Simpson-Housely, 2001) and *Mixed Messages: Materiality, Textuality, Missions* (with Gareth Griffiths, 2004).

Arthur M. Smith is librarian with the Royal Ontario Museum. His earlier writings on Annand have appeared in *Acadiensis* and the *Journal of the Royal Nova Scotia Historical Society.* His research sabbaticals have been devoted to transcribing Annand's orginal diaries at Nova Scotia Archives and Records Management.

Illustration Credits

Florence Jessie Murray and hospital staff, UCA 94.030C; Dr Frank W. Schofield and Korean Christian, UCQ 76.001 P/5828; Nova Scotia couples in New Hebrides, UCA 95.035 P/34; excavation of Anyang, UCA 1999.001 P/1592.

Wrong family: Margaret Wrong.

Index

Xuzhou (formerly spelled Hsü-chou), Jiangsu province. *See* Jesuit missions in China

yamen (magistrate's office), China, 12, 135–7, 139–42, 148
Young Men's Christian Association (YMCA), 113–14, 124, 153, 163, 256, 284, 285
Young People's Forward Movement

for Missions, 10, 76, 114, 130. *See also* Methodist Church of Canada
Young Women's Christian Association, 113, 163
Yukon, missions in, 46, 48–51, 54, 58–9, 62–3

Zhangde. *See* Henan, Canadian Presbyterian mission in North Henan; 'Waste of Yin'